"Jenkins' *Maya Cosmogenesis 2012* presents a fascinating, meticulously researched, exquisitely reasoned, scholarly yet readable account of the development of ancient Mesoamerican astro-spirituality, and offers an inspiring poetic vision of humanity's future."

—Douglas Gillette, author of *The Shaman's Secret:*
Lost Resurrection Teachings of the Ancient Maya

"With [Jenkins] scholarly effort of comparative calendric research and investigation into Mayan cosmology, we may all ascend to new levels of insight concerning the wealth of coded messages that remain in the Mayan legacy to modern mankind in this age of transformation."

—Jim Reed, The Institute of Maya Studies

"In the process of reading the account to this fascinating solution to the reason for the famed Mayan end-time date, Jenkins takes the reader through a well-researched psychoarcheological and astronomical excursion of the Mayan mind field of time."

—Dr. José Argüelles, author of *The Mayan Factor*

"Looking in the right direction makes all the difference in what one sees. Historians tend to look to the past, considering that in the nature of their job; but Maya culture has always been arguably future-oriented, naming time cycles small and large for their end-dates, and so investigators have tended to look the wrong way in their interpretations of those cycles, especially the largest: precession. Building on the pioneering work of de Santillana and von Dechend (*Hamlet's Mill*) and Schele (*Maya Cosmos*), repeatedly tested by his own observations at key sites, Jenkins here lays out the impressive results of 14 years of dedicated study and inspired synthesis."

—Stephen Eberhart, Department of Mathematics,
California State University, Northridge

"*Maya Cosmogenesis 2012* is not a work of speculation or wishful thinking, it is a clearheaded piece of well-documented research . . . using facts, not fancies, Jenkins leads us into the complex world of Mesoamerican iconography, cosmology, astrology, and astronomy and shows us how ancient insights are relevant to today's world."

—Bruce Scofield, author of *Signs of Time: An Introduction*
to Mesoamerican Astrology

ONE HUNAHPU

Source of matter, source of spirit
Spiraling in and spiraling out
Thirteen phases—numbers, vectors
Twenty hieroglyphic pictures
People growing toward the sun
Grow together and live as one
Hunab Ku, Hunahpu
Hub of everything we do
Search the stars for what we are
And find we need not look so far
Inside of us, deep down inside
Are kept the secrets of all time
Finding rhythm, speaking rhyme
Renew the ancient paradigm
Movement and measure
Sowing and dawning
Star of the evening
Star of the morning
One Ahau will start the churning
Watch for Venus, begin the learning
Teaching us the way to see
And how to climb the Sacred Tree
Tzolkin, Haab, and Calendar Round
Spherical music, magical sound
Eye at the center, dawn of our face
Edge of the cosmos, heart of all space
Mysterious day-sign
Bringer of Birth
It comes from the stars
And springs from the Earth

Other Books by John Major Jenkins

JOURNEY TO THE MAYAN UNDERWORLD

MIRROR IN THE SKY

TZOLKIN:
Visionary Perspectives and Calendar Studies

THE CENTER OF MAYAN TIME

MAYA COSMOGENESIS 2012:

THE TRUE MEANING OF THE MAYA CALENDAR END-DATE

John Major Jenkins

BEAR & COMPANY
ROCHESTER, VERMONT

Library of Congress Cataloging-in-Publication Data

Jenkins, John Major.

    Maya cosmogenesis 2012 : the true meaning of the Maya calendar end date / John Major Jenkins.

        p.   cm.

    Includes bibliographical references.

    ISBN 978-1-879181-48-9

    1. Maya calendar.   2. Maya astronomy.   3. Mayas—Religion. 4. Cosmology.   I. Title.

F1435.3.C14J45   1998

529'.329784152—dc21   98-11076
                                                            CIP

Copyright © 1998 by John Major Jenkins

All rights reserved. No part of this book may be reproduced by any means or in any form whatsoever without written permission from the publisher, except for brief quotations embodied in literary articles or reviews.

Bear & Company
Rochester, VT 05767

Cover concept: John Major Jenkins

Cover design: © 1998 by Lightbourne Images

Interior illustrations (unless otherwise noted):
© 1998 by John Major Jenkins

Interior page design and typography: Beth Hansen-Winter

Editor: Barbara Hand Clow

Copy Editor: Joan Parisi Wilcox

Printed in Canada

15 14 13 12 11

FOR THE TWO ELEANORS

PERMISSIONS

Quoted material from *Forest of Kings* (copyright © 1990 by Linda Schele and David Freidel) by permission from William Morrow and Company, Inc. Quoted material from *Skywatchers of Ancient Mexico* by Anthony F. Aveni (copyright © 1980 by University of Texas Press) by permission of the University of Texas Press. Quoted material from *The Fifth Sun* by Cartwright Brundage (copyright © 1979 by University of Texas Press) by permission of the University of Texas Press. Epigraph for Part III from Gordon Brotherston's article "Astronomical Norms in Mesoamerican Ritual and Time Reckoning" in *Archaeoastronomy in the New World* (Copyright © 1982 by Cambridge University Press) by permission of Cambridge University Press. Quoted material from *The Transformations of the Hummingbird* by Eva Hunt (Copyright © 1977 by Cornell University Press) by permission of Cornell University Press. Diagram 184 from *Living in Time* (copyright © 1987 by Palden Jenkins) Gateway Books, Bath England. Quoted material from *General History of Things of New Spain* by Bernardino de Sahagun, trans by Arthur J.O. Anderson and Charles E. Dibble (copyright © 1953 by the School of American Research, Archaeological Institute of America, Santa Fe, New Mexico. Diagrams 109 and 110 from Susanna M. Ekholm's "Mound 30a and the Early Pre-Classic Ceramic Sequence at Izapa, Chiapas, Mexico" in *Papers of the New World Archaeological Foundation, No. 25* (copyright © 1969 by Brigham Young University) by permission of the Papers of the New World Archaeological Foundation. Diagrams 111, 112, 134, 146, 154, and 171 from Gareth W. Lowe, Thomas A. Lee, Jr., and Eduardo Martinez Easpinoza's "Izapa: An Introduction to the Ruins and Monuments" in *Papers of the New World Archaeological Foundation, No. 31* (copyright © 1982 by Brigham Young University) by permission of the Papers of the New World Archaeological Foundation. Quoted material from *Fingerprints of the Gods* (copyright © 1996 by Graham Hancock) Crown Publishers. Day-sign names from *Breath on the Mirror* (copyright © 1993 by Dennis Tedlock) Harper San Francisco. Epigraph poem for Part V from "Winter Solstice" in *alcheringa* (copyright © by Dennis Tedlock). Excerpt of Hopi poem from *Book of the Hopi* (copyright © 1963 by Frank Waters) Penguin Books.

CONTENTS

PART I. PRECESSION ASTRONOMY

PART II. THE UNION OF CAPTAIN SERPENT AND CAPTAIN SUN DISK

PART III. MAYA COSMOGENESIS

PART IV. IZAPA COSMOS

PART V. GAZING INTO THE GALAXY

APPENDICES

LIST OF DIAGRAMS

APPENDIX DIAGRAMS

END NOTE DIAGRAMS

ACKNOWLEDGMENTS

Ellen, thank you eternally for loving me and believing in me throughout the grueling and uncertain process of turning this vision into a reality. Many thanks to Barbara Hand Clow for her understanding, encouragement, and suggestions on how to restructure the book, and for believing in the timeliness and value of my work. And Carl Lehrburger, who by hailing me when the doors of opportunity began to open, may be solely responsible for this book being published. Thanks to Terence McKenna for proving that visionary philosophers can make a living in a world gone trendy. Blessings and Dharmic obeisances to Kurt Joy for having the cosmic eye of the visionary shaman, for laughter, and for keeping me on the path.

For her thorough editing, restructuring of ideas, the text, and her extra effort on a project that certainly needed special attention, I greatly appreciate Joan Wilcox. Thanks to all the people at Bear & Company for their enthusiastic support and jobs well done, including John Nelson and Jody Winters. Special thanks to Beth Hansen-Winter for her wonderful interior design.

Great heartfelt thanks to Jim Reed, friend, believer, and Maya ceremonialist to whom I dedicate the poem entitled *One Hunahpu*. I would not be who I am without my family: Dad, Mom, Ralph, Grama Alice and Grama Bea, Cindy and Barry, Bill, Don and Erika, Deb, Jessica, Sarah, Kim, Leah, Jillian, Ken and Keith—with encouragement and interest, they've seen my passion for the Maya grow and bear many fruits. And to my Boulder friends, who saw me start with nothing and who never gave up on me: Steve and Kelly, Erik and Shara, Sharon and Joe, and all my friends at the Lighthouse Coffee Shop in Louisville. Special thanks to Kathy Pate, who has seen me through a dozen other projects, for appreciating the needs of a rebel scholar and for her support during the time of discovery. Gratitude also is due to Mayanists past and present, whose dedicated studies of Maya cosmology and culture have provided the foundation of my new synthesis.

Finally, thanks to the unknown ancient shamans and skywatchers, those who gazed into the cosmic center, and to the modern Maya people who have inspired and taught me by their lives and words. They continue to offer us profound insights into the cosmic order.

FOREWORD

We live in a time of unarguable and enormous change. And it is portentous change which was, in the era before mechanized technology ruled the world, the special province of seers, shamans, and prophets. We have, through the modern sciences of archaeology and linguistic analysis, sifted the world of the past for data, ideas, and visions pertinent to our own dilemma. I would argue that the most enduring and substantial legacies that we inherit from those ancient and far off times are the Maya calendar and the I Ching. Both of these inventions, when properly understood, move the heart nearer to the sources of all life.

As we investigate the past we find to our surprise that we are encountering its understanding of our immediate future. This is an unprecedented situation, full of awe-inspiring emotion and intellectual excitement. Our planet is in the process of transforming itself; this process is at a critical juncture, and to the degree that we can widen our mental screens to admit the ever-larger context in which our lives and our civilizations exist, we appreciatively participate in a great leap forward in the revelation of the Tao.

With these ideas as a driving force in my own journey, naturally it was with a great deal of pleasure that I accepted the invitation of traveler and scholar John Major Jenkins to write a foreword to *Maya Cosmogenesis 2012*, a revolutionary work of discovery and synthesis. In 1975, as Jenkins generously recalls, I was the first person to realize and to suggest in print (*The Invisible Landscape*) "that in our time, the winter solstice is placed in the constellation Sagittarius, only about 3 degrees from the Galactic Center which, also coincidentally, is within 2 degrees of the ecliptic. Because the winter solstice node is precessing, it is moving closer and closer to the point on the ecliptic where it will eclipse the galactic center." The reason that the notion of the importance of a heliacal solstice rising with the Galactic Center was even available to me was because I, like Jenkins himself, was inspired and challenged by the ideas and speculations that had been put forth earlier by Giorgio de Santillana and Hertha von Dechend in their pathbreaking book *Hamlet's Mill*, published in English in 1969.

My path of discovery was different from Jenkins', a fact that I believe gives greater credence to both our individual conclusions. By 1974 I was aware of the approach of a heliacal solstice rising of the Galactic Center and its potential as a time of renewal, yet astonishingly this was before I was aware that the astronomer-shamans of the Olmec/Maya had reached the same conclusions more than two millennia ago. A different chain of logic led me to the same celestial events and the same moment in time, and I recognized it as a moment of potential transformative opportunity.

In the early 1990s, while in correspondence with John Jenkins, we discussed the possibility that the end-date of the 13-baktun Great Cycle was intentionally chosen by the Maya because of the conjunction of the sun with the intersection of the ecliptic and the plane of the Milky Way on December 21, 2012—the 13.0.0.0.0 of the Long Count calendar. In my revised 1993 edition of *The Invisible Landscape*, I stated that the end-date for my own mushroom-revealed model of the cosmos ended on the same date as the Maya calendar but that the calculation of my end-date had been done by different methods than those of the Maya and without knowledge of those methods.

In the present work, John Major Jenkins has been able bring a new level of detail and a much greater clarity of understanding to a complicated academic situation, which is nevertheless fascinating. He has clarified and expanded these basic intuitions into a true decipherment of the intention behind the Maya calendar and its ending date. This is a signal accomplishment, on a par with the decipherment of the Maya texts that has paralleled and enriched Jenkins' conclusions. His commitment to this problem has been years long, and his careful scholarship has brought astonishing results. He, building carefully on the work of others, has shown that the intention of the Maya calendar makers was prophetic and eschatological. The Maya believed, for reasons which are perhaps forever lost, or perhaps soon to be revealed, that the coincidence of the winter solstice sunrise with the part of the Milky Way that they called *xibalba be* would not be, as some have stated, the end of the world, but its moment of true creation. The Maya believed that creation would only truly occur at a predictable moment in the future: our December 21, 2012.

In *Maya Cosmogenesis 2012*, Jenkins has shown that this precessional alignment of the winter solstice sun with the galaxy is the phenomenon in nature to which the ancient Olmec/Maya anchored their great calendar. *Maya Cosmogenesis 2012* sets the stage for us to ask the deeper question: "Why?" This would be an interesting question under any circumstances; for us in these times it is doubly interesting, for we, by chance or design, actually live in the end time anticipated by the ancient Maya shaman-prophets. Their bones and their civilization have long since gone into the Gaian womb that claims all the children of time. Indeed, their cities were ghostly necropoleis by the time the Spanish conquerors first gazed upon them, five hundred years ago. Yet it was our time that fascinated the Maya, and it was toward our time that they cast their ecstatic gaze, though it lay more than two millennia in the future at the time the first Long Count dates were recorded.

This is hair-raising stuff. Our own civilization, with its cults of the ephemeral and the material, might easily miss the point. And the task of appreciating the Maya is not made any easier by the fact that the specious archaeological fantasies of the New Age have poured scorn on all ancient knowledge that does not flow from the putative founts of lost Lemuria, high Atlantis, and even more dubious realms that are far away indeed. The Maya confound all this with the same imperturbable ease that they have confounded the Eurocentrism and condescension of academic archaeology. The Maya really are an ancient civilization that may have made discoveries and achieved an understanding deeper than our own in areas which we have tended to claim as our own.

This is the astonishing news that Jenkins brings: Modern astronomy is apparently not the first community of scholars to appreciate and study the structure of the greater cosmos. We can marvel over the "coincidence" of our own physicists' discovery of a black hole at the center of our galaxy and the Maya belief in a great black hole in the same spot, and thereby miss the point. This is no coincidence. Our minds and our mathematics are not so different from the ancient Maya that by different but convergent paths our science and theirs could not reach the same perspective.

This being said, what then of the Maya prediction/assumption/discovery of A.D. 2012 as the time of the transformation of the world? First of all, is there some scientific basis for the idea that when the winter solstice sunrise "stands" on the Galactic Center that any unusual physical effects might be expected? Today science answers in the negative. But science, unlike religion, is ever-growing and re-visiting and revising its own past simplifications. Do the spiral structure of the galaxy and the spiral structures of the molecules that create and maintain all life exist in a relationship of resonance? This should be investigated. "As above, so below" taught the alchemists of our own esoteric traditions. Did the Maya make more than a metaphor out of the perception that man is the mirror of the macrocosm? Is human fate and the larger drama of the galaxy somehow linked? Coupling mechanisms may be difficult to prove, but elucidation of subtle coupling mechanisms is what the new science of dynamics is designed to do.

We do not need the Maya and their prophetic calendar to know that we are living in times in which the ways of the world are being hammered and recast upon the anvil of fate. Our own calendar, rational in conception and intent—yet by its own millennial turning now upon us—inevitably directs our attention to larger scales of time and larger possibilities of being than those that claimed the attention of our recent ancestors. We know that we have come to a time of shift and renewal. We need, in this time more than any other, to understand and draw hope from the faith of the Maya that our time—this time now upon us—is the time of true creation. For it must be so.

Over millennia the Maya observed the drama of the approach of father sun toward the vagina of mother sky and, though the cosmic event itself was calculated to occur many centuries in the future, the Maya made the future conjunction the anchor point of their machinery of cosmic time keeping. Their myth, they would say the machinery of cosmic fate, chose our time as the quintessential moment of creation. And in reality our times have lived up to that expectation. To the rational mind this congruence is a coincidence, of little, if any interest at all. Yet as we decipher the monuments and texts of the Classic Maya it becomes ever more clear that they envisioned a world ruled by myths, they saw myths as the primary rudders of statecraft and civilization. The Maya sought to change and influence history through the power of myth, and their most powerful myth was the myth of the precessional drama and the end-time renewal. Collectively, as the twenty-first century dawns, we feel the ennui and exhaustion of the millennia-long practice of Western religion, politics, and science; we encounter the pollution and toxification that is the legacy of our particular style of being in the world. And we also find, among the endless bric-a-brac of the spiritual marketplace, the cosmogenic calendar of the ancient Maya. Can their temporal alchemy, which failed in the time of their own cultural climax and left their cities empty by the time of the Conquest, work for us? Can the Maya dream of renewal at the conjunction of winter solstice and Galactic Heart redeem our civilization? I believe that it can play a significant part, and that part of the resacralization of the world that must accompany any valorization of post-historical time involves the recognition of the deep power and sophistication of the aboriginal mind—not only the ancient aboriginal mind but the contemporary aboriginal mind as well.

As we awaken to the power of the moving sky, as we awaken to the powers that inform and illuminate many of the plants that have found their way into aboriginal medicine, as we struggle with the vastness of the universe of space and time and our place in it, as we do these things, we follow in Maya footsteps. In doing so we should celebrate the wisdom of the Maya, ponder its depths, and wonder after its most persistent perception: that the world is to be born at last on December 21, 2012 A.D.

Terence McKenna
Honaunau, Hawaii
January, 1998

INTRODUCTION

FIXING OUR SIGHTS

My fascination with the Maya began when I visited Mexico and Central America in 1986. This was the first of several journeys I undertook, "traveling on a shoestring" through the remnants of a vast and mysterious civilization. I explored dozens of ruins, many of them over a thousand years old. From the Yucatán in the north to Honduras in the south, from Belize in the east to Mexico City in the west, a vast civilization presented itself to me, and I was awestruck by its unfathomed mysteries. This region is called, appropriately enough, Mesoamerica—the middle of America. It is here that the Maya civilization arose, and it has tenaciously defied being fully understood.

That first journey south of the border was a turning point in my life, a commitment to learning about the profound history of my home continent. Leaving Chicago on a dismal December day with a thousand dollars in my pocket, I looked forward to several months of adventure, exploring ancient ruins and making friends among the contemporary Maya. Above all, I hoped to catch a glimpse of that elusive ancient knowledge, find some direction for my own life and, perhaps, to discover a personal mission. My travels led me from Mexico City through Oaxaca, where I visited the Zapotec capital of Monte Alban. After a few weeks dreaming on the coastal beaches of Oaxaca, I made my way to the highlands of Chiapas, where I welcomed in the New Year, 1987. Then I was ready for the heart of the journey: Guatemala, with its volcanic peaks, beautiful Lake Atitlan, and dozens of ancient ruins. Most importantly to me, the traditional Quiché Maya—some six million of them—continue to live in the highlands, in remote villages where they still count the days according to the ancient calendar and follow age-old traditions. And deep in Guatemala's northern Petén rain forest, accessible only by a bone-jarring sixteen-hour bus ride on muddy and dangerous roads, I found Tikal, my personal mecca.

I can remember a moment when, seven weeks into the trip, I was overcome by the sprawling former metropolis of Tikal. Sitting on the steps of the Central Acropolis, I looked around me at the towering sentinels of stone, their upper platforms stretching above the jungle canopy like altars to the stars, and I listened carefully to the wind whisper messages of a far-off time, and of another world. I thought about the expanse of time and the depth of space above me. This place had been home to some fifty thousand people at a time when London was a dirty market town of a thousand. Questions began to stir in my mind: What drove the Maya to such feats of accomplishment? What was their understanding about human nature, the stars, and the cosmos? Where did they come from? What caused the demise of their thriving cities? My questions were a natural outgrowth of a lifelong search for answers about the nature of life, death, and human spirituality.

From an early age I had been fascinated by the world of ideas. I had devoured everything I could on philosophy and cosmology. To me, cosmology involves more than just the study of the cosmos and the nature of the world; it also includes the role of human spirituality. My youthful curiosity led me through readings in science and philosophy, and deeper into Eastern mysticism. I soon found myself puzzling over what was happening in the world, where we were all headed, and what role human beings play in the evolution of life and consciousness. Ultimately, I became interested in Native American beliefs, the Hopi prophecies, and then the Maya. These interests led me to a contemplative moment at Tikal when, at age twenty-two, I intuited that the knowledge of the ancient Maya was going to play a significant role in the future development of Western philosophy and culture. There was something deep and profound in the stones on which I sat, and I sensed that the Maya were advanced in ways that my own world could barely appreciate or understand. Their minds seemed attuned to the cosmic spaces. Scholars had recognized Maya kings as priests, fully involved in both the political and spiritual life of their culture, but I envisioned Maya kings as time travelers, scientists, skywatchers, and magicians, capable of feats recognized only in ancient Hindu and Buddhist texts. While gazing at the carved monuments of the temple plazas of Guatemala's ruined cities, I saw Maya king-shamans journeying along sky ropes, passing between worlds, and communicating with other times and places. A lost knowledge echoed among the stones, fragmented, awaiting rediscovery.

But what was this ancient knowledge? At that point on my path, I still wasn't sure. I felt it had something to do with the sophisticated calendar systems used by the Maya, and I remembered reading in my guidebook that one of the Maya calendars was due to "end" on December 21, 2012. That date wasn't very far off. Why did the ancient Maya choose that date, I wondered. What is the true meaning of the Maya calendar end-date in A.D. 2012? The answer to this question became my personal quest. A brief reading of the literature on this topic did not offer much apart from unsatisfying generalizations. My gut feeling was that astronomy was involved, and yet I could not locate any academic books that directly addressed this possibility. That was over ten years ago.

Since 1986, the study of Maya science and religion has progressed by leaps and bounds. Archaeologists continue to uncover ancient ruins and have excavated thousands of carved monuments, jade artifacts, rich burial tombs, painted ceramic vases, and examples of the hieroglyphic writing invented by the Maya. Scholars have made enormous progress deciphering the Maya script. Specialists can now read almost all of these hieroglyphs, which reveal detailed histories for each Maya kingdom. In addition, scholars have found and deciphered sacred texts that describe events that occurred during the world's creation and successive re-creations. Many of these texts have direct bearing on the meaning of the 2012 end-date. Another recent breakthrough occurred when scholars realized that Maya myth describes astronomical events. In other words, there is a secret cosmological dimension encoded into Maya mythology. The Creation myth of the Maya, the *Popol Vuh*, recounts the adventures of their most important deities and culture heroes. Since these Maya deities represent astronomical objects such as stars and planets, their activities thus describe astronomical processes. All of this evidence would provide a key to interpreting the true scope of Maya knowledge, but it was not widely known back in 1986. It wasn't until the 1992 Austin Hieroglyphic meeting that Maya scholar Linda Schele revealed her interpretation of Maya Creation myth, in which she emphasized the relationship between myth and astronomy. Her work was hailed as a breakthrough, and was fully rendered in her 1993 book *Maya Cosmos*, coauthored with David Freidel and Joy Parker. I immediately saw the value of this new mytho-astronomical perspective, and it became my guiding principle as I searched more deeply into the Maya mysteries.

Upon returning from that first trip south of the border, I began a course of study that has resulted, over ten years, in seven books devoted to exploring the esoteric secrets of Maya calendar science and religion. It is amazing what you can do with a library card. I waded through popular and academic writings on Maya astronomy, culture, religion, and calendar science. In my book *Tzolkin: Visionary Perspectives and Calendar Studies*, I reconstructed the Maya Venus calendar and explored the nature of the 260-day Maya sacred calendar, called the *tzolkin*. In so doing, I was led to a closer look at another Maya calendar, the Long Count. The Long Count calendar operates separately from the tzolkin and tracks very large periods of time. I learned that the cycle of time that ends in A.D. 2012 is a period of some 5,125 years. The Maya called this a period of 13 "baktuns," in which each baktun lasts about 394 years. This large cycle began back in 3114 B.C. However, I realized that this does not mean the Long Count was invented that far back. In fact, I discovered that the Long Count calendar was invented only about 2,100 years ago, when monuments dated in the Long Count start appearing in the archaeological record. For example, the very first "Long Count monument" dates to 37 B.C. As such, the 3114 B.C. "beginning" date appears to have been a back calculation. The Maya astronomers calculated that between 3114 B.C. and A.D. 2012, a total of 13 "baktuns" would elapse.

But why, I asked myself, did this 13-baktun Great Cycle of the Long Count calendar end in A.D. 2012? Why not A.D. 1712, or A.D. 2650? What determined the placement of the 13-baktun Great Cycle in real time? I noticed that the 2012 end-date occurs precisely on the December solstice. Could it be that the "end" date was the intended anchor for the placement of the Long Count calendar, rather than the "beginning" date? I eventually found that some authors have attempted interpretations of the end-date. For example, Frank Waters, in his 1975 book *Mexico Mystique*, analyzed astrology charts for the end-date.[1] These were standard earth-centered charts, and a professional astrologer described the configuration of planets as being rare. This was intriguing information, yet somehow it just wasn't satisfying to me. I felt that, certainly, astronomy was involved in the Maya end-date, but it would have to be something really *big* to justify the end of a cycle of more than 5,000 years. Standard horoscope interpretations just do not address the Maya belief that a World Age would be ending. More recently, *The Mayan Prophecies* by Maurice Cotterell and Adrian Gilbert proposed that the 2012 end-date was chosen because of sunspot extremes and their effects on human fertility.[2] Theirs is an interesting hypothesis, but in my view their theory has problems. I reviewed their book carefully in 1995, interviewed Adrian Gilbert, and concluded that some doubt hung over the sunspot hypothesis.

One thing was certain: The Maya believed the world will "end" in A.D. 2012.

But what does this mean? The end-times doctrine can be interpreted in two ways: metaphorically and literally. My metaphorical interpretation is that the Maya believed that around the year we call 2012, a large chapter in human history will be coming to an end. All the values and assumptions of the previous World Age will expire, and a new phase of human growth will commence. Ultimately, I believe the Maya understood this to be a natural process, in which new life follows a death. We all experience this cycle of death and rebirth in our own lives: Our most difficult experiences of suffering and loss are ultimately our best teachers. Imagine this principle taking effect on the level of the entire human race.

The literal interpretation of the Maya concept of a World Age shift in 2012 is emphasized by many writers for the sheer drama of it. In this scenario, humanity literally is going to experience cataclysm and upheaval, earthquakes, disasters, famine, and plague. This Earth cleansing, however, is the prelude for a global renewal. While this scenario may seem bleak, the Maya doctrine of World Ages extends back over four previous epochs, each of which ended in cataclysm and the transformation of humanity into something completely new, a new being better suited for life in the new world. So even in this catastrophic scenario, the cyclic renewal of the Earth and the spiritual unfoldment of humanity prevail.

With so many questions still unanswered, I continued trying to satisfy my thirst for understanding the true meaning of the Maya end-date. Two considerations led me to see the end-date in a larger context. First, Western astrologers, that is, astrologers who specialize in non-Maya astrology, are saying that we are entering the Age of Aquarius, that a new World Age is, indeed, about to begin. A concept that originated in ancient Greek and Egyptian science, the "shifting of the ages" is based in an astronomical phenomenon called the precession of the equinoxes. The precession of the equinoxes, or simply precession, is caused by the fact that Earth wobbles on its axis. Earth spins on its axis once every twenty-four hours, resulting in the sunrise and sunset that define our day. However, the Earth, like a spinning top, also slowly wobbles or "precesses" on its axis. According to modern astronomical calculations, one full "wobble" (one full precessional cycle) takes about 25,800 years. For observers on Earth, this wobbling gives the impression that the sun rises against the background of different constellations as the centuries elapse. The result is that the equinox sun will soon be rising in the constellation of Aquarius rather than in Pisces, as it has for the past 2,000 years. Thus, we are moving out of the Age of Pisces and into the Age of Aquarius. Precession seemed to provide the "big event" I was looking for. I wondered if the Maya astronomers recognized the same twelve constellations that Western astrologers do, and if the Long Count calendar end-date marks our passage into the Aquarian Age.

The second consideration that emerged in my research also points to precession as being associated with the Long Count calendar. As already mentioned, the cycle that ends in A.D. 2012 is a period of 13 baktuns. A baktun is the fifth-place value in the base-twenty Long Count calendar, and it equals 144,000 days. Thirteen of these baktuns equal a 5,125-year "Great Cycle." Maya and Aztec documents relate a belief in four or five World Ages, and we currently live in the last one. Amazingly, five Great Cycles equal one precessional cycle! Early on in my research I thought the Maya end-date simply reflected our movement into the Age of Aquarius. However, as I searched deeper into the Maya wisdom I learned that ancient Maya astronomers looked at the heavens differently than their Western counterparts in Greece: They used thirteen constellations rather than twelve. This fact would result in a different timing for the anticipated shift in World Ages, one that would not agree with the dawn of the Aquarian Age recognized in Western astrology. I had to rule out the dawning of the Age of Aquarius as an explanation for the Maya end-date in 2012. Besides, most modern astrologers were putting off the advent of the Aquarian Age until the twenty-third century—over 200 years *after* the Maya end-date! Something else seemed to be going on, something involving precession but that was alien to the Western assumptions I was encountering in my readings.

I reformulated my guiding question: What event in the cycle of precession does 2012 represent? As fate would have it, the right book appeared before me at the right time. The year was 1993. The book was *Hamlet's Mill*. Authored by two respected scholars, Massachusetts Institute of Technology professor Giorgio de Santillana and University of Frankfurt history of science professor Hertha von Dechend, *Hamlet's Mill* turned out to be a treasure trove of ideas. The book's subheading says a lot about its contents: "An Essay on Myth and the Frame of Time." The "frame of time" refers to the celestial frame—the contents of the sky, including the stars, constellations, and the Milky Way. Our orientation to this "stellar frame" changes over time with precession. Myth is involved because the authors identify descriptions of this slow shifting of the sky in ancient myths from cultures around the globe. The basic premise of the book, then, is that myth and astronomy go hand in hand, that myth describes astronomical processes and, more specifically, that ancient cultures were aware of the precession of the equinoxes. Moreover, the authors contend that ancient cultures believed precession to have a primary influence on the changing destinies of humankind.

As mentioned, precession is usually tracked with the changing constellations in which the equinox sun rises. In Western astrology, there are twelve constellations, and thus each "constellation age" lasts about 2,160 years. However, the authors of *Hamlet's Mill* also noted that, during the precessional cycle, the equinox and solstice suns periodically line up with the Milky Way—the band of stars we see arching through the night sky that is also our home galaxy. One direct clue in *Hamlet's Mill* jumped out at me, and pointed me in a promising direction. The authors wrote that some 6,400 years ago (4400 B.C.), the fall equinox sun coincided with the Milky Way, and this was the fabled Golden Age found in many myths. In other words, this was a time when the sun, on the fall equinox, was in conjunction with the Milky Way, an era when a harmonious alignment existed in the sky. Of course, precession eventually caused this alignment to end, fostering a kind of celestial disharmony. Imagine how our ancient ancestors would have responded to this ever-increasing cosmic disharmony. The authors suggest this "untuning of the sky" resulted in our descent into history, with its increasing wars and fading memories of an ancient paradise in which cosmic harmony prevailed. Historically, the ancient paradise may be a collective memory of the Great Mother–worshiping culture of our Neolithic ancestors, in which the ideal of partnership and peaceful coexistence reigned. Moreover, 4400 B.C. does match up pretty well with when partnership culture was disrupted and a patriarchal system based upon hierarchies of dominance began arising in the Middle East—the forerunner of our own Western Tradition.

Interestingly, Santillana and von Dechend also discuss the ancient myths that relate a belief in a future time when cosmic harmony would return and an earthly paradise would resurface. In 1993, I began to carefully think through the implications of these ideas. If the fall equinox sun conjuncting the Milky Way was considered to be a precessional era of harmony, and a future return of this type of alignment was projected, what could it be? Well, the astronomical fact is that the alignment described above occurred some 6,400 years ago. Since the equinoxes and solstices divide the year into quarters, I reasoned that one-quarter of a precessional cycle later (6,450 years), *the December solstice sun will be joined with the Milky Way. In other words, the December solstice sun will be conjuncting the bright band of the Milky Way around the year* A.D. *2012!* I felt I had found the answer to my question about the true meaning of the Maya end-date, and quickly sought to confirm it. I studied star charts and proved to myself that, yes, despite it never making the morning newspaper headlines, a very rare alignment in the precessional cycle will occur on the December solstice of A.D. 2012—the end-date of the Maya calendar! Precession brings one of the seasonal quarters (either the March equinox, the June solstice, the September equinox, or the December solstice) into alignment with the Milky Way once every 6,450 years. However, the alignment of 2012 occurs only once every 25,800 years! Furthermore, the alignment involves the December solstice, the traditional "beginning" point of Earth's yearly cycle. Earth itself, and by extension its citizens, was involved in the alignment. This was certainly an event worthy of being recognized by the ancient Maya as a rare World Age shift. Could it be, I thought to myself, that the ancient Maya knew about precession thousands of years ago? And did they understand something about the Milky Way and our alignment with it that has escaped detection by modern science? My discovery answered one question but raised a host of others: Where exactly was the Long Count invented? Is the alignment of 2012 somehow encoded into Maya myths? Is it discussed in Maya hieroglyphic texts? Is it portrayed on Maya carvings? If so, how?

I now had the key to understanding the meaning of the Maya end-date, but it was clear that I was venturing into uncharted territory. I dove further into the academic literature, but nothing I read had anything to say about an astronomical alignment on the 2012 end-date. I felt bewildered because my discovery was not based on conjecture but was simply making a connection between two facts. First, the 13-baktun cycle of the Maya Long Count calendar ends on December 21, 2012. Second, a very rare alignment in the cycle of the precession of the equinoxes culminates on that day. Given this compelling "coincidence," in 1994 I asked esteemed Maya scholar Dennis Tedlock what he thought of it. He replied that he too had noticed this unusual situation in 2012, but did not know what to make of it. Were the ancient Maya aware of precession? Did they purposefully fix the end of their Long Count calendar to a rare alignment in the precessional cycle? If so, how were they able to accurately calculate the rate of precession? I had the impression that this train of thought was off limits in academia, that the implications were just too tantalizing to be credible.

However, I remained undaunted by the silence of the "ivory tower," and by early 1994 I was making progress sorting out the data. I had been studying Maya cosmology for almost seven years, having published three books on the subject, so I already had a good understanding of Maya myth, calendrics, and astronomy. I continued to review pertinent academic studies, looking for connections between astronomy and Maya myth. I focused my attention on the astronomy associated with the end-date alignment: the December solstice sun, the Milky Way, and the stars of Sagittarius and Scorpio. Three facts loomed before me:

- The ecliptic is the path traveled by the sun, moon, and planets through the sky. Twelve constellations lie along the ecliptic, and the sun passes through all twelve during the course of one year. The ecliptic crosses over the Milky Way at a 60° angle near the constellation Sagittarius. As such, it forms a cross with the Milky Way, and this cosmic cross was called the Sacred Tree by the ancient Maya.[3] (The cross form was also known as the "crossroads.") Amazingly, the center of this cosmic cross, that is, right where the ecliptic crosses over the Milky Way, *is exactly where the December solstice sun will be in* A.D. *2012.* This alignment occurs only once every 25,800 years.
- The Milky Way is observed as a bright, wide band of stars arching through the sky. In the clear skies of ancient Mesoamerica, many dark, blotchy areas could be observed along the Milky Way's length. These are "dark-cloud" formations caused by interstellar dust. The most prominent of these is called the "dark-rift" or the "Great Cleft" of the Milky Way. It looks like a dark road running along the Milky Way, and it points right at the cosmic crossing point, the center of the Maya Sacred Tree, right where the sun will be in 2012! The Maya called this dark-rift the Black Road, or the Road to the Underworld. They seem to have imagined it as a portal to another world, and the December solstice sun can enter it only in A.D. 2012.
- The area of the sky where all of these symbols and celestial objects converge is the center of our Milky Way Galaxy. This was perhaps the most astounding thing I discovered. The part of the Milky Way that the December solstice sun will conjunct is also where the center of our Galaxy (the Galactic Center) is located. It is the cosmic womb from which new stars are born, and from which everything in our Galaxy, including humans, came.

It is important to visualize our relationship to the Milky Way. The Milky Way is saucer-shaped and appears to us as a white band of stars. When we look at the Milky Way in the night sky, we are looking out along the edge of a spinning disk, as if looking at the edge of a spinning bicycle wheel. If we look away from the center of this "wheel," we look toward Gemini and Orion, where we gaze into the vastness of open space outside our Galaxy. The Milky Way is thin and diffuse in this direction, and we see only wispy strands of white. If we look in the other direction, however, toward the center of the wheel, at its "axle," we see a plethora of stars and a rich caldron of creation. Here is the cosmic oven of the Milky Way's center, and the dark-rift points right to it. The Milky Way is very bright and wide in this area, as if pregnant, and for this reason, I realized, the Maya recognized it as the womb of the sky. They considered this bulging area of the Galactic Center to be the cosmic source and center, the Womb of All.

I was extremely intrigued with what I was finding, and felt I was unlocking long-lost secrets of Maya cosmology. I had answered my guiding question about what event in the cycle of precession occurs in A.D. 2012. The answer: a rare conjunction of the December solstice sun with the Galactic Center. I published my initial findings in late 1994.[4] Thereafter, I was intensely engaged in tracking down the answers to the other questions that were popping up. My initial discovery opened up even more bizarre avenues of inquiry. For example, could the 2012 alignment cause Earth's poles to shift, resulting in sudden global catastrophe? Could the "field effects" of our changing relationship to the Milky Way stimulate genetic or spiritual evolution on Earth? If so, why are these possibilities not recognized in our supposedly superior Western science? Did the Mayas' focus on the Galactic Center have anything to do with the fact that astrophysicists have discovered a Black Hole—a possible portal through space and time—located there? It was obvious I had my work cut out for me, and I determined to look into these mysteries as deeply as I could.

For two years, 1995 and 1996, I was immersed in research, obsessed with the labyrinthine Pandora's Box I had opened. These were very busy and introspective years, and I felt charged with a mission and full of enthusiasm. Throughout, I had the obligations of life to attend to, working and paying the bills. Fortunately, I lived simply and efficiently, and so had time to cosmologize. And I was making progress. It seemed at times as if mysteries were solved almost by magic. The more I learned, the better I was able to formulate questions. As soon as I had framed a question correctly, the answer appeared. Soon, a general theory emerged: *The ancient Maya* understood something about the nature of the cosmos and the spiritual evolution of humanity that has gone unrecognized in our own worldview. This understanding involves our alignment with the center of our Galaxy, our cosmic center and source, and identifies A.D. 2012 as a time of tremendous transformation and opportunity for spiritual growth, a transition from one World Age to another.

The bottom line of my theory is that *the ancient Maya chose the 2012 end-date because this is the date on which occurs a rare alignment of the solstice sun with the Galactic Center.* I tested my theory, corresponded with Maya experts, and found that by synthesizing recent advances in the fields of archaeology, ethnography (the study of culture), archaeoastronomy (the study of the relationship between astronomy, archaeology, and cultural beliefs), epigraphy (the study of the Maya hieroglyphic writing), and iconography (the study of symbols and pictures), I could strongly support my ideas. Knowing the controversy my work might arouse in the academic community, I felt compelled to document my arguments so that my theory could not be dismissed as vague speculation. My self-published book *The Center of Mayan Time* presented the case as of early 1995, but more evidence continued to emerge, until a unified vision of the profound scope of Maya knowledge began to gel. By early 1997 I finished a magnum opus study—the original version of *Maya Cosmogenesis 2012*. It was huge, exhaustive, and covered a broad spectrum of related questions. I had identified how the 2012 alignment manifests in the symbolism of the Maya ballgame, in birthing rituals, and in king accession rites. Furthermore, I had traced the origins of the Long Count calendar to the little-known site of Izapa, and decoded its monuments as initiatory devices into a forgotten Galactic Cosmology. I began to solicit academic commentary on my book, openly inviting critique, by sending out abstracts to selected scholars. There was little response. Most of them simply did not have time to comment. However, I remembered that Robert Bauval, author of *The Orion Mystery*, had advised me to be persistent.

By this time (mid-1997), I had published over a dozen articles on Maya cosmology and the precession question. Finally, my friend Jim Reed convinced the Institute of Maya Studies that it would be worth bringing me to Miami to present my pioneering work. The Institute of Maya Studies is associated with the Miami Museum of Science and Planetarium, and has hosted Maya scholars such as Dennis Tedlock and Munro Edmonson. I was honored to be invited to present my theory at such a prestigious venue. I suspected I was on the cutting edge of where the Maya experts themselves were going and, in the end, my presentation on August 20, 1997, was well received. It had the feel of a breakthrough, especially in regard to the acceptance of my work by academia.[5] Nevertheless, I was not naive, and I knew that it would take years for an "outsider" like myself to make inroads into Maya scholardom. I had stormed the Ivory Tower, left my message, and that was enough for now.

Fortunately, around the same time, Barbara Hand Clow, a long-time believer in my work and copublisher at Bear & Company Publishing, encouraged me to begin revising the work for publication. The challenge of transforming what was originally an exercise in academic schematizing into something that is actually readable has been daunting at times. Many people have helped in this endeavor, and I am grateful to them. At last I was blessed with an opportunity to share my discovery with a much larger readership.

My work fits into an emerging trend of independent researchers decoding ancient precessional mysteries. Importantly, there have been many key breakthroughs in understanding ancient Egyptian cosmology. Jane B. Sellers' *The Death of Gods in Ancient Egypt* carefully outlines a compelling argument that certain astronomical phenomena, including the precession of the equinoxes, were understood by ancient Egyptian skywatchers. In *The Orion Mystery*, Robert Bauval and Adrian Gilbert explain how the Great Pyramid of Egypt is a precessional star-clock. Sight tubes within the pyramid, usually called "air-shafts," point to Sirius, but only during a specific era of precession. In *Fingerprints of the Gods*, sleuth-scholar Graham Hancock adds to this discovery by showing that the constellation Leo the Lion was rising on the vernal equinox at the "Zero Time" of 10,500 B.C. Hancock believes the lion-like Sphinx may have been the earthly symbol of the constellation Leo. Based upon this insight, and other evidence that suggests the Sphinx was constructed much earlier than previously thought, perhaps even during the Egyptian Zero Time, Hancock suggests that the builders of the Sphinx lived during the astrological Age of Leo—around 10,500 B.C. The Sphinx then looms as a mute witness to an era of precession long past, and that suggests precessional knowledge goes back to the very dawn of human civilization.

The idea that the Egyptians were aware of precession is not new. In compelling and original studies published in the 1940s and 1950s, many of them stemming from field observations, Alsatian researcher R.A. Schwaller de Lubicz defined Egypt as the great parent culture from which Old World wisdom emanated. In his book *Sacred Science*, de Lubicz shares the data that led him to conclude that the ancient Egyptians were aware of the precession of the equinoxes.

The Babylonians also seem to have been aware of precession. As early as 1906, historian of science J.L.E. Dreyer noted that three Babylonian tablets, each from a different era, give three different positions for the equinox, proving that the Babylonian astronomers were aware of precessional movement.[6] The Vedic astronomers of ancient India, according to Vedic scholar David Frawley, were also aware of precession—a knowledge possibly going back 6,000 years. Moving to the New World, William Sullivan's book *The Secret of the Incas* decoded precessional mysteries in the mythology and beliefs of the Inca in South America. Sullivan's work is well researched and adds a great deal to our understanding of how precessional knowledge manifested in the New World. Among independent scholars, at least, it appears as if there is a genuine revolution astir in how we view prehistoric peoples.

This revisioning has fought a persistent bias that survives in the assumptions of scholars as well as laypeople. Were our ancestors primitive, graceless cave dwellers, unaware of their relationship to the larger cosmos? Or did they gaze into the night sky with an appreciation for the majesty of it all, possessing insights into cosmic processes that are now lost to us? The new perspective championed by many independent thinkers favors the latter view.

For example, Barbara Hand Clow, in her book *The Pleiadian Agenda*, explores the deeper implications of the alignment in A.D. 2012. Going beyond strictly Egyptian or Maya perspectives, her insights into the history and future of our multidimensional cosmos testify to the deeply profound relationship that humanity has always had with the cosmos. According to Clow, we are entering a phase of human spiritual growth with galactic implications. Also taking a larger view of these intriguing ideas are Dennis and Terence McKenna, who in their book *The Invisible Landscape* mentioned the eclipse of the Galactic Center by the solstice sun in 2012. The McKennas arrived at the 2012 date using sources that did not involve the Maya calendar. This book was an underground classic upon publication in 1975, and was revised and republished in 1993. The McKennas write that the alignment in 2012 could "implicate the galaxy as a major formative influence upon the structure of the molecules that maintain and define life."[7] I can trace my interest in precession back to my encounter with this book in 1984. *The Invisible Landscape* and *Hamlet's Mill* are the two earliest sources that recognized the impending alignment of the solstice sun with the Milky Way Galaxy. I outline the history of the discovery of this idea in Appendix 1.

Despite the wider implications of this discovery, in my work I focus on how the precession of the equinoxes was mapped and calibrated among the ancient civilizations of the New World, specifically in Mesoamerica. What has emerged from my research is nothing less than the recovery of a lost worldview containing insights we are just beginning to appreciate. *Maya Cosmogenesis 2012* is devoted to exploring the Mayas' understanding of the 2012 end-date and the philosophy and cosmology that go with it. I have reconstructed what I term a lost Galactic Cosmology, and I explain its formulation, content, and the mythological language used by the Maya to encode its meanings. This is a book about cosmogenesis, the creation of the world. The Maya believed that the world will be reborn, in a sense "re-created," in the year we call 2012. Why did the Maya believe this? Where did this profound knowledge originate? What does it mean for the world to be "created" in 2012? And what are the implications for us? My book goes deep into previously unfathomed areas of the ancient Maya mind, and speaks to an event that is right around the corner. In addition, I offer an interpretation of what this rare cosmic event portends for those of us who will live through it. I believe, and I suspect that the Mayas believed, that we are all indispensible participants in the adventure of cosmogenesis. We cocreate the world, and what looms before us is a great opportunity for spiritual growth, both individual and planetary.

Maya Cosmogenesis 2012 is divided into five parts, each rigorously unveiling the archaeological and mythic dimensions of my theory. The text contains the flow of ideas as described below, as well as end notes. For readers interested in documentation, the end notes contain citations and more detailed arguments. The appendices are more technical still and explore academic considerations that should appeal more to the Maya specialists. For example, Appendix 5 contains my response to arguments against my theory that Maya scholars are likely to put forward. Likewise, Appendix 2 is a thorough examination of the academic literature pertaining to what the ancient Maya knew about precession.

Part I of my book provides a basic orientation to Mesoamerican civilization: the timeline of its development, its calendars, and its cosmology. Charting time was a central concern of the Maya, as was "finding the center" of the cosmos. Driven by a shamanistic interest in knowing the sky, the ancient Mesoamerican skywatchers discovered the astronomical phenomenon known as the precession of the equinoxes, and this knowledge was encoded into their Creation mythology. I introduce the two basic calendar systems used by the Maya and discuss how astronomy developed at various Mesoamerican sites, including those of the Olmec, Zapotec, Toltec, Izapan, and Maya people.

It is my contention that understanding the nature of precession became the central interest of Mesoamerican shaman-astronomers. They believed that specific types of alignments in the cycle of precession stimulate evolution for life on Earth. In my research, I determined that the Toltecs and the Maya devised two different methods for tracking precession. In other words, two different and competing cosmologies emerged—one involved the Long Count calendar, with its end-date in A.D. 2012, and the other involved the New Fire ceremony. The true meaning of these traditions is reconstructed. Furthermore, I show how the two systems were merged at Chichén Itzá in the ninth century A.D., and how the schism in the Mesoamerican psyche was healed. Thus, Part II encapsulates a "unified Mesoamerican cosmology" based upon precessional insights discovered by the ancient Maya skywatchers.

I will show how the Galactic Alignment of A.D. 2012, pinpointed by the Long Count end-date, was encoded into Maya Creation mythology. The Hero Twin myth is the original Creation myth of the Maya. In Part III, I reveal the deeper symbolism of the Hero Twin myth, a symbolism that encodes precessional astronomy. My interest here is in getting to the heart of how the Maya understood cosmogenesis—the birth of the world and its rebirth in A.D. 2012. Ultimately, the Maya envisioned the alignment to occur in 2012 as a union of the Cosmic Mother (the Milky Way) with First Father (the December solstice sun). Woven into Maya astronomy, mythology, and cosmology is a profound understanding of Earth's evolving consciousness. As my conclusions began to gel, I realized that the ancient Maya developed a sophisticated cosmological paradigm that modern science has yet to recognize.

Part IV is devoted to exploring the little known pre-Maya site of Izapa. Whereas traditional Maya scholarship interprets Izapa as an important site in the development of pre-Maya and Maya culture, I will reveal it to be the most innovative center of Mesoamerican astronomical, shamanic, calendric, and religious activity. I will show how ancient Izapa was the ceremonial site where the Galactic Cosmology was discovered. In fact, I believe Izapa to be the location where thousands of ancient calendar-priests were initiated into Galactic Cosmology. My interpretation of Izapa's more than fifty carved monuments reveals the highest esoteric secrets of ancient Maya cosmology.

Finally, I summarize the profound implications of this newly reconstructed

Galactic Cosmology and take the reader on an initiatory journey around the monuments of Izapa to reveal the ancient mysteries of Galactic Cosmology. I end with an understanding of why the Maya calendar ends in 2012, how this knowledge was built into Maya mythology and institutions, and what it means for us today.

I hope this book will open up new vistas in our understanding of the Maya, and preserve for the appreciation of future generations the amazing genius of their civilization. We are *just beginning* to understand what they knew. The importance of the foundation principle of this ancient cosmovision—the precession of the equinoxes—must be recognized as having a formative influence on the evolving life of Earth. And yet, modern science refuses to acknowledge this, and the fact that a rare Galactic Alignment looms before us has no place in our short-sighted technocracy. Perhaps our limited sight will be our undoing. We know about precession today, but, as the authors of *Hamlet's Mill* write, "The space-time continuum does not affect it [precession]. It is by now only a boring complication."[8]

To the Ancients, precession had the most profound of implications. To their understanding, it was involved in nothing less than the evolution of life on Earth, propelling Earth's lifeforms to higher levels of organization and complexity. The end result is the full unfolding of spirit and consciousness on a planet that began as molten rock. The Maya understood that whereas the 260-day sacred cycle is our period of individual gestation, the 26,000-year cycle is our collective gestation—our collective unfolding as a species. Their calendars and myths encode these truths. Furthermore, 2012 is the Zero Point of the process—the moment of collective spiritual birth. And how can we say that they are wrong? One thing is for sure, in this case time *will* tell. The era of transformation is upon us.

It appears as if a long chapter in human history is coming to a close, one that began perhaps 13,000 years ago. At the dawn of agriculture in the Paleolithic Age, human beings began to understand the nature and potential of the yearly cycle. They discovered planting and harvesting. As their time-concept was enhanced, they planned for a future barely appreciated by their immediate ancestors, and the resultant effects on human culture were transformative. The same might be said for us in regard to our understanding of the larger Galactic Season of precession: If we can enlarge our space-time concept and appreciate the immanent potential of this Great Year, the future of the human race might be brighter than we can presently imagine. Suffice it to say that we are, in fact, living in the Maya end-times, and something completely unprecedented does appear to be going on. *Maya*

Cosmogenesis 2012 endeavors to resurrect and restore the ancient Galactic Cosmology of the Maya. It is a "first reconnaissance" into a profound knowledge that once flowered in Mesoamerica, and promises to again. According to this ancient knowledge, a door into the heart of space and time opens in 2012. May we all take a step forward.

PART I:
PRECESSION ASTRONOMY

To me the most interesting result of the present investigation is the fact that, having once started on an unpremeditated course of study, I found an unsuspected wealth of material and finally attained one, totally undreamed-of conclusion, concerning the law governing the evolution of religion and civilization. This leads me to think that, as I groped in the darkness, searching for light, I unwittingly struck the key-note of that great universal theme which humanity, with a growing perception of existing, universal harmony, has ever been striving to seize and incorporate into their lives.

— Zelia Nuttall, *The Fundamental Principles of Old and New World Civilizations*

CHAPTER 1

A TIMELINE OF
MESOAMERICAN CULTURE

B efore we delve into the Maya period, we need to journey back in time, to the origins of Mesoamerican civilization. This journey will take us from the humble beginnings of hunter-gatherers in the Paleolithic to the complex high civilization of the Maya—and beyond. Eight thousand years ago, the embers of New World civilization began stirring in Middle America. Nomadic tribes wandered the wide valleys of what is now Central Mexico, hunting bison and other free-roaming game. At night, these people tracked the movements of the planets and stars, as their ancestors had for thousands of years before them. They gave the sun and the moon names. In fact, they recognized these celestial giants as deities, capable of nurturing and guiding life, but also capable of terrible acts of cruelty and destruction. The sun provided life-giving warmth, but also could be brutally hot. The planets, too, were observed as celestial wanderers, gods and goddesses sometimes involved in human affairs, and their motions were carefully charted. The Milky Way stretched overhead, spanning the horizons, and the river of white light that flowed from its womb embraced Earth with nurturance attributable only to the Great Mother of Creation. Even at this early phase in the development of Mesoamerican culture, the night sky loomed as a cosmic backdrop on which the concerns and questions of humanity were projected.

As long as six thousand years ago, villages began to form as maize was domesticated, through selective breeding, from a wild grain. This great accomplishment of the early Mesoamericans testifies to their innate genius and persistence. The achievement of coaxing juicy maize kernels out of teosinte, a skinny wild grain, required hundreds, if not thousands, of years of ongoing effort—a goal-focused continuity of effort over many generations. It seems reasonable for us to entertain the possibility that early skywatchers possessed a similar capacity for persistence and continuous effort. They could have relayed an accurate accounting of star positions and constellation lore from the earliest times. The ancient Mesoamerican astronomers even may have noticed the slow shifting of the stars, the precession of the equinoxes, at a very early date. The minds of the early Mesoamerican people were sharp, complex, and endlessly curious. Their vigilant attention to life, to evolving food sources, and to the stars imbued them with a sense of connection to both Earth and sky.

For the Maya, maize has an ancient mythological association with the origin of human beings. They believe to this day that the flesh of the first human beings was made from white maize and yellow maize. Today, maize cannot reseed itself without the help of human beings. A deep truth about humanity's relationship to Divinity is hidden within this fact: The Maize Deity—the source of life—needs human beings to further the ongoing process of life on Earth. The Maize Deity and human beings are cocreators. Thus, in a very real sense, the birth of New World civilization can be traced to the domestication of maize. From a mythological viewpoint, the domestication of maize suggests that early cultures in the New World had entered into a pact with the Maize Deity, a contract that would carry them to the lofty heights of a sophisticated and complex civilization. The Flute Song of the Hopi suggests what this contract might have been about:

We we lo lo, We we lo lo	There at the center of the universe
Ah yum tu wa, Na sa vu eh	Blue Corn Girl came up
Sa qua ma na, Ku yea va	Growing and maturing
Nah tuk se na	Beautifully[1]

This song recalls what seems to be a universally held indigenous idea that culture is like a beautiful child, growing outward from the center of the universe, maturing in time. This image also serves as a key to understanding a basic insight into human nature and time: Our spiritual natures unfold, in time, like flowers. That ancient people understood this profound truth gives us pause, and makes us wonder what else they knew. We know that some five thousand years ago the early

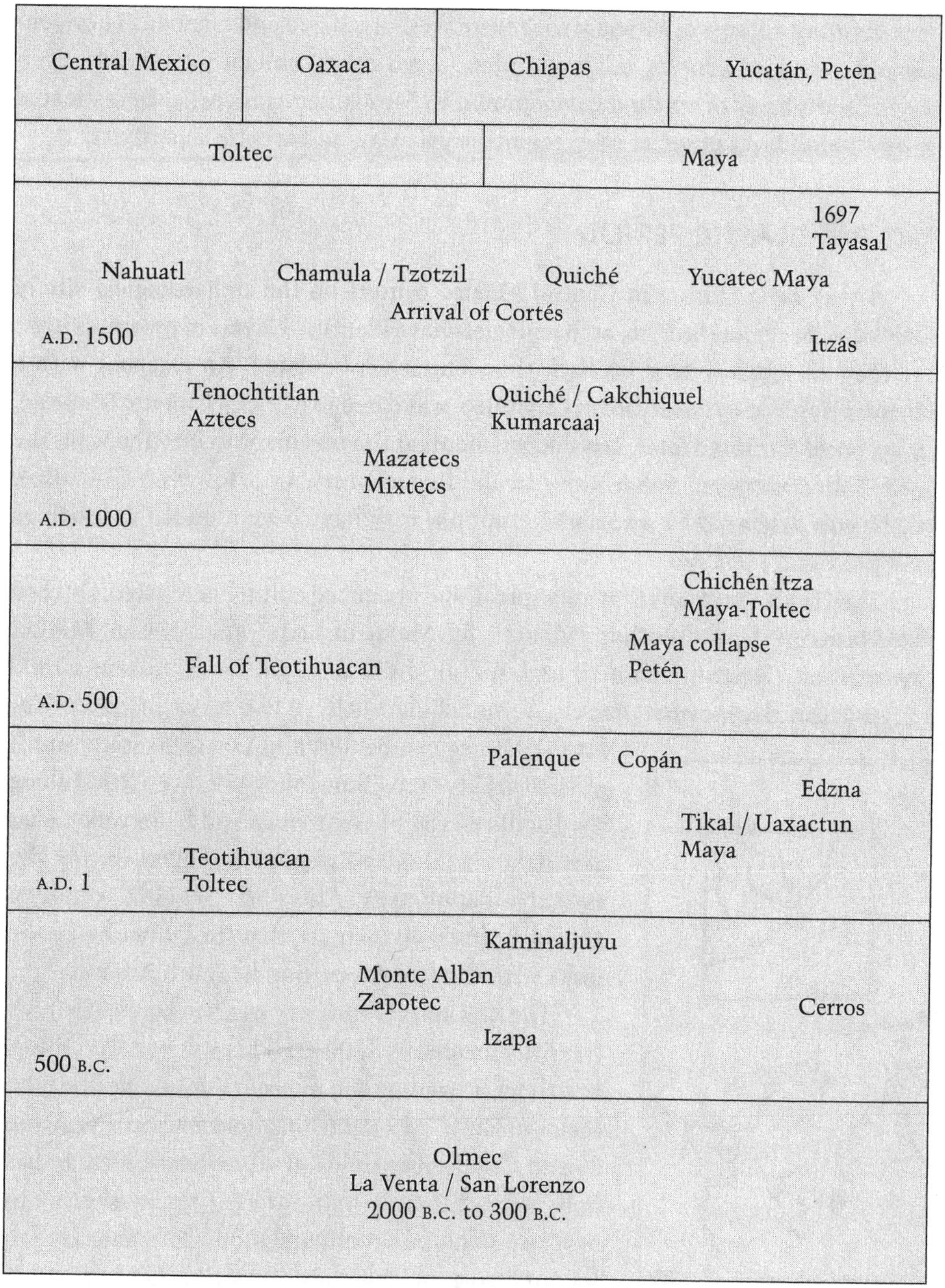

Central Mexico	Oaxaca	Chiapas	Yucatán, Peten
Toltec		Maya	

			1697 Tayasal
Nahuatl	Chamula / Tzotzil	Quiché	Yucatec Maya
	Arrival of Cortés		
A.D. 1500			Itzás
Tenochtitlan Aztecs		Quiché / Cakchiquel Kumarcaaj	
	Mazatecs Mixtecs		
A.D. 1000			
			Chichén Itza Maya-Toltec
			Maya collapse Petén
Fall of Teotihuacan			
A.D. 500			
		Palenque Copán	
			Edzna
			Tikal / Uaxactun Maya
Teotihuacan Toltec			
A.D. 1			
		Kaminaljuyu	
	Monte Alban Zapotec		
		Izapa	Cerros
500 B.C.			
Olmec La Venta / San Lorenzo 2000 B.C. to 300 B.C.			

Diagram 1. The timeline of Mesoamerican civilization

corn-farming villages of Mesoamerica were well-organized and planned. They contained ceremonial centers, religious cults, sacred rulers, and burial mounds. Even the earliest phases of cultural development in Mesoamerica reveal a sophisticated and profound level of social ease, scientific capacity, and artistic sensitivity.

THE PRE-CLASSIC PERIOD

A very early culture in Central Mexico centers on the archaeological site of Cuicuilco. In typical fashion, archaeologists have identified layers of pyramids here, but they are unclear how far back this center can be dated. An earspool with a calendar glyph on it, unearthed at Cuicuilco, was dated to 679 B.C.[2] Laurette Séjourné, in her book *Burning Water*, considers Cuicuilco the precursor to Teotihuacan, the great Toltec metropolis that arose in the first century A.D. However, Cuicuilco, which was destroyed by a volcanic eruption, may have been founded as much as four thousand years ago.

The Olmecs were the first widespread and organized culture in Mexico. Dubbed the Mesoamerican "mother culture" by Mexican artist and scholar Miguel Covarrubias, Olmec civilization took root in the Gulf Coast swamps around 1800 B.C. Its origin is somewhat obscure. Some scholars believe that an earlier precedent for the Olmec can be found in Guerrero state, south of Mexico City.[3] But Olmec sites have been found along the Pacific coasts of Guatemala and El Salvador, suggesting a vigorous and expansive empire during the second millennium B.C. Amazingly, scholars even have argued, rather convincingly, that the Olmec had trade links with the Chavín culture in South America.[4]

The first great Olmec city was San Lorenzo, which was fully formed by 1200 B.C. This site is in the Olmec heartland, a swampy and inhospitable region along the Mexican Gulf Coast stretching from southern Veracruz east to Campeche. Colossal stone heads were found here, some of them weighing forty tons, in addition to over two hundred ceremonial mounds. Strangely, San Lorenzo was suddenly destroyed by human hands around 900 B.C.

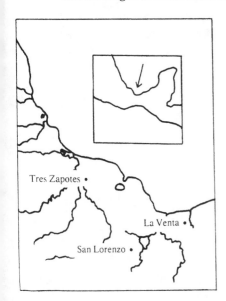

Diagram 2. Towns of the Olmec

La Venta is another important early Olmec site in this region. A cone-shaped pyramid almost a hundred feet high occupies the central precinct of the city, which was built on a small island surrounded by swamps. This pyramid is thought to be Mesoamerica's first large pyramid, built around 1200 B.C., although the structures at Cuicuilco in Central Mexico may be older. La Venta was a thriving ceremonial and market center, and even at this early period in Mesoamerican culture, there is evidence at La Venta of a sophisticated astronomical knowledge. Archaeoastronomical investigation has shown that the pyramid at La Venta was intentionally aligned toward the polar area of the sky and to specific stars in the Big Dipper.[5] The level of precision in these alignments is quite impressive. However, the effects of precession inevitably caused these alignments to "go out of sync," and the Olmec astronomers and temple-builders responded by periodically reorienting the pyramid. Their solution, however, was bound to be temporary, for precession would once again cause a misalignment between the stars and the pyramid. Nevertheless, the realignments of La Venta's pyramid provide persuasive evidence that Olmec astronomers were aware of precession.

As mentioned in the Introduction, precession is caused by the wobbling of Earth's axis and results in a shifting of the rise times of stars. Many Maya specialists believe that early Mesoamerican cultures such as the Olmec were not sophisticated enough to notice precession, because it is a very slow phenomenon. However, precession causes the rising time of a prominent star such as Spica to shift about 1° in seventy-two years. One degree actually spans a fairly large amount of space—consider that the full moon covers one-half of a degree. In the course of only 150 years—a period of time spanning only two or three lifetimes—Spica would shift very noticeably by the distance of about four full moons! If the Olmec skywatchers and others were indeed passing astronomical information down from one generation to another, they could very well, and fairly easily, have tracked precession. And tracking the *rising time* of a single, bright star is only one method early skywatchers may have used to discover precession. At the latitude of La Venta, the polar area of the sky (specifically, the North Celestial Pole) is very close to the horizon. Precession affects the rising *position* of circumpolar stars, and, given La Venta's precise orientation to the circumpolar stars in the Big Dipper, Olmec astronomers easily could have tracked precession-caused changes in the rising position of those stars. The pyramid realignments at La Venta make sense only if we allow that the Olmec were keenly interested in calibrating precession.

But why should the Ancients' understanding of precession be so important to us? This is a complicated question, and it will be answered in detail as the book progresses. Briefly, my research shows that precession was of immense interest to early Mesoamerican astronomers because it changed their relationship to the heavens, exerting dramatic effects on evolving humanity. The Maya were interested in the *big* picture, and, as sophisticated cosmologists, they endeavored to formulate a holistic model of time, evolution, and human nature. As often stated in the literature, the Maya were obsessed with time. Precession, a cycle of almost 26,000 years, was the largest astronomical time cycle that the Maya encountered. It thus represented to them the most profound of mysteries, and their cosmological sights were fixed on figuring out what precession meant for human beings. The Maya recognized that one heavenly object, the Galactic Center, was a key reference point for precessional change. In other words, we might say that precession shifts our "angular" orientation to the Galactic Center, and, as I will show, the Maya believed this to change—indeed, to intensify—evolutionary potential on Earth.

Ultimately, the discovery of precession gave rise to a Maya doctrine of World Ages—the *Popol Vuh* Creation myth—in which Earth and humanity experience cycles of destruction and re-creation over long periods of time. Anticipating realizations that our own science has yet to make, the Maya understood that precession represents a 26,000-year cycle of biological unfolding—a type of spiritual gestation and birth—that Earth and its consciousness-endowed lifeforms undergo. But we are getting ahead of ourselves. Let us return to La Venta and the early skywatchers, for they have more to teach us.

I believe that the evidence at La Venta for the discovery of precession represents a watershed event in the development of Mesoamerican cosmology. But how was this discovery incorporated into Olmec symbology? We can look to the many artifacts excavated at La Venta to get a sense of the Olmecs' mythological and cosmological preoccupations. The jaguar was the primary animal totem of the Olmec. The mouth of the jaguar represented the portal to the Underworld, as did terrestrial caves, where the Olmec priests engaged in shamanistic rituals. Toads, serpents, and birds also were important features of the Olmecs' shamanistic pantheon. Toads were the source of a vision-producing drug and also were the earthly animal totem of the Great Mother Goddess. Attuned to the rhythms of the Earth Mother, toads croak wildly before it rains, announcing the Earth Mother's water blessing. Snakes were symbols of rebirth and immortality, because they shed their skin every year yet do not die. In addition, the snake was also a symbol of the Milky Way.

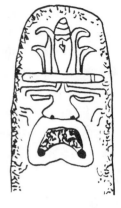

Many Olmec artifacts depict human heads with a small V-shaped cleft in their foreheads. This "cleft-head" motif is very revealing of Olmec ideas about life, birth, and death.

Sacred maize plants are often shown sprouting from these clefts, suggesting they represent a type of divine birthplace. The cleft head, as a divine birthplace, was believed to symbolize the portal between worlds—the doorway between the realm of the living and the realm of the dead, an entrance to the Underworld. The mouth of the jaguar and the cleft head both symbolize a portal to another realm that is also a birthplace. Here we begin to see how different mythological symbols can represent the same underlying concept. When it comes to astronomical concepts, we will find that many mythological symbols may refer to the same astronomical object. For example, Mesoamerican thinkers mythologized the Milky Way as a snake, a road, a river, a toad, and a Cosmic Mother. As we will see later, the cleft-head motif is an Olmec symbol that represents a very important "cleft-like" feature of the Milky Way—a "birthplace doorway" that the December solstice sun will enter on the 2012 end-date.

Diagram 3. The Olmec cleft-head "birthplace" with sprouting maize

At La Venta, as at later Mesoamerican cities, mythology and astronomy were closely related to ideas of political rulership. The emphasis on the relationship between the city's central ceremonial precinct and the ruling king-shaman indicates the presence of sacred kingship at La Venta, an institution central to later Maya society. The king was typically associated with the highest deity, sometimes the sun, but, more importantly, he was associated with the center and origin of the world. This association might take the form of the king's throne being located in—that is, aligned with—the "cosmic center." The Sacred Tree or World Axis was visualized extending down to Earth from this cosmic center. As the polar orientation of La Venta's pyramid suggests, the Olmec probably thought of the polar region as the cosmic center and source. This is not surprising, because the entire sky appears to revolve around the North Celestial Pole. In addition, the Neolithic ancestors of the Olmec who migrated into the New World from the far north of Asia worshiped the Pole Star as the highest deity. This notion survives today in Asia. The symbology and orientation of the sacred ruler's central palace within the Forbidden City (Beijing,

China) reflect an ancient interest in identifying the shaman-ruler with the Pole Star.[6]

In Mesoamerican symbology, in addition to being associated with the cosmic center, the king-shaman was also associated with caves. At Chalcatzingo, a late Olmec site dated to 600 B.C., Monument 1 portrays the sacred ruler, a king-shaman, sitting in a cave.

Shamanic rites, which were central to Mesoamerican religion, were performed in caves by calendar priests and probably even by sacred rulers themselves. You may recall that Maya kings, as shamans, were responsible for mediating knowledge and power flowing between Earth and the invisible, otherworldly domains. The Mesoamerican king-shaman had a foot in both worlds, and is thus depicted enthroned in the cosmic cave, the "portal" between worlds. The cave thus symbolizes the divine throne, a nexus between worlds. In later Maya hieroglyphic writing, caves were indicated by a "cleft-in-hill" glyph, a symbol corresponding to the Olmec cleft-head motif.

Diagram 4. Monument 1 from Chalcatzingo: The Olmec king-shaman enthroned in a cave

As mentioned, the mouth of the jaguar also represented an entrance to the Underworld. In addition, temple doorways, cenotes (sinkholes where water collects), and a woman's birth canal were all symbolic portals to the Underworld—the realm of the ancestors.[7]

Significantly, the Maya of today equate the terrestrial symbols of the Underworld portal with a specific place in the sky. The modern Quiché Maya identify the Great Cleft or "dark-rift" in the Milky Way, which looks like a black road running down its middle, as the "Road to the Underworld."[8] It runs from the stars of Sagittarius northward along the Milky Way, beyond the Aquila constellation. The Quiché term for this dark-rift in the Milky Way is *xibalba be* (*xibalba* = underworld; *be* = road). They also call it the Black Road. Though it may seem unusual

Diagram 5. Temple doorway as monster mouth portal

to locate the Road to the Underworld in the sky, the Maya believe that every night the Underworld rotates above the Earth and becomes the night sky.[9] As such, the dark-rift is the lowest point of the Underworld, but is also the highest point of the night sky. As we will see, recognition of this astronomical feature is critical to understanding the true meaning of the Maya end-date in A.D. 2012.

As the first millennium B.C. drew to a close, both the New World and the Old World were in transition, with conflicting mythologies and political ideologies battling for supremacy. In the Old World, a new paradigm, Christianity, emerged. In the New World, between 400 B.C. and 100 B.C., a great shift occurred in the flow of Mesoamerican civilization. The Olmecs had faded. A cultural style that would come to define the Maya, clearly different from the earlier Olmec tradition, began to emerge. The Pacific coastal regions of Chiapas and Guatemala saw a brief but important upsurge in cultural activity, which centered upon the site of Izapa. Izapa exerted enormous influence for at least three hundred years (250 B.C. to A.D. 50), and it was there that the Long Count calendar, with its intriguing 2012 end-date, was invented.

Over fifty standing carved monuments (stela, pronounced "stee-lah"), altars, and thrones depict scenes from the Maya Creation myth, the *Popol Vuh*, otherwise known as the Hero Twin myth. Dated to the first century B.C., these Izapan monuments are the first representations of the Hero Twin saga to appear in Mesoamerican art. Scholars recognize Izapa as an important archaeological site for what it reveals of Mesoamerica's cultural and political changes, but I came to realize that the knowledge encoded on Izapa's monuments was more astronomical than anthropological. I first noticed that the entire site-plan of Izapa was aligned to the December solstice horizon, suggesting that many of Izapa's monuments may portray astronomical events occurring in that direction. Izapa's ballcourt is aligned to the December solstice horizon, and may have represented the Milky Way. Several monuments depict the rebirth of the First Father solar deity, called One Hunahpu in the *Popol Vuh*. Putting the pieces together, I began to suspect that Izapa's monuments offered a mythic narrative, carved in stone, describing the astronomical alignment charted by the Long Count calendar.

Another major factor in understanding the role of Izapan culture in the development of sophisticated cosmological ideas involves the discovery nearby of many "mushroom stones" (ritual stone effigies of hallucinogenic mushrooms), dated to the era of Izapa's beginnings. The entire Chiapas-Guatemalan Pacific coastal region, with Izapa at the center, apparently was the site of a lengthy experiment in ritualistic and/or scientific use of hallucinogenic mushrooms around 300 B.C. They are evidence that the innovative ideas pioneered at Izapa were informed by the use of psychoactive drugs. As we shall see, an advanced cosmological knowledge emerged at Izapa, suggesting that the Izapans were not just ahead of their own time, they were even ahead of ours.

THE CLASSIC PERIOD

The Classic period (200 A.D. – 900 A.D.) refers specifically to the Maya realm. However, the Teotihuacan-Toltec tradition of Central Mexico (100 A.D. – 750 A.D.) closely paralleled the ascendancy of Maya civilization. These two traditions nurtured trade and political alliances. Although the Toltecs and Maya spoke different languages, they shared many basic beliefs about time, nature, and cosmology. The Maya occupied eastern Mesoamerica and the Toltecs lived some eight hundred kilometers directly to the west, in Central Mexico. As we will see, variations in calendrical tradition between these two realms defined a fundamental underlying difference in their respective conceptualization of World Ages.

Maya civilization has been thoroughly discussed in many popular books.[10] Recent work by archaeologists shows that very early Proto-Classic Maya sites emerged in the lowlands of the Petén (in northern Guatemala) around 100 B.C. Cerros is one of them, thought to be a place where the institution of sacred kingship became standardized. The great Maya cities of Tikal, Uaxactun, and Yaxchilan followed closely. Palenque, a little further to the west, contains astounding carvings and hieroglyphic texts, and today is a beautiful place to visit. In the seventh and eighth centuries A.D., Palenque was ruled by Pacal the Great and his son Chan Bahlum.[11] Many of the sanctuaries and buildings found today at Palenque were dedicated by these rulers. Interestingly, Palenque was ruled by Pacal's mother for a time in the early seventh century, before he effectively took the throne. Among the Classic Maya cities of Chiapas and Petén, a unique form of warfare emerged. Scholars call it Tlaloc-Venus warfare, or "Star Wars," because raiding campaigns were timed by the movements of Venus.[12]

The great southern city of the Maya was Copán, which is in present-day Honduras. William Fash is directing the archaeological project for the Peabody Museum at Copán, and many interesting new discoveries have come to light in recent years. Within the main temple Fash found a sequence of earlier pyramids, built by successive rulers of Copán between A.D. 430 and A.D. 800. Fash's team painstakingly reconstructed Copán's ornately sculpted buildings, revealing some of the esoteric facets of Copán's worldview. A dance platform and surrounding buildings depict episodes from the *Popol Vuh* story of Hunahpu and Xbalanque, the heroic twin sons of the First Father solar deity, One Hunahpu. The Hero Twin myth was the primary element of Copán mystery rites, which included the sacred ballgame, ceremonial dances, plays, and initiations into esoteric knowledge involving astronomical cycles. Fash and other researchers report that the iconography and architectural alignments at Copán reveal an interest in celestial bodies such as the Milky Way, Venus, and the moon.

Fash recently discovered a stela under the Temple of the Hieroglyphic Stairway dated 9.0.0.0.0 in the Long Count, which supports a founding date for Copán around the completion of the ninth baktun (December 9, 435). The ruling dynasty of Copán was founded in A.D. 426 with the accession of Yax-Kuk-Mo' (Blue-Quetzal-Macaw). A total of sixteen kings descended from Yax-Kuk-Mo' and ruled Copán for the next four hundred years. The thirteenth successor was a powerful man named Eighteen-Rabbit who, with his predecessor Smoke-Imix, ruled during Copán's zenith, from A.D. 628 to A.D. 738.

Conservation is a high priority for the directors of the Copán project. A virtual museum housing exact replicas of Copán's sculptures and building façades is being built near the site. Copán's progressive educational museum was inaugurated and opened on July 22, 1996.

In the lowland areas of the Yucatán to the north, in places like Chichén Itzá, Uxmal, Labnah, and Kabah, Maya culture took different forms, especially in regard to architectural design. These sites are impressive, and reveal that the people who built them were interested in Venus, the moon, and other astronomical bodies and events. For example, the Nunnery Complex at Uxmal contains a total of 584 windows, which is the number of days in a Venus cycle.[13] Uxmal also contains an interesting and unique oval-shaped pyramid, called the Pyramid of the Magician. Chichén Itzá contains the Caracol observatory and the Pyramid of Kukulcan (the "Castillo"), on which an amazing shadow-play cast by the late afternoon sun can be viewed every spring equinox. During this celestial "hierophany," the late afternoon equinox sun casts a shadow-image of the Maya snake deity Kukulcan against the balustrade of the north stairway, heralding the return of the life-giving serpent power and the continuance of life. Since the 1970s, this event has drawn increasingly large numbers of observers, who witness firsthand the amazing architectural and astronomical abilities of the ancient Maya. In looking closely at the esoteric symbology of this event, I discovered an alignment between the sun, the Pleiades, and the zenith that has until now gone unnoticed. I explore the implications of this lost cosmology, encoded into the Pyramid of Kukulcan at Chichén Itzá, in Part II.

In the ninth century A.D., Maya civilization began to disintegrate. Central autonomy and control fell apart due to a variety of factors including warfare, environmental degradation, drought, and diseases. Scholars attribute the Classic Maya collapse primarily to the proliferation of minor princedoms, each seeking its piece of the pie. In other words, *greed* contributed to the Maya downfall, a sobering message for our own times. By A.D. 950 the former glory of the Maya was no more. However, the Maya did not simply disappear, as has often been written. Their style of living changed, and their culture became decentralized, adapting to the effects of the collapse. In fact, certain Maya areas of Mesoamerica thrived after the collapse.

THE POST-CLASSIC PERIOD

The period between the Maya collapse and the arrival of the Spanish, roughly A.D. 900 to A.D. 1520, is called the Post-Classic period. Around A.D. 1200 the highlands of Guatemala were colonized by the Quiché and Cakchiquel people, who by 1520 had established an impressive empire. In the Yucatán peninsula, Toltec refugees from Teotihuacan arrived around A.D. 800, following long-established trade routes, and inspired a Post-Classic renaissance that we may call hybrid Toltec-Maya. The east-west cultural division we identified for the Classic era Toltec and Maya cultures thus shifted to a Post-Classic north-south division in which certain basic Toltec concepts and beliefs were transferred to the former lowland Maya realm of the Yucatán, while uniquely Maya traditions were preserved to the south, in Chiapas and Guatemala. This distinction will be important as we look at the calendric and cosmological traditions from these different areas, how they were designed to calibrate alignments in the precessional cycle, and how they were synthesized at Chichén Itzá.

The Post-Classic period also saw a flowering of Toltec-derived cultural traditions in Central Mexico. By the time of Spanish contact, Mixtec, Huastec, Mazatec, Aztec, and Zapotec people dominated the cultural scene. These groups lived in the mountains and wide valleys of Central Mexico, claimed Tollan (probably Teoti-huacan) as their ancestral homeland, and spoke various dialects of the Nahuatl language. In this way, Toltec traditions continued to grow and had spread as far east as the Yucatán. As mentioned, the Quiché and Cakchiquel Maya settled areas of the Guatemalan highlands in the Post-Classic period. The Quiché capital was at Kumarcaaj (near present-day Santa Cruz del Quiché). Kumarcaaj became known as Utatlán, and detailed dynastic histories of the Quiché are preserved in the *Popol Vuh* and various colonial documents.[14] After Spanish contact and a dramatic battle between conquistador Pedro Alvarado and the Quiché leader Tecun Uman, in which Tecun Uman was killed, the Spanish established and administered a new capital at Iximché. Today the Quiché are a vital people, despite being marginalized and perse-cuted by the Guatemalan government.

With all the intercultural activity in the Post-Classic Yucatán, Chichén Itzá and its sister city Mayapan experienced a series of political intrigues. Mayapan was founded in the tenth century A.D., and eventually formed a triple alliance with Uxmal and Chichén Itzá, called the League of Mayapan. These three strong cities were to exert equal power, but from the beginning Mayapan sought sole control. While peace lasted, the land prospered, art flourished, and architecture soared. Even-tually, because of the treachery of Hunnan Ceel, leader of Mayapan, the league erupted into civil war. The Itzás warred with Mayapan, but Hunnan Ceel brought in Mexican-Toltec allies and defeated the Itzá. The Xiu lineage began at this time, and is traceable up to the present day. In the 1450s Mayapan was utterly destroyed. All the Xiu nobility were killed except for one son, Tutul Xiu, who happened to be away at the time. Tutul Xiu reestablished his lineage at nearby Mani, and when the Spanish arrived, he was ruling that province.

THE POST-CONTACT

After contact with European invaders lusting after gold, Mesoamerica was radi-cally changed. This period was nothing short of a holocaust for indigenous peoples, many dying of disease and many others subjected to a quick journey into Christian hellfire by way of torture and dismemberment. Many material artifacts of Maya culture and genius were destroyed at this time. As documented in recent ethno-graphic studies, it is miraculous that many indigenous peoples of Mesoamerica have been able to preserve their traditions to the present day. The highland Maya in particular have continued to follow many central traditions of the ancient Maya religion, including the 260-day sacred calendar. In fact, they preserve the ancient Classic-period placement of the 260-day calendar, itself based upon the earlier Olmec placement, indicating a Mesoamerican continuity of calendar tradition extending over 3,000 years.[15] In comparison, the continuity of tradition in Central Mexico and in lowland Yucatán, areas subjected to greater persecution, has not fared so well. In Mexico, Maya tradition is preserved to a large extent in the highlands of Chiapas, and in Tzotzil and Tzeltal towns such as San Larrainzar, Chamula, and Zinacantan. But recent events in Guatemala and Chiapas have devastated traditional Maya culture. Probably more disruption and destruction of Maya culture has taken place since 1970 than in the last three hundred years. Sadly, these events result from our movement into a type of transnational feudalism driven by Wall Street and other U.S. money-engines. In other quarters, observers report a healthy resurgence of Maya culture and an avid interest among young Maya in their own history and cultural identity.[16]

The epic span of Mesoamerican history is impressive, reminding us that here, in this "new" continent, a self-sufficient and vital civilization once lived. The descendants of this civilization are still with us, and we can learn much by listening to them and studying their culture. Mesoamerican civilization pioneered many original traditions, a complex hieroglyphic writing system, and brilliant cosmo-conceptions not found elsewhere in the world. The unique calendar systems developed in Mesoamerica most clearly testify to the genius of Mesoamerican thinkers, who wove together mythology, political organization, religion, and astronomy into one seamless whole. As the true implications of ancient Maya cosmology resurface, the renaissance of indigenous cultures should be stimulated even further. The year 2012 may be a rallying cry for the modern Maya to understand and reclaim the greatness of their peoples' past achievements.

CHAPTER 2

CALENDRICS: MAPPING METHODS

Calendars were, and still are, used by the Maya to map and structure various aspects of human experience, from agricultural activities to observed cycles in the sky. The 260-day Mesoamerican calendar is used for both of these purposes, and this is where its greatest function can be found—it unites the processes of heaven and earth. The Nahuatl-speaking people of Central Mexico called the 260-day cycle the *tonalpohualli* (the book of days). Among the Maya people and academic specialists, it became known as the *tzolkin*.[1] In this book I will refer to it as the tzolkin or the sacred cycle. The tzolkin consists of twenty day-signs combined with a number from one to thirteen, thus creating a total of 260 unique units. The day-signs and numbers of the tzolkin are counted alongside each other, the same way our own month days and weekday names are tracked. For example, we would say for the month of April 1998 that Wednesday the 1st is followed by Thursday the 2nd, Friday the 3rd, and so on. The day name and the number click off simultaneously. Likewise, April 1, 1998, was 8 Iq' in the Quiché Maya tzolkin calendar, followed by 9 Aq'ab'al, 10 K'at, and so on. The combined cycles of thirteen and twenty make the tzolkin a mystical "time tool" for those who count it and track life events by its rhythms. Contemporary Quiché Maya daykeepers name the days as follows:[2]

QUICHÉ	ENGLISH
Kej	Deer
Q'anil	Yellow
Toj	Thunder

Tz'i'	Dog
Batz	Monkey
Eb	Tooth
Aj	Cane
Ix	Jaguar
Tz'ikin	Bird
Ajmak	Sinner
No'j	Thought
Tijax	Blade
Kawuq	Rain
Junajpu	Marksman
Imox	Lefthanded
Iq'	Wind
Aq'ab'al	Foredawn
K'at	Net
Kan	Snake
Kame	Death

Significantly, the modern Quiché Maya follow the same placement of the tzolkin (its location in real time) as did their Classic-period ancestors. In other words, a continuity of tradition has reached through the centuries, undisturbed by the Classic-period collapse and the ravages of the Conquest. This survival reveals how durable the Maya calendar is, and makes us wonder how much else of the ancient knowledge still survives in the remote villages of Central America.

The tzolkin has many rich and varied uses. In the 1970s, Quiché calendar-priest Andres Xiloj told ethnographers that the tzolkin's origin was based upon the nine-month period of human gestation. A period of 260 days very closely approximates the interval between when a woman first stops menstruating and her child is born. Maya midwives to this day calculate birth dates with the tzolkin. Maya daykeepers—those who follow the tzolkin—believe the day on which a child is born within the 260-day cycle determines personality characteristics. In this way, the tzolkin serves as an astrological oracle—a "book" that reveals a person's weaknesses and virtues.

The tzolkin calendar also is used in divination. Contemporary Quiché Maya calendar-priests in highland Guatemala use the tzolkin to answer questions for clients, such as the location of a stolen object, the wisdom of entering into a business deal, or marriage prospects. In addition to these magical properties, the 260-day sacred calendar also has astronomical uses. Because two tzolkin periods (520 days) equal three eclipse half-years (during which exactly three eclipses will occur), the tzolkin was used to predict eclipses. Through the tzolkin's many uses we see how Maya cosmovision weaves together biological Earth cycles (human gestation) and celestial sky cycles (eclipses). This parallelism reveals a fundamental principle recognized by the Maya, also acknowledged in Western mystery religions: as above, so below. Long ago, the Maya intuited that celestial cycles harmoniously reflect cycles on Earth. These Maya insights into the organizational tendencies of nature, what we might call an indigenous holographic paradigm, can be traced back at least to the invention of the tzolkin calendar, to the Olmec roughly 3,000 years ago.

As already mentioned, thirteen and twenty are the key numbers of the tzolkin, the "building blocks" of Maya time philosophy. Thirteen refers to the waxing phase of the moon—its new-to-full phase. Although one-half of a lunar phase–cycle mathematically equals 14.8 days rather than 13, the Maya placed greater importance on actual observations. The moon reappears as a sliver in the western skies *one day after* "moon dark" (the day on which the moon is too close to the sun to be seen). Likewise, for all observational purposes the full moon can be observed for at least two days. Thus, the count from new appearance to fullness is thirteen days. The number twenty refers to a human being's twenty fingers and toes, and also to the twenty-day *uinal* period of the Long Count calendar. In fact, the Maya words for "person" (*uinac*) and "month" (*uinal*) are similar. The 260-day tzolkin calendar is thus an ingenious multivalued "cosmic key," uniting human, agricultural, and astronomical cycles.[3]

The yearly cycle of the sun, known to the Maya as the *haab* (the "cycle of rains"), approximates the 365.2422-day solar year to 365 days. Probably one of the first astronomical cycles tracked by early Mesoamerican farmers, the haab consists of eighteen months of twenty days each, with a five-day "extra" month at the end. The haab is called a secular calendar because it was used primarily to time mundane agricultural activities, such as the planting and harvesting of maize. The tzolkin and haab were tracked simultaneously, each scheduling its own ritual or agricultural agenda. According to Maya scholar Munro Edmonson, the Olmec were using both the "sacred" tzolkin calendar and the "secular" haab by the seventh century

B.C. Thus, these two basic Mesoamerican calendars were in place even before the Long Count calendar was invented.

THE CALENDAR ROUND

Combined, the tzolkin-haab system defines a cycle of just under fifty-two years, called the Calendar Round.[4] Some scholars have dubbed this period the Maya or Aztec "century," but to eliminate confusion caused by forcing indigenous concepts through Western filters, I prefer the terms Calendar Round or the tzolkin-haab calendar, both of which I will use in this book.

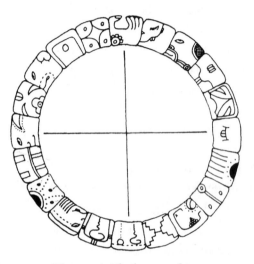

As with our own yearly cycle, the first day of the haab was thought of as New Year's Day. When the haab is combined with the tzolkin, four day-signs of the tzolkin are highlighted as being very important, because they are the only day-signs on which New Year's Day (in the haab) can fall. This fact arises from the mathematical dynamics of the two combined cycles. In the Quiché calendar still in use, these special day-signs, called "year-bearers," are *Kej* (Deer), *Eb* (Tooth), *N'oj* (Thought) and *Iq* (Wind).[5] Refer to the table of day-signs given on pages 17 and 18 to see how these four year-bearers

Diagram 6. The four year-bearers quarter the circle of twenty day-signs

are each five days apart. When you place the twenty day-signs in a circle, the four year-bearers quarter the circle.

In Maya cosmo-conception, the year-bearers were associated with the four sacred mountains of the four directions, as well as the four seasonal quarters (the two equinoxes and the two solstices). As such, a direction, a sacred mountain, and a seasonal quarter are associated with each year-bearer. This will be important to remember when we explore the calendric and mythological identity of the December solstice sun.

As mentioned, the Calendar Round of roughly fifty-two years is derived from the large cycle resulting from combining the tzolkin and the haab calendars. The ancient Maya used it, as did their Toltec cousins in Central Mexico. The later Aztecs also adopted the Calendar Round, and adhered to its esoteric meaning as a World Age calendar that was defined by the earlier Toltecs. The importance of this Calendar Round cycle to the Toltecs and the Aztecs is related to their concept of World Ages. In the Toltec-Aztec New Fire ceremony, the end of the world was expected to occur at the end of a Calendar Round, but only if the Pleiades failed to pass through the zenith (the exact center of the sky overhead) on the appropriate night. The zenith is an important feature of this World Age doctrine, and in my work to reconstruct Mesoamerican cosmology I determined that both the Calendar Round and the New Fire tradition were used to track precession. I will have a lot more to say about this in Part II. For now it is important to understand that the tzolkin-haab framework, the Calendar Round, was only one method used by Mesoamerican skywatchers to structure their expectations of future World Age shifts. The second major tracking method, or calendar of World Ages, is the Maya Long Count calendar.

THE LONG COUNT: THE GALACTIC CALENDAR

The ancient pre-Maya skywatchers of Mesoamerica created a sophisticated system of timekeeping known as the Long Count calendar. Long Count dates first start appearing in the archaeological record in the first century B.C., although the Long Count's formulation may have been in process for hundreds of years prior to that. The Long Count system is based upon nested cycles of days multiplied at each level by that key Maya number, twenty:

NUMBER OF DAYS	TERM
1	kin (day)
20	uinal
360	tun
7,200	katun
144,000	baktun

Notice, however, that the only exception to multiplying by twenty is at the tun level, where, in order to approximate the solar year, the uinal period is instead multiplied by 18 to make the 360-day tun. The Maya employed this counting system to track an unbroken sequence of days from the time it was inaugurated.

Munro Edmonson believes that the Long Count was put in place around 355 B.C.[6] However, the oldest Long Count date as yet found corresponds to 37 B.C. Of course, the Long Count may have been recorded on perishable materials for a long time before it began to be recorded in stone, but a conservative appraisal of the evidence, incorporating the archaeological, calendric, and ethnohistoric material, strongly suggests that the Long Count began to be officially counted in the first century B.C. Given that the Long Count appears to have been designed to calibrate precession, an endeavor that may have taken hundreds of years of astronomical observations to perfect, it is probably safe to say that the Long Count calendar was being perfected between 400 B.C. and 100 B.C., and was inaugurated in the first century B.C.

Although the Long Count calendar can be extended beyond the 13-baktun end-date, and, indeed, huge Long Count numbers have been identified in Maya codices and elsewhere, 13 baktuns is recorded on Maya monuments as the great Creation cycle of World Ages. We know this because Classic-period Maya Creation monuments record the end of the last Creation cycle, over 5,000 years ago, as the end of the thirteenth baktun. Furthermore, we find most Long Count dates in the archaeological record beginning with the fifth place value, the baktun.

Modern notation separates Long Count place values with a dot. For example, 6.19.19.0.0 equals 6 baktuns, 19 katuns, 19 tuns, 0 uinals, and 0 days. As can be seen in the chart given above, each baktun has 144,000 days, each katun has 7,200 days, and so on. If we add up all the values, we find that 6.19.19.0.0 indicates that a total of 1,007,640 days has elapsed since the Zero Date of 0.0.0.0.0. The much-discussed 13-baktun cycle is completed 1,872,000 days (13 baktuns) after 0.0.0.0.0. This period of time is the so-called Maya "Great Cycle" of the Long Count and equals 5,125.36 years. The Maya conceived of the Great Cycle as one World Age, one growth cycle, at the end of which humanity reaches the next stage in its spiritual development. As the life of an individual goes through distinct stages, so too the collective lifewave of humanity grows through several distinct phases. These "phases" are the five World Ages, or "Suns," spoken of in Mesoamerican mythology. Furthermore, thirteen baktuns reflect the thirteen numbers of the tzolkin, which, as we saw earlier, represent the new-to-full process of the moon. As such, the microcycle of the moon's unfolding parallels the macrocycle of 5,125 years—the seed-to-flower cycle operative on the level of human civilization.

Thus, according to Maya calendric science, the Great Cycle times our collective unfolding as a species, as well as the cycles of culture. But how are we to relate the 5,125-year Great Cycle to a time frame we can understand? When did it begin, and why? How does the Long Count relate to our Gregorian calendar?

The problem of correlating the Maya calendar with the Judeo-Christian Gregorian calendar has intrigued scholars for a hundred years. The standard question became: What does 0.0.0.0.0 (the Long Count "beginning" date) equal in the Judeo-Christian Gregorian calendar? When this question is answered, archaeological inscriptions can be put into their proper historical context and the end-date of the 13-baktun World Age cycle can be calculated. By 1950, after years of considering data from varied fields such as astronomy, ethnography, archaeology, and iconography, scholars determined that 0.0.0.0.0 corresponded to August 11, 3114 B.C. in our Gregorian calendar. This "correlation" became known as the GMT, named after the three scholars who contributed to its reconstruction: Joseph T. Goodman, Juan Martinez Hernández, and J. Eric S. Thompson. The GMT correlation determines that the Long Count end-date of 13.0.0.0.0 is December 21, 2012.[7] Significantly, of all proposed correlations, the GMT is the only one validated by both carbon-14 dating and the fact that it is synchronized with the surviving Quiché Maya count.

The Maya used Long Count katun periods, each lasting about twenty years, to celebrate significant junctures in a king's reign. Some kings ruled for two or more full katuns, a measure of stature and success. But these katun intervals are relative to when the king took office. Katun shifts in the Long Count are really determined by the fixed beginning date, similar to our own unavoidable decade-ending or century-ending transitions. Katun endings were sometimes celebrated with the smashing of stelae and sculpture, a symbolic gesture of a new beginning. Baktun endings, coming every 394 years, were especially important to the Maya, because they marked the end of a large cycle of time. A baktun ending occurred in A.D. 830, just as the Maya civilization started disintegrating. Some scholars have suggested that the Maya collapse was in part caused by a type of self-fulfilling apocalypse.[8] In the same way that an impending katun ending stimulated anticipation and fears about letting go of the old cycle and its concerns, the larger baktun-cycle ending catalyzed even greater fervor, excitement, and end-of-the-world fears. Remember, the Maya considered the end of the full 13-baktun cycle to herald a major World Age shift. But up until now no one has correctly identified and explored the reason for this belief. As my work shows, the fact is that a rare astronomical alignment in the cycle of precession is due to occur in A.D. 2012, and the Maya knew of it and understood its implications.

I have come to understand the Calendar Round and the Long Count calendars as precession-tracking tools, but each system uses a different methodology. While the Calendar Round was the unit of World Age calculation for the Toltecs and Aztecs of Central Mexico, for the Maya the unit was the katuns and baktuns of the Long Count. The important concept in the Long Count calendar for understanding how World Ages were tracked involves the position of the sun on the end-date and the "cosmic center" marked by the Maya Sacred Tree. As Maya scholar Linda Schele has shown, the four-directional Maya Sacred Tree is the cosmic crossroads formed by the Milky Way and the ecliptic (the path followed by the planets, moon, and sun).[9] As already mentioned, the astounding property of the Long Count end-date, revealing how it structures World Ages, is the simple fact that *the December solstice sun will be in conjunction with the center of this Sacred Tree on the Long Count end-date.* This convergence is caused by the precession of the equinoxes, and defines a rare "alignment era" in the cycle of precession. Given that the Sacred Tree also targets the Galactic Center within its crosshairs, I began to call the Long Count the Galactic Calendar. Furthermore, I termed the complex of ideas associated with the mythology and astronomy of the Long Count end-date the Galactic Cosmology.

The implications of the Long Count calendar were mind-boggling. However, as I reconstructed the lost precession astronomy of Mesoamerica, it became clear to me that the Toltecs recognized and tracked, with the Calendar Round and the New Fire ceremony, a precessional alignment that was different from the one tracked by the Maya with the Long Count calendar. Although this new discovery threatened to complicate my thesis, I could not ignore it. Since the Toltec system involved a rare alignment in the zenith, I termed it the Zenith Cosmology. Ultimately, I discovered that both methods were unified at Chichén Itzá in the ninth century A.D., and, amazingly, both astronomical alignments will occur in the early twenty-first century, thus mutually supporting each other. Here we catch a glimpse of the profound esoteric content of Mesoamerican cosmology, perspectives that are just beginning to come into view. My pioneering reconstruction of this lost cosmology opens up a greater appreciation for the true scope of ancient Mesoamerican science and religion. As A.D. 2012 approaches, a hidden knowledge is bursting forth, ready to be recognized and integrated into a world dying for new life. And, perhaps, a last chance.

A critical component of the two methods for tracking precession that I discovered and will explore more deeply in Part II is the concept of the "cosmic center." As will become clear, Mesoamerican skywatchers tracked alignments in precession in relation to a chosen cosmic center. But which cosmic center? Was it the North Celestial Pole that, as we saw earlier, was of interest to the Olmec at La Venta? Was it the zenith center (the exact center of the sky overhead) recognized in the Toltec-Aztec New Fire ceremony? Or did Mesoamerican skywatchers place primary significance on the Galactic Center? If so, what evidence is there for such a thesis?

The cosmic center is a significant, overarching concept in Mesoamerican cosmology. Finding the center was important not only to Mesoamerican skywatchers but to political leaders, because the cosmic center (also understood as a divine birthplace) was the "sacred throne" symbolically occupied by political rulers. Maya kings, who were really king-shamans, were required to journey into the cosmic center to retrieve sacred knowledge and the otherworldly power of rulership. But because the movements of celestial bodies are extremely complex, Mesoamerican skywatchers ultimately had to entertain three possible cosmic centers. As we shall see, they determined one to be false, another to be valid but limited to a specific latitude of observation, and the third to be supreme.

CHAPTER 3

COSMOLOGY: FINDING THE CENTER

W e have taken a look at the timeline of culture in Mesoamerica and briefly introduced the role of two different types of World Age calendar systems invented by Mesoamerican thinkers, the Calendar Round and the Long Count. I pointed out how the Calendar Round tradition was used primarily by the Toltecs and the Long Count belonged to the Maya. Another consideration, which will synthesize some of the ideas we have been discussing, falls under the heading of cosmovision or cosmology. Cosmology involves knowledge about the world's origins and its processes of development. The Maya were attuned to spiritual considerations, and for them the world's developmental processes must have included humanity's spiritual unfolding, a process described in their World Age mythology. The doctrine of World Ages is basically a philosophy of change, an insight into the nature of time and reality, such that the world is perceived to periodically renew itself. This insight, which also applies to the ups and downs of human civilization, is derived from observing nature. Nature is filled with affirmations about the cycles of time. The seasons wax and wane throughout the year. Birth, growth, death, and rebirth occur in unending cycles. Likewise, long-range chapters in human development give way, during brief periods of intense change, to a new "era" or "age" in which different aspects of human nature are emphasized. These are concepts intrinsic to Maya as well as Buddhist and Hindu religion. In comparison, the Judeo-Christian worldview espouses a doctrine of linear time, with a distinct beginning and a distinct, apocalyptic end. What is amazing about the basic tenets of the Maya worldview is that they are shared by religions currently followed by over half the planet.

WORLDMAKING, WORLDCENTERING, WORLDRENEWING

Despite the many varieties of cosmological traditions in Mesoamerica, we can distill some general universal principles. Following the work of Mesoamerican scholar Davíd Carrasco, we can identify three basic processes or concerns that apply to Mesoamerican culture as a whole: *worldmaking, worldcentering* and *worldrenewing*.[1] In Mesoamerican thought, the layout and orientation of each city were understood to be a reflection of the cosmic order. To mirror the important philosophical concept of a cosmic source and center located in the sky above, the socio-political realm was ordered by authority emanating from the city center. Likewise, the cosmic center, functioning both on Earth and in the sky, was considered to be a symbolic birthplace and source of universal order. Worldmaking is the first act in creating universal order, and in Mesoamerica it was accomplished through deity sacrifice. The Aztec myth describing the creation of the Fifth Age is a good illustration of how this happened:

Before the first sun had risen, before the first dawn, the gods assembled themselves at the ceremonial city of Teotihuacan. For four days they performed penances around a sacred fire, symbol of the divine center. Their sacrifices were intended to conjure the world into being. It soon became clear that a very great sacrifice would be necessary to succeed in such an ambitious endeavor. So, in a blissful moment of inspired self-sacrifice, two of the deities hurled themselves into the fire. The gods then halted their rites and looked around for where the sun would rise, sensing that the immolation might have been enough to create the dawn. One of the gods, Quetzalcoatl, faced the east, and there, off in the distance, the sun rose just over the horizon. Thus the world was made through the self-sacrifice of two deities, through offerings to the central axis mundi. *The first act of cosmogenesis, of creating the world, had been accomplished.*

The sun now sat in the east, but there was a problem. It did not move; it just hovered there. The dawn had come, but the world was going nowhere. The world, unfortunately, had "no stability, no process, no center."[2] In other words, the world still needed to be centered, something that can only be accomplished in the field of movement, of time. In the act of worldcentering, the pressing question is: How can the world "find a pattern, orbit, process?"[3] At this unfinished stage, the sun can only remain motionless, hovering, without process. In other words, *centering is a function of time.* This point will become important when we look at the evolution of cosmology after the Olmec era, when a very large time factor—precession—became undeniable.

Because the worldcentering act can occur only in reference to time, movement, and process, the Aztec gods had to make a greater sacrifice. In the Aztec myth, *all* of the remaining gods sacrificed themselves to set the world in motion. But Ehecatl, god of wind, was the one who really got things moving. As god of wind, he sacrificed himself by releasing himself into the world, stirring up a storm to get things turning. Thus, through a total self-sacrifice of the gods, releasing themselves fully into their desired creation, the world was set in motion, and time began. Theirs was an act of centering because time and motion, *process*, could now keep the world in balance.

Centering the village, centering the body, centering the sky—in effect, centering the cosmos on all levels—was a primary concern to Mesoamerican society, affecting the health and balance of each region's ritual and socio-political existence. The astronomical component of this endeavor, finding the center of the sky, was the province of the calendar-priests and skywatchers. Among the Quiché Maya these astronomer-priests are called *nik' wakinal*, "those who look into the center." Like the gods of the first time, the modern priests perform sacrifices to keep the world rolling, to keep time moving forward to its hoped-for, but not inevitable, recycling at the end of the age.

World rebirth is the third time principle in Mesoamerican thought which, in Carrasco's model, is called "worldrenewal." As cultural, calendric, and political eras came to a close, new rituals and myths emerged as creative adaptations to changing conditions. These were implemented at appropriate intervals in the cyclic calendar. Mesoamerican calendar cycles defined renewal intervals, from daily renewal to intervals of thirteen days, twenty days, up to the uinal, tun, katun, baktun, and even larger cycles. These times of calendric recycling told the Classic-period calendar-priests when to make worldrenewing sacrifices, and included the ritual destruction of old monuments and the inauguration of new ones.

Both worldmaking and worldrenewal are rooted in the concept of cosmogenesis. Creation and re-Creation happen in endless cycles, an idea implicit in the Mesoamerican doctrine of World Ages. Thus, if cosmogenesis (the birth of the current World Age) occurred back in 3114 B.C., then A.D. 2012 represents a new cosmogenesis. In short, the Maya believed the world, the cosmos, will be reborn, or re-created, in A.D. 2012. This is why my book is called *Maya Cosmogenesis 2012*.

Worldcentering occurs in the field of time, in the phase of universal unfolding that occurs between Creation (worldmaking) and re-Creation (worldrenewal). In Mesoamerica, the passage of time was charted with the cyclic motion of astronomical events.[4] Considering the close relationship between time and world-centering, only by gaining an understanding of astronomical time cycles could the Mesoamerican skywatchers approach an understanding of where the true cosmic center was located. Furthermore, only upon locating the "center" of the world—the celestial center and its earthly counterpart—could the Ancients "anchor" time and thereby orient themselves to the cosmos in the correct way. In other words, it was critical for Mesoamerican calendrics and cosmology, as well as socio-political orientation, to understand cosmic cycles, and this naturally included the precession of the equinoxes. In fact, accurately calculating the rate of precession probably emerged as the greatest enigma for Mesoamerican skywatchers, the solution to which would define the proper orientation to the cosmos, an orientation necessary for the well-being of all.

As mentioned earlier, alignments in precession were tracked in relation to the concept of a cosmic center. We are not talking here about a vague metaphysical concept. Rather, we are tuning in to the mindset of the ancient Mesoamerican skywatchers and divining what their interests and goals were; we are talking here about astronomy. When Mesoamerican astronomers looked up at the cosmic ocean of the night sky—that vast expanse they believed to be the inverted Underworld—three regions attracted their attention, seductively offering solutions to the cosmic-center mystery. To the north, low on the horizon, they saw the sky revolving around the North Celestial Pole. This must have been a compelling candidate for the cosmic center. However, the zenith[5] (the exact center of the sky overhead) also represents a compelling center. In the tropical latitudes, the sun passes through the zenith at high noon twice a year. Because the exact date of the sun's zenith passage depends on one's latitude of observation, ambiguity exists in the zenith-as-center concept. For example, at Chichén Itzá the second annual solar zenith passage occurs on July 26. Hundreds of kilometers to the south, at Copán, the second annual solar zenith passage takes place on August 13.

The cosmic center was believed to represent not only the center of Creation, but the source of Creation. The search for the center thus had to somehow satisfy these two criteria. In many Mesoamerican myths, the Great Mother in the sky—the cosmic birther and source of manifestation—was envisioned as the Milky Way, and the bright and wide part of the Milky Way near Sagittarius (its "great bulge") presents itself as the womb of the sky, the pregnant belly of the Milky Way Mother, the center and source of Creation. In fact, as mentioned in the Introduction, this area of the Milky Way is where the Galactic Center is located, which is, in fact, the center of our Galaxy and the source-point of everything in it. There is ample evidence to suggest Mesoamericans recognized these three cosmic centers, each of which vied for recognition as the true Heart of Sky. The Maya skywatchers had a difficult problem to solve, one based upon a careful and conscious consideration of these facts.

When were these compelling and sophisticated facts recognized? For example, when did the Mesoamerican skywatchers discover the zenith concept? When did they begin to understand the Milky Way as an important axis and its great bulge as a cosmic source? What evidence do we have that the early Mesoamerican people were at all interested in these concepts? To answer these questions, we have to do some historical detective work, and take a look at how cosmology evolved in the New World. We can begin with the early migrations of Asian people into the New World, determine what their cosmological ideas were, and then track how ideas about the center of the sky changed as people migrated southward in the New World.

THE POLAR GOD GOES SOUTH: EARLY ASIAN MIGRATIONS INTO THE NEW WORLD

Scholars generally agree that Asian people migrated from the Far North across the Bering Strait into the New World at various times, depending upon glaciation that formed land bridges. These migrations probably came in distinct waves sixty, thirty-five, and ten thousand years ago. Geographer and historian Paul Shao suggests that more recent migrations from northern China may have occurred along this route.[6] Even trans-Pacific voyages to the New World by ancient Polynesians cannot be ruled out. Basically, however, people primarily moved from the northern latitudes eastward and southward into the Americas. These people originated in or passed through northern China and followed a land route through northeastern Siberia and Alaska.

Because indigenous cultures in these areas today are intrinsically shamanistic, and because Neolithic cultures have been shown to belong to an ancient global shamanism, we can surmise that the ancient cultures who migrated into the New World were shamanistic as well. As such, their basic cosmological ideas were probably very similar to those surviving today among Siberian tribes and other cultures in the Far North. Shamans of these groups undertake visionary journeys into the cosmic center, the Pole Star, to retrieve sacred otherworldly knowledge and powers. For them, the North Celestial Pole is believed to be the highest god, the source and center of existence, as well as their visionary destination. The Pole Star is recognized as the undeniable cosmic center because, at northern latitudes, it is very high in the sky and the stars spin around it. In these northern regions, the zenith-as-center concept does not threaten the Polar God for supremecy because, outside of the tropical latitudes, the sun never passes through the zenith.

For the shamanistic cultures migrating into the Americas, religious ideas about journeying to the cosmic center were no doubt very time-resistant. The hazards of entering new bioregions, the development of migration myths, and the human fears and worries that accompanied their journeys all required that the shamans retained a strong link with the Polar God. The concept of the Polar God among these shamanistic people already had a long history, probably extending far back into the Paleolithic Era. But what happened as these groups moved southward through the Americas? What happened to their ancient concept of a high Polar Deity as the cosmic center? Clearly, migrations southward must have had some effect on these cosmological ideas. The polar area loses its prominence in the Tropics; as you move further south, the North Celestial Pole gets lower and lower on the horizon. Its declination (angular distance above the horizon) varies from 0° at the equator to 90° at the North Pole. (Interestingly, this means that the North Celestial Pole is in the zenith at the North Pole.) A celestial object's declination always equals the latitude of observation. So, at the 18°N latitude of La Venta, for instance, the North Celestial Pole was observed some 18° above the horizon, resulting in a very different sky than was observed in the Far North. The sky there appears more like a spinning barrel than a revolving, upward-pointing merry-go-round.

In astronomical terms, the North Celestial Pole is identified by Earth's polar axis. It is the Earth's axis projected onto the celestial sphere; this is why the stars appear to revolve around it. The North Celestial Pole is not always occupied by a star. Precession causes the position of the North Celestial Pole to shift, so sometimes there is a Pole Star but sometimes there is not. Some 4,600 years ago, the

Pole Star was Draco. Currently, it is Polaris. Nevertheless, ancient shaman-skywatchers of the Far North continuously recognized the North Celestial Pole, whether occupied by a star or not, as the cosmic source and center. That is, they did until southward migrations threatened the sovereignty of the Polar God with more complex considerations, namely, precession.

My model is basically this: With human migrations southward into the Americas, cosmological ideas about the cosmic center changed and evolved. The Polar God went south and was exposed as being an illusion. My model is not without basis in at least one documented migration legend. In his book *Star Trek to Hawa-i'i*, Clyde Hostetter describes the legend of Maui, who lengthened the day in order to give the Polynesians more time to do their work. Hostetter argues convincingly that the story of Maui's accomplishment commemorates a time in the ancient past when a seagoing people followed their leader from northern latitudes to Hawaii, a land nearer the equator where the days are never short. In a similar fashion, the *Popol Vuh* story of the "false" god Seven Macaw, who corresponds with the Big Dipper, illustrates how Mesoamericans determined the ancient Polar God to be untrustworthy. The Hero Twins had to shoot Seven Macaw out of his polar perch, and it is quite clear that this myth reflects astronomy. I will have a lot more to say about the mytho-astronomical fall of Seven Macaw in Part IV. But for now, let's continue exploring how Mesoamericans sought to determine the true cosmic center from among the three candidates.

LA VENTA: A POLAR CULT

I believe another example for a latitude-related shift in cosmological orientation can be found among the Olmec, at La Venta. There, the ancient interest in the Polar God was institutionalized, but it fell from grace when the Olmec astronomers realized that the sky was shifting. As mentioned, at the 18°N latitude of La Venta, the North Celestial Pole and the circumpolar constellations such as the Big Dipper and Little Dipper are very low on the northern horizon. The primary axis of La Venta, including its pyramid, is oriented toward the polar area, 8° west of north. Mesoamerican scholar Marion Popenoe Hatch wrote an important research paper on Olmec astronomy at La Venta in which she determined several facts about the site.[7] La Venta's heyday was around 1000 B.C., although Hatch proposes that the astronomical knowledge that defined the orientation of La Venta probably goes back

Diagram 7. The center point of the Big Dipper's bowl stars

to roughly 2000 B.C. Her theory is based on the position of the stars in the bowl of the Big Dipper and the "center point" defined by connecting those stars.[8]

According to Hatch, at midnight on the June solstice in the 2000 B.C. era of precession, the center point of the Big Dipper's bowl lay almost precisely on the north meridian (the vertical line extending from the horizon through the North Celestial Pole). At this midnight moment, the observer from the great pyramid at La Venta would see the Pleiades in the eastern sky and Scorpio setting in the west. Without complicating things too much, we can distill some basic perspectives from Hatch's findings, which are derived from astronomical facts. The 8° west of north baseline of La Venta was aligned to the setting point of the center point of the bowl of the Big Dipper. Around 2000 B.C., Olmec skywatchers had determined that the Big Dipper's meridian transit *as well as its first contact with the horizon* occurred at midnight on the June solstice. In this way, the solar year (of 365.2422 days) was "keyed" to the sidereal year (of 365.25 days).[9] The most mundane result of this "keying" was the timing of agricultural events, festivals, and so on. The deeper implication, however, arises when we understand that this solstice alignment of 2000 B.C. would not last forever. Precession is constantly moving stars and constellations out of their former positions and relationships to the solar year. As a result, for the Olmec astronomers, the Big Dipper event described above, which was apparently central to La Venta's ceremonial and cosmological orientation, stopped occurring on the June solstice. Thus, precession could not have gone unnoticed.

As Hatch reports, in the five hundred years following 1000 B.C., the stars in the bowl of the Big Dipper underwent complex changes and regressions in their declinations wrought by precession. The precise rate of change experienced by a star depends on its celestial location. Circumpolar stars in particular experience rather strange precessional alterations. In comparison, stars near the ecliptic shift a uniform 1° every 72 years. If these changes were being tracked by Olmec skywatchers, which, given the facts sketched above, they most certainly were, a great interest in what was really happening in the sky must have arisen. There is archaeological evidence that La Venta's pyramid was periodically realigned, probably to account for the precessional changes that threatened the long-cherished Polar God. These periodic realignments strongly suggest that the Olmec were trying to get a handle on the rate of precessional slippage.

By 900 B.C., when another prominent Olmec site, San Lorenzo, was destroyed by human hands, the Olmec must have realized that the polar area was not a stable cosmic center. In other words, they must have become aware of the precession of the celestial frame. I believe that this discovery eventually led to the accurate calculation of the rate of precession, though it may have taken hundreds of years. In fact, it may not have been fine-tuned enough to be carved in stone until the first century B.C., when the first monuments dated in the Long Count calendar appear in the archaeological record. Although by 900 B.C. the Olmec culture was disintegrating, for the Olmec shaman-astronomers, and for any skywatcher, esoteric interests transcended cultural and political vicissitudes. Star knowledge and any high goal of shamanistic science—such as calculating the rate of precession—would be preserved and passed down. As we will see, the goal of calculating precession survived in the skywatching agenda of the Izapans.

MONTE ALBAN AND CAPELLA: STELLAR SHIFTINGS AND THE ZENITH TUBE

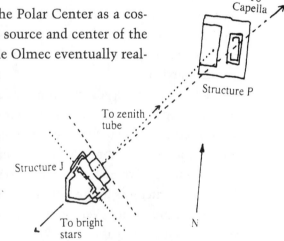

Diagram 8. Zenith observations and alignments at Monte Alban

The early Olmec were oriented to the Polar Center as a cosmological focal point for ideas about the source and center of the world. However, as we have just seen, the Olmec eventually realized this cosmic center to be false. In terms of empirical correctness, this realization was a very real scientific breakthrough: The North Celestial Pole is not, in fact, the center of the sky nor is it the "source" of the world. Meanwhile, activity at another Pre-Classic Mesoamerican city, Monte Alban, suggests another cosmic center was being examined.

The early Zapotec capital of Monte Alban is located on a mountaintop outside of present-day Oaxaca. Most structures at Monte Alban are oriented 4° to 8° east of north. Structure J, a strange, arrow-shaped building, is different. Archaeoastronomers Anthony Aveni and David Linsley determined that this building loosely points to the setting positions of the five bright stars of the Southern Cross.[10] This alignment occurred in the precessional era of 250 B.C., when these structures were built. Overall, the loose 3° range of the alignment is not very impressive. However, Aveni noted another alignment that yields more interesting results. The perpendicular to Structure J's baseline shoots through what was an opening or doorway in Structure P, a platform on the other side of the plaza.

The sight line through the doorway in Structure P points northeast to where the bright star Capella was seen to rise in the precessional era of 275 B.C. During this time, Capella made its first reappearance in the predawn sky (its heliacal rise) on May 8, which is the first solar zenith-passage date at the latitude of Monte Alban. Solar zenith passages (when the sun passes through the zenith at high noon) were important indicators of the zenith center and told the Mesoamerican farmer when the rainy season was about to commence. Solar zenith passages occur only within the Tropics, that is, between latitudes 23.5°S and 23.5°N. (As mentioned earlier, and a point important for our discussion of the Zenith Cosmology in Part II, the precise dates of solar zenith passages depend on one's latitude of observation.) Amazingly, platform Structure P, through which the Capella observations were sighted, houses Monte Alban's famous zenith tube. This vertical tube leads into an underground chamber where zenith-passage measurements of the sun (and stars) could be made.[11] Zenith tubes have been found at other sites, such as Xochicalco in Central Mexico.

Solar zenith passages were thus no doubt tracked at Monte Alban, demonstrating that Zapotec astronomers were interested in a cosmic center that was different from that of the earlier Olmec, one that is unique to the tropical zone. It seems that the astronomers of Monte Alban also had abandoned the ancient Polar God and were looking elsewhere for the true cosmic center. They probably understood that the zenith center was located *in time* as well as in space, because solar zenith passages occur only twice every year. The solar year (the haab), the tzolkin, and intervals between zenith passages all contributed to the ancient Mesoamericans' developing calendric cosmology. It was the synchronization *in time* of key points in these different cycles that would define the center of time and space. However, it might be better to say that key alignments in large time cycles *open the doorway to* the center of spacetime, rather than *define* that center.

Clearly present in the archaeological study of Monte Alban is evidence for the realigning of buildings to compensate for precession. This strongly suggests that, as at La Venta, the skywatchers of Monte Alban were at least aware of precession. Tracking the changing rise times of a star such as Capella would be a good way to get a handle on the rate of precession. These astronomical phenomena must have been very important to the ancient astronomers, for they are central to locating the center of the sky. Apparently there were several centers to contend with, each depending on one's perspective. Clearly, appearances could be deceiving. The solution to finding the true cosmic center required a genius that we can barely appreciate today and insights into the cosmic order obtained with methods we are only beginning to understand.

PRECESSIONAL CONSIDERATIONS AT TEOTIHUACAN

Teotihuacan, the great Toltec metropolis where the Fifth Sun was born, also contains evidence of having been constructed according to an astronomical plan. Several scholars have argued that an alignment with the Pleiades was responsible for the founding orientation of Teotihuacan.[12] The axis perpendicular to the famous Street of the Dead pointed to the setting position of the Pleiades. The two "pecked crosses" that scholars believe were used to lay out the city lie along this axis. The pecked cross in the group of structures called the Viking Group is just east of the Street of the Dead, and the Cerro Colorado pecked cross is some distance to the west.

The significant fact that defined the orientation of Teotihuacan is that, during the era of Teotihuacan's construction (A.D. 150), the heliacal rise of the Pleiades (the day of its annual reappearance, rising before the sun) occurred on the first solar zenith-passage date (May 17 at the latitude of Teotihuacan). In other words, on the first day of the year that the sun passed through the zenith at high noon—itself a significant event—the Pleiades made their first reappearance in the east, after having been lost in the sun's rays for some six weeks. Two significant cosmological events were occurring on the same date: the heliacal rise of the Pleiades and the solar zenith passage. It is an astronomical fact, however, that the date on which the Pleiades rise heliacally changes with precession. In time, perhaps as little as one hundred years, this cosmological "double feature" moved out of sync. Quite simply, within one hundred years of Teotihuacan's founding, the Pleiades ceased to undergo heliacal rise on the May 17 solar zenith-passage date. As a result, the astronomical mandate that defined Teotihuacan's orientation as a sacred "city of the gods" expired. The Teotihuacan astronomers must have noticed this, and they probably began devising ways to track the Pleiades' shifting. As I will show in Part II, the tradition designed to track the precessional slippage of the Pleiades (toward the zenith) is none other than the New Fire ceremony.

If, indeed, the quest for finding the true cosmic center is what drove the development of astronomy and cosmology in Mesoamerica, the solution proved to be problematic, involving as it did the slow shifting of the celestial frame due to precession. Astronomer-priests from different times and towns worked with either the zenith center or the polar center, tirelessly trying to calculate the sky's slippage. Finally, the skywatchers of Izapa discovered a cosmic center beyond all others, one that was unassailable. The invention of the Long Count calendar attests to this, and points to the third cosmic center identified by the ancient skywatchers: the Galactic Center, the center of our Milky Way Galaxy, and the source and origin of everything in our Galaxy, including us. For the Mayas, it is located at the center of the Sacred Tree, the crossing point of the Milky Way and the ecliptic near Sagittarius. They came to understand the Galactic Center as the true cosmic center, the Womb of All, which renews the world in A.D. 2012.

COSMIC CENTERS: POLAR, ZENITH, AND GALACTIC

As cosmological thinking became more sophisticated in Mesoamerica, and as ancient astronomers asked the right questions and sought new answers, so too did the solution to locating the cosmic center become deeper, more complicated, and more profound. If we trace this esoteric journey back to the Neolithic Siberian shamanism from which New World peoples descended, we can understand that the North Celestial Pole, and its occasional occupant, the Pole Star, was, for Northern Asian cultures, the obvious choice as the cosmic center. At more northerly latitudes, the Pole Star is higher up in the sky, causing the stellar dome to spin around it like a top or a mill, and so they did not have to deal with competing cosmic centers (such as the sun-in-the-zenith) present farther south in the Tropics. In the tropical zone, that is, south of Texas and Key West, and certainly at La Venta, the polar area lies very low in the sky. The celestial dome is less of a dome and more of a spinning barrel. As a result, the rise and set positions of stars are more pronounced for the earthbound observer, and stars appear to rise quickly.

One can imagine how, as people migrated south, the esoteric cosmology devel-

oped over thousands of years in Asia underwent a strange transformation, a transformation that, I believe, fully broke forth when astronomers at La Venta confirmed
that the cosmic axis of the polar area was not only not very "high" anymore, but
moved![13] In any case, suddenly time became a factor in the great endeavor of finding the cosmic center. In the tropical zone, the polar area as a valid cosmic center
must have been disqualified on two counts: It is too low in the sky and it shifts.
Since the North Celestial Pole lies close to the horizon at the latitude of La Venta,
it was easier for skywatchers to notice changes in the rise and set dates of circumpolar stars, such as those in the Big Dipper. They could have observed one-day
shifts almost within one lifetime, and because of a star's steep vertical rise within
the Tropics, they could have identified its rising point along the horizon with good
precision. Eventually they would have realized that the circumpolar stars were, for
some reason, shifting position. The Polar God began to reveal his true face: The
Polar God was false!

After San Lorenzo fell around 900 B.C. and Olmec civilization began to wane,
Mesoamerican skywatchers embarked on a fantastic adventure and rose to a great
challenge. Unable to deny the new cosmological knowledge unfolding before them,
they were forced to look elsewhere for a cosmic center, preferably one that could be
tested and trusted. Because the cycle we call precession now factored into their
search, time became a consideration in the quest to find the center. As the Aztec
myth of cosmogenesis described earlier suggests, worldcentering can occur only
when time—movement and process—begins.

We have already seen how the skywatchers at Monte Alban tracked the zenith
passages of the sun. Within the Tropics, the sun passes through the center of the
sky on only two days every year. In this method, time is indeed a factor indicating
the center of space. In this Zenith Cosmology, the zenith is a particularly compelling cosmic center because it is, quite simply, the exact geometrical center of the
celestial dome overhead. But zenith passages of the sun occur only within the Tropics. Furthermore, and what complicates the zenith-as-center model, the dates of
solar zenith passages change with latitude. However, solar zenith passages can, in
fact, be used to track precession, if not identify an *absolute* cosmic center. In fact,
in my research I realized that an important Mesoamerican group, the Toltecs, pursued and developed the zenith-as-center concept—the Zenith Cosmology. As we
will see in Part II, the Zenith Cosmology resurfaced at Chichén Itzá and was encoded into the Pyramid of Kukulcan.

Roughly two hundred years after the zenith tube and Building J at Monte Alban were built, the Long Count calendar appears in the archaeological record. With this calendar, and the astronomical alignment that occurs on its end-date, the emerging Maya (specifically, the Izapans) claimed the prize of identifying the ultimate time-dependent cosmic center. They succeeded in locating the true cosmic birthplace and celestial throne. Their space-time map, preserved in the fragmented artifacts of their ancient calendar-science, leads us right into the Galactic Center.

The thread weaving through these cosmic centers is the thread of time. Time became the primary factor in determining the location of the cosmic center and the date of worldrenewal. The ultimate time cycle was the precession of the equinoxes, and precession now looms as a very important factor in understanding Maya cosmogenesis. What exactly is the precession of the equinoxes? How does it work, and what do Maya scholars have to say about it? How does it manifest in Maya myth? An introduction to the Mystery of the Ages is in order.

CHAPTER 4

PRECESSION:
THE MYSTERY OF THE AGES

The idea of periodically shifting World Ages is found in the myths of many cultures. Human beings are naturally interested in the vast cycles of time and the changing seasons of life on Earth. To ancient societies, the sky was understood to be intimately linked with the changing modes of human culture. Long ago, skywatchers in many parts of the globe tracked a vast astronomical cycle, and they believed that this Great Cycle determined transformational eras in human culture. But there is a great mystery around this topic, almost as if the original story somehow got muddled. How far back does this knowledge go? New interpretations of ancient history are forcing us to accept that our distant ancestors understood the true astronomical meaning behind the doctrine of World Ages. Thousands of years ago, people were tuned into the night sky to a depth that we cannot comprehend, living as most of us do in urban areas that are so polluted as to veil the stars.

Among ancient cultures, and especially in Mesoamerica, the World Age doctrine was a fundamental belief. It engendered an appreciation for the vast nature of time and a curiosity about the mysteries of ages long gone and soon to come. Among independent researchers and students of ancient civilizations, it is now becoming very clear that the Mystery of the Ages is solved in the astronomical fact of the precession of the equinoxes. Precession changes our relationship to our Milky Way Galaxy, and ultimately brings us back to the starting point. The Greek philosophy of the Eternal Return speaks clearly to this obscured source of the World Age doctrine, as does Plato's Spindle of Necessity.[1] Astronomical cycles, sooner or later, are always expected to come back around to their "zero" point. The same holds true for the precession of the equinoxes and, as the Maya knew, the Zero Point arrives in A.D. 2012.

PRECESSION: THE BASICS

What exactly is precession, and how does it relate to the World Age doctrines of the Maya and the Toltecs? The precession of the equinoxes, also known as the Platonic Year and the Great Year, is caused by the slow wobbling of the Earth's axis. The Earth's wobble causes the position of the equinox sun to slowly precess west-ward against the background of stars, thus the term "the precession of the equinoxes."

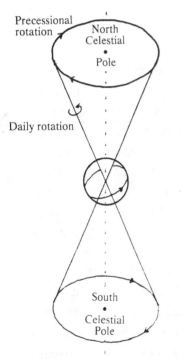

Diagram 9. The Precession of the Equinoxes

Right now the Earth's axis (the North Celestial Pole) points roughly to Polaris, the Pole Star, but five thousand years ago the North Celestial Pole pointed roughly to Alpha Draconis. By A.D. 11,000 the Pole Star will be Vega. The precessional shift of the equinoxes applies equally to the solstices. For example, currently the December solstice point is in the constellation of Sagittarius. But 2,000 years ago it was in Capricorn.[2] Since then, it has precessed backward almost one full astrological sign. Modern astronomers estimate the full cycle of precession to be between 25,600 and 26,000 years. The Maya estimate of precession, if we assume that five Great Cycles (65 baktuns) were intended to represent a full precessional cycle, is 25,626 years. Since the end-date of the 13-baktun cycle of the Long Count calendar identifies a rare alignment in the cycle of precession, and Long Count dating first started appearing in the archaeological record in the first century B.C., the ancient skywatchers apparently had already calculated precession at that time. Their forward projection, some 2,100 years into the future, was very accurate and reveals that the ancient skywatchers possessed an advanced cosmological knowledge.

PRECESSION OLD AND NEW

It is commonly thought that the Greek astronomer Hipparchus was the first to discover precession, in 128 B.C. However, recent books by independent thinkers who are unfettered by the limitations of scholardom have shown that the ancient Egyptians were aware of precession.[3] Between the era of Egypt's glory and the rise of Platonic science and astronomy just prior to the Christian era, there was probably a hiatus in the understanding or appreciation of precessional knowledge. Perhaps Egyptian Mystery Schools preserved this knowledge up until the time of Pythagoras and early Greek philosophers. Many early Greek thinkers, including Pythagoras, were initiated into these Mystery Schools.

It is interesting to note that when Hipparchus rediscovered precession, the effects on then-current cosmological ideas were dramatic. A world that believed the stars to be eternally fixed realized that they in fact underwent a slow celestial shifting. This situation, no doubt unwelcome in some quarters, demanded a radical rethinking of basic ideas about the cosmos. New ideas also require new explanatory myths, and the mystery cult known as the Mithraic Mysteries is now understood to have had the revelation of the profound meaning of the precession of the equinoxes at the center of its most coveted initiatory ceremonies.[4] In other words, the Mithraic Mysteries arose in direct response to the rediscovery of precession, as a World Age doctrine to describe the vast cycles of cosmic time. It spread throughout the civilized world wherever the Romans went, establishing sanctuaries from North Africa to Scotland. Mithraism competed with early Christianity for future status as World Religion, and its adherents worshiped one supreme deity—Mithras, the great architecton who was responsible for the slow shifting of the heavens. In the Mithraic Mysteries, the slaying of the bull by Mithras, the supreme God of Time, symbolized the precessional shift out of the Age of Taurus—the death of the bull god.

In the example of Mithraism, we can see how easily precessional knowledge lends itself to a World Age mythology. In fact, one begins to suspect that wherever the World Age doctrine is prominent—as in Mesoamerica—precessional knowledge is lurking in the shadows. By the end of this book, it will be clear that the Maya Creation myth, the *Popol Vuh*, is an esoteric World Age doctrine that arose with the discovery of precession over 2,100 years ago. Ironically, this apparently took place in Mesoamerica around the same time as the Hipparchus-Mithras link emerged in the Old World.

PRECESSION: FOREGROUND AND BACKGROUND

How did precession look to the ancient skywatchers? Before we can answer that question, we must be clear about how precession is viewed in the heavens and how the Mesoamericans developed different precession-tracking methods.

As explained earlier, the ecliptic is the path followed by the sun, moon, and planets. Viewed as an arch in the sky, it stretches, for observers in the Northern Hemisphere, from the southeast to the southwest. The ecliptic circles the sky and the twelve constellations that lie along its "road" are the well-known zodiacal constellations. The sun journeys around the ecliptic once every year, and four "solar stations" lie along the ecliptic—the two solstices and the two equinoxes. These solar stations are like the anchors or "pillars" of the year, the "corners" of the cosmic house, and they are located in specific constellations. As precession causes the equinoxes and solstices to shift, the position of these solar stations against background constellations slowly moves. For example, currently, the solar station of the March equinox sun is about to move backward from Pisces into Aquarius.

Therefore, we can distinguish foreground features of the sky, which move with precession, from background features, which stay fixed. Foreground features include, as mentioned, the four seasonal stations (the position of the sun on the equinoxes and solstices). Background features include the stars, constellations, and, most importantly, the Milky Way. Since precession causes the foreground features to move in relation to the background features, the background features can be used as "markers" to track precession. In Western astrology, constellations are used for this purpose. However, the dividing point between constellations is very loose. We understand that constellations are each 30° wide, but this is an ideal, average measure. As observed in the sky, the sizes of individual zodiacal constellations vary greatly, and thus they cannot be used to accurately demarcate precessional movement. The Milky Way, on the other hand, is a band in the sky, and is much less ambiguous as a marker. The Maya used the Milky Way as their World Age marker. They calculated precession based upon the observed movement of the December solstice sun (a foreground feature) toward the Milky Way (a background feature). One way to visualize this is to measure the distance of the Milky Way above the dawning December solstice sun (see diagram 10).

As the ancient skywatchers observed, over many years, the solstice sun and the Milky Way drawing closer together, they realized that a synchronization or conjunction would happen during some future epoch. The calculation of when this

Diagram 10. The precession-caused convergence of the Milky Way and December solstice sun

conjunction was to happen was encoded in the Long Count calendar.

The astronomical synchronization I just described involves one method used by the ancient Mesoamerican skywatchers to track precession. The other method can be explained with the same "foreground-background" model, in the following way: Besides the four seasonal quarters as foreground features, there are also the two dates of the solar zenith passage. We can call these the sun's "zenith stations." (As mentioned earlier, the exact dates of the sun's zenith passage depend upon the latitude of observation; Appendix 3 contains detailed tables for these latitude-dependent dates.) Like the seasonal quarters, the sun's zenith stations are foreground "anchors" against which precession can be tracked. The background feature used in this method was a constellation, the Pleiades. The New Fire ceremony of the Toltecs is a critical key to understanding how this tracking method worked. In addition, the Pyramid of Kukulcan at Chichén Itzá provides another missing link. I will discuss this Zenith Cosmology in more detail in Part II. For now, suffice it to say that as I reassembled the forgotten Zenith Cosmology, I realized that the Pyramid of Kukulcan is a precessional star-clock, and the synchronization of the Pleiades with the zenith sun is the Zero Point of this alternate precession-tracking method.

DID THEY OR DIDN'T THEY?

It is quite apparent that precession, the slow shifting of the stellar frame of time, was of great interest to Mesoamerican astronomers. Because modern astronomers recognize that precession is relatively hard to detect and measure, many Maya scholars casually dismiss the idea that Mesoamerican stargazers knew anything at all about it.[5] And yet, the end-date alignment alone strongly suggests that they did. My interpretation of the Long Count calendar, as a system that pinpointed an align-

ment in precession to occur some 2,100 years after its invention, may appear unlikely or fantastic. It may even be met with scoffing skepticism despite the simple
fact that the 13-baktun cycle end-date does, without any help from me, very accurately identify a glaringly obvious and compelling alignment in the cycle of precession. Coincidence? This is what must be considered unlikely.

Since the Mesoamerican understanding of precession is a potentially controversial topic, I decided I had to carefully survey scholarly opinions about this. I
was delighted and surprised to find that the scholars most qualified to comment
on this question consider it quite likely that ancient Mesoamerican skywatchers
were aware of precession. For example, elder Maya scholar Gordon Brotherston,
author of numerous books and essays and professor of literature at the University
of Essex, wrote that "the great year of equinoctial precession emerges as a missing
link between the local and political chronology of our era and the vast evolutionary philosophy of time so vividly testified to in the Popol Vuh."[6] Here we find an
eminent Mesoamerican scholar saying, rather matter of factly, that the *Popol Vuh*
contains a "vast evolutionary philosophy" derived from the Mayas' understanding
of the nature of precession. And why shouldn't the ancient Maya have understood
precession? In terms of mathematics, astronomy, and calendrics, the Maya are
recognized as the most advanced of all the New World cultures. Mayanists talk
routinely of the "year-drift formula," developed over 2,000 years ago, which en-
abled ancient skywatchers to calculate the solar year to an accuracy of four deci-
mal places. Future eclipse dates were calculated with great accuracy. Maya scholar
J. Eric S. Thompson noted that the Venus Calendar of the Classic-period Maya
used a correction mechanism that lost only .08 days in 468 years! Overall, Brotherston's assessment is fair and accurate: "From a practical point of view, a culture as ancient, numerate, and chronologically sophisticated as that of Mesoamerica
is more likely than not to have detected and then measured the phenomenon of
precession."[7]

On this question, I have collected a host of additional comments by scholars in
Appendix 2, "Mesoamerican Precessional Knowledge: In the Literature." The point
of this brief overview is simple: The ancient Mesoamerican skywatchers independently discovered and calculated precession. But let me conclude with one final
statement on whether or not the ancient skywatchers knew about precession. It is
by archaeoastronomer and Maya scholar Anthony Aveni, probably the Mayanist
most qualified to comment on this point. In his definitive book *Skywatchers of*

Ancient Mexico, Aveni writes that "Ancient astronomers easily could detect the long-term precessional motion by witnessing changes in the *time of year* at which the bright stars underwent heliacal rising. . . . Through myth and legend the earliest skywatchers transmitted their consciousness of the passage of the vernal equinox along the zodiac from constellation to constellation."[8]

CHAPTER 5

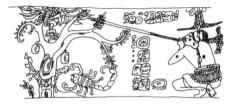

MYTHOLOGY AND ASTRONOMY

Maya Creation mythology is rooted in celestial events involving stars, the Milky Way, and certain constellations. Mythological stories, especially those that involve cosmogenesis—the origin of the world—are derived from observations of celestial movements. This is not strictly a Maya phenomenon, for many ancient cultures naturally followed similar developmental pathways. For example, Roman gods such as Jupiter and Saturn refer to planets. As mentioned in the last chapter, Mithraism was a mystery cult that had precession as its highest mytho-astronomical revelation. In this chapter I will sketch, with examples, how many ancient cultures wove their mythologies with the information gathered by observing the sky.

For most of the twentieth century it has been somewhat unfashionable in scholarly circles to see astronomy in ancient myth. Events around the turn of the century reveal a source of bias. The Panbabylonians were a group of German scholars who believed that all myth descended from the astronomical discoveries of the Babylonians. They proposed, along with politically incorrect metaphysical doctrines, that the ancient Babylonians had discovered the precession of the equinoxes and that this knowledge gave rise to Creation myths and a doctrine of World Ages that spread to other cultures, including the Egyptians and the Greeks. On the eve of World War I, however, the Panbabylonians were discredited and disbanded. As many scholars had shown interest in this group, it was a somewhat embarrassing debacle. The effect of this episode on academia was that it became taboo to see astronomy in ancient myth. And there the situation rested for several decades.

In the 1940s and 1950s, the work of anthropologist Hertha von Dechend persistently fought this bias. Her research led to the writing and publication, in 1969, of *Hamlet's Mill*, coauthored with Giorgio de Santillana. In the 1960s and 1970s, the new field of archaeoastronomy dealt seriously with the relationships between astronomy, architectural orientation, mythology, and culture. Gerald Hawkins' book *Stonehenge Decoded*, published in 1970, contributed to the revival of recognizing mythic astronomy in the artifacts of ancient cultures. In the 1980s and early 1990s, a revolution in understanding Maya cosmology took place when scholars explored, once again, the likely relationship between ancient astronomy and ancient myth. Maya epigrapher and art historian Linda Schele contributed a great deal to this revolution, and her work was published in 1993 in *Maya Cosmos*.

Still, *Hamlet's Mill* was the single most important book to pioneer an accurate reappraisal of how cosmologically advanced our ancient ancestors truly were. The recurring leitmotif in *Hamlet's Mill* is that astronomy and mythology were closely related in the thinking of many ancient cultures. By unraveling the threads of how myth and astronomy were woven together by ancient skywatchers, Santillana and von Dechend exposed precession as a central consideration. With exhaustive documentation and erudition, the authors of *Hamlet's Mill* provided comparative analyses of astronomical features involved in the precession question. They endeavored to decode the mythic language of astronomy and proposed several core principles or rules.

- Animals, gods, and goddesses frequently represent planets, stars, or other astronomical features.
- Adventures ostensibly taking place on the surface of the Earth are metaphors for events actually taking place in the sky, revealing a belief in parallel, or synchronized, action between heaven and Earth.

In my own research I have confirmed von Dechend and Santillana's work and I realized the importance of another core principle: One astronomical feature may be mythologized in several different ways. For example, the Aztec deity Quetzalcoatl refers to Venus as morning star whereas his dark twin, Tezcatlipoca, refers to Venus as evening star. Here we are reminded that Mesoamerican deities typically rule sectors of time rather than objects. For example, though the sun appears every day, the December solstice Sun Lord appears only on the December solstice. The March equinox Sun Lord is a completely different deity. In this way, we see how different deities manifest through the same physical object.

In Maya thought, gods represent intangible forces or principles that can manifest in many different events at different times. The Lightning God is present during thunderstorms, but is also present when a human being has an orgasm. The Fire God is present during violent volcanic eruptions, but also during a calm, cozy evening around the family hearth. Predictably, this cornucopia of deities engendered confusion among early ethnographers, to the point that some considered Maya mythology itself to be hopelessly degenerate and fragmented. However, the confusion was based on the Western assumption that a planet, being an "object," must be ruled by one deity.

These cosmo-conceptions, many of which seem unorthodox to our own assumptions, reveal a progressive worldview that recognizes the underlying spiritual realm as primary to the realm of physical, material manifestation. Like the Hopi, whose kachina spirit controls the manifestation of rain, the Maya believed that spiritual forces and their ruling deities underlie and control material manifestation. Therefore, in our exploration of Maya cosmogenesis, we must recognize and decipher the different representations of the same astronomical events in Maya mythology, rather than erroneously attempt to identify the "real" one.

In the following illustrations, I have chosen to focus on the astronomical features that are relevant to the end-date astronomy, which include the Milky Way and dark-rift. The Mesoamericans mythologized the Milky Way as a cosmic tree, a cosmic mountain or volcano, a cosmic ballcourt, a Great Mother, a snake or crocodile monster, a white road, and a river. The mythic identities of the dark-rift can be paired with these mythic identities of the Milky Way in the following way:

MILKY WAY	DARK-RIFT
Cosmic Tree	Cleft in Tree
Cosmic Mountain	Cave in Mountain
Cosmic Volcano	Crater in Volcano
Ballcourt	Ballcourt and/or Goalring
Great Mother	Birth Canal
Snake / Monster	Mouth or Cleft Head
White Road	Black Road
River	Canyon or Cleft

These identifications often cross over in the symbol system of Mesoamerican

Diagram 11. Ballcourt glyph and Cauac monster

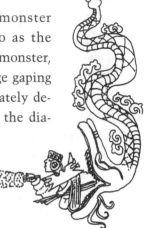

Diagram 12. Mixcoatl, the Milky Way

art. For example, the glyph for a ballcourt resembles, in its basic structural arrangement, the image of the Solar Lord emerging from the cleft head of a "cosmic monster."

The cosmic monster also is referred to as the Cauac (Kah-wok) monster, a deity with a huge gaping mouth that alternately devours and births deities and worlds. In the diagram above, the Cauac monster has a stepped forehead, a symbol that, in other contexts, represents the steps of the ballcourt. The cosmic monster also is visualized as a snake with a large mouth out of which deities and ancestors emerge. According to scholars, this sky-snake is Mixcoatl, the Milky Way.[1]

If we can take this symbology a step further, the mouth of this Milky Way snake is probably the dark-rift. And the solar warrior that emerges from the mouth represents the sun. So, in this simple image, the astronomical event of the sun within the dark-rift in the Milky Way is portrayed.

For now, the cross-comparative chart given above is intended to introduce some unusual aspects of Mesoamerican cosmo-conception and illustrate how astronomical features, especially those associated with the end-date alignment, were mythologized in a rich variety of mutually supporting ways. There is additional evidence that the dark-rift was mythologized as the mouth of the Milky Way sky-snake, which I will address in the next section.

NEW WORLD MYTHIC ASTRONOMY

Scholars in many fields of study identify the astronomical features involved in the end-date alignment as being significant in Mesoamerican thought. A cosmological model proposed by Maya scholar David Kelley targets the dark-rift in the Milky Way as a place where time cycles begin and end.[2] Most significantly, his model highlights the dark-rift as a Creation Place, which it certainly is if we accept the cosmology defined by the end-date alignment. His work also shows that the Mesoamericans used the Milky Way as a calendric division line—a cosmic axis.[3] Kelley wanted to locate the celestial placement of specific deities, the key deity being Xiuhtecuhtli, Lord of the Year and Lord of Fire, because that god's calendric associations are well-known. The three basic time-cycles in the Mesoamerican calendar are:

- The nine Lords of the Night cycle
- The thirteen day-number cycle
- The twenty day-sign cycle

The Lord of Fire, Xiuhtecuhtli, like all Mesoamerican deities, has a host of attributes including color, number, and direction. Significantly, he is the first of the thirteen day-numbers, first of the nine Lords of the Night, and ninth of the twenty sacred day-signs. Kelley argues that Xiuhtecuhtli's astronomical location is the belt stars of Orion, which, in Aztec myth, are associated with the fire sticks and the primal fire. This constellation is located close to where the Milky Way crosses the ecliptic in Gemini. Given the connections between astronomy, number, and deity, the basic cycles of the Mesoamerican calendar can be placed in the sky as shown in diagram 13.

The Milky Way with its dark-rift clearly resembles a snake monster with gaping maw. Notice how the dark-rift serves as an end-place for the thirteen-day cycle as well as for the nine-day cycle. It also serves as

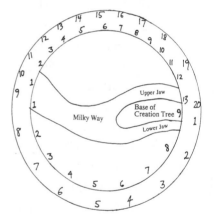

Diagram 13. David Kelley's Milky Way model

the *beginning and end* of the twenty-day cycle. Kelley calls the split in the Milky Way defined by the dark-rift as the upper and lower jaws of the Cauac monster—the cosmic monster that is the Milky Way. He also calls the Milky Way the Tamoanchan Tree, which is the Creation Place of Central Mexican mythology. This cosmic monster's head and mouth form the base of the Tamoanchan Tree. Significantly, many trees at Izapa, the city where the Galactic Cosmology was formulated, were marked with a monster mask at their base.

Since astronomically the base of the tree is the dark-rift near Sagittarius, then conversely, the top of the tree would be located in Gemini. Overall, Kelley's model tells us that the Milky Way serves as an end-beginning divider in Mesoamerican cosmology and calendrics. Specifically, the part of the Milky Way where the dark-rift is located is seen to be the mouth of the Milky Way monster, a Creation Place where time ends and begins anew.[4]

Diagram 14. Izapan cosmic monster and the Creation Tree

Additional examples add to the Milky Way's many roles. In the 1970s, ethnographer Gary Urton studied the cosmology of the Quechua Indians from the Peruvian village of Misminay, a short distance from Cuzco. In his book *At the Crossroads of Earth and Sky*, he reports his discovery of an amazingly complex geo-cosmic mapping system based upon sky lore. These ideas found among the Quechua of Misminay are probably late survivals of ancient Inca cosmology. The ancient people of Peru were very interested in the Milky Way, in its different widths and varying brightness as well as in its dark spaces. The Quechua recognized several distinct "dark-cloud" constellations within the Milky Way.[5] These constellations are different from the "connect the dot" asterisms of Western astronomy. The Quechua dark-cloud constellations consist of the dark ridges and spaces within the Milky Way, similar to the dark-rift in the Milky Way recognized in the mythology of the Maya.

For the Quechua, the dates when the sun conjuncted the Milky Way were of great interest, for then the sun would pass into the road of souls. In Gary Urton's diagrams we see a hint of the fact that the December solstice sun is currently close to conjuncting the Milky Way.

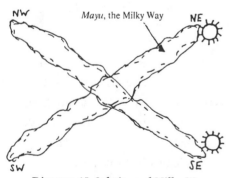

Diagram 15. Solstice and Milky Way

During the time of conjunction, the Quechua believe, as do the Maya, that the sun enters the road that leads to the land of the dead. On the other hand, the Quechua also recognize that the terrestrial counterpart to the Milky Way is the sacred Vilcanota River, which runs through Misminay village. Rather than contradicting the Milky Way's identity as a celestial road, this new identity as a river enriches the Milky Way's power. Also, it reveals how the Quechua mapped the sky onto geographical features.

In South America, the relationship between myth and astr. profound. William Sullivan's recent book, *The Secret of the Incas*, de sional myths among the Inca, in which a dark-cloud constellation called Atoc located close to the Maya dark-rift, was used as a marker to track precession. A. cording to Sullivan, a precessional alignment event occurred around A.D. 650 that was incorporated into an Inca myth called "Why Fox's Tail is Black." See Appendix 6 for a closer look at Sullivan's contribution to elucidating precessional mythlore in the New World.

Moving north from Peru to Honduras, we find the Chortí Maya, who still live near the ancient Maya site of Copán. They perform a ritual to reenact the creation of the world, called "raising the sky," which tracks the yearly movements of the Milky Way. They named the Milky Way the "Camino de Santiago" (The Road of St. James), after the patron saint Santiago, who controls thunder, rain, and the rainbow. On the Chortí saint day of Santiago, July 25, the intersection of the Milky Way and the ecliptic (the one near Gemini) passes straight overhead through the zenith, forming a cross in the sky that is recognized as the Wakah-Chan, the Sacred Tree of the Maya. This event defines the quadrated division of the cosmos, a model employed by most Mesoamerican cultures.

Ethnographer Charles Wisdom explained that the Chortí see the Milky Way as a wheel.[6] This sounds strange, but when we understand how the Milky Way moves through the sky in a single night, we can appreciate the Chortí image: the sky and the Milky Way appear as a fish-eye lens spinning upon some invisible axis. In general, the Chortí are very interested in the changing movements of the Milky Way throughout the night and the year. They are no doubt aware of its brightest and widest area near Sagittarius and its dimmer, more diffuse area near Orion. In addition, if they are aware of the Sacred Tree cross in Gemini, they most certainly are aware of the other cross in Sagittarius.

In these examples we find that the Milky Way was mythologized as a road, a tree, a river, a cosmic monster, even a wheel. Let's narrow down our focus now and look at the *Popol Vuh* for more examples of the Milky Way's mythic identities, and let's also try to determine the astronomical identities of other *Popol Vuh* characters.

STRONOMY IN THE POPOL VUH MYTH

The Quiché Maya book called the *Popol Vuh* is a Creation epic with a long history. It recounts the adventures of the Hero Twins, among other deities, and although it was recorded by the Quiché in the 1550s, some of its primary episodes appear on Classic-period ceramics as well as on monuments at Izapa, which are dated to about 100 B.C. No doubt, during its long history the *Popol Vuh* and the astronomical identities ascribed to its characters have undergone changes. However, by comparing the monuments of Izapa with Classic-period ceramics and the Quiché *Popol Vuh*, we find that the astronomical meaning of several key episodes in the Hero Twin myth, notably the demise of Seven Macaw, was preserved throughout its history.

The *Popol Vuh* refers to the dark-rift in several different mythological contexts. The black cleft (or dark-rift) in the Milky Way and the crossing point of the Milky Way and the ecliptic in Sagittarius are extremely important celestial features because of their involvement with the astronomical alignment that occurs on the 13-baktun cycle end-date. Maya scholar Dennis Tedlock notes the identity of the dark-rift and many other astronomical and calendric references in the *Popol Vuh*, and has compared them to information in the Maya *Dresden Codex*. In his 1985 translation of the *Popol Vuh*, we find that *ri be xibalba* ("the road Xibalba") also is known as "the Black Road." This is the road that beckoned One Hunahpu and Seven Hunahpu (the Hero Twins' father and uncle) when they were on their way to Xibalba, and it led to their deaths. Today, *xibalba be* ("the road to Xibalba") is the Quiché term for the dark-rift in the Milky Way.[7] Barbara Tedlock reports these same identifications for the dark-rift in her ethnographic work among the Quiché Maya.[8]

In one *Popol Vuh* episode, the Black Road speaks to the Hero Twins, suggesting that the Black Road (the dark-rift) either has or is a mouth. This makes sense when we remember that the dark-rift is the Road to the Underworld, and the mouths of jaguars and snakes were also recognized as Underworld portals. As a result, when we look at Maya carvings and see Maya lords being birthed from the mouths of snakes, toads, or jaguar deities, we should suspect that they are being born from the dark-rift—appropriately enough, since the Milky Way is the Great Mother and the dark-rift is her birth canal.

A phrase in the *Popol Vuh*—*cahib xalcat be*—means "four junction roads" or simply "crossroads." These four roads emanate from the Milky Way/ecliptic cross-ing point, the cosmic navel, which is the place where the "fourfold siding, the stretching of the cord" occurs, explained as the very first Creation event in the *Popol Vuh*. According to Dennis Tedlock, Maya Creation "took place at a celestial crossroads," and it is clear that he is referring to this information.[9]

Each of the four cosmic roads is associated with a color. The Black Road is, as has been shown, the northward pointing part of the Milky Way containing the dark-rift. The White Road is the white, star-rich part of the Milky Way that extends south from the ecliptic. The Green and Red roads refer to the arms of the ecliptic extending east and west from the Milky Way. The Maya intentionally mapped the four cosmic roads onto the local environment. Typically, a village would have four roads departing from its center, which served to divide the surrounding fields into ritual and agricultural districts. Further afield, shrines in the distant mountains were visited on specific days in the tzolkin calendar, and four sacred mountains were each associated with a direction and a year-bearer. The organizational nucleus for Maya culture was the central axis extending down to the city center from the Heart of Sky—the center of the cosmic crossroads. As the title of Gary Urton's book *At the Crossroads of Earth and Sky* suggests, indigenous New World cultures mapped and organized their societies according to a celestial blueprint.

In another episode from the *Popol Vuh*, after One Hunahpu was killed, his head was placed in the crook of a calabash tree which "stands by the road." Dennis Tedlock writes that the calabash tree symbolizes the Milky Way, and the road near the tree is the ecliptic.[10] The crook or cleft in the tree near the ecliptic is thus the dark-rift. Hanging in this spot, One Hunahpu's skull impregnates Blood Moon with the Hero Twins. Later, the Hero Twins facilitate the resurrection of their father in the Under-world ballcourt, which is another metaphor for the dark-rift. In this important and defining context, the dark-rift is a place of conception and, ultimately, rebirth.

But who is this One Hunahpu? What is his astronomical identity? In recon-structing the astronomical identity of One Hunahpu, I had to look at the era in which he emerged into Maya consciousness. Since he is a central deity in the Hero Twin myth, and episodes from this myth first appear on the monuments of Izapa, I placed his origin at roughly 300 B.C. to 100 B.C. Earlier, David Kelley decoded the astronomical identity of Xiuhtecuhtli, the Aztec Fire God, based upon calendric and directional attributes. We can do the same for One Hunahpu.

The calendric day that represents One Hunahpu is One Ahau. The linguistic transformations of One Hunahpu suggest his relationship with other Mesoamerican deities over a 2,200-year history:

> Hun-rakan
>
> Hu-rakan (Hurricane)
>
> Hun Hunahpu (One Hunahpu)
>
> One Ahau
>
> Hun-Ahpu
>
> Hun abku
>
> Hunab Ku[11]

During the Classic period of the Maya, One Ahau was the Sacred Day of Venus, the tzolkin day that marked the beginning of a Venus Round period of 104 haab. In the dim mists of the Mesoamerican past, however, before the Venus Calendar came along, One Ahau had another very important meaning. Ahau was one of the year-bearers in the earliest year-bearer system, the one probably used at Izapa. The year-bearers in this system (known as the Type V system) are Ahau (Solar Lord), Chicchan (Serpent), Oc (Dog) and Men (Eagle). As we saw earlier, year-bearers are associated with the four geographical directions and also with the four seasonal quarters (the two equinoxes and two solstices). One of the year-bearers is always considered to be the senior year-bearer, and, of the Type V year-bearers listed, Ahau was without doubt the most revered. Every fifty-two years the coefficient 1 comes around to combine with the senior year-bearer on New Year's Day, thus initiating a new Calendar Round cycle. Clearly, One Ahau/One Hunahpu would have been the senior year-bearer and Calendar Round initiator.

The next question is "which *seasonal quarter* is senior?" Although some may argue for the March equinox, my research reveals that the December solstice fills this position *because it begins the return of the sun, the resurrection of the Ahau-Sun-Lord.* We also may recall that the Long Count end-date is the big *4 Ahau* day, and its creators knew it corresponds to a December solstice. The rebirth of the sun on the December solstice is a widespread Maya belief.[12] That the Maya believed the winter solstice to be New Year's Day is suggested by the fact that it is still the focus of a midnight ceremony among the Chamula Maya.[13] Moreover, the Aztec sun god Huitzilopochtli, in some contexts, appeared as the newborn sun on the December solstice.[14]

Therefore, it is highly likely that the December solstice was considered to be the "senior" seasonal quarter, a miniature place of rebirth if you will, while Ahau was clearly the senior day-sign. By linguistic, calendric, and astronomical evidence, it is deeply probable that One Hunahpu symbolizes the December solstice sun. A simpler form of this argument is as follows: As an "Ahau" or Lord, One Hunahpu is a representative of the sun. As a First Father or "First Sun" deity, he represents the first sun or "day" of the year, and therefore he symbolizes the December solstice sun. Furthermore, in the *Popol Vuh*, One Hunahpu's resurrection signals the beginning of a new World Age. Since the December solstice sun is what gets reborn, we are drawn to recognize the end-date alignment as what the *Popol Vuh* Creation myth describes.

To illustrate the astronomical dimensions of another important episode in the *Popol Vuh*, the conception of the Hero Twins, we must remember that deities, as symbols of intangible forces, can manifest in different objects and events. The conception of the Hero Twins is the event that ultimately leads to One Hunahpu's resurrection. Conception, birth, resurrection, and rebirth all partake of the same principle that we may simply call "Creation," and One Hunahpu, as the primal First Father progenitor, rules this Creation principle. In the episode of the Hero Twins' conception, according to Dennis Tedlock, One Hunahpu's severed head symbolizes the conjunction of Jupiter and Venus.[15] Jupiter and Venus become the source of a creation, because the skull that represents them will impregnate Blood Moon with the Hero Twins. When we remember that One Hunahpu's head is hung in the dark-rift, we have an astronomical picture of the conception of the Hero Twins: Jupiter and Venus conjunct in the dark-rift. Furthermore, Dennis Tedlock identified Blood Moon as the waning moon in the east, adding another celestial body to the conjunction.[16] As a result, the *Popol Vuh* provides us with a temporal sky map with which we can pinpoint when the Hero Twins, and their story, were created. In other words, I realized that information in the *Popol Vuh* encodes the date of the Hero Twin's conception. I consulted my astronomy software and, to my amazement, found a December solstice date in the second century B.C. that beautifully portrays the cosmic conception of the Hero Twins. I will explore these findings in more detail in Part III.

Additional mythic players in the *Popol Vuh* beckon to be identified astronomically. What of the 400 Boys? Or Seven Macaw? As we will see, these stars of Maya mythology were associated with specific astronomical features, and their behavior, although complex and varied, suggests they were involved in ancient descriptions of precession.

In the *Popol Vuh*, the story of the death of the 400 Boys recalls Old World precessional imagery of a tent being pulled down. This image derives from the polar axis being understood as the central pole of a cosmic tent. Zipacna, son of Seven Macaw, finds the 400 Boys laboring to erect the central pole for their tent. He helps them by digging a deep hole, and aborts their plan to kill him by hiding in a side tunnel he dug

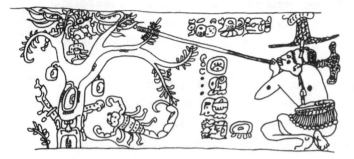

Diagram 16. Classic-period depiction of Seven Macaw and Hunahpu

to save himself. When they slam the pole down into the hole, the 400 Boys congratulate themselves by getting drunk, thinking they have killed Zipacna. However, Zipacna surprises them by bringing the house tent down on their heads. Here we see the familiar theme of the central axis being yanked out of its fixture, an image of the shifting Pole Star, which defines "the end of the world." According to Dennis Tedlock, the murdered 400 Boys ascend into the sky and become the Pleiades.[17]

The father of Zipacna, Seven Macaw, was thought of as a vain and false ruler of a previous World Age, the age of the wooden people. The Hero Twins had to do away with him before they could begin their work to resurrect and instate their father, One Hunahpu, as the true World Age ruler. A painting on a Maya vase (above) illustrates one of the Hero Twins shooting Seven Macaw out of his throne. Although this painting is from the Classic period, it contains the same information as this image from Izapa, carved some six hundred years earlier (see diagram 17).

Both illustrations depict Seven Macaw about to fall from his throne in the polar center, and both preserve the same underlying astronomical meaning. Seven Macaw has been identified by ethnographers working among the highland Maya as the Big Dipper, while his wife

Diagram 17. Izapa Stela 25. Hunahpu with Seven Macaw in his polar perch

Chimalmat is the Little Dipper.[18] The latter constellation contains the Pole Star, and both may be said to be regents of the polar zone.

In the *Popol Vuh*, Seven Macaw was a false god—a ruler of a previous World Age—suggesting that the Pole Star is a "false" Heart of Heaven. His demise signifies the downfall of a previous worldview, that of the Olmec. If the polar region was realized to be a "false" celestial center, a mistaken place of creation, in what way does Seven Macaw fall away from his polar perch? We saw earlier how the Olmec of La Venta determined, as a result of discovering precession, that the polar area was not a valid cosmic center. In Part IV we will find out exactly how precession causes Seven Macaw to fall from his polar perch.

THE UNDERWORLD ROAD TO BAKTUN 13

The Black Road, the crook in the calabash tree, the cosmic birthplace, the crossroads, the jaguar's mouth, the Sacred Tree, *xibalba be*—all of these mytho-astronomical concepts point to the same location: the dark-rift in the Milky Way. In its deepest meanings, the dark-rift is a place of connection between life and death, the Earth and the Underworld—a place where Creation occurs. It is the portal to the Otherworld and a birth-death nexus. The dark-rift is a central player in the Maya myth of cosmogenesis, as well as in the precession-caused astronomical alignment that culminates in A.D. 2012.

The rich astronomical information provided by the Quiché *Popol Vuh* allows us to expand how we understand the dark-rift's meanings. In general, it can be seen as a black spot at the top of the sky—a dark "hole" near the cosmic crossroads formed by the Milky Way and ecliptic. The cosmic center associated with this area of the sky is, as was sketched earlier, the Galactic Center. We also saw earlier how the Mesoamerican astronomers recognized two other cosmic centers, one in the zenith and one in the North Celestial Pole. Let's return to the Chortí and Yucatec material and see how the concept of the hole in the sky also applied to the zenith.

The modern Chortí, as well as the modern Yucatec Maya, erect a ceremonial house in which four poles are lashed together at the top. An offering plate is hung from the centerpoint, which is thought of as a hole in the sky, a sacred doorway at the center of the sacred crossroads. The Yucatec Mayas' term for this centerpoint is *u hol Glorya*, translated as the Glory Hole.[19]

Located at the top of the sky in the center of the cosmic crossroads, the Glory

Hole is a sacred conduit between Earth and the inner planes of the sky. The Yucatec ceremonialists explicitly associate it with the zenith, which makes sense when we remember that the Zenith Cosmology flowered at Chichén Itzá after the Toltecs arrived in the Yucatán in the ninth century A.D. The point is that the ritual structure of the Yucatec ceremonial house also could apply to the Galactic Cosmology, in which the dark-rift would be the Glory Hole and the four lashed poles would represent the four roads formed by the Milky Way/ecliptic cross. Given the Chortí interest in this cosmic crossroads, the Chortí ceremonial house may, in fact, be ori-

Diagram 18. Ceremonial house with top-knot "hole" as an image of the cosmic center as a hole in the sky

ented to the Galactic Center rather than the zenith. Nevertheless, in both examples, the celestial dome of the night sky is envisioned as a house.

The Maya equate the four-cornered celestial dome with a house for other reasons. Houses "belong" to women. When a Maya woman marries and becomes a mother, she "owns" the family house. Symbolically, she is the house. In fact, in the Yucatec language and elsewhere, *na* means both house and mother. As a result, if we expand these ideas to the level of the cosmos at large, the cosmos is a house, the house is the mother; in other words, *the cosmos is the Great Mother.* The Milky Way itself is the arched frame of the Cosmos-Mother, and her birth canal would thus be the dark-rift—the "hole" at the deepest center of the night sky—that is, the Underworld.

The same symbolic association is found among the Tzutujil Maya people of Guatemala. They use sweat baths for practical health reasons as well as for ceremonial rebirthing. When they emerge from the door of the sweat house after a purifying cleanse, they believe they are reborn from the Great Mother. Their word for the sweat house door is the same as their word for the cervix.[20]

These examples demonstrate that, in Mesoamerican cosmo-conception, an entire complex of mythological meanings is associated with the dark-rift and the Milky Way/ecliptic crossroads. The central meaning, however, can be distilled by cross-comparing all of the metaphors. The dark-rift and the cosmic center clearly have to do with birth and rebirth, the portal to another world, and World Age Creation. The four-cornered house symbolizes the celestial dome centered upon the central hole of Creation and, depending on your cosmological training, this could refer to either the zenith or the dark-rift. Most importantly, it is clear that the dark-rift in the Milky Way was mythologized as the birth canal of the Great Mother. It is the Underworld Black Road to baktun 13.

OF FIRE DRILLS AND POLE STARS

The authors of *Hamlet's Mill* briefly discuss Mesoamerican symbology as it relates to precession. Unfortunately, the Mesoamerican interpretations are somewhat vague, understandable given the state of Maya studies when the authors were writing in the late 1960s. However, they do mention the Aztec Fire Drill ceremony and the Aztec god Tezcatlipoca. The fire drill symbolizes the cosmic axis, and Tezcatlipoca, the one-foot deity, spins upon the Pole Star. Clearly, in this Aztec cosmology, the cosmic axis of the fire drill shaft was fixed to the Pole Star.

The Maya counterpart to Tezcatlipoca is Hunrakan (or Hurakan), the twisted "one-leg" god of the Quiché and other Maya groups. He is famous in the *Popol Vuh* for bringing down destruction on a previous age, the age of the wooden people. He wipes the slate clean by sending a universal flood down to Earth. Interestingly, the English word *hurricane* is derived from Hurakan. The fact that Hunrakan is thought of as being "caught in a whirlwind"—that is, spinning around—and literally means "one-leg," associates him with the polar axis. This association is not limited to Mesoamerica, and its universality attests to its validity. For example, Prince Dhruvi in India was the World Age ruler who stood on one foot, and symbolized the North Celestial Pole.[21]

The fire drill is the primeval machine. It spins and generates friction, fire, heat, and preserves life. Furthermore, it may wear out and is subject to failure, which brings about the end of a World Age. Robert Carlsen and Martín Prechtel, who lived with the Maya for many years, illuminate the symbology of the fire drill in their article "Weaving and Cosmos amongst the Tzutujil Maya of Guatemala." Among the Tzutujil Maya, neighbors to the Quiché, the fire drill was operated with a bow by pulling a cord wrapped around the shaft back and forth. The base of the shaft went into a notch, and the back-and-forth process resembled both sex and weaving. The base is female and the shaft is male, and the top of the shaft was hooked on the celestial navel, the location of a high celestial deity.

Large fire drills needed two operators, one on each side, and many Mesoamerican images are based upon a structural arrangement I call the fire drill symbol.

Notice here that the drill shaft, symbol of the World Axis, is flanked by two operators, who serve as caretakers of time. Early Long Count monuments are similarly structured, with two attendants flanking a vertical glyph column containing the Long Count date (see examples in Part IV).

Diagram 19. Fire Drill gods from the Dresden Codex

Diagram 20. Churning of the Milky Ocean. India

The fire-drill symbol is ancient and global. In Hindu cosmology, the image of the churning Milky Ocean (the Milky Way as the generator of all manifestation) is structurally identical to the fire-drill symbol. The fire-drill symbol is also found in Egyptian symbolism, in which, again, the cosmic axis of time is operated, like a fire drill, by attendants on the right and the left.

The polar axis, extending down from the North Celestial Pole to the Earth, manifests in easily recognized mythic symbols. It usually takes the form of a World Tree, a cosmic fire drill, or a spinning "one leg" god. For many cultures in the Far North the Pole Star that secures the cosmic axis is called the "Nail of the North." In Finnish mythology, the celestial axis centered upon the Pole Star is symbolized by the Sampo, a magic spinning mill with a "many ciphered cover" that represents the twinkling stars of the night sky. Significantly, in Runo 42 of the Finnish *Kalevala*, the Sampo is stolen, that is, removed from its former place of residence. As argued in *Hamlet's Mill*, this story probably represents a knowledge of the shifting frame of time, an awareness of precession among the ancient Finns. Likewise, in the Egyptian and Hindu images, the same knowledge is implicit, because the common element of the myths surrounding the fire drill symbol is that the shaft eventually wears out its "hinge" and the spinning skies go out of kilter.

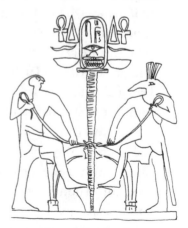

Diagram 21. Egyptian fire-drill brothers, Horus and Set

The fire drill found in Mesoamerican art and symbolism is especially common at Izapa. Izapan Stela 2 clearly depicts the fire-drill symbology and also illustrates an event in the Hero Twin story—the demise of Seven Macaw.

This stela shows the Hero Twins Hunahpu and Xbalanque, as the World Axis attendants, facilitating the demise of Seven Macaw. As mentioned earlier, Seven Macaw was a polar deity, confirming that this Izapan fire-drill image does, like the other examples given above, symbolize the polar axis and the North Celestial Pole.

Diagram 22. Stela 2, Izapa. Maya fire drill brothers, Hunahpu and Xbalanque

The comparison here of Izapan, Maya, Aztec, Finnish, Egyptian, and Indian symbology suggests a universally shared concept: the maintenance of time and the continuation of the cycles of heaven facilitated by two important twin beings, the fire-drill gods. Encoded in these images is an underlying knowledge that the fire drill and its ruling deity periodically must be replaced, that precession will cause the polar axis to point to different Pole Stars over long periods. For example, we mentioned that Tezcatlipoca was the one-legged polar deity for the Aztecs. In fact, there are four Tezcatlipocas, and scholar Eva Hunt has argued that these four Tezcatlipocas represented four different eras of precession during which the North Celestial Pole pointed to four different Pole Stars over a very large period of time.[22]

As can be seen from all of the examples in this chapter, mythology and astronomy were intimately related in the beliefs of many ancient cultures around the globe. In Mesomerican cosmology, the polar center was an important focus and represents an older worldview, one that was superseded by new astronomical discoveries. Mesoamerican skywatchers were working with three cosmic centers, the polar, the zenith, and the Galactic, and in Part IV we will return to the meaning of the polar god Seven Macaw and understand how his "fall" symbolizes precessional movement. But as we have already seen, over 2,400 years ago the zenith and the Milky Way's great bulge (the Galactic Center) became especially interesting to Mesoamerican skywatchers, more so than the old polar cosmology. Therefore, it is time that we focus on the Galactic Center and the zenith center, and explore how the cosmologies surrounding these two cosmic centers were developed in separate regions and were eventually unified at Chichén Itzá.

PART II:
THE UNION OF CAPTAIN SERPENT
AND CAPTAIN SUN DISK

The Day of the Cross (May 3rd) appears linked directly to the concept of the astronomic cross, since it celebrates in thought the zenith position of the sun in conjunction with the Pleiades.

— Susan Milbrath, *Star Gods and Astronomy of the Aztecs*

CHAPTER 6

THE PYRAMID OF KUKULCAN:
A COSMIC MYTH IN STONE

Mesoamerican cosmologists hailed different alignments in the precessional cycle as rare eras of change and accelerated evolution on Earth, or World Age shifts. In my work with the ancient cosmologies of Mesoamerica, I identified two different alignments in precession that were being tracked by the ancient skywatchers. The Toltecs preferred an alignment centering on the zenith, whereas the Maya claimed the one oriented toward the Galaxy. Each culture explained the astronomical alignment with a myth: The Toltecs used the New Fire myth and its attendant ceremony, and the Maya created the Hero Twin myth. As my search into the mysteries of the ancient past deepened, I realized that these two World Age traditions were in conflict. Although both are rooted in the precession of the equinoxes, the Toltec and Maya timings of the future World Age shift were, in their original formulation, not in agreement. Culturally and politically, this disagreement created a fundamental schism in the Mesoamerican psyche that lasted over eight hundred years. The Toltec empire centering on Teotihuacan fell in the eighth century A.D., around the same time the Maya empire to the east began experiencing instability. However, as Mesoamerican civilization approached its apocalyptic meltdown in the eighth and ninth centuries, Chichén Itzá emerged as the place where the Toltec and the Maya World Age systems (the Zenith Cosmology and the Galactic Cosmology) were both preserved and, moreover, unified. The Maya-Toltec reconciliation is portrayed on murals at Chichén Itzá in the union of two deity-rulers,

Captain Sun Disk and Captain Serpent.[1] By the end of Part II, it will become clear why these avatars, or cosmic representatives, symbolize the two World Age cosmologies of the Maya and the Toltec cultures.

My research shows that the Toltec method of tracking precession involved the New Fire ceremony and the movement of the sun and the Pleiades in relation to the zenith. This method of sky charting was transplanted to Chichén Itzá in the Yucatán with Toltec migrations beginning in the eighth century A.D. The Pyramid of Kukulcan at Chichén Itzá was built in the early ninth century and encodes a profound message derived from the Toltec precession-tracking system.

CHICHÉN ITZÁ: SHADOW PLAY ON THE EQUINOX

Chichén Itzá is the site of several phases of Maya culture, beginning over 2,000 years ago. The city was founded and originally inhabited by the Maya. However, in the eighth century A.D., the great Toltec city of Teotihuacan in Central Mexico collapsed, and many Toltecs migrated east to the Yucatán. This influx of foreigners stimulated new growth at Chichén Itzá, but at a cost. As recorded on fantastic murals near Chichén Itzá's famous ballcourt, the Toltec invaders occupied the city and began to implement their own skywatching agenda. A vigorous blending of the Maya and Toltec cultures ensued, resulting in the building of Chichén's best known structures, including the Caracol observatory, the Great Ballcourt, and the Pyramid of Kukulcan. The hybrid Toltec-Maya culture, as portrayed in the art and architecture of the Yucatán, is especially present at Chichén Itzá. As such, we can think of Chichén Itzá as the headquarters for the unique ninth-century merger of the Maya and Toltec cultures.

Chichén Itzá is probably the most visited and best known site in the Yucatán. One can visit the Great Ballcourt, the Pyramid of Kukulcan, the Hall of Atlantean Columns, the Caracol observatory, and the Sacred Well (the cenote). But

Diagram 23. The Pyramid of Kukulcan when discovered in the nineteenth century

the city's biggest attraction is an amazing astronomical event that occurs every spring equinox. On this day, March 21, thousands of visitors pack in around the Pyramid of Kukulcan and prepare to watch the shadow-play caused by the afternoon sun. Around 4:00 p.m., the rays of the sun cast a shadow that looks like an undulating snake onto the side of the north stairway. A serpent's head carved in stone at the base of the stairway completes the picture of an upside-down serpent—a deity-serpent descending from the sky—that is quite common in Mesoamerican art. One can imagine that the snake's tail, or rattle, points through the roof of the little room on top of the pyramid. Visitors go away from this experience amazed at the sophisticated and ingenious people who could build a mythological story into their monumental architecture. It is the story of the return of the solar warmth and life energy at the spring equinox, the annual renewal of the serpent-power in the agricultural, religious, and political affairs of the city.

The head of the snake points to the nearby cenote, and part of the mystery-play enacted by the ancient Maya-Toltec priests every March equinox no doubt involved processions from the Pyramid of Kukulcan to the Sacred Well, where ritual sacrifices took place. Stone carvings of inverted serpents are found throughout Chichén Itzá, often as roof supports or stylized doorjamb ornaments.

The solar-snake of Yucatec Maya mythology is Kukulcan, whose counterpart in Toltec mythology is Quetzalcoatl, the Plumed Serpent.

Diagram 24. Inverted Serpent at Chichén Itzá

According to Mexican researcher José Diaz-Bolio, the Yucatec rattlesnake (*Crotalus durissus durissus*) was the focus of ancient Maya ceremonies and symbolized the sun.[2] During Diaz-Bolio's intimate study of these snakes he noticed that a little round design resembling a "solar face" can be found near their rattle (see diagram 26).

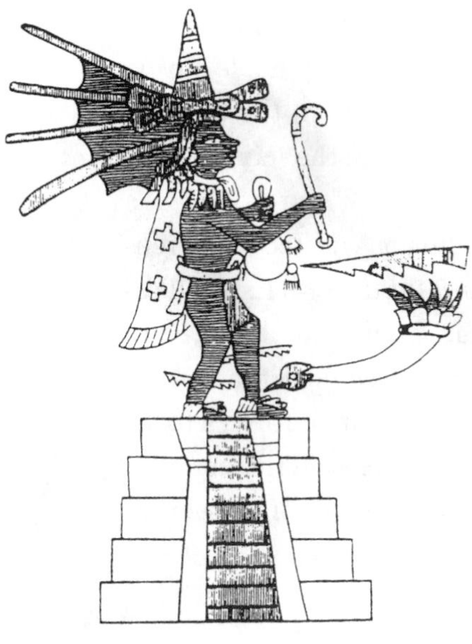

Diagram 25. Quetzalcoatl, from the Codex Telleriano- Remensis

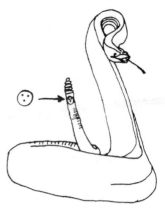

Diaz-Bolio believes the Maya recognized these natural designs as symbols of the sun deity, and the nearby rattle represented the sun deity's crown. The number of segments in a snake's rattle increases every year, and thus the rattle, for the ancient Maya, was a perfect symbol of time. Maya kings were avatars of the sun and were especially revered if they ruled for many years, or, metaphorically speaking, if their "rattle-crowns got longer." In addition, snakes shed their skins at the height of the hot season, which symbolizes the sun's annual rebirth. As such, for the ancient Maya the snake was a compelling symbol of time and renewal, as well as of rulership.

*Diagram 26. Solar face on **Crotalus durissus d.***

In his independently published book *The Geometry of the Maya*, Diaz-Bolio provides further evidence that the ancient Maya recognized the little solar "Ahau" faces on the serpent's tail and incorporated this symbol into their mythology. On a decorative panel found near the Governor's Palace at Uxmal, Diaz-Bolio notes several tiny solar faces, each surrounded by a stylized rattle resembling a stepped pyramid. The equation between the segmented rattle and pyramid steps is significant, given the fact that the shadow-serpent appears on the balustrade of the north stairway of the Pyramid of Kukulcan. He found a similar motif on the Palace at Palenque, in which he interprets the four stylized rattles around each solar face as symbols of the four directions (and, I would add, the four year-bearers). More significantly still, Diaz-Bolio's research led him to examine drawings of ancient carvings made during an early expedition to Palenque, and he notes a tiny human face in the tail of a serpent that is held by two priests. For Diaz-Bolio, the solar face in the serpent's tail symbolizes the sun, time, the calendar, and renewal.

Given Diaz-Bolio's findings and a general understanding of Yucatec Maya religion, it is not surprising that the Maya chose *Crotalus durissus d.*, with its provocative natural markings, to represent a major deity, Kukulcan-Quetzalcoatl. The equinox shadow-play event is an astronomical and architectural wonder that tells a story about the annual reappearance of Kukulcan. And this event continues to astonish thousands of visitors every year, who come to witness the esoteric secrets of Maya cosmology. However, the shadow-serpent has not revealed all of its secrets. At least, not until now.

My interest in the deeper cosmological meaning of the equinox shadow-play event increased when I realized that the Yucatec Maya word for the Pleiades is *tzab*, which also means "rattle."[3] In other words, for the ancient Yucatec Maya, the Pleiades were symbolized by the rattle of the rattlesnake, and the rattle's place during the equinox event at Chichén Itzá is at the very top, the apex, of the pyramid. I wondered if something else might be going on here, something a little more obscure and much more profound. How are the Pleiades associated with the top of the pyramid, and what might that have to do with the sun and snakes? And how might Maya and Toltec cosmology fit into this scenario? I began to feel that the deeper meaning of the mythic drama of Kukulcan's manifestation on the spring equinox still needed to be decoded.

TROPICAL ASTRONOMY AND THE ZENITH CENTER

The answer to the enigma of Chichén Itzá's lost cosmology, as symbolized by the equinox shadow-serpent, requires that we understand the sun's movements within the tropical latitudes. The entire region defining Mesoamerica is completely within the Tropics, that is, within 23°26' of the equator. Much of what seems so obscure in Mesoamerican *astrology* will become more clear if we learn to appreciate the unusual dynamics of tropical *astronomy*.

At the tropical latitudes, the sun's daily and annual motion is much different than what we would observe from Seattle, London, or New York. The tropical zone is delineated by the tropic of Cancer (running through northern Mexico) and the tropic of Capricorn (running through Chile in South America).[4] The U.S. and Europe are at northern latitudes, and when we watch the sun move through the sky during a single day, it traces an arc to the south of us. It rises in the southeast and sets in the southwest. On the December solstice, the arc is very low in the sky. On the June solstice, the arc is much higher and longer, accounting for the longest day of the year. But still, at our northern latitude, the sun never passes through the center of the sky; it always makes an arc to the south of the zenith. The sun can pass through the zenith only within the Tropics, and the exact dates of the solar zenith passage vary with latitude. At latitude 23°26'N (the tropic of Cancer), the sun passes right through the zenith only on one day—the June solstice.[5] At noon on this day, no shadows are cast, and the Toltec and Maya astronomers considered these "no shadow" days to be very sacred. As you move south from the tropic of Cancer, the dates of the solar zenith passage change, and there will be two days every year when the sun moves through the zenith, one on its journey from winter solstice to summer solstice, and one on its return journey from summer solstice to winter solstice. At the latitude of Chichén Itzá (20°40'N), zenith passages of the sun occur on May 23 and July 23. A little further south, at latitude 19°40'N, a solar zenith passage happens on July 26, and this is why the Yucatec Maya celebrated July 26 as New Year's Day.[6] The sixteenth-century Yucatec Maya chief Juan Pío Pérez confirmed this when he wrote "To this day the Indians call the year Jaab or Haab, and . . . they commenced it on the 16th of July. It is worthy to notice that their progenitors . . . sought to make it begin from the precise day on which the Sun returns to the zenith. . . ."[7] July 16 in the older Julian calendar is equivalent to July 26 in our Gregorian calendar—the traditional and authentic New Year's Day for the Yucatec Maya. The use of this date as New Year's Day, although significant only for a specific latitude, provides clear evidence that solar zenith passages were very important in Yucatec cosmology and

Diagram 27. The sun and the Pleiades conjuncting in the zenith over Chichén Itzá on May 20, 2000. All of the inner planets are nearby

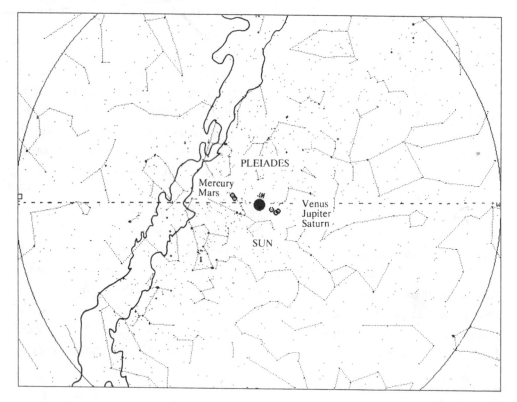

calendrics. The uniquely compelling attribute of this date is, of course, that the sun is in the precise center of the sky, in the Heart of Heaven.

The other zenith-passage date at latitude 19°40'N is May 20, which is sixty days after the March equinox. Significantly, zenith-passage dates do not change with the precession of the equinoxes. At latitude 19°40'N the first zenith passage of the sun has always taken place sixty days after the spring equinox. Notice that there is a slight difference between this May 20 date and the date of the solar zenith passage a little further to the north, at Chichén Itzá. The difference amounts to three days; however, in terms of observing "no shadows at high noon," one would not be able to distinguish any difference between May 20 and May 23.[8] The fact is that zenith-passage observations, given the "no shadow at high noon" criterion, allow for a range of days. If you go to Chichén Itzá on May 20, you will observe no shadows at high noon. For a detailed look at the nature of zenith-passage observations, see Appendix 3, "Space-Time Maps of the Sun and Pleiades in the Zenith."

I am emphasizing this point to associate the May 20 zenith passage of the sun with the mythic cosmo-drama encoded into the pyramid at Chichén Itzá. And here is the key to understanding its deeper cosmological meaning: *The importance of May 20 lies in the fact that the sun and the Pleiades are currently in conjunction on this day.* Thus, on May 20, both the sun and the Pleiades, together, pass through the zenith directly over the Pyramid of Kukulcan.

This alignment is compelling in terms of World Age concepts because it changes with precession. In other words, one hundred years ago this alignment was not in effect at the latitude of Chichén Itzá; only in our current era is it coming into resonance. But how does this relate to the equinox shadow-play event? Remember, the snake's rattle symbolizes the Pleiades and

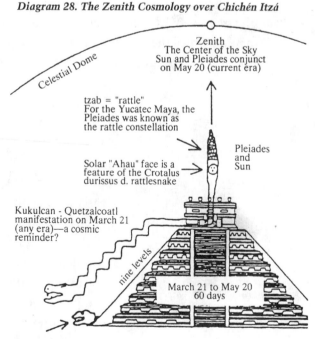

Diagram 28. The Zenith Cosmology over Chichén Itzá

Zenith
The Center of the Sky
Sun and Pleiades conjunct
on May 20 (current era)

Celestial Dome

tzab = "rattle"
For the Yucatec Maya, the
Pleiades was known as
the rattle constellation

Pleiades
and
Sun

Solar "Ahau" face is a
feature of the Crotalus
durissus d. rattlesnake

Kukulcan - Quetzalcoatl
manifestation on March 21
(any era)—a cosmic
reminder?

nine levels

March 21 to May 20
60 days

Serpent head
carved in stone

the "solar face" design near the rattle symbolizes the sun. During the equinox manifestation of Kukulcan, the sun-Pleiades tail of the serpent-shadow points into the center of the sky, the zenith.

The cosmic myth at Chichén Itzá, as encoded into the famous shadow-serpent event, thus involves a previously unrecognized World Age context, in that the symbology of the serpent's tail points to a rare precessional alignment of the sun and the Pleiades in the zenith.

MAYA PYRAMIDS: COSMOGRAMS IN STONE

A general facet of pyramid symbolism among the Maya is that they are cosmograms (symbols of the cosmos) in stone. The Pyramid of Kukulcan, when viewed from above, represents the quadrated "completion" hieroglyph and symbolizes the five cosmological directions—four at the corners and one in the center. The central direction is the astronomical zenith.[9]

The apex of any Maya pyramid points to the zenith and might indicate certain dates in the year on which astronomical events happen in the zenith, usually the solar zenith passages. At Chichén Itzá, the equinox appearance of the serpent-shadow with the Pleiades tail indicates that the Pleiades are supposed to occupy the central zenith direction of Kukulcan's pyramid. As we will see in Chapter 8, Classic-period Maya rulers timed their accession ceremonies to coincide with astronomical events happening in the zenith. Furthermore, these accession ceremonies took place on the top of a pyramid, in the symbolic center of the cosmos, the zenith center.

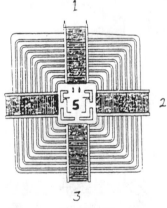

Diagram 29. Five directions: Pyramid as cosmogram, zenith in the center

When the Pyramid of Kukulcan was built around A.D. 830, it was designed to indicate a sun-Pleiades alignment in the zenith. However, at the latitude of Chichén Itzá, this alignment does not begin until the early twenty-first century A.D. The precession of the equinoxes is responsible for bringing the sun and the Pleiades together in the zenith, revealing that Kukulcan's pyramid is a precessional clock with its alarm set for the twenty-first century. Significantly, the precessional alignment of the Zenith Cosmology is different than the one targeted by the Long

Count end-date in A.D. 2012. But how does this zenith alignment work? And how was it tracked? As mentioned, zenith-passage dates vary depending on latitude, and they do not change with precession. The sun has always passed through the zenith over Chichén Itzá on May 20.[10] However, the date on which the sun and the Pleiades conjunct does change with precession. Five hundred years ago, they were conjunct on May 13. The conjunction of the sun and the Pleiades has begun to occur on May 20 in our present era, which, significantly, corresponds to the solar zenith-passage date at Chichén Itzá. This convergence of separate phenomena is what makes the early twenty-first century a rare era of precessional alignment for Chichén Itzá.

What I call the Zenith Cosmology is a forgotten paradigm that could only be reconstructed from looking carefully at Mesoamerican traditions, symbology, and cosmological priorities. The best way to envision the converging phenomena of the Zenith Cosmology is with the following diagram:

Year (A.D.)	1436	1508	1652	1724	1796	1940	2012	2084	2228
Date on which the sun and Pleiades join in year shown	5.12	5.13	5.15	5.16	5.17	5.19	5.20	5.21	5.23

At the latitude of Chichén Itzá, the date of the solar zenith passage is May 20. Thus the sun-Pleiades join in the zenith on May 20.

Diagram 30. Alignment eras of the sun-Pleiades in the zenith

As will become clear, I believe that Kukulcan/Quetzalcoatl, the Plumed Serpent, was the symbol of the sun-Pleiades conjunction. Notice in the diagram that for the latitude of Chichén Itzá, the culmination of the Zenith Cosmology—that is, when the sun and the Pleiades join in the zenith—is the twenty-first century A.D. Thirteen hundred years ago the sun-Pleiades-zenith conjunction occurred on May 1, which highlighted the latitude of Copán as the region blessed by the Plumed Serpent. The nature of zenith phenomena is complicated. In general, the location of the sun-Pleiades-zenith conjunction has moved from southerly latitudes (e.g., Copán) during the Maya Classic period northward to Chichén Itzá, where it presently occurs.

For Chichén Itzá, the May 20 sun-Pleiades-zenith alignment speaks clearly to the aspect of Maya cosmology having to do with World Age shiftings, great celestial alignments, and vast epochs of time. The equinox shadow-play event thus seems to be the annual reminder to look to the heavens, to remember the place from where the Plumed Serpent springs, and to patiently await his return. The future return of Quetzalcoatl, the Plumed Serpent, is one of the best-known Mexican myths. In the popular literature, Quetzalcoatl has been variously identified as Saint Patrick, Jesus, Hernán Cortés, or a space alien. But if we examine the early Toltec mythology, we find that Quetzalcoatl was originally identified with the Pleiades.[11] He also has always had solar attributes, which does not create a conflict if we think of Quetzalcoatl as that unique being who manifests when the sun and the Pleiades are joined. Given that the deity Quetzalcoatl was first conceived at Teotihuacan, and that city, as we saw previously, was oriented to an alignment with the Pleiades on the May zenith-passage date, the return of Quetzalcoatl myth would seem to have everything to do with a future era during which Quetzalcoatl (the sun and the Pleiades united) takes his throne in the zenith center. In other words, the sun-Pleiades deity (Quetzalcoatl) has been slowly marching toward the zenith center, moving one degree closer every seventy-two years, to ultimately reclaim his ruling station in the Heart of Heaven.

CHICHÉN ITZÁ REVEALED

The sun-Pleiades-zenith alignment is currently within range at Chichén Itzá. However, we can't pin this alignment down to a specific year, because of the six-day range for zenith-passage observations at the latitude of Chichén Itzá. The sun-Pleiades alignment over Chichén Itzá begins around the year 2000, but continues, for all observational purposes, for over two centuries. This entire period may represent a period of renaissance for Maya culture in the Yucatán, during which the ancient knowledge is reclaimed. Michael Coe, accomplished Maya scholar, relates that the contemporary Yucatec Maya believe the world will end "at the year 2000 plus a little."[12] Although this may be a memory of the Long Count end-date of A.D. 2012, we should not overlook the possibility that the sun-Pleiades-zenith alignment over Chichén Itzá (in the same era of the Long Count end-date) may have been understood as separate confirmation of the older Long Count end-date calculations.

Here we begin to suspect something very interesting going on at Chichén Itzá. Is it a coincidence that the Zenith Cosmology just described points to the early twenty-first century, as does the Long Count end-date, the Galactic Cosmology? As revealed on the murals of Chichén Itzá, a union of opposed political/cosmological ideologies took place in the ninth century A.D.; we will examine this reconciliation more closely in Chapter 12 in order to solve this enigma of conflicting World Age cosmologies.

If we take the year A.D. 2012 as a good marker for the era in which the sun and the Pleiades are conjunct on May 20, something doubly interesting is found. First, on May 20 of A.D. 2012, there will be a solar eclipse that will sweep across central and western North America. This means that the sun and the Pleiades will pass through the zenith *with the moon!* Second, that date in the 260-day tzolkin calendar will be 10 Chicchan, and Chicchan means serpent. The Pyramid of Kukulcan has nine levels and the top, central platform (the "zenith") is the tenth. Thus 10 Chicchan, May 20, 2012—the date of a solar eclipse—would be a most auspicious day to consciously celebrate the ancient cosmic myth at Chichén Itzá.

The pyramid at Chichén Itzá is the site of an incredible mytho-cosmic story set in stone. Until now, only part of this incredible story has been recognized. The pyramid itself is a World Age calendar, pointing to a unique alignment in the Great Cycle of precession. Many of us are familar with the shadow-play event that takes place there on the spring equinox. In fact, it has become the annual pilgrimage site of groups performing solar ceremonies and initiations. On the equinox day, Kukulcan manifests and slithers down the stairs, tail up in the air, heading toward the cenote—and then is gone! My understanding of this event has expanded to incorporate the fact that Kukulcan's rattle—the Pleiades—points to the zenith where the sun and the Pleiades will be found sixty days later. But this conjunction only begins to occur in our current era, extending through the next two centuries. The equinox shadow, on the other hand, is not affected by precession and occurs in any era. Thus, the serpent manifestation is, literally, the pointer to a zenith conjunction of the sun and the Pleiades. The sun-Pleiades-zenith convocation, now beginning to occur over Chichén Itzá, may in fact herald the fabled "return of Quetzalcoatl."

If you go to Chichén Itzá at high noon on May 20, know that the sun and the Pleiades are up there, together, in the exact center of the sky. This may be the real manifestation of Kukulcan signified by the equinox event. The citizens of ninth-century Chichén Itzá believed their city would be bathed by the light of the great alignment sometime in the remote future. As such, the visible equinox manifestation seems to be a perennial clue to help those who are alive during the Maya end-times to get the message. The complete message. And the complete message appears to be that when the sun and the Pleiades join forces in the Heart of Heaven, Quetzalcoatl will return and a new era will dawn.[13]

CHAPTER 7

~RUE MEANING
OF ~ ~W FIRE CEREMONY

~he esoteric knowledge encoded into the Pyramid of Kukulcan came from Toltec
~kywatchers originating from Teotihuacan in Central Mexico. But how did
~ncient skywatchers track the ever-changing dates of the sun-Pleiades con-
~ As competent astronomers and insightful cosmologists, they noticed that
~f the sun-Pleiades conjunction was slowly moving toward the date of the
~n passage. The nature of the convergence in some remote future epoch,
b~ ~alignment in the Great Year of precession, most certainly would have
bee~ ~red justification for a World Age shift. But how did the early Teotihuacan
astron~ ~riests pinpoint the exact day of the sun-Pleiades conjunction? After
all, the Ple~ ~s are lost in the rays of the sun for more than four weeks, until they
rise heliacally ~ early June. The answer to our question comes from the most significant and best-known ritual event performed at Toltec Teotihuacan and Aztec
Tenochtitlan: the New Fire ceremony.

My reconstruction of the full meaning of the cosmic myth at Chichén Itzá
identifies the relevance of the astronomy of the sun-Pleiades-zenith conjunction.
However, the tracking method used by Mesoamerican astronomers eluded me until I thought carefully about the nature of the New Fire observation of the Pleiades.
As a result, another unrecognized aspect of Mesoamerican cosmology came into
focus, and now adds to our understanding of ancient Mesoamerica's lost cosmology.

THE ZENITH COSMOLOGY TRACKING METHOD:
THE NEW FIRE CEREMONY

At the Central Mexican site of Teotihuacan, the New Fire ceremony was being performed as early as the fourth century A.D.[1] As mentioned earlier, when Teotihuacan was built in the first century A.D., it was aligned with the Pleiades on the May zenith-passage date. The Toltecs are called "the people of the Pleiades" because this constellation played a major role in their ritual ceremonies and cosmological doctrines. As archaeologists have shown, Toltec traditions from Teotihuacan were brought to Chichén Itzá in the ninth century A.D., and the New Fire ceremony was being performed at Chichén Itzá in late Classic times (A.D. 700 – A.D. 900).[2] In the fourteenth century, the Aztecs of Central Mexico adopted the New Fire ceremony, and it was still being practiced at the time of the Conquest. As documented by Conquest-era commentator Bernardino Sahagún, the New Fire ceremony, also known as "the Binding of the Years," involved the careful observation of the Pleiades at the end of each fifty-two-year Calendar Round. Sahagún's indigenous informants described for him the rites of the New Fire ceremony performed at Aztec Tenochtitlan (Mexico City) in 1507: "These are representatives of the Pleiades which mark the fifth cardinal point [the zenith]. At the beginning of a period of 52 years, fire was newly kindled when the Pleiades were at the zenith at midnight. The flaming up of this fire was a sign to the anxious waiting multitude that the world was not, as they had feared, to be swallowed up in darkness. . . ."[3]

Let us take a closer look at a typical New Fire ceremony as performed by the Aztecs. During the time of the New Fire, when a Calendar Round was about to end, the Aztec people ritually extinguished all fires, swept houses clean, and cast statues and other relics into the water. The day before the beginning of the new Calendar Round era, a procession of Fire Priests and a captive warrior solemnly filed out of Tenochtitlan toward the sacred Hill of the Star. Arriving at the Hill of the Star as midnight approached, they watched the Pleiades nearing the zenith and prepared their captive for sacrifice. In the city, the people climbed onto their roofs. Fear and anticipation gripped every citizen, because if the Pleiades did not reach the center of the sky at exactly midnight, they believed that "the world would end." When midnight came and the Pleiades passed through the zenith, the warrior's heart was sliced out. The Fire Priests immediately kindled a fire in the warrior's chest cavity and anointed his still-beating heart in the sacred flames of the New Fire. The New

Fire and the precious heart were simultaneously bathed in the light of the zenithal Pleiades, and the continuation of time was assured. The highest offering on Earth—the human heart—was made at the correct astronomical moment. The god of the zenith center was appeased, and the world would not be destroyed. The Aztec people breathed a sigh of relief, because time would continue for at least another Calendar Round. The New Fire was then used to rekindle all the main fires throughout the city, and even those in distant towns of the Aztec empire.

This dramatic Mystery Play is thick with many levels of meaning. It involves astronomy, human sacrifice, world renewal, and calendars. That human sacrifice is involved in the ceremony has typically been what commentators have focused on, but few scholars have looked closely at the astronomical dimensions of the New Fire tradition.

One astronomical element in the New Fire ceremony, evident in Sahagún's report given above, is critical to understanding what this tradition was really about. The Aztec astronomer-priests observed the Pleiades pass through the zenith *at midnight*. At Mesoamerican latitudes the Pleiades pass through the zenith quite often. However, the Pleiades pass through the zenith *at midnight* on only one day, currently in mid-November. I wondered what this may have signified to the ancient Fire Priests, and why the precise midnight observation was so critical. Looking closely at the astronomy of the midnight zenith passage of the Pleiades, I realized that this event *defines the day exactly six months later when the sun and Pleiades are in conjunction!* It thus appears likely that the New Fire ceremony was used to identify the precise date of the sun-Pleiades conjunction, an event central to the Zenith Cosmology I reconstructed at Chichén Itzá. Calibrating the exact date of the sun-Pleiades conjunction in May was a continual concern because that date moves forward with precession. Thus, every 52 or 104 years, the day had to be corrected. Clearly, the New Fire ceremony was really about the astronomical calibration of precession, despite its gory sideshow.

In 1507, the sun and the Pleiades were in conjunction on May 14, and the Aztecs knew this because they observed, during the New Fire ceremony that took place on November 14, the Pleiades pass through the zenith at midnight.[4] But why did they need to know the precise date of the sun-Pleiades conjunction? At the latitude of Tenochtitlan, the first solar zenith passage occurs on May 18, four days after the sun-Pleiades conjunction in 1507. Since precession moves the date of the sun-Pleiades conjunction forward one day every seventy-two years, it would not be for another three hundred or so years that the two dates aligned, and then the sun and the Pleiades would occupy the zenith together. As we saw previously, the May solar zenith-passage date was involved in the founding orientation of Teotihuacan, the city that was hailed by the Aztecs as their ancient origin place. That the Toltecs inaugurated the New Fire tradition at least 1,700 years ago and the later Aztecs were still performing it proves that the cosmological traditions of the earlier Toltecs were adopted by the later Aztecs. As a result, an interest in solar zenith-passage dates as indicators of the zenith center was shared by both traditions, which means both the Aztecs and the Toltecs ascribed to what I have termed the Zenith Cosmology.

Within the Zenith Cosmology, the future convergence of the sun-Pleiades conjunction date with the local zenith-passage date was recognized by ancient cosmologists as a rare alignment in the precessional cycle, and was thus thought of as an era of historical, cultural, and spiritual change. For the Toltecs and the Aztecs, the future synchronization of the sun and the Pleiades with the zenith was the primary concern of the New Fire ceremony. The great anxiety for the Aztec peasantry was that the world would end if the Pleiades failed to pass through the zenith at midnight. However, I believe that the Aztec astronomer-priests knew that this simply meant that they would then have to adjust one day forward for precession. The ultimate target, the era of the great alignment, was what the end-times anxiety was really about. We can distinguish here between the detailed scientific calculations performed by the Aztec astronomer-priests and the generic message designed to control the masses. As such, the populace was in great mortal terror during the New Fire ceremony, not knowing the real story, while their astronomer-priests carefully fine-tuned their alignment cosmology. The original Toltec "alignment era" was targeted for a sun-Pleiades zenith passage to occur at the latitude of Teotihuacan on May 18. This places the original Toltec alignment era in the late eighteenth to the early nineteenth century. However, when the Toltecs transferred their New Fire Zenith Cosmology to Chichén Itzá, which is a little further north, the era of the World Age shift was recalibrated to when the sun and the Pleiades conjunct on May 20. This recalibration highlights our own era as being cosmologically significant for Chichén Itzá, because May 20 is when the sun and Pleiades currently join in the zenith over the Pyramid of Kukulcan. The Toltec move to Chichén may have been intentional because Chichén's latitude supplies the necessary solar zenith-passage date to bring the Zenith Cosmology into alignment with the 2012 end-date of the Galactic Cosmology. In this interpretation, the ancient Mesoamerican need for correct orientation to the cosmic center may have driven the Toltecs to relocate their headquarters to Chichén Itzá.

EARTHQUAKES AND ENDINGS AT LATITUDE 19°40'N

The 19°N to 20°N latitude is significant for several reasons. As just described, it is currently the latitude at which the sun-Pleiades-zenith alignment occurs. Another reason for its importance involves geometry and the Earth grid. The latitude and longitude lines used by mapmakers can be imagined as a grid system laid over the Earth. Certain geometrical forms placed within the Earth sphere identify specific latitudes as "sacred" places. The ley line theory of the sacred harmonic Earth grid proposes that certain locations on the Earth's surface are power points derived from spherical geometry. For example, the Earth's poles and the equator are fundamental "power areas." As mentioned, certain geometrical shapes placed within the Earth sphere define specific points or latitudes on the Earth's surface where increased geophysical, magnetic, or geothermal energy may be found. For example, the base of an equilateral four-sided pyramid with a vertex on the South Pole reaches the 19°40'N latitude.

According to Earth-grid harmonics, the placement of this geometric shape identifies the 19°40'N latitude as a power band along which increased Earth energies are found. An equilateral four-sided pyramid, like the one in diagram 31, is a Platonic Solid, one of the few three-dimensional forms derived from equilateral shapes such as triangles and pentagons. These shapes have a unique symmetry to them, and are constructed from the sacred ratio called the Golden Mean, a mathematical proportion used by the Egyptians in constructing the Great Pyramid.[5] The point here is that the science of Earth-grid harmonics highlights the 19°N to 20°N latitude as a significant power place.

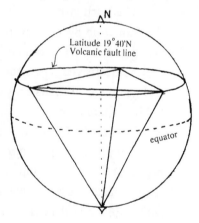

Diagram 31. A Platonic Solid points to latitude 19°40'N

The Zenith Cosmology also focuses on the 19°N to 20°N latitude. The sun-Pleiades-zenith alignment currently occurring at the 19°N to 20°N latitude has meaning not only for Chichén Itzá, but for Teotihuacan in Central Mexico, where the ancient Toltecs devised the New Fire tradition. Both of these ancient cities are within one degree of 19°40′N. There is something else very special about this latitude, apart from the Earth-grid theory and the Zenith Cosmology. Geologists have noted that the chain of high volcanic peaks in Central Mexico (which occasionally threaten civilization in that region) lie on an east-west rift at latitude 19°30′N.[6] These active volcanos include the smoldering Popocatepetl, which looms over Mexico City and is the usual cause of earthquakes there. As such, a dangerous volcanic fault line runs through Central Mexico at the 19°30′N latitude. Did the ancient Toltecs know of this, and did they try to appease the volcanic Fire God in order to delay the destruction of the Fifth Sun, the current World Age inaugurated at ancient Teotihuacan?

The famous Aztec Sunstone encodes the meaning of the New Fire ceremony and the fifty-two-year Calendar Round. It depicts five World Ages, each one destroyed by various natural cataclysms including floods, wind, and fire (see diagram 32).

The Fifth World Age, the one we are currently in, is portrayed in the center of the Sunstone by the seventeenth day-sign, Ollin, which means "movement" or "earthquake." The standard reading of this symbol is that the current World Age will be destroyed by earthquakes. One begins to wonder about the astronomical and geophysical focus on the 19°30′N latitude, supported by geophysical studies, ley line theory, and the ancient Toltec Zenith Cosmology. Perhaps the Toltec prediction that the Fifth Sun will be destroyed by earthquakes has to do with an astronomical pressure applied to the unstable 19°30′N latitude that will catalyze volcanic eruptions and earthquakes? If we were pressed to make a prediction based upon these suggestive scientific facts and archaeological clues, we could suggest that Mexico City will be destroyed by a violent earthquake in the early twenty-first century. Perhaps the ancient Toltec Fire Priests are beginning to stir in their resting places. Perhaps they feel the ancient prophecy is about to be fulfilled. And thus, the most literal interpretation of the secret message hidden within the New Fire tradition may, indeed, come to pass.

Diagram 32. The Aztec Sunstone

CHAPTER 8

ZENITH IMAGERY IN MESOAMERICA

We just explored how zenith passages and their relationship to the sun and the Pleiades manifest at Chichén Itzá. The zenith concept was most significant in the Toltec New Fire ceremony, in which the Pleiades were observed passing through the zenith at midnight. But how widespread was the zenith concept? How old is it? In what other ways do zenith passages and the movements of the Pleiades manifest in Mesoamerican art and ideas? How were solar zenith passages portrayed, and what meanings did they have?

ZENITH TUBES AND CHULTUNES

Mesoamerican astronomers used several methods to track solar zenith passages. One way was to measure the shadow cast from a vertical pole, called a gnomon. When the sun is directly overhead, the pole casts no shadow. Another way was to use a zenith tube, a deep vertical hole in the ground leading to an underground cave. When the sun is in the zenith, it projects a vertical beam onto the floor of the underground chamber against which measurements are made. Structures containing zenith tubes were found at Monte Alban and Xochicalco in Central Mexico. In the Yucatán, archaeologists found many bottle-shaped underground chambers called *chultunes*, and it is still unclear what they may have been used for. Maya ceremonialist Jim Reed, who has spent a great deal of time in the Yucatán, told me that the local Maya believe you can climb into a chultune and, under certain conditions, observe stars passing through the zenith in the middle of the day. One wonders if some kind of refraction effect is possible, a phenomenon not understood by modern science. In one of those strange coincidences, I encountered a passage in my reading that provided a precedent for this "daytime telescope." In his opus *Dialogue on the Great World Systems*, Galileo Galilei, in referring to the activities of Aristotle, wrote, "Having his works brought, he turned to the place where the philosopher gives the reason why, from the bottom of a very deep well, one may see the stars in heaven at noonday."[1] Perhaps chultunes served as *daytime zenith tubes*.

SUN-PLEIADES-ZENITH IN MESOAMERICAN THOUGHT

As mentioned earlier, the Aztecs (and the earlier Toltecs) observed the passage of the Pleiades through the zenith *at midnight*. My own interpretation of this, considering the exactitude implied by the precise midnight observation, is that this observation was used to define the *exact date* of the sun-Pleiades conjunction six months later, in May. In Mesoamerican thought, the zenith concept is inextricably related to the movements of the sun and the Pleiades. In fact, there is evidence in the *Madrid Codex*, one of the few surviving Maya books, that the Maya were interested in the conjunction of the Pleiades with the first zenith-passage date of the sun.[2] As noted in Part I, the horizon position of the Pleiades on the May zenith-passage date defined the orientation of that great early Mesoamerican city, Teotihuacan, built in the first century A.D. This zenith-Pleiades relationship is an ancient concept, and probably was pioneered at Izapa around 100 B.C.[3] Archaeoastronomer Anthony Aveni wrote that it has been suggested that the "zenith principle" was discovered at Izapa and passed along to Copán, which is on the same latitude.[4]

As I explained earlier, the Toltecs and the Aztecs thought of the zenith as a cosmic center and in keeping with common Mesoamerican doctrine, they believed cosmogenesis occurs at a cosmic center identified by a celestial cross.[5] According to one scholar, the Maya believed ". . . in the cross as a symbol of the first solar zenith sun. . . ."[6] This symbology identifies the May solar zenith passage as a

The accession of the Maya king Bird Jaguar is recorded on Yaxchilan Lintel 30 as occurring on 11 Ahau 8 Zec 9.16.1.0.0, which is May 1, 752 A.D.—the date of a sun-Pleiades conjunction. Bird Jaguar is shown holding a serpent-footed sceptor. Elsewhere, on Lintel 41, Bird Jaguar holds a long vertical pole. The date on this lintel is May 7, 755 A.D.—a solar zenith-passage date at the latitude of Yaxchilan. According to Maya scholar Arthur Schlak, the vertical spear or staff held in these depictions is a gnomon used for identifying the "no-shadow" date of solar zenith passage.[11] Diagram 34 depicts such a zenith-passage measuring staff.

Monuments dated in the Long Count calendar frequently record astronomical events. Records of eclipse dates and Venus risings are quite common. However, scholars have frequently neglected to recognize solar zenith-passage dates and sun-Pleiades conjunction dates in Long Count inscriptions. I just related examples from Yaxchilan and Tikal, and here are a few more: Stela 10 from Xultun records the date 10.3.0.0.0, on which the sun and the Pleiades were in conjunction. Katun 9.16.0.0.0 fell near a solar zenith passage at Tikal. Katuns 9.15, 9.16, and 9.17 all have Mars and the Pleiades conjunct, but only 9.16 also fell near a solar zenith passage.

Chan Bahlum, son of the Palenque king Pacal, celebrated his thirty-third birthday by recognizing the solar zenith passage and the Pleiades. According to Arthur Schlak, the kilt in diagram 35 symbolizes the Pleiades

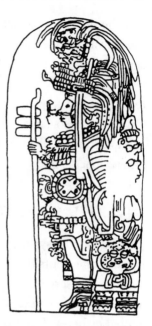

Diagram 34. Tikal Stela 20 showing a vertical staff used to identify the solar zenith passage

Diagram 35. Chan Bahlum's thirty-third birthday

and the upright staff denotes a solar zenith passage.[12] These examples prove that the Maya considered it propitious to coordinate important ceremonies with solar zenith-passage dates and sun-Pleiades conjunctions. The serpent-footed sceptor, which appears to signify the accepting of kingship (accession to the cosmic center), resembles the serpent-shadow that appears on Kukulcan's pyramid at Chichén Itzá. Given this association, the serpent-footed sceptor, as a symbol of divine power and rulership, probably symbolizes the sun-Pleiades-zenith alignment and bestows Quetzalcoatl's blessing upon those chosen to hold it.

INVERTED SERPENT COLUMNS AND YEAR-BEARERS

Additional symbols found in Maya art suggest that the inverted serpent symbol also represents the beginning and ending of time cycles. At the ruins of Chichén Itzá, many "serpent column portals" were found, carved from local stone. Generally, these are inverted snakes, heads at the bottom, tails up in the air, which served either as functional supports for platform-altars or as decorations on the sides of buildings. Along with the so-called "Atlantean columns" present at Chichén Itzá, serpent columns also were found at the Central Mexican site of Tula, a Toltec site with many similarities to Chichén Itzá. The serpent columns at Chichén Itzá bring to mind the solar shadow-image that appears on the equinox.

Diagram 36. Serpent column (left) and Atlantean columns (right) from Chichén Itzá

I described earlier how the symbology of the upward-pointing rattlesnake tail was intended to indicate a sun-Pleiades conjunction in the zenith. The abundance of the same image in stone, as a decorative and functional convention, suggests that the inverted rattlesnake was a well-understood mythological motif. Mayanist George Kubler studied the serpent columns at Chichén Itzá and wrote, "Most directly related to the serpent-columns are their sky-bearer capitals [representatives]."[13] In other words, since serpent columns serve as platform corner supports, they represent the four "pillars of the cosmos." Therefore, the serpent columns correspond to the directional *bacab* (sky-bearers), which in turn are related to the four calendric year-bearers. New Year's Day—the first day of the 365-day haab—always occurred on one of these calendric year-bearers. Considering that the Yucatec Maya New Year's Day was celebrated, at the time of the Conquest, on one of the solar zenith-passage dates, we can easily understand how serpent columns are thus substitute symbols for the year-bearer, for New Year's Day. Also, the Pyramid of Kukulcan at Chichén Itzá has ninety-one steps on each of its four sides, making a total of 364 "base" steps. The 365th step—or "day"—is at the very top of the pyramid, in the zenith position. Now imagine turning this metaphor upside-down, so that the zenith is the first day—New Year's Day—and one descends the pyramid by spiraling down the remaining 364 steps, or days.

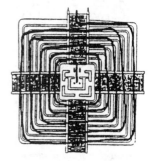

Diagram 37. *Spiraling out from the center on the Pyramid of Kukulcan. Four directions, 365 steps, zenith in the center (the top)*

Here we have confirmed the idea that the cosmic center (the zenith), being associated with New Year's Day, is an important beginning point for time. With the first day of the solar year located at the top of the pyramid—in the central zenith direction—we are also reminded that time begins in and, ultimately, returns to the cosmic center.

Another important mythological serpent was known as Hapaycan, derived from the Yucatec Maya verb *hap*, which means "to open the mouth, swallow, absorb."[14] In a reference from the sixteenth-century Motul dictionary, *hapaknak u chi'* means "open like a viper's mouth." The stem *-nak* also has the meaning of "throne," and *nak* is the sound-inversion of *kan*, which means "serpent, four, and sky." (Sound inversion words are from the language of Zuvuya, a mystical poetry developed by Yucatec Maya shamans.)

Given these symbolic connections, in some essential sense the serpent's open mouth is related to the concept of the throne. The idea of "mouth as throne" makes sense when we understand that the crossroads mark the cosmic center, the cross indicates the doorway into another world, and these doorways were envisioned as "mouths." Most importantly, kings were enthroned on cross-marked thrones, and were intended to symbolically occupy the cosmic center. As discussed previously, serpent and jaguar mouths were both understood as portals to the Underworld. The ubiquitous Mesoamerican motif of solar kings emerging from snakes' mouths is thus a statement of rulership, stating in effect, "I am the newly born king, enthroned in the mouth of the Otherworld."

Yet another family of serpent-forms at Chichén Itzá is called Xiuhcoatl, which

Diagram 38. Solar king emerging from a snake's mouth

literally means "blue serpent."[15] According to Kubler, in the imagery of Highland Mexico, the source of Chichén tradition, "Xiuhcoatl appears often as a descending serpent with trapezoidal overlapping body segments, and the rattler tail converted into the 'year-sign' of trapeze and triangle."[16] This important symbolic connection confirms what I proposed earlier: The Pleiades (the snake's rattle) represents the year-bearer. This association makes sense when we remember that the Pleiades was observed in the New Fire ceremony, passing through the zenith at the beginning of the Calendar Round cycle. These related concepts support my theory that the convergence of the Pleiades with a solar zenith-passage date (one of which was New Year's Day) underlies the World Age doctrine at Chichén Itzá, and it was encoded into the Pyramid of Kukulcan.

In diagram 39, we see the rattle (the Pleiades) transformed into the Central Mexican symbol for the year-bearer. Since the primary year-bearer at Chichén Itzá coincided with a solar zenith-passage date, the coincidence of "sun, Pleiades, and zenith" implies questions that my Chichén hypothesis already answers.[17] Notice that further up the serpent's tail are four bundles, which symbolize the four solar

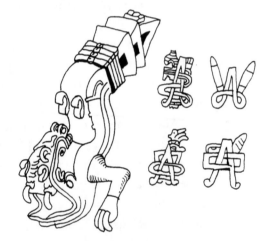

Diagram 39. The Xiuhcoatl serpent with year-sign tail (left). Examples of Aztec trapezoidal year-signs (right)

year-bearers. As with the "solar face" near the *Crotalus durissus* rattlesnake's rattle, here we have combined imagery depicting a united sun and Pleiades. As mentioned, the concept of the zenith is also present in this imagery.

On the famous Aztec Sunstone, there are two Xiuhcoatl snakes rimming the perimeter of the stone. Their heads meet at the bottom, and the headdress of each contains seven stars—the seven stars of the Pleiades (see diagram 40).

The body of each Xiuhcoatl serpent is divided into eleven segments in which can be seen the flames representing the New Fire. But why eleven segments? Since each block represents a New Fire (i.e., a Calendar Round period of fifty-two years), the total number of years per serpent is thus 11 x 52 = 572. Significantly, 572 years equal 8 periods of 71.5 years, which is roughly the amount of time it takes for one degree, or day, of precessional shifting. Within the New Fire tradition's concern for making precessional adjustments, an even eight days of correction for every eleven New Fire ceremonies could have been implemented. This whole number accounting is com-

Diagram 40. Xiuhcoatl serpent with Pleiades headgear on the Aztec Sunstone. The stars are on the snout of the serpent

pletely in keeping with the Mesoamerican interest in finding whole number commensuration between time cycles, rather than using fractions, and results in a very accurate precessional cycle value of 25,740 years.

THE TRAPEZOIDAL YEAR-SIGN: AN ASTRONOMICAL INSTRUMENT

How else might the Central Mexican year-sign be related to the zenith? In pursuing this line of inquiry, we must review what we have discovered so far. What will emerge is an underlying pattern that unites all the seemingly unrelated symbols we have been discussing. To begin, the trapezoidal year-sign form is not limited exclusively to Central Mexico. The "trapezoid instrument" has been identified at Uxmal, Copán, Piedras Negras, and other Maya sites.[18]

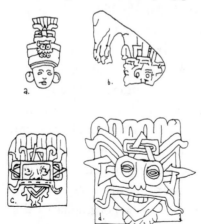

The year-sign is usually attached to the head of a deity figure, but can also be found elsewhere, for example, on the lower back of a figure from Tehuacan (see diagram 42).

In addition, at Uxmal archaeologists found many faces in the form of the trapezoidal year-sign, called "Tlaloc images."[19] Many of these had year-signs for ears, in addition to one on the forehead. The prevalent head placement of the year-sign on these artifacts recalls the cleft-head

Diagram 41. The trapezoidal year-sign symbol outside of Central Mexico: (a) Copán, (b) Piedra Negras, (c) Uxmal, and (d) Maya

motif of the Olmec[20] and the "witz mountain," which symbolizes the "broken place, bitter water place" where corn was born
(according to the *Popol Vuh*).

I have already pointed out the connection between the
year-sign tail of the Xiuhcoatl serpent and the Yucatec rattlesnake rattle. Since *tzab* (the rattle) is also the word for the Pleiades in Yucatec Maya, I noted a connection between the Pleiades
and New Year's Day (symbolized by the year-sign "tail"). In addition, since New Year's Day was celebrated on one of the solar
zenith-passage dates in the Yucatán, a connection between the
Pleiades and New Year's Day is implicit. This association cycles
back to, and is supported by, the basic fact that in the New Fire
ceremony (at the beginning of not just any year but the fifty-
two-year Calendar Round) the Pleiades was carefully observed

Diagram 42. Year-sign on lower back (tail) of deity figure

passing through the zenith at midnight. Thus, the related transformations include
the Pleiades, the rattlesnake rattle, the year-sign, New Year's Day, and the zenith.

The Central Mexican year-sign is directly related to the zenith by way of an
interesting discovery offered by Maya scholar Adrian Digby. Digby found that the
trapezoidal year-sign symbol portrays an "unrecognized astronomical instrument."[21]
He reconstructs two versions of what the shadow-casting trapezoid instrument
looked like, one based upon a drawing from the Pyramid of the Plumed Serpent at

Diagram 43. Trapezoidal year-sign de-signs projected into three dimensions become shadow-casting astronomical instruments

Xochicalco and the other from Tenango. As
mentioned earlier, there is a zenith tube at
Xochicalco, clearly demonstrating that solar
zenith passages were of interest there.

Digby tracked the shadows cast by these
reconstructed three-dimensional trapezoid
"year-signs" on the solstices and the equinoxes.
He found that the patterns formed could be used
to keep very accurate solar observations.
Clearly, although Digby did not emphasize this,
the instrument is perfectly suited for identifying solar zenith-passage dates, on which the
zenith sun will project a simple cross downward
from the trapezoidal "crosshairs." In fact, this

cross is explicitly portrayed below the trapezoidal year-sign glyph found on the Pyramid of the Plumed Serpent at Xochicalco.
The shadow-cross is none other than the
quadripartite "quincunx" design, which portrays the four directions with the fifth—the
zenith—in the center.

*Diagram 44. Shadows cast on the solar
zenith-passage project the Mesoamerican
quincunx design or, alternatively, the
eight-sided figure*

This shadow-symbol on the Pyramid of
the Plumed Serpent at Xochicalco is similar in nature to the serpent-shadow on the
Pyramid of Kukulcan at Chichén Itzá. Remember, the Plumed Serpent (Quetzalcoatl)
is the Central Mexican version of the Yucatec Maya deity known as Kukulcan.
Since the Xochicalco and Chichén Itzá pyramids were both used as zenith calendars, the fact that both are dedicated to the same deity is no doubt significant. At
Xochicalco, the trapezoidal year-sign with the zenith-passage indicator projected
below it (the shadow cross), when combined with the Pleiades/rattle/year-sign
symbol-complex, suggests only one scenario: *the Pleiades and the sun in the zenith on New Year's Day.* This is precisely the event that occurs at Chichén Itzá.[22]
Clearly, the Zenith Cosmology involving the sun, the Pleiades, and the zenith was
shared between Central Mexico and Chichén Itzá.

PLEIADES-SCORPIUS POLARITY: THE TAIL AND THE MOUTH

The symbolic meanings of the inverted serpent columns, with a special focus
on the meaning of the serpent's rattle, should now be clear. The astronomical reference is to the Pleiades and, in related symbology, to the year-bearer (New Year's
Day), which was celebrated in the Yucatán on one of the solar zenith-passage dates.
But what about the other end of the snake, its mouth? We have already seen that
the mouth of the Hapaycan snake deity was akin to a throne. In Mesoamerican art
and iconography, deities are often shown emerging (or being born) from serpent
mouths. At Chichén Itzá the mouth of the shadow-serpent points to the nearby
cenote, as if that is its destination. Both the serpent's mouth and the cenote were
considered to be portals to the Underworld.

We should remember that the Quiché Maya call the dark-rift in the Milky Way
(located near Scorpio and Sagittarius) a doorway to the Underworld. South American mythlore related to the Scorpio constellation might help us clarify Mesoamerican

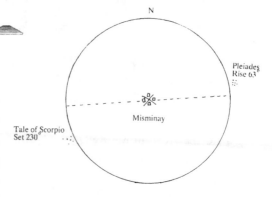

concepts. The Barasana people of North-western Amazonia recognize a polarity between the Pleiades (called *nyokoara*, Star Thing) and Scorpius. An ethnographic study of Barasana star lore reveals: "A snake constellation identified with Scorpius is found throughout the Vaupés region and, in many parts of Amazonia, Scorpius is identified with Boiassu, the Great Serpent."[23] The polarity is a function of the roughly opposed rising and setting times of the Pleiades and

Diagram 45. The "collca" axis: Pleiades-Scorpius polarity. The mouth and tail of the Milky Way serpent

Scorpio throughout the agricultural year. Although these two constellations are not precisely 180° apart, their polarity is functional in terms of seasonal activities and observations. Ethnographer Gary Urton identified a similar Pleiades-Scorpius polarity among the highland Quechua in Peru, in which both constellations are understood as *collcas*, or storehouses.[24]

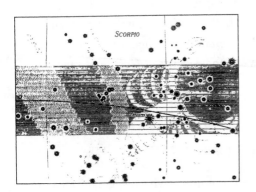

Diagram 46. The Scorpion constellation. Bayer (1603)

But what do these South American traditions have to do with Chichén Itzá? And what does Scorpio have to do with the mouth of a serpent? The South American material on the Pleiades-Scorpius polarity suggests a perspective that any agricultural people might adopt, and suggests a way we can understand the Pleiades rattle and the opposed snake-mouth in Yucatec cosmology.[25] Scorpius is near Sagittarius, both are near the Milky Way, and, more to the point, both are very close to the dark-rift in the Milky Way. The illustration above from Johann Bayer's seventeenth-century astronomical treatise, *Uranometria*, demonstrates the close relationship between the Scorpion constellation (especially its tail) and the dark-rift "mouth" in the Milky Way snake.

In this illustration, the stars of Sagittarius are just above and to the left of the tail of Scorpius, and the dark-rift in the Milky Way is clearly visible. The band of the Milky Way is roughly 10° wide and is tolerably close to both Sagittarius and Scorpio. This is the area of the Milky Way where the Galactic Center is located. In

Nicaraguan and Maya mythology, the Mother Scorpion at the end of the Milky Way is located in Scorpio[26] and her tail is identical to the scorpion's tail in diagram 46. That the Scorpion Mother, who houses the souls of the dead and the unborn, is located in the region of the Galactic Center is significant, as it suggests the Central American Indians deified the Galactic Center as a birthplace or Otherworld storehouse of souls.

The Scorpio tail is very close to the dark-rift "mouth." The Pleiades, on the other side of the sky, were thought of as a rattlesnake rattle, or tail, and this tail-mouth polarity is connected by the Milky Way. The Pleiades are fairly close to where the Milky Way crosses through Gemini, and, of course, the dark-rift mouth in the Milky Way is near Sagittarius-Scorpio. If we bring these facts back to our thesis of multiple cosmic centers, we can piece together what may be a lost paradigm. If the Pleiades (the snake's rattle) reveals one type of cosmic center (the zenith) and the dark-rift in the Milky Way (the snake's mouth) conceals another cosmic center (the Galactic Center), a complex cosmological model uniting the zenith center with the Galactic Center seems in order. Although it is still a stretch to say with any certainty that the inverted serpent-columns at Chichén Itzá, with their tail-mouth polarity, encode this interpretation, they just might. An advanced shamanistic paradigm? A sophisticated cosmogonic map involving skylore lost for centuries? There may be a lot more to Kukulcan than we have been led to believe. In fact, these very considerations are what led me to suspect Chichén Itzá as the place where the Zenith Cosmology and the Galactic Cosmology were synthesized.

We have traced meaningful connections between many symbolic motifs that relate to zenith imagery. It is often necessary to wade through the academic data and synthesize what is really going on. Our search has uncovered significant relationships between the solar zenith passage, the Pleiades, the year-sign, New Year's Day, and the Kukulcan-Quetzalcoatl deity that contribute to elucidating the nature of the Zenith Cosmology in Mesoamerica. The associations can be summed up as follows:

- The snake's rattle (*tzab*) refers to the Pleiades.
- The Pleiades and the New Fire ceremony are related to solar zenith passages.
- In the Yucatán, a solar zenith-passage date was celebrated as New Year's Day around the time of the Conquest.

- Maya kings coordinated important rituals to occur on solar zenith-passage dates and sun-Pleiades conjunctions.
- Serpent-footed sceptors of rulership may have represented the sun-Pleiades-zenith event, which in turn symbolized Quetzalcoatl (sun-Pleiades) taking his throne in the zenith.
- Inverted serpent columns are secondary symbols for the directional *bacab* and the year-bearer symbols of New Year's Day.
- The Central Mexican trapezoidal year-sign depicts an astronomical instrument suited to identifying solar zenith-passage dates, gives rise to the ubiquitous quincunx design, and is found on the tail of the Xiuhcoatl snake.
- The Hapaycan snake's mouth refers, by sound inversion, to the concept of a deity-ruler's throne. (The serpent's mouth is the portal to the Otherworld and is the place where Maya kings are reborn upon taking their throne of office.)
- As suggested by South American examples and Mesoamerican clues, a polarity between the Pleiades and Scorpio may have been recognized in Mesoamerican cosmology. In this interpretation, the serpent's mouth (the dark-rift near Scorpio) was counterposed to the serpent's tail (the Pleiades), and the Milky Way was the Great Serpent that unites them.

So, what is really going on in all this? First, a Zenith Cosmology existed throughout Mesoamerica. The Pyramid of Kukulcan is the most clear and profound example of the Zenith Cosmology, a cosmic myth in stone. The symbolic connections between all of these snake motifs, the Pleiades, and year-bearer signs cannot be coincidence, and my interpretation of how they were synthesized makes sense in terms of what scholars already know about Mesoamerican traditions. Furthermore, the related concepts I have sketched suggest a kind of Maya "unified theory" that connects two cosmic centers—the zenith and the Galactic Center—via the Milky Way serpent-tree axis.[27]

TWO COSMOLOGIES UNITED?

Mesoamerican cosmologists must have organized and ordered the complicated relationships among these metaphors into a profound cosmological system. Chichén Itzá preserves a lost method of tracking the precession of the equinoxes that I call the Zenith Cosmology. But we can't separate the Zenith Cosmology from other facets of Mesoamerican cosmology, namely, the overwhelmingly important cosmology of the end-date, the Galactic Cosmology. The presence of the Galactic Cosmology at Chichén Itzá is undeniable, hidden within the symbols and myths we have been discussing—for example, the dark-rift "mouth" of the snake. In the next three chapters we will explore the underlying astronomy and mythology of the Galactic Cosmology in more detail.

What seems to be emerging from our examination of Mesoamerican mytho-astronomy is a complex and extremely sophisticated paradigm in which the Zenith Cosmology of the Toltecs was somehow unified with the Galactic Cosmology of the Maya Long Count calendar. The World Age calendar utilized in the Zenith Cosmology was the Calendar Round, whereas the Galactic Alignment to occur in A.D. 2012 was tracked with the Long Count calendar. Evidence suggests that the Mesoamerican cosmologists were interested in unifying these two systems. Whatever this was about, it seems to have taken place at Chichén Itzá. In the final chapter of this part of the book, we will return to Chichén Itzá and explore how and why Chichén was the place where the Zenith Cosmology and the Galactic Cosmology were unified.

Long before Chichén Itzá emerged as the place of reconciliation, almost a millennium before the Pyramid of Kukulcan was built, the Long Count calendar was invented by the Izapan culture in southern Chiapas. Why do I call the Long Count calendar a "Galactic Cosmology"? What exactly is involved in the astronomy of its end-date in A.D. 2012? It is time we took a closer look at the astronomy of A.D. 2012 and the area of the sky involved in the end-date, for the Scorpio-Sagittarius region contains many stellar mysteries, ones that the ancient Maya gazed into deeply.

CHAPTER 9

THE LONG COUNT: GALACTIC ALIGNMENT IN 2012

O ver 2,000 years ago, ancient cosmonauts in southern Mesoamerica invented the Long Count calendar. They began dating carved monuments with this calendar in the first century B.C. The Long Count calendar is a galactic calendar because it pinpoints a rare alignment with our Milky Way Galaxy, due to occur in A.D. 2012—a date written as 13.0.0.0.0 in the Long Count. As we have seen, astronomy and mythology are deeply interwoven in how the ancient skywatchers thought about this Galactic Alignment, and the Maya Creation myth, the *Popol Vuh*, encodes the astronomy of the end-date, depicting it as a time of great transformation and world rebirth. And look around us, we do live in an era of great transformation. Space flight, computers, and sophisticated data technology have all emerged in the last fifty years. It does seem that human civilization is being propelled into increasingly complex forms of organization. Time, in a sense, is accelerating. Innovative changes are occurring at a faster and faster rate as we approach the 2012 date. Human civilization is transforming at a rate without precedence. The ancient Maya believed that our impending alignment with the Galactic Center is responsible for this transformation. However, modern science does not recognize any connection between the current state of the world and the larger galactic context. Could it be that the ancient Maya were privy to a cosmological knowledge that we are just beginning to understand?

THE FACTS OF THE MATTER

Let us take a look at the astronomy involved in the end-date alignment. What astronomical features are involved? Where exactly is the Galactic Center, and how can we visualize the 2012 alignment?

The 13-baktun cycle end-date of the Long Count calendar (December 21, 2012) pinpoints a rare astronomical alignment determined by the precession of the equinoxes. The alignment occurs when the December solstice sun conjuncts the crossing point of the Milky Way and the ecliptic in Sagittarius. This crossing point is where the dark-rift in the Milky Way is located, and it is known to the Quiché Maya as the *xibalba be* (the Road to the Underworld) or simply "the Black Road." Maya scholars have identified the nearby crossing point of the Milky Way and the ecliptic as the Maya Sacred Tree, and the modern Quiché call that spot the "Crossroads." In short, the Creation Place was believed to exist at a cosmic crossroads. And the Galactic Center, the true Creation Place, is found right next to the cross formed by the Milky Way and the ecliptic.

Underlying the importance of the 2012 end-date is an astronomical process, the precession of the equinoxes. Having already explained how precession works in Part I, I would like to review here how precession was tracked. As explained earlier, precessional tracking involves the identification of foreground and background features in the sky. Foreground features include the seasonal quarters (the equinoxes and solstices), that is, the sidereal position of the solstice or equinox sun. Background features against which the precessional movement of the foreground features can be tracked include stars, constellations, and the Milky Way. The 2012 alignment involves specific astronomical features: the Milky Way, the Galactic Center, the dark-rift in the Milky Way, the December solstice sun, and the ecliptic. What exactly are these, and how are they related?

THE MILKY WAY

The Milky Way is a perfect background marker for precession. When we go outside on a moonless night, preferably far away from the light pollution of cities, we look up and see the breathtaking expanse of the Milky Way across the sky. When we see the Milky Way, we are actually looking out along the edge of our own galaxy. Since we are *within* our galaxy, the Milky Way appears to circle the entire sky, and if we look at the Milky Way at different times of the year, we can chart its different forms. We will notice that the area of the Milky Way that crosses through the constellation Gemini is relatively thin and diffuse. In comparison, on the oppo-

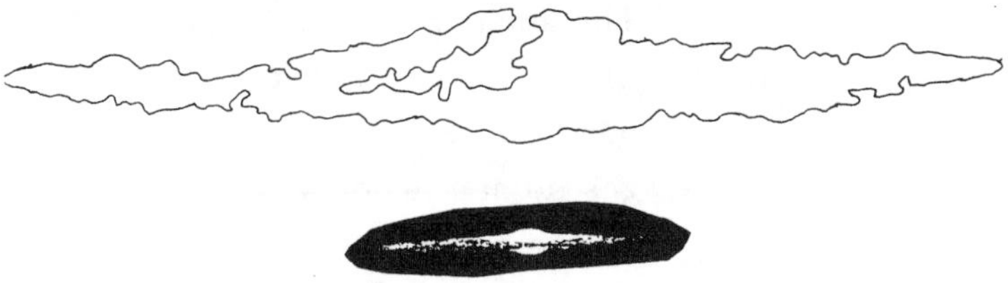

Diagram 47. Our Galaxy and its central bulge, compared with spiral galaxy below

site side of the sky from Gemini—in Sagittarius and Scorpio—the Milky Way is very bright and quite wide. The bright, wide, and dense part of the Milky Way that crosses through Sagittarius and Scorpio is where the Galactic Center is located—that hyperdense region out of which the Milky Way and everything in it, including us, has poured.

Notice the Milky Way's central bulge in the diagram above. This is the bright and wide part of the Milky Way that runs through Sagittarius. It makes us think of an engorged, womblike area, easily giving rise to the idea that the Milky Way is a huge, pregnant being, and the central bulge is thus the womb or birthplace of the sky. The Maya understood this dense, bright bulge as a Cosmic Center and Creation Place, a conclusion based solely upon naked-eye observation that is, in fact, very true: The center of our saucer-shaped Galaxy lies within this bright and wide part of the Milky Way.

THE ECLIPTIC

The ecliptic, which is roughly 14° wide, is the path followed by the sun, moon, and planets. The Maya saw the ecliptic as a double-headed serpent, as frequently portrayed in Maya sculpture and art.[1] It is a foreground feature, and the four "stations" along the ecliptic—the two solstices and two equinoxes—are important markers. Their slow movement toward the Milky Way is an indication of the phenomenon of precession. Where is the ecliptic in the sky? Where is the ecliptic in relation to the Milky Way? These are important questions. The ecliptic crosses the Milky Way through the constellations of Gemini and Sagittarius at roughly a 60° angle. When we discuss Maya Creation mythology in the next chapter, it will be important to remember that there are two areas in the sky, opposite each other, where a cross is formed by the Milky Way and the ecliptic. The cross in Sagittarius is the one that concerns us right now.

This cross is recognized by the Maya and the Indians of South America today.

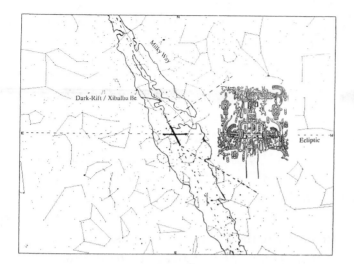

Diagram 48. Ecliptic through the central bulge in Sagittarius

The ancient Maya called it the Sacred Tree, and it is depicted on Pacal's sarcophagus lid at Palenque. Notice that the ecliptic crosses over the Milky Way near its central bulge. But why? There is no law of physics that says it has to. This drawing involves the relationship between a local foreground feature (the ecliptic) and a distant background feature (the Milky Way). Astrophysicists, when confronted with the fact that the ecliptic crosses over the Milky Way near its central bulge, consider it a coincidence. However, because the Milky Way can be thought of as an enormous magnet, we might postulate some kind of magnetic field "entrainment" to explain it. At any rate, the ecliptic's location is quite fortuitous, as it allows the celestial "deities" traveling along the ecliptic to come into periodic conjunction with the central bulge of the Milky Way—the great galactic power-station itself. As for the ecliptic's solar "stations"—the equinoxes and solstices—these approach the Galactic Center very slowly, and Maya astronomers con-

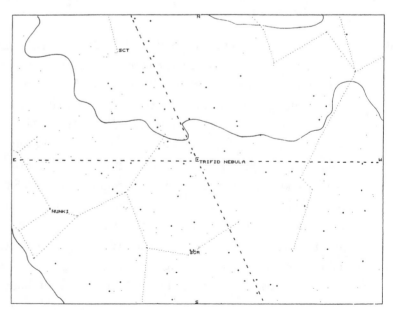

Diagram 49. Cross in Sagittarius: Galactic equator crossing over the ecliptic near the Trifid Nebula (M20)

sidered the eras in which these quarter-stations conjunct the Milky Way through its center to be transformative, signaling a World Age shift. These eras of transformative shift, affecting all life on planet Earth, include A.D. 2012, 4500 B.C., 10,800 B.C., and 17,300 B.C. According to Maya cosmology, which recognizes the December solstice as the most important solar station, A.D. 2012 represents the most significant of these four possible eras.

Star charts such as *Norton's 2000.0*[2] allow us to plot where the ecliptic crosses over the Milky Way (see diagram 49). To seek exact precision would be inappropriate because, you may remember, the ecliptic path is 14° wide. However, we can afford to be a little more precise because the sun's path along the ecliptic is less subject to variation than the planets' paths along it.

In addition to the width of the ecliptic, the width of the Milky Way allows an expanded range for the crossover zone, but we can use the precise meridian of the Galactic equator to chart diagram 49. As previously discussed, a very significant feature of the Milky Way runs right along the Galactic equator—the dark-rift.

THE DARK-RIFT

The dark-rift, also called the Great Cleft, is a dark band running along the Milky Way. It begins where the ecliptic crosses the Milky Way in Sagittarius and stretches some distance northward, past the constellation of Aquila. The dark-rift is created by interstellar dust clouds, so prevalent in that dense region near the Milky Way's central bulge, and it can be seen in diagram 48. The Indians of South America recognize many dark-cloud forms within the Milky Way, one of which is the pregnant llama. This formation happens to be quite close to the central bulge, thus reinforcing the idea that the central bulge was recognized in indigenous cosmologies as a fertile Creation Place or cosmic womb. The Maya recognize the dark-rift as a Road to the Underworld, which is a very important element in Maya Creation mythology. It was seen as a passageway into the central bulge of the Milky Way, the cosmic "Otherworld" of the Creation Place.

Where exactly is the dark-rift? Does it actually touch the crossing-point in Sagittarius? These are difficult questions, because there are variations in how the Milky Way and its dark clouds are represented in star charts and computer software. Even planetariums do not provide unambiguous data. It is best to go into the field and chart the position of the dark-rift, with special attention to its southern terminus. The months of July and August provide optimal viewing, and in the United States the high mountains of Colorado provide clear stargazing conditions. The "edges" of the dark-rift vary with viewing conditions, especially ambient light caused by distant cities and the moon's varying phases. The ancient Maya astronomers enjoyed optimum stargazing conditions, comparable to or even better than what is possible today in the Rocky Mountains. On August 5, 1996, I was camping in the Holy Cross wilderness area near Leadville, at 11,400 feet. The night sky was ablaze with stars, and I had a beautiful view of the Great Cleft and Sagittarius. The experience was awesome, and I breathed in and felt the infinite depth of black sky that loomed above me. Jupiter was 8° east of the crossing point, and using other stars as markers, I was able to get a good map of the extent of the Milky Way and the dark-rift. I can attest that a saucer-shaped mind-map of the Milky Way can be constructed from naked-eye observations and that the idea that the Milky Way is a uniformly wide band is false.[3] Combining all the charting tools available, especially the field observations made in August 1996, I have come up with a good positional map of the dark-rift near the crossing point.

Diagram 50. Parameters of the dark-rift's southern terminus near the crossing point in Sagittarius. Observations around midnight, August 5, 1996

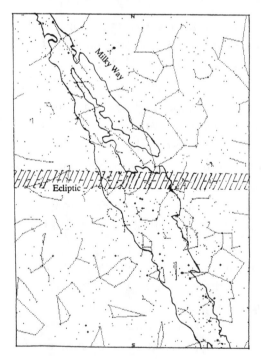

From my observations, the darkest area of the dark-rift does appear to be somewhat north of the ecliptic. The Great Cleft is quite wide at this point. Tracing it farther north, it extends well beyond Aquila as its width decreases. The southern terminus of the dark-rift is somewhat ambiguous; there is not a clear division between the darkness of space and the edge of the Milky Way. In the diagram, I have expanded the width of the ecliptic to 14°, the actual width of the band through which the sun, moon, and planets travel, and the dark-rift is at least 6° wide. The crossroads is thus less a point in space and more a zone. Because of the diffuse nature of the Milky

Way near the southern terminus of the dark-rift (just north of the precise crossing point), we are technically correct in saying that the dark-rift touches the ecliptic. In all fairness, the sense one gets from seeing it is that the roundish, darkest area of the dark-rift is clearly north of the ecliptic.[4] One should consider, however, that in the mythic consciousness of the ancient skywatchers, astronomical precision was less important than the mythological and calendric meaning ascribed to this area.[5]

In general then, the dark-rift is suitably close to the crossroads, the cosmic Place of Creation. The idea then is that the sun, in one of its quarter stations, could "enter the road" and travel into the Otherworld—the cosmic Creation Place. This alignment is, of course, time dependent because it is a function of precession. All this evidence leads to one conclusion: For the Maya, 13.0.0.0.0 (A.D. 2012) represented the era in which the doorway into the Heart of Creation opens.

DECEMBER SOLSTICE SUN: THE SLOW APPROACH

How can we best visualize precession and its effects on the position of the sun in the sky? This can be illustrated very simply:

In the diagram, position A indicates the position of the December solstice sun 5,000 years ago. It is some 70° from the dark-rift crossing point in Sagittarius. Position B indicates the December solstice sun 2,000 years ago. Notice that the phenomenon of precession is causing the position of the December solstice sun to converge with the Creation Place. This diagram is a clear illustration of the way we can track precession by watching the movement of a foreground feature (the December solstice ecliptic "station") in relation to the background feature of the Milky

Diagram 51. Convergence of the December solstice sun with the Creation Place over a period of 5,000 years

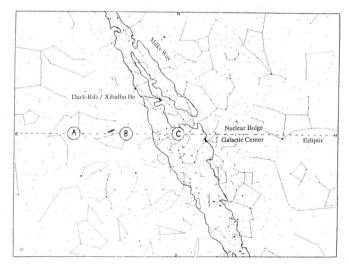

Way. Position C shows the culmination of the process in A.D. 2012, when the December solstice sun will be in conjunction with the Galactic Center.

The Creation Place we have been discussing is not just a fanciful fairy tale of the Maya. It is an actual location in the sky, a place that indeed can be called a cosmic womb or Creation Place; it is the Galactic Center. I have argued that this area of the Milky Way could have been recognized as a womb or Creation Place simply by naked-eye observation, because the "central bulge" in the area of the Galactic Center suggests this identification. Let me clarify that the term Galactic Center refers to *the center of our Milky Way Galaxy*, not the center of all galaxies. Astronomers and Maya scholars may be very skeptical that ancient Mesoamerican skywatchers could have been aware of the Galactic Center. In this book, I propose two possibilities. The first involves the scenario just described, that the observable central bulge imagistically suggests the womb of a huge pregnant being. Thus, the same part of the sky that modern science calls Galactic Center was understood by the Maya for what it truly is—a Creation Place and cosmic center. The other possibility is more challenging.

From studies in iconography and ethnobotany, we know the ancient Maya radically altered their perceptions in order to have visions of the underlying nature of reality. They achieved this heightened awareness through the use of hallucinogens collected from sacred plants or the *Bufo marines* toad. Some powerful hallucinogens, particularly psilocybin mushrooms and Dimethyltriptamine (DMT and its derivative 5-MEODMT), can enhance one's visual acuity, giving one brief access to subtle energy fields not normally visible to the eye. If the Maya cosmonauts gazed into the night sky while in such a state, and evidence I will present later suggests they did, the Galactic Center might have become overwhelmingly obvious, a blazing energy-knot in the night sky.

A constantly recurring mythological motif in Mesoamerican ideas is that of the Night Sun. In Central Mexican picture books the Night Sun is depicted as a spiderlike being—a black sun with dark rays shooting out in all directions. Scholars have traditionally identified this motif as the sun during its nightly journey underground, that is, through the Underworld. However, as we have seen, the Maya thought of the night sky as the Underworld, and thus the Night Sun would not be the sun under the earth, but a "dark sun" in the highest point of the night sky. As such, the Night Sun may indeed refer to the Galactic Center. Of course, the Galactic Center does not resemble a blazing sun—at least, not in normal states of consciousness.

It is a fact of astronomy that the December solstice sun will be in conjunction with the great bulge of the Galactic Center in the years around A.D. 2012. Astrophysicists now believe that a Black Hole—a hyperdense object from which even light cannot escape—exists at the center of our Galaxy. Amazingly, evidence that the Maya were aware of the Black Hole in the Galactic Center is found in hieroglyphic texts describing the creation of the world, and this evidence will be explored in more depth in Chapter 16 and Appendix 4.

THE GALACTIC EQUATOR PASSOVER

Precision-oriented thinkers may notice by looking closely at the diagrams in this chapter that the December solstice sun will make its closest pass to the Galactic Center sometime during the next two hundred years. Because the precise location of the Galactic Center is slightly south of the ecliptic, and the ecliptic crosses over the Milky Way at a 60° angle, the December solstice sun will be slightly closer to the Galactic Center in about two hundred years. However, the spatial difference between the solstice sun and the Galactic Center in 2012 versus the twenty-third century is negligible, and other considerations, which I will discuss below, indicate era 2012 as the true alignment era. A close view of the sun's movement through the region of the great bulge of the Galactic Center reveals the spatial and temporal parameters of the Galactic Alignment.

In A.D. 2012 the sun will be some 3° from the Galactic Center (and 3° is considered to be within conjunction). We can calculate that its closest pass, in about two hundred years, will be 2°45'. In the most generalized scenario, the spatial parameters of this solstice sun-Galaxy alignment can be expanded to include the moment the solstice sun first began to conjunct the eastern edge of the

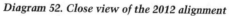

Diagram 52. Close view of the 2012 alignment

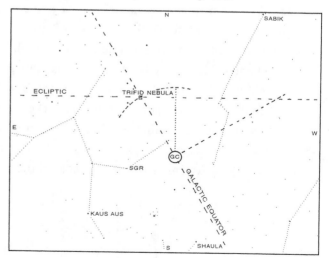

Milky Way, which was something like 450 years ago. The temporal range of the alignment, depending on how we define conjunction, can therefore be on the order of 900 years. On the other hand, our search for an exact date of conjunction is hampered by the fact that there are several astronomical factors involved. The problem with looking too closely for a precise solstice sun-Galactic Center alignment is that the Galactic Center is not a point in the sky but a region, and it has identifiable gravitational and magnetic centers that do not share the same location. Thus, for very real empirical reasons, it is misleading to envision the Galactic Center as a precise point in the sky; it is more realistic to see it as the large field covered by the visible great bulge. Overall, that the Galactic Center, the Galactic equator's crossing point with the ecliptic, and the December solstice sun's position in A.D. 2012 are all located within 3° of each other, provides a relatively small zone, or window, in which the alignment phenomenon occurs.

More importantly, astronomical considerations allow us to suspect that the real trigger of the World Age shift occurs when the solstice meridian crosses over the Galactic equator, which is complete by the end of 1999.[6] However, since the sun is one-half of a degree wide, that final half-diameter of the sun (one-fourth of a degree) will not be clear of the Galactic equator until A.D. 2018. Again, calculating precise alignments between abstract meridians and points disregards the fact that actual astronomical features, with size and shape, are involved. We can certainly debate the fine points regarding the exact year of the World Age shift, but, as mentioned, this approach stems from too great a need for precision, and we can get lost in micro-scrutinizing the data. I believe and emphasize that the era of transformation is defined by the December solstice sun's alignment with the equatorial band extending out from the Galactic Center, which is some 3° away. I will discuss the social and evolutionary implications that this passage through the Galactic equator will have for life on Earth in greater detail in Part V.

Maya Creation cosmology involves the precession of the equinoxes and the astronomical features discussed in this section. Now that we have explored how precession works and the parameters of the astronomical factors near the Creation Place, it is about time we put the pieces of the puzzle together.

CHAPTER 10

MAYA CREATION:
THE STELLAR FRAME AND WORLD AGES

Having examined and clarified the astronomical factors of the 2012 alignment, we can now look more closely at how this event was incorporated into Maya cosmology. How did the ancient skywatchers observe the slow convergence of the sun and the Milky Way, over 2,000 years ago? How were those astronomical players depicted in Maya myth? What did the alignment look like to them? And why did they conceive of this as a future rebirth of the world? What are the late-breaking ideas about Maya Creation mythology emerging in academic circles?

The sky defined the Maya understanding of cosmogenesis. Celestial events were mythologized into stories for the masses that nevertheless had deeper esoteric underpinnings. For example, the resurrection of the *Popol Vuh* deity One Hunahpu (First Father) as the Maize God was an annual event, commemorated with each year's corn harvest. Yet First Father's resurrection also had a celestial component of much larger scope, a rebirth of the world on a scale of epic proportions. My research emphasizes the importance of the larger perspective, one necessary in consideration of the alignment pointed to by the Long Count end-date. Maya scholar Linda Schele recently offered a revolutionary mytho-astronomical interpretation of the celestial origins of Maya Creation myth,[1] although the full story is still emerging. In the book *Maya Cosmos*, Schele recounts the process by which she came to her important discoveries. She drew from the body of ethnographic evidence that shows that mythological beings have astronomical identities. For example, the vain and false ruler Seven Macaw corresponds to the Big Dipper and his wife, Chimalmat, corresponds to the Little Dipper, which contains the Pole Star. As such, they are regents of the polar area. In the Maya Hero Twin myth (the *Popol Vuh*), the Hero Twins are destined to destroy Seven Macaw. In doing so, they make way for the resurrection of their father, One Hunahpu, otherwise known as First Father. This long-anticipated rebirth ushers in a new World Age, one of many described in the Maya Creation myth.

Linda Schele identified the birth of First Father/One Hunahpu on Classic-period ceramics, where he is depicted emerging from the cracked back of a turtle—a symbol of the Earth. According to star-glyphs found in Maya codices, the turtle also is found in the sky, the three stars of Orion's belt forming its back. Alnitak, the southernmost star in Orion's belt, combines with the two leg stars to make a cosmic triangle. Schele pointed out that the Maya call this triangle the hearth, and identify it with the three stones used in their hearths. They are thought of as the three stones of Creation, and the embers of the primal fire are seen to be the Orion nebula, located in the center of the triangle of hearthstones.[2] First Father's emergence from the nearby belt stars is connected to the lighting of the primal fire and the dawn of time. First Father is thus likened to the Aztec deity Xiuhtecuhtli, who, as we saw earlier is the Fire God that Maya scholar David Kelley identified with the Orion constellation. But First Father is also the Maize God, so the celestial movement of the sun past the Orion-Gemini constellations, in June, evokes the annual rebirth of life-giving maize during the growing season. In other words, when the solar fire passes through the hearth (the triangle formed from stars in Orion), life returns to Earth in the form of germinating maize. Schele's interpretation revolves

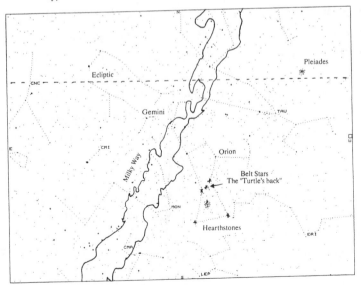

Diagram 53. Orion, the Turtle, Hearthstones, Sacred Tree, Milky Way, and the Maize God

around a cosmic Navel of Creation, the place in Gemini where the Milky Way crosses the ecliptic. Probably the most exciting identification explained by Schele involves this cosmic crossroads. She points out that the ecliptic corresponds to the many double-headed serpent bars found in Maya art, and the Milky Way is the cosmic axis, the "trunk" of the World Tree. Thus, the crossing point of the Milky Way and the ecliptic is the Maya Sacred Tree, the Place of Creation and rebirth.

In general terms then, Maya myth and astronomy complement each other, and, according to Schele, Creation revolves around the cosmic crossroads, the Sacred Tree—the crossing point of the Milky Way and the ecliptic. This in itself is a major breakthrough in understanding the profound sources of Maya cosmology. However, additional considerations not recognized until now paint an even more astounding picture.

THE OTHER CREATION PLACE

Schele focused her reconstruction of Maya Creation mythology on the crossing point of the Milky Way and the ecliptic in Gemini. This is a valid celestial origin point for the mapping out of the quadrated celestial divisions of the sky. As such, four roads should emanate from this spot. According to Maya cosmology, there is a Black Road in the sky, and a White one also, but they are not found at the crossing point in Gemini. They are found at the crossing point of the Milky Way and the ecliptic in Sagittarius. It is true: There are two crossroads. It just so happens that the crossroads in Sagittarius also is the location of the Black Road, known to the Quiché Maya as the *xibalba be*, the Road to the Underworld. This is the dark-rift in the Milky Way, extending north from the ecliptic as previously discussed. The part of the Milky Way stretching south of the ecliptic is called the *sac be*, the White Road. The Green and Red roads extend east and west along the ecliptic, with the Milky Way dividing them.[3] These are the four roads and the four directions of Maya cosmovision. In the Hero Twin Creation myth, the First God maps out the cosmos by stretching the cord, marking the corners, designing the four-fold siding and the four-fold cornering. The quadrated cosmos thus emerges from the navel-crossroads, the Place of Creation. With these initial identifications, we are fully justified in examining the Sagittarian cross as another likely place of Maya Creation. The region of Sagittarius is particularly compelling as a Place of Creation because that is where the Galactic Center is located.

As previously discussed, the *xibalba be* occurs in the Hero Twin myth in at least three contexts. The Black Road and the "four-junction roads" are first encountered when One Hunahpu and Seven Hunahpu journey to battle the Lords of Xibalba. They come to a crossroads and must decide which road to take. They choose the Black Road, which, of course, is the *xibalba be*. It was an appropriate choice, since it is the road that leads to Xibalba, the Underworld. In the Underworld, they encounter the Dark Lords, face trickery and trials, and ultimately are defeated and killed. The Dark Lords of Xibalba then hang One Hunahpu's decapitated head, now resembling a gourdlike skull, in a calabash tree. The skull rests in a crook or crevice in the branches of the Cosmic Tree, which stands "by the road." According to *Popol Vuh* translator Dennis Tedlock, this road is the ecliptic. Here is the second appearance of the *xibalba be*, in new mythic garb: The Milky Way is the World Tree, so this crevice in the tree is another metaphor for the dark-rift. The crossing point of Milky Way and ecliptic was, after all, identified by Schele as the Sacred Tree, and the tree near the ecliptic is the Milky Way.[4]

The third role of the *xibalba be* Creation Place occurs in the next scene. A woman named Blood Moon comes along, the skull spits in her hand and magically conceives the Hero Twins, metaphorically associating the *xibalba be* with sexual conception and the vagina of a cosmic Great Mother deity. Ultimately, the Twins avenge their father's death, paving the way for his rebirth, which is nothing less than the long-awaited dawning event of Maya Creation myth. Given the symbolic identification of the dark-rift as a cosmic birthplace, we are probably safe in deducing that One Hunahpu will be reborn from the *xibalba be* as well. Linda Schele deciphered First Father/One Hunahpu's birth as emerging from the back of an Earth turtle; however, these are Classic-period depictions. If we look at the early portrayals of One Hunahpu's resurrection, on the monuments of Izapa, he is shown emerging from the mouth of a jaguar-toad or other Earth deity. The mouth of the jaguar has been considered since ancient times to symbolize the entrance to the Underworld, as were terrestrial caves, and thus clearly refers to the dark-rift in the Milky Way. The toad motif goes back to the Olmec, and is related to concepts of the Cosmic Mother or Earth Goddess. The cleft head that is so prevalent in Olmec art is a portrayal of the triangular cleft in the head of the *Bufo marines* toad species,[5] which in turn signified the cave or "cleft" of Creation—the crater at the top of the cosmic volcano that is occupied by the ancient Fire God. Coatlicue, the name of the Aztec Mother Goddess, means Snake Woman, and the Milky Way was envisioned as a cosmic snake. Furthermore, the related goddess Citlalinicue was the Great Mother of the Stars who lives in the Milky Way.[6] Thus, the Milky Way was conceived as a Great Mother Goddess in many Mesoamerican myths. In a Creation scene from the Mixtec *Codex Vindobonensis*, First Father does not emerge from a turtle, he emerges from a tree, which, upon closer inspection, is the inverted Goddess. As such, he emerges from the Goddess's birth canal. In these mythic transformations, the dark-rift in the Milky Way symbolizes the cosmic birth canal.

Diagram 54. *Inverted Goddess, birth canal emergence*

I believe that Schele's Gemini/Orion-centered model of Maya Creation refers to the annual rebirth of the life-giving Corn God, which is played out in the sky on certain nights of the year. Remembering that the ancient Mesoamericans considered maize to be the source and origin of life, we can understand this annual resurrection of life as a celestial Mystery Play related to the June–August–September growing season of life-giving maize. However, Maya cosmogenesis is also about epic spans of time and World Age transformations, so we may suspect that Schele's reconstruction is incomplete. After all, she focused on only one of the crossing-point Places of Creation—the one near Gemini. When we examine the astronomy and mythology of the Sagittarian crossing point, we encounter more complex considerations, ones that nevertheless speak to the vast nature of World Age rebirth described in the *Popol Vuh*. While the annual resurrection of One Hunahpu as the Maize Deity is an important seasonal application of the resurrection myth, we find that it has a more startling, World Age component as well. In that the two readings related here (Schele's and my own) refer to two different temporal levels—a year and a "great year"—it seems appropriate that one myth was located at one crossing point, while the other was located at the opposite one.[7]

UNION OF FIRST FATHER AND FIRST MOTHER

In the Hero Twin myth, the rebirth of First Father/One Hunahpu signifies the dawning or creation of a new World Age. His calendric name is 1 Ahau, Ahau being the twentieth day-sign of the 260-day tzolkin calendar. In its oldest connotation, this day-sign means Lord or Sun. Thus, One Hunahpu is First Sun. The First Sun of the year is the December solstice sun.[8] The December solstice is the time when the sun begins its own resurrection, making the identification between One Hunahpu and the December solstice sun not only appropriate but clear. We must keep this identification in mind as we examine the following mytho-astronomical motifs. We have seen how the *xibalba be* has several mythic forms and how it appears in the *Popol Vuh* in three contexts. It is the road that One Hunahpu and Seven Hunahpu choose to take to the Underworld, and it leads to their deaths. It is the crook in the calabash tree where One Hunahpu's head is hung. It is the place where the Hero Twins are conceived. It is a road, it is the crevice in a tree, it is the cosmic birth canal. It appears self-evident that One Hunahpu will be reborn from this place as well. In related contexts, we have seen how the image of the Cosmic Mother's birth canal maps onto the astronomical image of the dark-rift in the Milky Way. Water is life-giving, the activator of fertility, and we have seen how the Milky Way, in addition to its other identities, was conceived of as a river. In another image from *Codex Vindobonensis*, a deity emerges from a cleft in a river that contains a four-junction crossroads. In the illustration above, notice the footprints in the quadrated circle, indicating the four cosmic roads.

Diagram 55. Cross and cup: River of Apoala emergence

In this image, again we see the crossroads near the cosmic birth portal. All of these mythic images attest that the dark-rift in the Milky Way was imaged in many ways and appears in many different forms of Mesoamerican myth. But they all indicate that the dark-rift was conceived of as a place of magical conception and celestial rebirth. The parallel image of birthplace and crossroads relates to the oldest universal ideas about celestial rebirth, the laying out of the four directions, and World Age Creation. The crossroads and the birth portal: the cross and the cup. These two powerful metaphors work together and provide a compellingly clear map to the true astronomical place of Maya Creation.

If we now look again at the astronomy of the end-date in 2012, the pieces of the puzzle begin to fall into place. On 13.0.0.0.0, December 21, 2012, the December solstice sun is dead center in the *xibalba be,* right at the crossing point of Creation in Sagittarius. The December solstice sun is First Father and the Milky Way is Cosmic Mother. Mythologically speaking, on this date First Father and Cosmic Mother are joined. Actually, it might be more accurate to say that Cosmic Mother rebirths Cosmic Father, our star, the sun. Here we see a reflection of a very ancient cosmogonic Creation myth, attributable to a substratum of history prior to patriarchal overlay: The Cosmic Mother is the head-point of a trinity involving the birth of a male deity who is also her mate. This Trinity Principle involves the dynamic between mother, father, and child, and shares with many Old World traditions the idea that the Great Mother, as the first principle of Creation, must give birth to her mate, First Father, and only then can engender the multiplicity of created beings. On the cosmic level, the astronomical trinity is Galactic Center, solstice sun, and humanity.

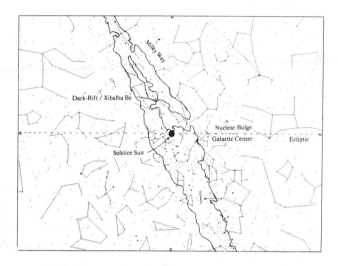

Diagram 56. 13.0.0.0.0, the end-date of the 13-baktun cycle of the Long Count. December solstice sun enters the Milky Way dark-rift

It is initially strange to think that Maya Creation occurs on what we are calling the "end-date." But Maya concepts of weaving, birthing, and dawning declare that Creation (birth) occurs *at the end* of a time cycle. The birth of a child occurs at the end of the nine-month period of human gestation. Furthermore, the Maya utilized "end naming," such that periods of time were named after their *last* day. For example, we are presently in the 4 Ahau katun of the Great Cycle, because it ends on the tzolkin day 4 Ahau. On Creation Day, the New Sun emerges from the Cave of Creation. The astronomical event of the 13-baktun cycle end-date is perfectly evocative of World Age transformation and cosmological re-creation.

The alignment of the December solstice sun with the dark-rift in Sagittarius is caused by the precession of the equinoxes, a cycle of almost 26,000 years. It is probably no coincidence that the 13-baktun period is exactly one-fifth of this precessional cycle. The ancient Mesoamerican skywatchers clearly anticipated and calibrated the future celestial juncture—an epic, cosmic collusion of male and female Creation forces. This new cosmological knowledge was encoded into the Hero Twin myth as the story of Creation. It is an essential key to understanding my reconstruction of the Galactic Cosmology formulated by Mesoamerican skywatchers.

THE MONUMENTS OF IZAPA

Some straightforward questions arise in considering the implications of this discovery. For example, when and where was the Long Count invented, and who devised it? And, if the Hero Twin Creation myth is a type of esoteric doctrine that, in its deepest meaning, describes the nature of the Long Count end-date, when and where was it developed? Amazingly, it turns out that the answers to these questions are the same. Both the Long Count and the *Popol Vuh* emerged at the same time, in the same region, in the same cultural context. The answer points us to the pre-Maya Izapan civilization of southern Mesoamerica.[9]

Izapa was a ceremonial site in southern Chiapas that flourished some 2,100 years ago. It was the transition culture between the older Olmec and the emerging Maya. Michael Coe and other scholars credit the Izapan civilization with devising the Long Count. Many of Izapa's carved monuments depict distinct episodes from the *Popol Vuh*, the earliest examples in the archaeological record. Nearby sites such as Abaj Takalik yield Izapan-style art and the first Long Count dates. In examining the monuments of Izapa, we find iconographic evidence that supports my end-date thesis. On over fifty carved monuments found at this pre-Classic site, there is a preoccupation with the demise of Seven Macaw at the hands of the Hero Twins and the resurrection of First Father.

Scholars identify the crocodile-tree depicted on several Izapan stelae as the Milky Way.[10] The mouth of the crocodile monster is the dark-rift. Several monuments at Izapa and related sites depict the emergence of First Father from the mouth of an Earth deity with treelike and reptilian features, as in the jaguar-frog/Milky Way/Mother Goddess complex of mythic forms.

One of the most compelling depictions from Izapa is Stela 11, which clearly portrays the astronomical meaning of the Long Count end-date:

Here we have First Father performing the primal measuring act. The durability of this Mesoamerican deity is evident when we realize that the later 1 Ahau of the Maya Venus Calendar is derived from our "Hunahpu." The small circular symbol on First Father's nose is a "star" symbol. The four sky-streaks emanating from behind First Father, though not in a crossroads format, may be the Four Roads. He is emerging from the "mouth" of the jaguar-toad, who represents the cosmic Milky Way Goddess. This monument is one of many at Izapa that portray the alignment of the end-date. In fact, as will be shown in more detail in Part IV, Izapa was the home of the Initiation Mysteries into Galactic Cosmology, where astronomer-priests utilized Izapa's many carved monuments as teaching tools for initiates.

Diagram 57. Stela 11 at Izapa

THE ANCIENT SKYWATCHERS' VIEW OF CREATION

What were the ancient skywatchers of Izapa actually looking at? And how does Stela 11 portray the future alignment? It is extremely interesting that Stela 11 faces the rising position of the December solstice sun, where the following skyviews were visible over a seven-hundred-year period.

In this diagram, we can see how the Milky Way and its dark-rift looked to Mesoamerican skywatchers on the December solstice of 700 B.C. I chose this date because this is when the pre-Maya site of Izapa was on the rise.

By 200 B.C., again on the December sol-

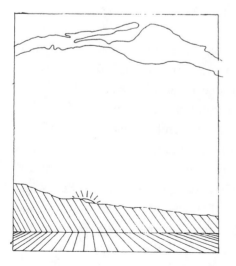

Diagram 58. The cross and dark-rift as viewed from the latitude of Izapa, 700 B.C.

stice, the dark-rift "Creation Place" was noticeably closer to the horizon.

The difference in the dark-rift's position
is some 7°—a very noticeable change. By the
first century B.C., Long Count dates start appearing in the archaeological record. If Mesoamerican skywatchers continued to chart the
convergence of the solstice sunrise with the
Milky Way as it appeared on the December
solstice, they would find an impasse around
the year A.D. 650. Around this era, they would
find that the rising Milky Way was too close
to the horizon to be seen as the rays of the
December solstice sun began to brighten the

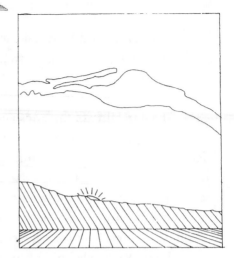

Diagram 59. View from Izapa, 200 B.C.

sky.[11] In other words, morning came on before the Milky Way was high enough
over the horizon to be seen. However, the phenomenon could still be tracked by
watching the skies days or weeks before the solstice, as well as by other, more
complicated means. The point is that the phenomenon—precession—was tracked
and calculated long before this impasse occurred. The date of the future "Zero Time"
of Galactic Alignment was calculated by *at least*
37 B.C., when the Long Count first appears in the
archaeological record. By that time, the following skyview was seen from Izapa on the December solstice:

*Diagram 60. December Solstice, 37 B.C.,
viewed from Stela 11, Izapa*

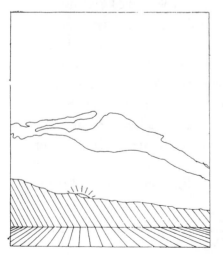

Here we have the Cosmic Milky Way Monster with her dark-rift "mouth" some 30° above
the dawning December solstice sun. Throughout
the process, the precession of the stellar frame has
been causing the December solstice sun to slowly
converge with the "mouth." Izapan skywatchers
of the formative period (400 B.C. to 100 B.C.) certainly could have noticed the process. They would
have realized that when the alignment occurs, at
dawn on Creation Day, the Milky Way rims the
horizon. The sky will then sit upon the Earth,

touching it at all points around the horizon. This alignment of solar and Galactic planes may define a subtle Earth-rhythm, empirically measurable, propelling transformations of life on Earth at distinct intervals, an arcane artifact of ancient cosmology that points to our immediate future. The precession-defined alignment highlighted by the Maya end-date occurs only once every 26,000 years. We are living in the shadows of a rare celestial juncture.

THE MAYA END TIMES

The full meaning of the celestial origins of Maya Creation should now be clear. In addition to Linda Schele's interpretation of Maya Creation revolving around the crossing point in Gemini, there is a more far-reaching esoteric component that becomes apparent when we examine the crossing point in Sagittarius. During the archaic transition from Olmec to Maya culture, we may imagine that a new discovery defined the emerging Maya as unique bearers of a more sophisticated cosmological understanding, and heirs to a new era. They were, with great ingenuity, very far-seeing and pointedly focused on a vision of future rebirth. Anchored as this belief is to an actual stellar process, we cannot say that it is not going to happen. Our own millennial milestone is strangely mocked and modified by ancient Maya cosmology. For the ancient Izapans and the early Maya, and in the earliest version of the Long Count-*Popol Vuh* Creation myth, Creation occurs on 13.0.0.0.0, December 21, 2012, when First Father and First Mother join forces to engender a new World Age.

The Hero Twin story is one "myth" that encodes the astronomy of the Long Count end-date. Earlier, we saw how the New Fire ceremony was the "myth" that explained the Zenith Cosmology. There is another Mesoamerican tradition that encodes the alignment in 2012, one that involves heroic triumph and Mystery Play, as well as human sacrifice. Like the Hero Twin and New Fire myths, this esoteric tradition, with precessional knowledge at its center, was not a marginal aspect of Mesoamerican society. It had everything to do with the renewal of the sun, the rebirth of First Father, and the triumph of light over darkness. It is the Mesoamerican ballgame.

CHAPTER 11

THE COSMIC SYMBOLISM OF THE MAYA BALLGAME

A ballgame similar to the one played by the Maya has existed in the New World for thousands of years. Remains of ballcourts have been found throughout Mesoamerica and beyond, from Arizona to the isles of the Caribbean, though the rules of the game varied widely from region to region. The Maya developed the ballgame into a ritual Mystery Play filled with symbolism, which we can understand by studying its depiction in Maya books and on painted ceramics, murals, and sculpture. In addition, the ballgame's primary symbols and procedures are present in mythological sources such as the *Popol Vuh*. There is a mythological dimension to the game, and because the characters of Maya myth have astronomical identities, the ballgame ultimately describes specific celestial processes and events. Overall, scholars have come to a general understanding of the profound symbolism encoded into the Mesoamerican ballgame. We can apply these accepted academic ideas to the cosmic level of meaning, thus supplying a deeper reading that is overlooked in the mainstream interpretation. By "cosmic level of meaning" I mean the ballgame's clear reference to World Age rebirth and cosmogenesis.

One scholar who studied the ballgame in detail sums up its meaning this way: ". . . the human ballgame was considered a repetition of a divine one, constituting a kind of magic by analogy, to support the victory of the light against the darkness, the sun against the stars."[1] Thus, in the broadest terms, the ballgame is about the battle between the forces of darkness and light. Victory occurs when the ball passes through the goalring, symbolizing the triumphant rebirth of the sun. As scholars have noted, the ballgame evokes the sun's daily rebirth (at dawn) as well as its yearly rebirth. The time of the yearly rebirth is a matter of academic debate, usually being placed either on the December solstice or the March equinox. For reasons that will become clear, I believe the December solstice is the correct interpretation for the date of annual solar rebirth. Of course, this date is in agreement with some of the most commonly held ideas around the globe, for Western culture as a whole celebrates the New Year around the December solstice. As for the Maya, the end of the 13-baktun cycle of the Long Count calendar falls on the December solstice, thus suggesting that this point in the solar year was considered a major end-beginning nexus.

According to scholarly interpretation of the ballgame's symbolism, solar rebirth occurs on two temporal levels: daily and annually. Unfortunately, scholars have neglected the next higher level, that of World Age rebirth—solar rebirth in terms of the large-scale "Great Year" of the Long Count. This oversight is surprising, because world renewal is a major aspect of Maya Creation myth. I refer to this next level as the cosmic or galactic level, because it ultimately involves the galactic frame of time and the Galactic Alignment that occurs on the 13-baktun cycle end-date. As argued throughout the book, this end-date represents when the Maya believed the next World Age would begin, that is, when the current era or "Sun" would be reborn on the galactic level of time. As we will see, the astronomical and mythological features associated with the end-date (December 21, 2012 A.D.) apply directly to the symbolism of the ballgame. The three temporal levels of solar rebirth in the Maya ballgame, then, are as follows: daily rebirth, annual rebirth, and World Age rebirth.

FEATURES OF THE GAME

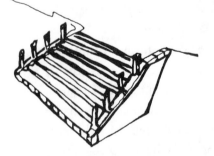

Diagram 61. Serpent-mouth stairway from Bilbao

With these three temporal levels in mind, we can now take a detailed look at the features of the Maya ballgame. The game included the following elements: the ballcourt, the players, the gameball, the goalring, the center marker, and the gaming gear or equipment. Symbolically, the ballcourt itself represents either an entrance to the Underworld or the Underworld itself, because ballcourts are literally "earth depressions," recalling other Underworld portals such as cenotes and caves. As diagram 61 reveals, stairways leading down into the ballcourt at sites such as Bilbao actually resemble serpent mouths.

We can see that each step has two serpent "fangs," likening the stairway passage to a serpent's mouth.[2] Like a jaguar's or a toad's, the serpent's mouth symbolizes the entrance to the Underworld. Images of Classic-period ballcourts show ritual activities occurring near the stepped-wall architecture of ballcourts. In these scenes the ball is often portrayed as the decapitated head or skull of a sacrificed deity, and in Maya myth, the ball-skull is the head of First Father/One Hunahpu, who in the *Popol Vuh* was killed and decapitated by the Lords of the Underworld.

As a symbol of the solar deity One Hunahpu, the ball-skull is the sun, a meaning almost universally accepted among scholars. Thus, the movements of the ball during the game reflect the movements of the sun. As mentioned earlier, in ballgame symbolism the sun moves along and is reborn on three temporal levels, with each level building upon the

Diagram 62. Ballcourt scene showing the ball-skull on the ballcourt stairs

"dawn point" of the previous level. For example, the sun's daily rebirth occurs at dawn, when the sun moves from the Underworld below the eastern horizon into the day sky. Its annual rebirth begins at dawn on the December solstice, when the sun begins to move from the deepest Underworld level of winter (the longest night of the year) into increasing daylight. Finally, its World Age rebirth begins at dawn on the December solstice of the year A.D. 2012, the Zero Point of the Galactic cycle.[3] At this highest level, the ballgame is a metaphor for precessional movement of the December solstice sun.

Another important aspect of ballcourt symbolism relates to the ballcourt's cross-shaped depiction in Central Mexican picture books.

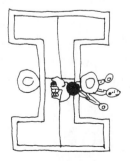

Diagram 63. I-shaped ballcourt with crossroads inside. From the Codex Columbino *and the* Codex Borbonicus.

The cross is a universal Mesoamerican symbol of the Creation Place. Classic-period ballcourts, being layed out in such a pattern, "essentially represented the surface of the earth, the four cardinal directions, and the symbolic entrance to the Underworld within its center."[4] In the *Popol Vuh*, the western ballcourt where the Hero Twins battle the Lords of Xibalba is actually in the Underworld. Crosses still used by the Tzotzil Maya in highland Chiapas represent doorways to the Otherworld. Skulls are often shown in the very center of ballcourts, and skulls represent the Underworld.

Quatrefoil shapes, such as those carved on ballcourt markers at Copán, enclose events taking place in the Underworld. These are less rigid than the I-shaped symbols of the ballcourt depictions from Central Mexico.

Ballcourts symbolically represent the intersection of the Upper and Lower worlds, and thus their crossroads format suggests the astronomical location of the crossing point of the Milky Way and the ecliptic. Side

Diagram 64. Quatrefoil scene in the Underworld

views of ballcourts also reveal a T-shape or a stepped design, like this one from the *Dresden Codex*.

In diagram 65, we see a god enthroned on the T-shaped ballcourt. This is not surprising, since thrones also were quadrated symbols of the cosmic center, upon which gods and kings were enthroned. Other associations paint an even stranger scenario. The stepped design is symbolic of a depression or cave and therefore relates to the concept of the Earth-womb, the birthing house of the Goddess. As we have already seen, the Maya associated caves

Diagram 65. Dresden Codex god enthroned on ballcourt

with the concepts of the womb and the vaginal passageway.[5] In the Tzotzil language, the word *ch'en* (cave) also means a woman's vagina.[6] The ballcourt, the cave, the goalring, the birth canal: these associations are rich and profound, and provide clues to help reconstruct the cosmic meaning of the Maya ballgame.[7]

There are also rich associations to explore with the stepped-wall symbol of the ballcourt. The stepped-wall design that indicates the Underworld portal to the Xibalban ballcourt is related to the "step-curl" motif that appears on the forehead of Classic-period Cauac monsters (see diagram 66).

Diagram 66.
Stepped wall of
ballcourt compared
to step-curl motif

The cleft-forehead design is derived from the Olmec cleft-head motif, and it ultimately refers to the "broken place, the bitter water place" where the Maize God (also known as First Father) is reborn. The step-curl of the Cauac monster is often portrayed as an emergence place, once again suggesting the womb environment.[8]

Variations in this cosmic monster display the same structural pattern: A round object or a deity is shown inside the cleft "Creation Place" at the top (see diagram 68). The basic structure of these varied cosmic monster symbols can be boiled down to a symbol that

Diagram 67. Cauac monster with step-curl forehead

Diagram 69.
Ballcourt
glyph

is none other than the glyph for ballcourts. This image portrays the game-ball in the goalring. However, it also looks like a cornseed in a pod. Since this "pod" or earth-cleft also is an entrance to the Underworld, the astronomical reference would appear to be to the *xibalba be*, the entrance to the Underworld identified with the dark-rift in the Milky Way.

Related depictions contain not only the ball and the cleft symbols, but also the crossroads motif. This image evokes the crossroads of Creation near the dark-rift.

All of these images are related, can be traced back

Diagram 68. "Cosmic Monster"
with step-forehead motif, from
Tikal royal temple. Cauac-Witz design with blood and corn symbols

Diagram 70. Cross in ball-court/
womb/step-curl motif

to the Olmec motif of the cleft head, and represent the birthplace of maize and the Maize Deity. Importantly, the ballgame victory was as much about the Maize Deity's rebirth as it was about the sun's rebirth; both represent life and light.[9] The astronomical features of the Maya ballgame are now becoming clear. The "cleft" and "cross" references in the diagrams above are to the dark-rift in the Milky Way and the Milky Way/ecliptic cross. As we will see, the primary ballgame symbol for the dark-rift is the goalring, and the December solstice sun (the gameball) must pass through the goalring to be reborn.

COSMIC SHADOWS AND ALIGNMENTS AT CHICHÉN ITZÁ

The ballgame and ballcourt symbolism were highly developed at the site of Chichén Itzá in the Yucatán, which contains no less than thirteen ballcourts, including the largest one yet found.

The Great Ballcourt at Chichén Itzá, located a short distance northwest of the Pyramid of Kukulcan, was oriented to the Milky Way on the June solstice in the era A.D. 865.[10] At midnight on every June solstice during this era, the long axis of the ballcourt pointed to where the Milky Way touched the horizon. The body of the Milky Way arched through the sky, mirroring the ballcourt itself, and the dark-rift in the Milky Way would have been observed overhead. In other words, it appears the designers of Chichén's ballcourt intended to mirror the dark-rift and the Milky Way with the orientation of the ceremonial ballcourt. This makes sense when we remember that the night sky and the Underworld are in essence the same.[11]

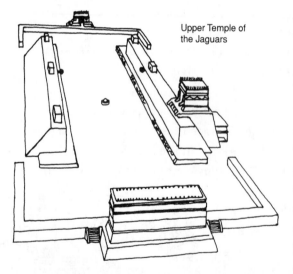

Upper Temple of the Jaguars

Diagram 71. The Great Ballcourt at Chichén Itzá

This is a little appreciated but very significant truism of Maya cosmo-conception: The Underworld was, in one sense, located under the Earth, but at night it rotated above the horizon to become the night sky.

Diagram 72. East wall mural with ball passing through the goalring's shadow. Noon on June solstice, A.D. 865

In the relationship between the Milky Way and the Great Ballcourt just described, the dark-rift is the "central hole" of the Milky Way ballcourt; in other words, it is the cosmic goalring. Its cosmological meanings include a center and navel of the sky, a portal to other dimensions, and a place of rebirth. This is where the solar deity—the big gameball—will be reborn at the end of the current era.

There is another interesting hierophany that takes place in the ballcourt on the June solstice. The ballcourt's east wall has a scene carved on it of a ballgame. In the lengthwise center of the wall, nearly underneath the actual goalring placed higher up on the wall, is a gameball portrayed as a skull. Around noon on the June solstice, a shadow cast by the sun stretches along the lower wall and, as noon approaches, it appears that the ball is passing through the ring's shadow.[12]

Imagine the game played on the June solstice around A.D. 865. During midday, while the Mystery Play unfolds on the court, the solstice Sun Deity casts a beam through the goalring, illuminating the gameball carved on the east wall. At the very least, this associates solar rebirth (symbolized by the ball passing through the goalring's shadow) with the solstice. Specifically, the June solstice and on this same day, at midnight, the dark-rift looms overhead as the Milky Way aligns with the ballcourt. Combined, these two events, one at noon and one at midnight, proclaim a clear message: The solstice Sun Deity goes into the dark-rift and the game is over. The image of the solstice goalring shadow moving along the ballcourt's east wall is similar to the equinoctial shadow-serpent that appears on the nearby Pyramid of Kukulcan. Given the hierophanies associated with the Great Ballcourt and the Pyramid of Kukulcan, equinox dates, zenith-passage dates, and solstice dates are all significant in the cosmologies represented at Chichén Itzá.

In one meaning, the dark-rift symbolizes the goalring, but, being overhead in the middle of the Milky Way ballcourt, it should also reflect an object located in the exact center of the ballcourt's playing field. If you visit the ruins today, you will not see anything there. What *was* there—a stone marker—was pulled out long ago

and was lost for decades, but has now been recovered. Maya scholar Linnea Wren reconstructed the discovery and rediscovery of the Ballcourt Stone.[13]

Diagram 73. Chichén Itzá's Ballcourt Stone

Among the fascinating facts associated with this artifact is the symbolism of its shape. It clearly shows a ball (the sun) in the goalring (the dark-rift overhead). This resemblance provides additional evidence for my interpretation of the astronomical dimension of the Maya ballgame.

Since the ballgame was played at Chichén Itzá in the ninth century, we might be tempted to determine on what date in the solar year the sun conjuncted the dark-rift in that century. If we consult astronomy software, we find the rather unspectacular date of December 3. But we must remember that the World Age myth—the final victory of the ballgame—involved the far future transformation or rebirth of the solstice sun at the end of the current era, December 21, 2012. Clearly, the Ballcourt Stone portrays the Great Cycle ending of 13.0.0.0.0, when the December solstice Ahau successfully passes through the birth portal—the goalring—to re-emerge from the Underworld into the next world.[14]

The Ballcourt Stone was found in the central spot of the ballcourt. At other sites, this spot is sometimes occupied by a simple marker. Sometimes these center markers contain a skull design or a commemoration date. The center marker from the ballcourt at Toniná, a Classic-period Maya site southeast of Palenque, provides astounding confirmation of the theory we have been discussing.

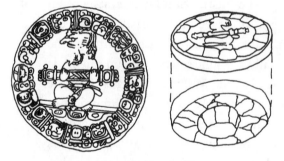

Diagram 74. The center marker in the Toniná ballcourt symbolizing the Milky Way/ecliptic cross, and the hole underneath

Toniná's center marker shows an Ahau Lord holding a double-headed bar. As explained earlier, Maya kings represent the World Axis (the Milky Way), and the "serpent bar" they hold in front of them symbolizes the ecliptic. This interpretation is especially relevant to Palenque, a site closely related to Toniná. So, this central marker plaque at Toniná says to us: Here is the spot that marks the cross formed by the Milky Way and the ecliptic. But what about the dark-rift "hole" within the cross—the end-date goalring? Lifting this center marker up reveals a deep hole, thought by scholars to be a "sacrifice" offering pit. This "hole" clearly represents the dark-rift within the cosmic crossroads, a significant association, but there's more. Toniná's center marker contains the dedication date of 9.17.5.0.0, which is December 27, 775 A.D. Dedication events usually stretched over a couple of days, placing the beginning of this ballcourt's dedication within a day or two of the December solstice.[15] So, the cosmic symbolism of the Chichén Itzá ballcourt, clearly pointing to the end-date astronomy, is validated at Toniná. If we combine the symbology of Toniná's center marker with the symbology of Chichén Itzá's Ballcourt Stone, and remember that the solstice sun is involved in both contexts, the following astronomical features are implicated:

- The cross formed by the Milky Way and the ecliptic
- The dark-rift in the Milky Way
- The solstice sun in conjunction with the dark-rift in the Milky Way

Ballgame symbolism clearly refers to the alignment that occurs on the 13-baktun cycle end-date in 2012. Despite the overwhelmingly clear picture that leads to this conclusion, my theory about the deeper meaning of the Maya ballgame is completely new. Scholars have narrowly skirted around putting the pieces together, but, strangely, they avoid making the connection. For example, Linda Schele and David Freidel analyzed hieroglyphs associated with the ballgame and deciphered an important glyph to mean "black hole." The Creation events played out in the ballgame "happened at the black hole."[16] These authors then proceeded to note that the "black hole" hieroglyph refers to Maya Creation events, as well as the place where Maya kings were enthroned, and points to "the Black Road, through the Cleft in the Milky Way . . . from the ballcourts of the Maya to the Court of Creation in the Land of Death."[17] Incredibly, these scholars note a connection between the "black hole" hieroglyph so central to ballgame symbolism and the dark-rift (the Black Road) in the Milky Way! However, this important insight never surfaces again in the writings of either Schele or Freidel, even though their book *Maya Cosmos* had everything to do with Maya Creation mythology. Instead, as we saw in Chapter 10, Schele chose to explore the astronomical features near the crossroads in Gemini rather than the ones near the "black hole" in Sagittarius. It seems, then, that academia is either biding its time or has overlooked an extremely important facet of Maya cosmology.[18] As a result, I have done all my pioneering work on this question in the face of almost total academic silence. The overarching importance of the Portal to the Underworld, the dark-rift near Sagittarius, though clearly stumbled across from time to time, has yet to be embraced in the hallowed halls of academia.

My reconstruction of the Maya ballgame addresses its highest, most esoteric function. I focused on astronomical and cosmological concepts, as that is where I feel its most profound and deepest meaning is to be found. In brief, the ball passing through the goalring represents the rebirth of the sun, and the Maya perceived this to occur on daily, annual, and galactic levels. The galactic level of solar rebirth involves the precession-caused movement of the winter solstice sun into alignment with the dark-rift (the cosmic goalring). The ballgame was a ceremonial Mystery Play, with the Galactic Cosmology as its central doctrine.

We can learn more about the inner secrets of the ballgame when we examine the role of the gameplayers. Evidence suggests the players may have used hallucinogenic mushrooms to heighten their coordination and reflexes, and to intensify the drama of the game. Generally, the players were required to make a sacrifice, to give their energy and even their lives so that the ball could reach its goal and the cosmic machinery of time and fate would continue to roll forward.

KEEP IT ROLLING

Scholars are still somewhat unclear as to who the gameplayers actually were. Were they captured slaves from other kingdoms forced to feed the gods? Were they a special class of athletic warriors, competing for the highest honor of being sacrificed to the gods? Were they the Maya kings themselves, impersonating deities and culture heros, as part of regularly performed pageantry and Mystery Play? Probably all of these possibilities were true at various times. However, if we look closely at the ballplayers' equipment, we can understand what their central role was.

Ballplayers used an array of equipment while playing. In the *Popol Vuh*, the Hero Twins' ballgame gear was stashed in the rafters of their grandmother's house. Since the upper domain of the cosmic house (i.e., grandmother's house) is the night sky, the gaming gear may represent constellations.[19] The ballplayers usually wore stone "yokes" with which they hit the ball. Archaeologists have found a few of these heavy U-shaped devices like that shown in diagram 75.

Notice the knot-curl on the forehead of the deity who is carved on the yoke's side, which symbolizes a place of emergence or birth. This is no doubt a variation of the step-curl forehead motifs discussed earlier. Scholars recognize the U-shape as a symbol for either the moon or the entrance to the Underworld (or both).[20] Thus, when the players wore the stone yoke around their hips, they were symbolically halfway in the Underworld, that is, between worlds. This means that they, like the sun during its strenuous rebirth on three temporal levels, were trying to emerge into another world. In a sense, they were halfway through the birthing experience. They were being born while trying to help the sun be reborn at the same time and so were engaged in a kind of sympathetic magic to help the sun move toward its goal. In short, the ballplayers

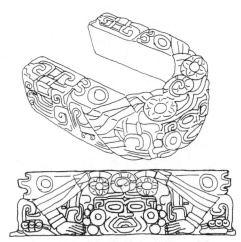

Diagram 75. Stone yoke worn by ball-players, symbol of the Underworld portal

were indispensible in keeping the end-date alignment moving toward its goal.

I interpret the gameplayers as heroic semi-human deities whose job was to keep the sun rolling toward its meeting with the dark-rift. In other words, they were in a sense like cosmic midwives, or vision-helpers, who must facilitate the emergence of the next World Age, the rebirth of the solar deity (and all life) into the galactic level. Through a kind of sympathetic magic, they kept the precessional frame rolling so that the doorway through to the source and center of the cosmos—which resides at the deepest foundation of the "Underworld" (the night sky)—can open. Through their efforts, an alignment between the foreground framework of the sky (the local solar system defined by the ecliptic, with its four seasonal quarter positions of the sun) and the cosmic background of the sky (the Milky Way) will occur in 2012. During the 2012 victory-era, the flood of new information and energy that pours forth will fuel the multiplication and regeneration of life on Earth. Said in traditional terms, "fertility" is heightened to the point of overload, thus stimulating transformation. The gameball in the dark-rift is a type of cosmic insemination. This is the highest level of cosmic rebirth, symbolized by the Mesoamerican ballgame. When considering the mytho-cosmic dimensions of the ballgame, we cannot separate its simplest level of operation (the sun's daily rebirth at dawn) from the larger scale process of World Age rebirth—the resurrection of First Father/One Hunahpu on the galactic level of time. The ballgame is the game of cocreation, a partnership between humans and higher forces in cosmogenesis. The ballfields truly are cosmic courts of Creation, where the forces of creation are "courted" and engaged, and where the role of human beings as cocreators in their own evolution is activated.

ONE MORE QUESTION

One final question emerged for me as I decoded the presence of the Galactic Cosmology at Chichén Itzá. The galactic ballcourt at Chichén is, indeed, an imposing structure. However, the Pyramid of Kukulcan is even more magnificent, and hides within it the ancient Zenith Cosmology of the Toltecs. Could both cosmologies exist side by side at Chichén Itzá? Since the Galactic Cosmology was followed by the Maya and the Zenith Cosmology was used by the Toltecs—two widely separate cultures—how could both co-exist at Chichén?[21] We are currently in the World Age of 4 Ollin (4 Movement or Earthquake), which emerged at Toltec Teotihuacan in the distant past. The end of this Fifth Sun was tracked with the New Fire ceremony, the Zenith Cosmology reconstructed earlier in chapters 6 and 7.[22] But does the end-date of the Aztec calendar coincide with the 2012 World Age end-date of the Maya? Here is the pressing question: Did the Zenith Cosmology and the Galactic Cosmology ever meet? Something appeared to be going on here, and I determined to look more closely at Chichén Itzá's history.

CHAPTER 12

CHICHÉN ITZÁ COSMOLOGY: MAYA-TOLTEC RECONCILIATION

The great city of Chichén Itzá, a magical center of Mesoamerican knowledge, is where the equinox manifestation of Kukulcan, the Plumed Serpent, occurs. This has become an annual event in which thousands of people from around the world gather to watch the sun cast its rays across the corner of Kukulcan's pyramid, projecting a shadow-image of a descending serpent along the balustrade of the north stairway. Viewers come away amazed at the sophisticated architectural engineering of the Maya, and with a feeling for their profound and little understood cosmology.

The cosmological insights of Chichén Itzá go even deeper than its shadow-play. There are other cosmic alignments at Chichén involving the Great Ballcourt, the Upper Temple of the Jaguars, and the famous Caracol observatory. We will look closely at these architectural cosmo-conceptions to reveal exactly what purpose Chichén Itzá served within the larger context of Mesoamerican civilization and its evolving cosmological knowledge.

A POLAR HISTORY OF MESOAMERICA

As discussed earlier, the Olmecs were the great Mesoamerican "Mother Culture," building an extensive civilization that existed between 2500 B.C. and 300 B.C. Olmec sites such as La Venta, San Lorenzo, and Tres Zapotes are located in the so-called Olmec heartland—the low, swampy, Gulf Coast areas of the modern states of Tabasco and Veracruz. According to historians and archaeologists, the Olmec represented a unified phase of Mesoamerican civilization that lasted from 900 B.C. to 500 B.C.[1]

But what happened after that? It appears that a split occurred, dividing a previously unified Mesoamerican civilization into two camps, each with different cosmological doctrines. Around 100 B.C., the rise of two major cultural traditions began, but in two widely separated regions. In Central Mexico, the Toltecs founded a metropolis called Teotihuacan, City of the Gods, aligning it with the Pleiades and the zenith sun. This great center of civilization grew and established many towns under its dominion, coming to control most of the area for six centuries. Teotihuacan is where the present, soon-to-end Fifth Sun was born, and it is believed to be the mythical Tollan of the Aztecs. (The Aztecs arrived on the cultural scene of Central Mexico much later, in the fourteenth century A.D.) At the same time that Toltec tradition and cosmology were being formulated in Central Mexico, the Maya, far to the east, emerged in the jungle-forests of Guatemala, Belize, and Yucatán, creating interrelated city states such as Cerros, Caracol, Calakmul, Uaxactun, El Mirador, and Tikal.

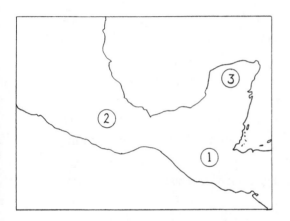

Diagram 76. Map of Mesoamerica: 1) Maya zone, 2) Toltec zone, 3) Maya-Toltec zone

The Maya and the Toltec civilizations developed at the same time and, although they nurtured trade links through which artistic forms and ideas were shared, they designed two different cosmological systems to track World Ages. The underlying calendar used by both groups was the 260-day calendar, but a basic disagreement in how large-scale cycles of time were to be tracked—the timing of World Ages—apparently drove a wedge between the Toltecs and the Mayas and prevented a harmonious reconciliation for many centuries.

We can envision this split as a natural dichotomy in the development of whole systems (including cultures), in which the Mystery Play of polarization and eventual reconciliation is the name of the game, an organic necessity much like cell mitosis. Polarization and reunification are a process that manifests on all levels of life. The process is identifiable in a person's life, in the dynamics of social and philosophical movements, within schools of thought, and in societies and civilizations as a whole. This model is in accord with the progressive science of whole systems dynamics. A schism may appear in what was previously a whole unto itself; a polarization of opposite tendencies or ideas then develops, until complete opposition defines the mutually arisen need for each other, thus initiating the move to reunification. We can identify eras in social movements or civilizations as either divergent or convergent. The questions that naturally arise upon considering these historical facts are: What defined the differences between ancient Maya and Toltec cosmo-conception, and how and where did those differences get reconciled? The answers are found when we look at the two different methods used by the Toltec and the Maya to track World Ages. I believe that these differences led to the age-old fundamental schism between Toltec and Maya thought—the rift in the Meso-american psyche.

So far in Part II, we have been concerned with reconstructing two different methods used by Mesoamerican skywatchers to track precession. One is called the Zenith Cosmology and the other is the Galactic Cosmology. The Toltecs of Teotihuacan, living in the early years of the first millennium of the Christian era, counted World Ages with a fifty-two-year period known as the Calendar Round. With it, they initiated the Fifth Sun (or World Age) at Teotihuacan and projected its end some time in the distant future. Their New Fire ceremony became critical to our understanding of how they used the Calendar Round to track precession. The Toltec Fire Priests, you will remember, performed the New Fire ceremony at the end of each Calendar Round, during which they carefully observed the Pleiades passing through the zenith at midnight. When the day on which it did this shifted (as a result of precession), the Toltec astronomer-priests adjusted their World Age calendar and knew they were moving closer to the much anticipated ending of the Fifth Sun.

The Toltecs believed that the next World Age would begin when the Pleiades aligned with the first zenith passage of the sun in May, and this is the phenomenon they tracked with their Calendar Round and New Fire ceremony. This zenith alignment was conceived as a World Age birth, but its precise timing is dependent upon one's latitude of observation. At the latitude of Toltec Teotihuacan, it occurred in the early nineteenth century. The Fifth Sun thus seems to have already ended. However, the timing shifted when the Toltecs transported the Zenith Cosmology to Chichén Itzá, whose latitude is a little further to the north and therefore offers a later calculation for the World Age shift.

As argued in Chapters 7 and 8, the high god of the Toltec pantheon that represented the Zenith Cosmology was Quetzalcoatl, whose earliest astronomical association is with the Pleiades.[2] According to scholars, Quetzalcoatl emerged into Mesoamerican consciousness at Teotihuacan around the third century A.D., the same time the New Fire ceremony began to be performed. The Pleiades were known as the serpent's rattle, and the flight of the Pleiades into alignment with the zenith sun evoked the image of a flying serpent—the feathered serpent Quetzalcoatl.

As for the Maya, they too were tracking precession as the basis of their World Age doctrine, but they were concerned with a completely different astronomical alignment, the solstice-Galaxy conjunction of A.D. 2012. They used the Long Count calendar (rather than the Calendar Round) to track this precessional alignment, which they calculated to occur on the Long Count date 13.0.0.0.0. The Mayas' World Age cosmology concerned itself with a rare and profound galactic synchro-

Diagram 77. Captain Sun Disk

nization—the convergence of our Earth-sun system's solstice meridian with the larger galactic frame of time. This is the Zero Point of the Galactic Cycle of precession, an event that previously occurred 26,000 years ago. The early Maya skywatchers understood this vast time cycle and brilliantly devised the Long Count calendar to end precisely on the Galactic Zero Point. Because this cosmology involved the movement of the solstice sun, the supreme avatar of the Maya pantheon was Ahau, the solstice Sun Deity, pictured at Chichén Itzá as a solar warrior within a Sun Disk. Among many Maya scholars, including Arthur Miller, Linda Schele, and David Freidel, the preferred name for this deity is Captain Sun Disk.[3]

Another "captain" of high rank in the Chichén Itzá murals was dubbed Captain Serpent, who is none other than the snake deity Quetzalcoatl-Kukulcan—the avatar of the Zenith Cosmology. Captain Serpent is portrayed with a rattlesnake wrapped around him.

Diagram 78. Captain Serpent

Significantly, as pictured on murals throughout Chichén Itzá, these two gods formed an alliance. As such, Chichén Itzá was the site of an ongoing cultural-cosmological experiment through which the schism in the collective psyche of ancient Mesoamerica was healed.

Historically, after Teotihuacan in Central Mexico fell around A.D. 750, Chichén Itzá (formerly primarily a Maya city) received a flood of Toltec immigrants, who brought with them their own brand of World Age cosmology and myth. By the end of the tenth baktun in A.D. 830, many of Chichén Itzá's most fascinating structures were built, aligned to the heavens in specific though complex ways. The new chapter in the history of Chichén Itzá was stimulated by fresh ideas from the west, resulting in the synthesis and reconciliation of the two primary cosmological systems previously described. We will see evidence for this pact between the Toltec and Maya worldviews as we proceed to explore some of Chichén's lesser-known cosmic alignments.

COSMIC ALIGNMENTS AT CHICHÉN ITZÁ

Any discussion of the astronomical alignments at Chichén Itzá must begin with the Caracol observatory, where astronomer Anthony Aveni and his colleagues identified several significant astronomical orientations. Windows in the ruined upper tower point toward the extreme northern and southern rise positions of Venus. The equinox sunset is visible through another window in the tower. The orientation of the base of the entire structure indicates that the astronomical positioning of the Caracol was intentional. The corner-to-corner alignment of the base corresponds with the solstice axis. A perpendicular line from the base of the upper platform points to the location on the horizon where the sun sets on the dates of its zenith passage at the latitude of Chichén Itzá—May 20–25 and July 22–27.[4] According to Aveni, around A.D. 1000 the last annual setting of the Pleiades could be viewed in late April from a window in the Caracol's upper tower. In addition to the Caracol's alignments with the Pleiades, the zenith sun, the solstice axis, the equinox, and the setting extremes of Venus, Aveni found fifteen other alignments that correspond reasonably well with astronomical events.

The shadow serpent that descends the Pyramid of Kukulcan on the equinox has already been discussed. Briefly, in my recent work on the astronomy and mythology of this event, I discovered an unrecognized facet that completes the mythic message. As previously explained, the serpent is a well-known symbol of the sun. In addition, Yucatecan rattlesnakes often have a natural "solar face" design near the rattle, reinforcing their meaning as solar divinities. In the Yucatec Maya language, the rattle is called *tzab*, which is also the name for the Pleiades. At ancient Chichén Itzá, New Year's Day was celebrated on one of the zenith-passage dates, suggesting that solar zenith passages were very important as temporal beginning and ending points. My reconstruction of the true meaning of the Toltec New Fire ceremony, transplanted to Chichén, proposes that this ceremony was really about tracking when, in the remote future, the Pleiades conjunct the sun on the solar zenith-passage date. Due to precession, this complex astronomical convergence now occurs at Chichén Itzá every May 20, when the sun and the Pleiades are conjunct within the prescribed six-day range for zenith-passage dates at Chichén. The mythology of Kukulcan descending, in relation to the symbology of the rattle (the Pleiades) and the snake (the zenith sun), points directly to the May 20 event, sixty days after the equinox. Thus, the Pyramid of Kukulcan is a cosmic myth set in stone, pointing straight up to the zenith, where an astronomical alignment suggestive of World Age transformation occurs in the twenty-first century A.D. As if the equinox shadow-serpent manifestation alone is not enough to inspire an awesome respect for ancient Maya cosmology, this World Age myth, clearly alluded to by the equinox event itself, is worthy of being called the greatest calendrical-architectural achievement known. A compelling event is beginning to transpire—the sun and the Pleiades joined in the zenith over Chichén Itzá—that will extend through the next century and then fall out of sync, never to happen again. This is the era of World Age transformation as formulated by the ancient Toltecs. The players, as with other alignments at Chichén, are the Pleiades and the zenith sun. As is now clear, however, this was only one method used by the ancient Mesoamerican skywatchers to track precession. The other involved the Maya Long Count calendar, the Milky Way, and the solstice sun. These mytho-astronomical players are found in Chichén's ballcourt alignments.

The High Priest's Grave, a small ruin in the old section of Chichén near the Caracol, is a miniature model of Kukulcan's pyramid. Scholars have been unable to precisely examine its orientation because of its eroded condition. Interestingly, however, they found a large chamber underneath the small pyramid and identified it as the tomb of a shaman or priest. A Long Count date found in this underground chamber is a solstice date from the ninth century.[5] As described in Chapter 11, the Great Ballcourt aligned with the Milky Way on solstice dates in the mid-ninth century, the point being that solstice dates as well as equinox dates were apparently significant for Chichén's calendar keepers.

Finally, scholars have determined that the Pyramid of Kukulcan was built around the end of the tenth baktun in A.D. 830, when the Toltec Calendar Round ending happened to synchronize with the Maya baktun ending.[6] This significant calendric convergence offered the Maya-Toltec thinkers a rare opportunity to reconcile the two main streams of cosmological thought in Mesoamerica—the recalibration of the Toltec Calendar Round with the Maya Long Count. The year A.D. 830, which is 10.0.0.0.0 in the Long Count, was the date of this incredible calendric opportunity, and this is when most of the amazing astronomical structures at Chichén were designed and built. For this reason as well as others, Chichén looms as a place of calendrical and cosmological unification.[7]

The Great Ballcourt, the largest ballcourt known in the ancient Maya world, lies a short distance to the northwest of the Pyramid of Kukulcan. As discussed in the previous chapter, it encodes many alignments, most notably ones involving the Milky Way and the solstices. For instance, the Great Ballcourt was aligned with the Milky Way at midnight on the June solstices around A.D. 865. This means that if you stood in the center of the ballcourt at midnight on one of these solstice dates, you would have seen the Milky Way arching overhead, touching the opposed horizons to which the lengthwise axis of the ballcourt points. Overhead, you would have seen the place where the Milky Way and the ecliptic cross.

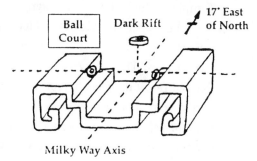

This intersection forms the cross-shaped cosmic ballcourt—a symbol important for its role in the Long Count end-date of A.D. 2012. Simply put, the center of this cosmic cross is where the December solstice sun will be in 2012.

Diagram 79. Ballcourt schematic showing cross formed by the Milky Way and the ecliptic

The mural on the east wall of the ballcourt shows the primary ballplayer—in reality a high deity—being decapitated. His severed head becomes the gameball, which the players then must kick into the goalring. This scenario is a metaphor for the December solstice sun moving slowly into its "goal"—the dark-rift near the cosmic cross formed by the Milky Way and the ecliptic. Within the metaphor of the ballgame, the dark-rift "cave" is the goalring, and the severed head or gameball is the December solstice sun.

You may recall that the actual stone goalring of the ballcourt's east wall is above and to the left of the mural depicting the severed head as the gameball. As high noon approaches on the June solstice, a shadow cast from this stone goalring slowly moves along the mural toward and finally through the gameball. The effect is that of the ball moving slowly through the goalring as high noon approaches on the solstice. This shadow-play alludes to the mythic meaning of the ballgame as a metaphor for the alignment of the 2012 end-date. The December solstice sun converges upon and conjuncts the dark-rift "goalring" in the center of the cosmic Milky Way ballcourt only in the years surrounding A.D. 2012. Like Chichén's Toltec Zenith Cosmology, this alignment is an effect of the precession of the equinoxes, and occurs in the early twenty-first century.

The astounding sophistication of this hierophany, in the architectural engineering as well as in the intended mythological meaning, almost eclipses the mind-boggling profundity of the shadow-serpent manifestation on Kukulcan's pyramid. But we are not finished with the Great Ballcourt yet. One more alignment, one that confirms Chichén's role as the site where the Zenith Cosmology and the Galactic Cosmology were merged, occurs above the east wall mural, in the Upper Temple of the Jaguars (see diagram 71).

The Upper Temple of the Jaguars is a small building constructed over the eastern wall of the Great Ballcourt. Its west-facing doorway provides a clear view of the flat horizon. The doorway is a wide portal leading into the inner chamber, and is flanked on both sides by serpent columns. These are stone sculptures of the inverted serpent image that is found throughout Chichén Itzá, reminiscent of the equinoctial shadow-serpent that appears on the Pyramid of Kukulcan. Inside the chamber, several murals were still visible in the late nineteenth century, but are now completely deteriorated. Luckily, Adela Breton made detailed drawings of them in 1906.[8] One of the murals within the Upper Temple of the Jaguars depicts two beings of equal stature and is situated such that the rays of the setting sun on its date of zenith passage illuminate it.[9] This is, literally, where the secret history of Chichén comes to light.

THE UNION OF CAPTAIN SERPENT AND CAPTAIN SUN DISK

Based upon Breton's drawings, there was enough information in the murals to identify the two beings as none other than Captain Sun Disk and Captain Serpent, the mytho-historical figures found throughout Chichén, who played an important

Diagram 80. Drawing from a Chichén Itzá mural showing Captain Sun Disk (Maya) and Captain Serpent (Toltec) together. From the Upper Temple of the Jaguars

role during the Maya-Toltec synergy of the ninth century.

Although these two characters may have had some meaning as actual historical figures, their mythological role, as representatives of the Toltec and Maya cosmologies, is more important. The biannual zenith illumination of their meeting symbolizes, and serves as a reminder of, the political and cosmological alliance formed between the Toltec and Maya civilizations. Captain Sun Disk represents the Maya ideal of a cosmic ruler and symbolizes the prevailing Maya cosmology of the solstice sun disk moving toward the Milky Way. Captain Serpent is the Toltec avatar associated with the feathered serpent, Quetzalcoatl (that is, with the World Age cosmology involving the Pleiades moving toward the zenith sun).[10] In that the Mesoamerican schism formed after the fall of the Olmec, the reconciliation of Captain Sun Disk and Captain Serpent was probably almost three baktuns in the making. And they came together to recognize and agree that it would be another three baktuns before the end times—the era of World Age renewal—would arrive.

The joining of these cosmic avatars of the Toltec and Maya peoples represents a reconciliation of the ancient schism in the Mesoamerican psyche, which I believe occurred at Chichén Itzá in the ninth century A.D. It was a reconciliation of two different branches of what was, after all, basically a shared cosmological discovery: the precession of the equinoxes. Both traditions competed to identify the future World Age transition by tracking the precession of the equinoxes. However, early in Mesoamerican history, perhaps around 50 B.C., the two different precession-tracking methods were formulated that resulted in two slightly different timings. This gave rise to a cosmological conflict—a disagreement on the very important and basic concept of when the next World Age would arrive. We might imagine this conflict to be similar to modern battles between Israel and Palestine, battles arising from serious social, religious, and political differences, even though these two traditions spring from the same source. In fact, a polarization of opposed ideals seems to be the underlying root of basic social and philosophical problems in the world today. The possibility of successfully reconciling such differences, on the scale of civilizations, is attested to by what was accomplished at Chichén Itzá.

The original Toltec tracking method, based upon calculations made at the latitude of Teotihuacan, resulted in a World Age shift to occur in the early nineteenth century. Early on, however, the Toltecs noticed their end-date cosmology was not in accord with the Maya Long Count system, which predicted the Zero Point of precession in the early twenty-first century. For the two systems and the schism in Mesoamerican civilization to be reconciled, some adjustment had to be made somewhere. What occurred is clear: The Toltec Zenith Cosmology was adjusted when the Toltecs relocated to the latitude of Chichén Itzá, effectively bringing it into line with the Long Count end-date.

Captain Sun Disk and Captain Serpent each represent the fully manifest ideal of their respective cosmologies. Having achieved full polarization and complete expression, they could then meet and be reconciled. This was no doubt a recognition by the Toltec-Maya alliance of the deeper process of civilization of which they were a part—an intentional decision to adapt, compromise, reconcile, and integrate into a new level of unity rather than violently break down into separatist camps. The successful reunification achieved by Chichén's Toltec and Maya inhabitants is evident in the intentional blending of their respective calendar cosmologies around A.D. 830. The pact between the Toltec and the Maya was formed at this time, anointed by solar alignment, and preserved in stone for future generations. The years following the alliance saw massive monuments built and dedicated to consecrate the pact, and to point anyone with eyes to see to the World Age shift now agreed upon by both systems.

The Pyramid of Kukulcan represents the Toltec New Fire system that points, after a slight adjustment upon the Toltec relocation to the latitude of Chichén Itzá, to the early twenty-first century. The Great Ballcourt's alignment with the Milky Way, as well as the symbology of the ballgame itself, reminds us of the solstice convergence with the portal to the next world—the Maya Galactic Cosmology that likewise identifies a World Age shift to occur in the early twenty-first century (A.D. 2012).

TIME WILL TELL

At Chichén Itzá, Captain Sun Disk (the cosmic avatar of the Maya) and Captain Serpent (the cosmic avatar of the Toltec) joined to create a new, hybrid cosmology, a meta-system synthesizing the best insights of both traditions. Their union is commemorated twice a year by the setting zenith-date sun that illuminates the mural depicting their pact. The Upper Temple of the Jaguars and the pact sealed inside combine the solar zenith criterion (its orientation to the setting sun on the date of zenith passage) with the Milky Way criterion (the Great Ballcourt) as symbols of unity and reconciliation. The mythology and astronomy of the Zenith Cosmology and the Galactic Cosmology were united: The Toltecs and the Maya began to act as one. Both cultural traditions joined in the powerful proclamation that what we call the twenty-first century, measured with two different cosmological alignments in the Great Year of precession, would be a great era of transformation for humanity, one in which an old world is destroyed and a new world rises from the ashes. According to both Maya and Toltec myth, humanity saves itself at these critical nexus points only by transforming, by mutating into something totally unrecognizable, a new being altogether. What this will be, only time will tell.

The two cosmological systems unified at Chichén Itzá drew together many aspects of Mesoamerican culture. Each system belonged to a specific culture, each had its own tracking calendar, and each had an explanatory myth or ceremonial tradition to go with it.

Diagram 81. Two Mesoamerican Precessional Cosmologies

	The Zenith Cosmology	**The Galactic Cosmology**
Site of Origin:	Teotihuacan	Izapa
Era of Origin:	First Century A.D.	First Century B.C.
Culture:	Toltec	Maya
Calendar:	Calendar Round	Long Count
Myth:	New Fire	Hero Twin/Ballgame
Astronomy:	Zenith Sun & Pleiades	Solstice Sun & Galactic Center
Captain:	Serpent	Sun Disk
Deity:	Quetzalcoatl	One Hunahpu

The Galactic Cosmology actually had several "myths" that encoded its concepts: the Hero Twin myth and the ballgame Mystery Play, as well as birthing symbols and king accession rites. We explored the ballgame in detail first because it directly implicates Chichén Itzá by way of its ballcourt alignments and it encodes the Galactic Cosmology in a straightforward way. We now need to explore the Hero Twin myth and related folklore in greater detail, to deepen our appreciation for how Maya mythology encodes the astronomical meaning of the Long Count end-date. This examination will lead us progressively into new insights about the nature of Maya shamanism, birthing rituals, and king initiations. We will see anew how the Maya conceptualized cosmogenesis, and get to the root of what the Galactic Cosmology is all about. What will emerge is persuasive evidence of the Mayas' ancient and profound understanding of cosmological processes, including galactic forces that impinge upon the evolution of life on earth—a paradigm that supersedes anything yet encountered by Western science.

PART III:
MAYA COSMOGENESIS

From a practical point of view, a culture as ancient, numerate and

chronologically sophisticated as that of Mesoamerica is more likely

than not to have detected and then measured the phenomenon of

precession . . . the great year of equinoctial precession emerges as a

missing link between the local and political chronology of our era

and the vast evolutionary philosophy of time so vividly testified to

in the Popol Vuh.

— Gordon Brotherston,
Archaeoastronomy in the New World

CHAPTER 13

THE BIRTH OF THE HERO TWINS

The magical conception of the Hero Twins is an important episode in the *Popol Vuh*. When we remember that myth and astronomy go together, it is not surprising that this mythic narrative is based upon astronomy, and that we may be able to identify the real-time astronomical event that signified the conception of Hunahpu and Xbalanque and, therefore, the era in which their story was created. An important question we will be able to answer is, who is the real mother of the Hero Twins? In the *Popol Vuh*, she is called X'quic, which means Blood Woman or Blood Moon. However, as we will see, other considerations suggest she is more than just the moon.

After One Hunahpu and Seven Hunahpu journey to Xibalba and fail at all the tests presented them, they are killed and One Hunahpu's head is hung in a calabash tree by a road. Soon thereafter, Blood Moon, a daughter of one of the lesser Lords of Xibalba, comes along and is intrigued with the skull-tree. She speaks with the skull but does not know it is One Hunahpu and Seven Hunahpu acting together "as one mind." The skull spits into Blood Moon's hand, magically impregnating her. She continues on her way, is eventually banished to the surface of the Earth, and gives birth to the Hero Twins, Hunahpu and Xbalanque.

If we can decipher enough astronomy in this myth, we can take what we find and search astronomy software for dates that represent the astronomical event corresponding to the conception of the Hero Twins. The works of Dennis Tedlock, translator of the Hero Twin myth, provide all of the key astronomical identifications involved in the Hero Twin story.[1] According to Tedlock's interpretation, Blood Moon is the waning post-full moon, the sliver-shaped moon that rises in the east just before sunrise.[2] The skull that speaks "belongs" to both One Hunahpu and Seven Hunahpu, and they speak through it with "one mind."[3] One Hunahpu (the calendric day 1 Ahau) represents Venus, and Seven Hunahpu represents Jupiter.[4] The skull that speaks therefore represents the conjunction of these two bright planets. As a calendric year-bearer associated with the seasonal quarters, the resurrected One Hunahpu represents the December solstice sun, and his rebirth was only possible through the efforts of his sons, the Hero Twins. Thus, in our search for the mytho-astronomical conception of the Hero Twins, we should be open to the possibility that a December solstice date may also be involved.

The Venus-Jupiter "skull" was hung in the fork of a tree. The tree itself is the Milky Way, and it happens to "stand by the road" (the ecliptic).[5] This astronomical configuration suggests a cross formed by the Milky Way and the ecliptic. According to Tedlock, this cross designates the entrance place to Xibalba, the *xibalba be*, which the modern Quiché Maya identify astronomically as the dark cleft in the Milky Way whose southern terminus touches the ecliptic near Sagittarius.[6] The dark-rift also was mythologized as a divine birthplace. Importantly, the crook or cleft in the calabash tree where One Hunahpu's skull was hung is identified by Tedlock as this dark-rift in the Milky Way.[7] So, the fork in the calabash tree where the conjunction of Venus (One Hunahpu) and Jupiter (Seven Hunahpu) occurs is synonymous with the dark-rift in the Milky Way. We now have identified a definite location for the Venus-Jupiter conjunction.

We can narrow down the astronomical scope even further because Blood Moon swings by for a visit. As mentioned, Blood Moon is the waning post-full moon, a sliver in the predawn eastern sky. Since Venus never swings more than 47° from the sun, in either its morning star or evening star phase, the Venus-Jupiter-moon syzygy must occur in the *xibalba be* less than 47° west of the sun. This puts them in the predawn sky in late fall or early winter. In fact, considering that we will be looking at likely dates beginning with the earliest version of the Hero Twin myth at Izapa, some 2,100 years ago, the required scenario must occur not more than twenty-five days before the December solstice and not more than eighteen days after the December solstice. The reason: 2,100 years ago the December solstice sun was 30° east of the *xibalba be* (the required place of Venus-Jupiter). So, twenty-five days prior to the December solstice defines a minimum 5° spread for predawn visibility; likewise, more than eighteen days after the December solstice exceeds the 47° maximum possible distance between the dark-rift (the conjunction place) and the sun. This temporal span is obviously precession-related, because by the year A.D. 2000 the December solstice sun is right in the *xibalba be*, while 2,100 years ago there was a 30° separation, allowing the Jupiter-Venus-moon conjunction to be visible in the predawn eastern sky.

With these constraints, we can next decide in what era we should begin the search. The conception of the Hero Twin episode in the *Popol Vuh* may have contained the astronomical meaning in its earliest form. Hero Twin adventures appear on the monuments of Izapa between 500 B.C. and A.D. 50, providing a range to guide our search.[8]

To begin, we should track when Jupiter conjuncts the *xibalba be*. Since Venus parameters limit this search to within twenty-five days before and eighteen days after the December solstice, we can narrow down the range even more. Also, remembering that the December solstice sun was the "first sun" or "first day"—a new beginning or birthtime—we should be on the lookout for what occurs on December solstice dates.

Searching my astronomy software[9] for Jupiter-Venus-moon conjunctions in the *xibalba be*, I found that there are distinct fifty-nine-year intervals at which our syzygy tends to repeat (a syzygy is a triple conjunction). Amazingly, the precision of this complex three-way conjunction tends to maximize around December solstice dates in the second century B.C. To make some tedious research brief, let me share

only the results. I checked all of the dates between 556 B.C. and A.D. 51 on which this triple conjunction occurred. Of the fifty-three dates that met the criteria, sixteen are worth mentioning, although only four or five provide a distinct picture of a Jupiter-Venus-moon syzygy in the *xibalba be*.

All of these star-map dates

Diagram 82. January 5, 532 B.C., 4:00 a.m.

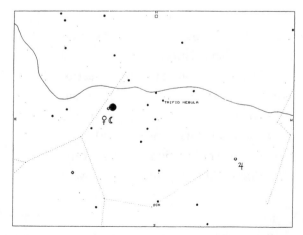

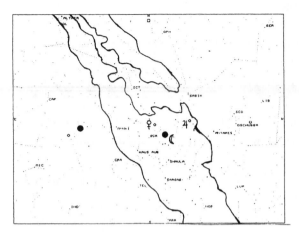

Diagram 83. January 9, 508 B.C.

were charted with the Gregorian calendar. The earliest syzygy of 532 B.C. was notable because it appears that the moon occulted Venus. In other words, the conjunction was so close that the moon passed right over, or occulted, Venus. This sky picture certainly illustrates the intimacy necessary for impregnation.

The next date shows a tolerably close conjunction of Jupiter-Venus-moon in the *xibalba be*. Notice that diagrams 82 and 83 depict a realistic representation of the Milky Way and its dark-rift—the mouth of the Cosmic Monster and birth canal of the Great Mother. Nothing notable occurs between 508 B.C. and 307 B.C. with the exception of a Jupiter-Mars conjunction with the dark-rift on the date December 25, 331 B.C. However, by 224 B.C., the sky once again gets interesting.

On this date, Jupiter, Venus, and the moon are nicely grouped in the dark-rift mouth, and Saturn is roughly 20° to the west of them. This is the first in a series of four especially notable dates, separated by fifty-nine years each.

On December 17, 189 B.C., Jupiter, Venus, and the moon were roughly conjunct, but were some 5° west of the dark-rift. I noticed that after a two hundred year period of inactivity between 508 B.C. and 307 B.C., notable dates were not only increasing but were approaching the December solstice date. The next date, December 22, 165 B.C., occurs right on the December solstice.

Diagram 85 shows the mytho-astronomical picture of Jupiter, Venus, and the moon in close conjunction in the dark-rift, with Mars some 15° further off to the west. The position of Mars means it rose first in the predawn sky, followed

Diagram 84. December 14, 224 B.C.

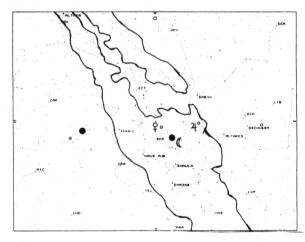

by Venus and then the closely paired Jupiter-moon. This is the second date in a series of notable dates, each separated by fifty-nine years. Neptune happens to be within 1° of Mars on this date but it would not have been visible to the naked eye.

The next notable date, December 28, 106 B.C., moves us further away from the December solstice date, showing a loose grouping of Jupiter-Venus-moon around the dark-rift, with Saturn in the mix. Finally, on January 6, 46 B.C., an unusual Jupiter-Venus-moon conjunction occurred near the dark-rift mouth, again with Saturn in the picture. However, Jupiter was some 7° further west of the dark-rift mouth, further out than Saturn, while Venus and the moon were very close.

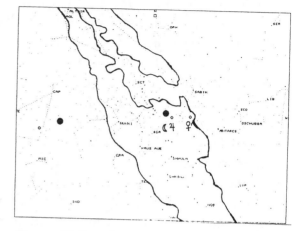

Diagram 85. December 22, 165 B.C.

A lot of theoretical mythic astronomy must have been occurring during the period between 224 B.C. and 46 B.C. The conjunctions in 46 B.C., 106 B.C., 165 B.C. and 224 B.C. all provide fairly good sky-pictures of what we know was mythologized in the Hero Twin Creation myth as the conception of the Hero Twins. This range of dates parallels the time of the Izapan civilization's development and growth. The 165 B.C. date in particular is intriguing because it occurred on the December solstice. It is also one of the most precise of all the sky pictures. At the very least, the astronomical events that occurred on these dates suggest ancient astronomer-priests were yoking their new myths to the Cosmic Mother's dark-rift "birth canal" in the sky—the *xibalba be*. If the Izapan skywatchers had been aware of the fifty-nine-year interval separating these triple conjunctions, they would have anticipated one in A.D. 13. That a compelling triple conjunction did not occur on this date may have disappointed them. Ironically, it was right around this time that Izapa is thought to have gone into decline. On the other hand, they might have been well aware that the sacred syzygy came in groupings that eventually fell out of synchronization.

The barrage of syzygy dates in the second and first centuries B.C. is very compelling, especially because they occurred after a two hundred year period devoid of meaningful conjunctions. For this reason alone, ancient skywatchers might have paid close attention to them. The new cycle of syzygies may even have been so provocative to the early skywatchers of Izapa that they felt compelled to mythologize them. What we do know for sure is that, at some point, the triple conjunction of Jupiter, Venus, and the moon in the dark-rift became the celestial signature of the mythological conception of the Hero Twins, Hunahpu and Xbalanque. I am fairly certain that this mythic formulation occurred on one of the most compelling dates listed, probably the one on the December solstice of 165 B.C.[10]

Diagram 86. Stela 10 from Izapa: The birth of the Hero Twins

Having decoded and applied the astronomical identifications in the Hero Twin myth, it seemed to me that I had successfully identified the astronomical event that signified the conception and birth of the Hero Twins. In the astronomical evidence rallied here, the dark-rift is reinforced as a conception place in ancient Mesoamerican mytho-astronomy, a Creation Place. Hunahpu's and Xbalanque's mythological conception, which I have located in real time with its astronomical signature, may also indicate their germinal entry into early Maya myth and folk consciousness. As such, their "conception" must go back to Izapa. Importantly, several Izapan monuments illustrate the Hero Twin conception myth. For example, the Milky Way calabash tree is depicted on Stela 10, under which the Hero Twins are shown umbilically connected to their mother, Blood Moon.

It seems that the dramatic conjunctions observed in the middle of baktun 7 inspired several ideas among the Izapan cosmonauts. One was that the dark-rift in the Milky Way was a Creation Place. Another was that the December solstice was a Creation Time. Since the Long Count ends with a conjunction also involving the dark-rift in the Milky Way and the December solstice sun, the Hero Twin astronomy might have lent itself to the formulation of the Long Count. Overall, however, we can suggest an answer for the question posed at the beginning of this chapter: Who is the real mother of the Hero Twins? She is the Milky Way, or the moon in conjunction with the Milky Way.

The skull of One Hunahpu spits into Blood Moon's hand, magically impregnating her with the Hero Twins. The astronomical syzygy between Jupiter, Venus, and the moon—the three brightest celestial objects after the sun—is a fairly frequent event. However, its occurrence in a specific sidereal location such as the Great Mother's birthplace is less frequent. In tracking this triple conjunction's occurrences with astronomy software, I noticed that it occurs at fifty-nine-year intervals for three or four cycles but then goes out of sync. Presumably, a different phase-cycle will then come to prominence, be useful for a few fifty-nine-year periods, and then also pass. At any rate, the skull spat frequently, and we might presume that, for the ancient astronomers, any time the celestial syzygy occurred, the conception of the Hero Twins was recalled. If so, it seems the ancient Mesoamerican skywatchers were capable of impressive and sophisticated astronomy, as well as imaginative myth-making based on those astronomical observations.

The fact that one of the most compelling triple-conjunction dates occurs on the December solstice leads us to recall Stela 11 (diagram 57), and its depiction of the Izapan December solstice sunrise that we examined earlier. Like the celestial rebirth of One Hunahpu on Creation Day, the conception of Hunahpu and Xbalanque also occurs near the *xibalba be*. In this way we can use that same skyview from Izapa to illustrate the astronomical meaning of the Hero Twins' dramatic, mytho-astronomical conception. The players are One Hunahpu and Seven Hunahpu (Venus and Jupiter), Blood Moon, the *xibalba be*, and the first day of the year, the December solstice.

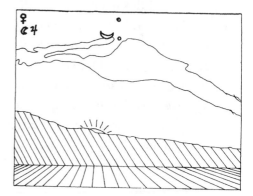

Diagram 87. The view over Izapa showing the cosmic conception of the Hero Twins, Hunahpu and Xbalanque. December solstice, 165 B.C.

As we have seen from this close look at the sources of the Hero Twins' mythological conception and birth, Maya myth speaks the language of the stars and planets, and its study can open us to a new way of relating to the cosmos, one that receives the whispered messages of far off celestial events. The Hero Twin myth itself is a rich source of calendric and astronomical information. Based upon our calendrical, astronomical, and mythological studies, it is becoming more and more clear that the Hero Twin myth and the Long Count calendar arose at the same time, in the same place, and that they work together to elucidate the end-date cosmology. Given that the Long Count is a calendar that calibrates precession, we can surmise that the Hero Twin

Creation myth encodes precessional knowledge and is therefore an esoteric World Age doctrine. But how exactly does the Hero Twin Creation story describe precession? How is it connected to the Long Count? And why do I assume that a myth must arise with the discovery of precession?

To answer these questions, we must understand that disparate ancient cultures who derived their worldviews from observing the natural world, a natural world that includes the sky, might have formulated very similar ideas. As archaeoastronomer Anthony Aveni said, "In ancient societies, the sky and its contents lay at the very foundation of human cognition,"[11] meaning that the shared backdrop of the night sky provides celestial dramas that were mythologized by diverse peoples in similar ways. Armed with this perspective, we can search the globe for cultures challenged by the discovery of precession to understand what took place in the New World as cosmological understanding evolved. For example, how did philosophical assumptions change when precession was discovered in the Old World? It just so happens, as we mentioned earlier, that Mithraism arose in the Old World upon the discovery of precession by the Greek astronomer Hipparchus. Amazingly, these Old World events took place in the first century B.C., precisely when the enigmatic Izapan civilization was in full swing, inventing the Long Count and devising the Hero Twin Creation myth. Let us pause for a moment and take a look at this strange trans-Atlantic parallel, which will help us understand that the development of the Hero Twin myth as an esoteric precession doctrine is not without precedent.

THE HERO TWIN MYTH AS PRECESSION DOCTRINE

The *Popol Vuh* describes a succession of World Ages, each one ending in cataclysm. The current age is the one in which the Hero Twins endeavor to resurrect their father, One Hunahpu, and it ends when the Lords of Xibalba are defeated in the Underworld Ballcourt and One Hunahpu is reborn. Before any of this takes place, however, the Hero Twins must do away with Seven Macaw, the vain and false ruler of the previous World Age. Seven Macaw, as noted earlier, was identified with the Big Dipper and this, in addition to the other facts already sketched, shows quite clearly that a great deal of astronomy was encoded into the Hero Twin myth.

World Age doctrines are not unique to Mesoamerica. From India to China to Finland to Egypt, a deep and profound Mystery of the Ages peeks out at us from the fragmented ancient myths of shifting epochs of humanity. The book *Hamlet's Mill* is now, after pioneering a new approach, only one book among many to argue that World Age myths are derived from knowledge of the precession of the equinoxes. The Hero Twin Creation myth is a classic Mesoamerican example of a World Age myth, and so we may expect that knowledge of precession lurks within it. And indeed that is the case. I have already argued that a primary event in the *Popol Vuh*, the rebirth of First Father/One Hunahpu, symbolizes the precession-caused end-date alignment. One Hunahpu's resurrection and his claiming of his throne in the cosmic center symbolize the December solstice sun's movement into conjunction with the great bulge of the Galactic Center, an event that culminates in A.D. 2012. In this way, the Hero Twin myth encodes a rare alignment in precession, and can thus be considered an esoteric World Age doctrine with precession as its deepest secret message. The larger question, however, is how and why the discovery of precession alters the worldview of its discoverers.

We can observe how the discovery of precession exerts changes on cosmological ideas by looking at the situation in the Old World at the time Hipparchus "discovered" precession in 128 B.C. Although the Greek astronomers were quite sophisticated, they believed in the erroneous doctrine that the stars are eternally fixed. It was inconceivable and heretical for them to accept that the stars actually belong to a slow shifting—that the constellations slip backward over long periods of time. But Hipparchus proved that this is the case—that the rise times of stars shift—and he calculated this "Platonic Year" to be 36,000 years long. He was wrong by a long shot, but the precise calibration is not the issue. The point is that his discovery shook the foundations of Greek cosmology. We can only imagine the distress this radical new doctrine must have caused the standard bearers of Greco-Roman science. They may have feared that this knowledge would cause a breakdown in society as a whole, should common people get wind of an unstable sky. They probably decided that this dangerous knowledge should be available only to the elect, to the few who could demonstrate their ability to comprehend its profound meaning.

And so Mithraism arose, a Mystery Cult whose highest initiatory experience was the revelation of precession as the cause for the shifting destinies of humanity through vast epochs. Mithraic ceremonies were closely guarded, taking place in caves and constructed underground chambers. Still, the new stellar religion spread wildly in the first century B.C., with sanctuaries springing up from North Africa to

Scotland, wherever the Romans went. The highest deity, Mithras, was often depicted slaying a bull, symbolizing his dominion over the axial shifting of the sky and elevating him as the one who ended the Age of Taurus (the Bull). As such, Mithras was the Prime Mover and God of Precession. His birthday was the December solstice.

Mithraism competed with Christianity for future status as a global religion, and there are many similarities between the two religions. Jesus and Mithras were both born on the December solstice.[12] Early Christianity is filled with astrological symbolism; Mithraic sanctuaries depict zodiac scenes. But Mithraism was an initiatory Mystery Play, a direct revelation and personal experience of divinity, akin to the earlier mysteries of Delphi and Eleusis. Christianity,

Diagram 88. Mithras as Aeon, the God of Time

on the other hand, came to espouse a path to God accessible only through Jesus. One can only wonder what the world would look like today had Mithraism succeeded in overcoming Christianity.

The Hipparchus-Mithras connection is a perfect example of how the discovery of precession gives rise to a new explanatory mythology. In Mesoamerica, it is clear that the Long Count encodes a knowledge of precession, because the 13-baktun-cycle end-date of A.D. 2012 pinpoints a rare alignment in precession. It also is clear that the Long Count calendar arose about the same time as did the new Mesoamerican Creation myth, the Hero Twin myth. As we have seen, this Creation story encodes the astronomical process that converges in A.D. 2012. The Long Count-Hero Twin complex is another typical example of how precessional knowledge is encoded into myth. The parallel to Mithraism in the Old World is striking, but not surprising.

One element of the Hero Twin story illustrates how the discovery of precession exerts changes on established cosmological doctrine. That the Hero Twins dispensed with the old Polar God, Seven Macaw, indicates an advance in cosmological thinking, one that abandoned a limited polar paradigm and then proceeded to formulate a cosmological orientation centered upon a new cosmic center, the Galactic Center. This Mesoamerican "change of the gods" suggests a doctrinal shift occurred, wherein Mesoamerican cosmologists shifted from a polar-oriented cosmology to a Galaxy-centered one. Furthermore, they apparently wanted to highlight the Galactic Center as a supreme organizing principle, with One Hunahpu as the Mesoamerican God of Precession.

In the Old World, Mithras had to destroy the Bull, the god of the zodiacal age of Taurus, before new zodiacal gods could have their turn. Although Jesus is the god of the current zodiacal age of Pisces, Mithras himself is the one who turns the axial wheel of precession and thus presides over the entire process. Likewise, One Hunahpu is the God of the Center, the Galactic Center, and rules during the eras of transformation in which the December solstice sun conjuncts the Galactic Center. These are the rare World Age eras in which Earth and humanity experience great suffering, tremendous change, and, ultimately, growth.

The ancient Hero Twin myth, formulated during the early days of Izapa, comes down to us today via the Quiché *Popol Vuh*, recorded in Guatemala in the 1550s. The *Popol Vuh* can be considered a late variant of the ancient Creation myth originally formulated 2,100 years ago at Izapa. Being both a myth and a star map, the Maya Creation myth encodes for us a "lost" Galactic Cosmology. We must ask ourselves, however, how much of this ancient knowledge was really "lost," for we can now decode the ancient cosmological paradigm as found in myths and on monuments, such as the stelae of Izapa and the Great Ballcourt at Chichén Itzá. Perhaps it was never lost; perhaps we just could not see it. More importantly, there are more than six million Maya living today in the highlands of Guatemala and Chiapas, and millions more in Yucatán, Belize, and Quintana Roo. The highland Quiché Maya, descendants of those who preserved the *Popol Vuh*, retain star lore that points to the Galactic Center as a place of profound significance. To this day, they tell stories that appear to be variants of those recorded in the *Popol Vuh*, stories of an ancient time when calendar-priests and vision-seeking shamans gazed into the cosmic center with full consciousness of a deep cosmic knowledge. Secret knowledge has a way of surviving in the ancient stories, even if the storytellers themselves have forgotten the true roots of their metaphors. We have uncovered the core of this "lost" knowledge, and can now pause to look with a discerning eye at some of the surviving stories in order to deepen our appreciation of the Galactic Cosmology.

CHAPTER 14

A HAWK, A CROSS, AND A MOUTH

In the 1970s, Maya ethnographers Barbara Tedlock and Dennis Tedlock were apprenticed to a Quiché daykeeper named Andrés Xiloj. They lived in the village of Momostenango, a traditional Quiché town where the ancient ways are still followed and the 260-day tzolkin calendar still survives. Barbara Tedlock collected star lore among the Quiché, and Andrés Xiloj told her of a curious legend involving a hawk and a cross. The story is tied to astronomical events that signal the appropriate times to plant and harvest corn. Although it is quite brief, it is filled with mytho-astronomical information.

Every year in April, Xic, the Hawk, arrives and lifts the Cross out of the ocean. Thereafter the rains begin, nourishing the newly planted corn. By October, the Hawk comes again, passing through the center of the sky. This time it drops the Cross into the southern ocean. This is when the rains cease, and corn plants are bent in preparation for harvest. The Hawk disappears in December and January.

Two constellations are involved in this myth, the Cross and the Hawk. The Cross, more commonly called the Thieves' Cross, consists of stars in Sagittarius.[1]

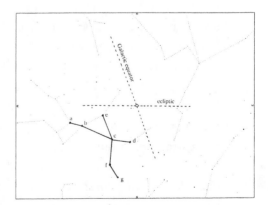

Diagram 89. The Maya Thieves' Cross constellation in Sagittarius

167

The striking thing about this constellation is that it resembles the nearby cross formed by the Milky Way and the ecliptic. Its vertical member is tilted to the left in the same way that the Milky Way crosses the ecliptic at an angle. Its east-west member is roughly parallel to the ecliptic just to the north. (Obviously, the ecliptic is not a visible feature, but the location of its path was known to the Maya). The visible Thieves' Cross constellation in Sagittarius probably served to remind the viewer of the less obvious cross of the Milky Way/ecliptic. The parallel seems unlikely to be coincidental.

In Maya cosmology, crosses symbolize the cosmic center and, in fact, the Milky Way/ecliptic cross is targeted on the Galactic Center. In Mesoamerican symbology, crosses are depicted as a source of rain.[2] In the story, when the Hawk picks up the Cross in its mouth and carries it out of the ocean in April, the rains come. Thus, crosses and cosmic centers are sources of rain, which sustains life and nurtures fertility.

As for the Hawk in our story, the Hawk—on one level, refers to the flocks of Swainson's hawks that migrate through Guatemala in April and October. Migrating northward by the thousands in April, they signal that the rains will soon arrive. Flying southward in October, they tell the Quiché farmer that the dry season is coming. But in what way do they carry a cross? Well, they don't, but their celestial counterpart does. The Hawk constellation recognized by the Quiché is found north of the Thieves' Cross and corresponds to the Aquila (Eagle) constellation of Old World astronomy. Although the Maya and Old World constellations share the same image—a bird—we should refrain from assuming that the Maya derived their image from post-Conquest influence. Aquila is a clear-cut constellation and easily lends itself to being viewed as a bird, so the Maya likely visualized this star grouping as a hawk, independent of the Aquila/Eagle identification for the same star grouping in the Old World. In fact, Barbara Tedlock points out that "Hawk" is a better designation for this constellation, because the wings sweep backward (mirroring the angles of the star group) whereas eagles (Aquila) extend their wings almost straight out during flight. As a result, the head of the Maya Hawk constellation points downward, or southward, that is, toward the Sagittarian crossing point of the Milky Way and the ecliptic. As with the Thieves' Cross, the Hawk constellation is closely associated with the Milky Way: The "body" of this constellation actually lies along the Milky Way. As such, it appears to fly along the Milky Way, its head pointing southward. When we chart out the relationship between the Hawk and the Thieves' Cross constellations, a hidden astronomical player becomes quite apparent.

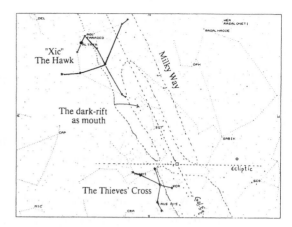

Diagram 90 visually illustrates the legend shared by Tedlock's teacher Andrés Xiloj, that of the Hawk dropping the Cross into the ocean. While Swainson's hawks are migrating south overhead in late October and early November, the Hawk constellation can be observed passing through the zenith just after sunset. Throughout the night, the Hawk-Cross combo moves westward, so the Hawk appears to carry the Cross up

Diagram 90. A Hawk, a Cross, and a Mouth: dark-rift as mouth

and over the sky. Before sunrise the Cross sets in the southwest and the Hawk sets almost directly west. The Pacific Ocean lies to the southwest of Momostenango, so the cosmic myth conforms to local geography. In this way, the Hawk is understood to drop the Cross into the ocean. By December the Hawk sets at sunset and the myth is no longer played out in the sky.

In charting the actual movements of this cosmic myth with astronomy software, I noticed that the dark-rift in the Milky Way connects the two constellations.

Diagram 91. Dresden Codex *flood scene*

In the myth, the Hawk carries the Cross in its mouth. Ethnographic information identifies the dark-rift as a portal to the Underworld, and related contexts suggest that the dark-rift was also understood to be a mouth. Given the astronomy thus far sketched, the mouth of the Hawk constellation must be the dark-rift.

Based upon this association, we can deduce that the cosmic mouth is also a source for rain in the myth. When the Hawk carries the Cross into the center of the sky, rains come. In the *Popol Vuh*, Huracan, also known as Heart of Sky, destroys a previous World Age when he sends a flood down upon the Earth. A famous scene in the Maya *Dresden Codex* shows a universal deluge pouring out of a deity's mouth.

Heroes of Maya myth often journey to Xibalba (the Maya

Underworld) to wage war on its evil denizens. In the *Popol Vuh*, One Hunahpu and Seven Hunahpu journeyed to the Underworld and when they come to a crossroads, they must choose the correct road. Of the four roads they encountered, only the Black Road spoke to them, saying, "I am the one you are taking. I am the lord's road."[3] They ended up choosing this Black Road, which is another name for the *xibalba be*—the dark-rift in the Milky Way.[4] The point here is that the Black Road spoke—it either has or *is* a mouth—which contributes to the veracity of our identification of the Hawk's mouth with the dark-rift. From this and other Maya sources we have examined, we know that the portal to the Underworld could be envisioned in many ways: It was at least a road and a mouth (and elsewhere it might be a temple door, a birthing passage, or something else). If we entertain the possibility that the dark-rift in the Milky Way was the unchanging celestial core of this many-faceted mythic structure, then we may find many mythic journeys to the Underworld involving different metaphors, but all referring to the astronomical fact of the dark-rift in Sagittarius.

Carvings and images from all over Mesoamerica show a warrior or king emerging from the mouth of a deity monster. This "monster" is sometimes birdlike, though sometimes it resembles a toad or a crocodile. Here, too, we have many mythic transformations and parallel metaphors being expressed. Symbolically, they are all equivalent and refer to the Milky Way. The underlying "fact"—the foundation of the mythic transformations—is the eternally recurring astronomical movement of the Milky Way and the dark-rift observable throughout the year.

The mouth of the Hawk constellation appears to be the background "mouth" suggested by the dark-rift, but the ethnographers who collected the Quiché myth of "The Hawk and the Cross" did not report that it contains an implicit reference to the Milky Way's dark-rift, an astronomical feature that plays an important role in Quiché mythology, Mesoamerican cosmology in general, and the alignment of the Long Count end-date.

THE HOLE IN THE SKY, THE MOUTH OF THE MONSTER

Other Maya groups today preserve myths and folktales that reflect concepts in the Quiché myth of the Hawk and the Cross. This parallelism suggests that there is a common basis for these stories, that each reflects a common, ancient cosmovision. By exploring several of these stories, we can get to the heart of their mythic structures and learn how to cross-compare their diverse mytho-astronomical metaphors.

In one Chortí Maya folktale that resembles "The Hawk and the Cross," a frog wants to see the world from the sky. A bird takes him up in its mouth, high into the sky. But then the frog is dropped and falls back to Earth, getting flattened upon impact.[5] Here, as in the Quiché tale, a bird carries an object into the sky, and then drops it. However, the objects the bird carries are different: The Quiché cross has been replaced with the Chortí frog. Sky-Earth polarity is present in both stories, for each contains an ascending stage and a descending, or dropping, stage.

But how are the cross and the frog metaphors related? In Mesoamerican art, frogs are sometimes depicted head-on, with the arms and legs forming the Kan-Cross symbol.

The frog's mouth serves as the central or fifth direction. The Chortí story may refer to the same astronomy as the Quiché myth—in this case, the frog's mouth is the dark-rift (the hole in the center of the cosmos), and the frog's arms and legs are the four directions formed by the Milky Way/ecliptic cross. The four-cornered frog thus represents the four-directional celestial grid centered on the

Diagram 92. Monument 9 from Chalcatzingo. Frog as Kan-Cross, mouth in center as fifth direction

crossing point of the Milky Way and ecliptic in Sagittarius, which has been identified by Dennis Tedlock as the "four junction roads," i.e., the celestial crossroads.[6]

In both of these myths, the Earth and the sky are connected through the ascending-descending movement of the frog, the cross, and the bird, and these mythic symbols are thus at home in both realms. This dual-nature motif is a common feature of Mesoamerican religious imagery. As one scholar put it, "Supernaturals have many characteristics, one of which is bilocality . . . the most important deities are located in both earth and sky."[7] In Mesoamerican thought, the realms of Earth and sky operate together, following the same cycles. The ascending and descending process in these myths suggests that *time* is an important facet of both realms. Furthermore, distinct up and down movements of stars are a characteristic of the Tropics, whereas at middle and northern latitudes stellar movements appear to move in a circular way, revolving around the North Celestial Pole. These myths thus accurately reflect the steep rise and set motions of stars as viewed within the

Tropics. In Mesoamerica, to the extent that time concepts are derived from sky observations, time is more like a roller coaster than a merry-go-round.

On sculpture from the Pacific Coast of Guatemala and Chiapas, archaeologists have found many images of birds holding a round object in their mouths. This object is probably a corn seed, which symbolizes the sun. The bird is usually depicted in flight.

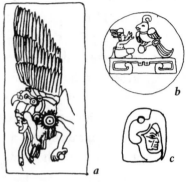

The sun and the cross motifs are directly related in Mesoamerican art and writing. For example, the ubiquitous Kan-Cross glyph denotes the sun in many contexts. The Ahau ruler is a solar deity, and therefore is an avatar of the sun. In the religious beliefs of the Maya from highland Chiapas, crosses are symbolic meeting points between this world and the realm of the dead. In other words, they are nexus points bridging the Underworld and the sky. Like the *xibalba be*, they are doorways to another world. And human beings, having two arms and two legs, are four-directional symbols incarnate, just like the frog. It is well-known that the macaw represents the

Diagram 93. a) Monument 17, Cotzumalhuapa, b) Altar 20, Izapa, c) Head-in-mouth from El Baúl

sun, and in many early Maya images, the bird holds a human figure, probably an Ahau Lord, in its mouth. These carvings probably depict some form of the Hero Twin myth, and thus the lords shown may be Hunahpu or Xbalanque. In any case, these heroes, and all political Ahau (or chiefs), are representatives of the sun. In fact, Hunahpu becomes the sun at the end of the *Popol Vuh*.[8] We can formalize the relational transformation of these symbols as follows: Cross:Frog-Bird:Sun:Ahau-Lord. The frog, with its two arms and two legs, is a cross symbol. The sun is portrayed as a cross in Mesoamerican art, and the Ahau Lord is enthroned on the cross situated at the boundary between the Upper and Lower worlds. This "formula" explains how human beings, with their four arms and legs, are symbols of the Sacred Cross centered upon the dark-rift.[9]

In looking at these various cross forms, we are concerned with identifying metaphorical parallels. Since myth and metaphor often describe astronomical events, we can build a cross-comparative database of astronomical road maps. Although it is difficult to reconstruct any developmental continuity in these representations, or describe the rationale of how these symbols are related, we can draw reasonable visual analogies. For example, the four-legged frog is like the solar lord, who has two arms and two legs; clearly, both symbolize the four-directional cosmos. It is this kind of analogy-based thinking that allows us to acknowledge how these symbols can vary tremendously yet still refer to the same astronomical phenomenon.

Linguistics also can reveal parallels and broaden our understanding of how mythological concepts are related. For example, in the Chortí material an oft-repeated term is *hol txan*. This is related to the Yucatec Maya phrase *hol can be*, the "hole in the middle of four roads." As Maya scholar J. Eric S. Thompson wrote, "*Hol can be* is an expression in the Books of Chilam Balam. Roys considered it to mean the opening (hol) between the four roads, the crossroads (can be)."[10] *Kan* or *chan* means four, sky, and/or serpent, and *be* means road. In other words, the *hol can be* is symbolically equivalent to the mouth of the frog, the hole where the four roads meet, the central fifth direction, the center from which the Maya cosmos emanates and from which Creation occurs.[11] This is about as clear a picture as we can get, and has exciting implications for our decoding of the astronomy in these myths. Hawks, crosses, and mouths point right at the crossroads in Sagittarius, exactly where we find the dark-rift "hole" or "mouth" known as the *xibalba be*.

As mentioned, *hol txan* refers to the same concept as *hol can be*. We can look at how this term is used in the Chortí myths collected by ethnographer John Fought. The first occurrence of *hol txan* in Fought's book is in the folktale called "Belief in Diviners." During a divination for the cause of illness, the speaker says, "Perhaps it just came. Perhaps it was sickening winds, perhaps it was winds over the peaks, it may have been Hol Txan winds, or Hol Txan clouds over the peaks. Perhaps it was hovering clouds, perhaps it was Old Angels over the peaks."[12] Here, *hol txan* seems to be associated with something over the peaks, 'Old Angels,' which probably means pre-Hispanic deities. The speaker continues, "Perhaps it [*hol txan*] is the Great Royal Temple, the Great Major Temple. Perhaps it is the hole where chilate is poured? [The hole where the ceremonial offering of *chilate* was poured symbolized the center of the Earth, the Earth's 'mouth'.] Perhaps our Holy Mother has joined up with the Hol Txan."[13] The story continues in this fashion with the diviner, searching for the cause of illness, reciting a litany of symbolic associations. For certain, mystery surrounds this *hol txan* concept, and the failure of Chortí storytellers to pin down the meaning of this term does not necessarily mean they did not know what it meant. We read elsewhere that *txih txan* means "serpent" in Chortí. This term is similar to its Yucatec counterpart *chic chan*, and *Chicchan* is the Yucatec day-sign that means serpent. This linguistic association reveals that the Chortí "tx" replaces the Yucatec "ch" (this is really a question of orthography; the spelling of the words is different but the sounds are identical). As mentioned, *chan* or *can* means four, sky, and serpent. Thus, *hol txan* seems to mean exactly the same thing as *hol can be*. Another Chortí story implies that the *hol txan* is a source of wind, which suggests a "hole" in the sky through which winds pour—a universal mythological motif.

In the story called "Curing," we are told: "Truly, you are the Kings of death . . . of disease . . . you seek [or search] the Silent Day [the night sky], the silent hour[14] so as to transform yourselves, to Hol Txan over mankind, since your waking is like a thief's presence. . . ."[15] Transformation, a Silent Day, a thief—here we have compelling and familiar motifs. In this last passage, the term *hol txan* is used as a verb, suggesting something like "to rule over," reinforcing the image of a king or a head chief enthroned in the cosmic center. In this light, the earlier mention of "Our Holy Mother" joining up with the *hol txan* is very suggestive. If the Holy Mother is a reference to the overarching cosmos (the Milky Way), then the topmost head chief (the sun) joining with the Milky Way describes a familiar astronomical scenario. And remember, in the ceremonial houses of the Yucatec Maya, the *hol can be* is at the very top, at the center of the symbolic cosmos. Elsewhere, Fought relates that his Chortí informant provided a folk etymology for the term *hol txan*, saying it is "like a rainbow."[16] Among the Chortí, rainbows are associated with the Milky Way because they both arch through sky, and—significantly—the Milky Way is prominent during the time of year when the rains come. Rains, and the croaking frogs that call them, are also associated with the nurturing fertility goddess, the Earth Mother. And the Milky Way, being a part of the four-directional map, is associated with the four color directions (primary rainbow colors).

Finally, there is a little known *hol txan* ceremony that is performed in secret by a man and a woman near a pit or hole in the ground that contains candles. According to Fought's informant, "They expose their genitals, fill in the pit, and thereby put a spell on someone."[17] Here we have the image of sexual union of male and female over the earth-pit, or perhaps a late variant of an ancient rite involving bloodletting from the genitals. Or, this may be a more generic shamanic technique. (Dennis Tedlock writes of a Quiché shaman who advised that a man and a woman seeking his counsel should wear the same shirt for a while, and then he would bury it in order to cure their incessant quarreling.[18]) Overall, the meanings of *hol txan* and *hol can be* operate in parallel and enrich our original reading of the Quiché story of "The Hawk and the Cross."

The term *hol* is found in many Maya languages, and generally means "head," as in chief or "topmost." We should remember that in Mesoamerican politics, "chiefs" or kings were enthroned in the center of the world, a cosmic center that has both terrestrial and celestial aspects; the king is the *axis mundi* uniting all levels. In the Maya village of Santa Eulalia in the western highlands of Guatemala, Holom Wits (head or chief mountain) was the name of one of the four crosses erected at the directional pathways out of town. In the same town, people worshiped an idol called Holom Konop, who was the symbolic head of the village. In the 1920s a controversial political intrigue took place around this figure: It was stolen by people who were against the ancient ways, but eventually it was recovered.[19] This Holom Konop deity is a modern variant of the ancient *Mam*, the year-bearer. Holom Konop also appears to be associated with the Earth Lord, the *dueño del mundo*, the "Earth owner." In the 1920s, ethnographers reported a cave ceremony near Santa Eulalia that involved welcoming in the new year-bearer (the *Mam*), and during the rites the Holom Konop icon was on the floor of the cave.[20] Oliver LaFarge, the ethnographer who visited Santa Eulalia, suggested this deity had a secret function when he wrote that the town shrine dedicated to Holom Konop "receives much attention from the Prayermakers but very little from the ordinary people, perhaps because of the extremely esoteric nature of the Holom Konop."[21]

Recent ethnographic work in the Yucatán[22] identifies the *u hol glorya* as the topmost and central level in the huts built for ceremonial rites (Linda Schele calls it the Glory Hole). These huts are made with four lashed poles (the four directions), tied together at the top. The top thus represents the crossing point, and hung from this central "hole" are religious ropes or cords. As Karl Taube put it, the *u hol glorya* is "a cosmic hole or conduit in the center and zenith of the sky."[23] It is a hole in the center of the crossroads, like the mouth of the frog or the mouth of the Hawk that carries the Thieves' Cross. Again, these mouths and cosmic holes symbolize the dark-rift in the Milky Way. Interestingly, the Chortí and Yucatec Maya share the ceremonial practice of erecting symbolic houses of lashed poles that are tied together at the top.[24]

Whether it be the *hol can be*, the *u hol glorya*, Holom Konop, or *hol txan*, the common thread in all of these phrases is the word *hol*. In one of those strange linguistic parallels, the Mesoamerican word-concept *hol* not only sounds like but also means "hole." But related meanings include "topmost" or "chief" and "conduit." This topmost conduit or offering hole occurs in relation to sacrifice rituals, the chief year-bearer, and is located at the center of the four-cornered cosmic house. The astronomical reference should now be clear. While one location for the offering "hol" could be, as in the Yucatec model, the zenith, another location could be the dark-rift "hole," that is, the center of the Milky Way/ecliptic cross near Sagittarius. Whether it be the zenith center or the Galactic Center, the point is that a dark mystery, the mouth of a monster, lurks within the cosmic center.[25] What this mystery is will become clear when we gaze more deeply into the Galactic Center.

Susan Milbrath provided an important additional discussion of the cosmic crossroads recognized by the Chortí Maya, having determined that this is none other than the cross formed by the Milky Way and the ecliptic. She wrote that the modern survival of the indigenous "Day of the Cross" festival (May 3) is a blend of zenith sun worship directly related to honoring the Milky Way/ecliptic cross, because "it celebrates in thought the zenith position of the sun in conjunction with the Pleiades."[26] She also noted an association between the modern Day of the Cross, the arrival of the rains, and the solar zenith passage in May.[27]

The Chortí Maya considered the center of the Milky Way/ecliptic cross to be "the heart of heaven and earth associated with the navel of the world and the mythic ceiba tree."[28] Being the center of heaven and Earth, the crossing point is thus the celestial marker of an axis that actually extends down from heaven to the center of the Earth. Milbrath encountered and clarified the confusion between the polar center and the zenith-as-center concept,[29] a confusion that results from Hunrakan (Heart of Heaven) sometimes being associated with the polar region. However, ethnographer Raphael Girard, working among the Chortí, also associated the central world axis of the ceiba tree with the zenith.[30] I feel that this conflict can be solved when we accept that Maya cosmology was very complex, and the Maya recognized both the zenith center and the polar center. Myths of a high deity of the cosmic center (such as Hunrakan) apply equally well to both. Furthermore, the mytho-astronomical motifs we have examined clearly indicate a third cosmic center, the Galactic Center. Remember, the Chortí Maya considered the center of the Milky Way/ecliptic cross to be the "heart of heaven and earth," indicating the Galactic Center as the centerpiece to this cosmogonic myth-map. Based upon my synthesis of the corpus of academic studies already completed, my conclusions are reasonable and even self-evident.[31]

More symbolic associations can be added to this metaphorical schema. On some Classic Maya stelae, kings hold the double-headed serpent bar at a slight angle. As mentioned earlier, the double-headed serpent bar is now understood by scholars to symbolize the ecliptic path of the sun and the planets.

According to Barbara Tedlock's ethnographic information, the sky-cross is described as "inclined to the left," an apt description of both the Thieves' Cross constellation and the nearby Milky Way/ecliptic cross. In the diagram, the ruler's body is the Milky Way, and the double-headed serpent bar of rulership is the ecliptic (probably assuming the place of his outstretched arms). The center of this crossroads incarnate is the human heart, the highest sacrificial offering in Mesoamerican ritual. In this example, the sacred ruler does not just sit on the throne symbolizing the cosmic center and crossroads; instead, he *is* the crossroads. And how is the king a cross? We saw earlier how the physical body forms a cross, but there are two other considerations: The sun is symbolized by the cross, and sacred rulers are Ahau Lords, representatives of the solar force. Thus, we have a king-sun-cross association. Most interestingly, we have

Diagram 94. Stela 10, Seibal. Ruler as Milky Way holding the ecliptic at an angle. From Turner (1985:31)

seen that crosses are still recognized by Maya groups as doorways or portals to the Underworld, the realm of the ancestors and supernaturals. Maya kings were not just political leaders, but were spiritual leaders as well—king and shaman—and one of their shamanic roles was to mediate knowledge flowing between this world and other realms. The king-shaman had a foot in both worlds; he bridged realms and was, literally, a doorway between worlds. He was one of the topmost chiefs, or Holom Konops, who reside in the highest cosmic seat—the center of the cosmic cross.

We have reviewed a number of symbolic forms and metaphor-complexes as they appear in Maya folklore and linguistics. We cannot be sure how many of these mythic inflections were intended or recognized by the Maya, but knowing the Maya penchant for word play, analogy, and metaphor, it would not be surprising if everything we have discussed was considered to be, at one time or another, a legitimate mythic transformation. The astronomical phenomena we have examined have multiple representations in Maya myth, revealing a continuity of underlying meaning that suggests a type of metaphoric parallelism — *conservation of referential core*. In other words, because the sources for these mythic concepts are found in the sky, we can identify similarities between the different mythic forms assumed by these astronomical features, as shown in the following table:

Astronomical Reference	*Mythological Metaphors*
Milky Way/ecliptic cross	Sacred Tree, crossroads, king w/serpent bar
Thieves' Cross constellation	terrestrial quincunx, frog, "Thieves' Cross"
Xic (Aquila) constellation	celestial quincunx, hawk, season bringer
Dark-rift in the Milky Way	mouth, road, birth canal, door, crook in tree
Galactic Center	cosmic center, throne, heart, cosmic womb
Milky Way/ecliptic crossing point	navel, umbilicus, center, hole, fifth direction

Diagram 95. Chart comparing astronomical and mythological identities

This careful scrutiny of parallels between mythological motifs can be applied to many folktales. We have looked at several examples, considered linguistic and ethnographic data, and found a common thread running through them all. But I have saved the best for last. In the next chapter we will examine the modern Maya folktale called "The Man Who Was Swallowed by an Alligator," which sheds new light on how certain episodes in the Hero Twin myth were long ago conceived in unexpected yet understandable ways, and became transformed after the Conquest. Ultimately, we once again find compelling evidence for a complex and sophisticated cosmological science that survives within a fragmented, enigmatic folktale.

CHAPTER 15

THE MAN WHO WAS SWALLOWED BY AN ALLIGATOR

The Quiché Maya folktale "The Man Who Was Swallowed by an Alligator" was recorded in the highlands of Guatemala in the 1970s. Told by F. Lucas Tepaz Raxuleu of Santa Catarina Ixtahuacán, it was collected and translated by William Norman at the Proyecto Lingüístico Francisco Marroquín in Antigua, Guatemala.[1] The legend clearly retains certain themes found in the Quiché *Popol Vuh*, which was recorded in the 1550s. Episodes and characters from the *Popol Vuh*, as well as unrecognizable scenarios involving the same characters, are found on ancient monuments at the Pre-Classic site of Izapa (400 B.C.–A.D. 100). Not surprisingly, given this long time span, although these three legends share a similar theme, some of their metaphors are different.

The earliest version of the Quiché Creation myth, identifiable at Izapa, contains motifs not found in the Quiché version but that are present in the modern tale. In the study of epic poetry, redactions (variant versions) often clarify what is really being talked about in the "standard" version. Thus, although a story and its telling may stretch over thousands of years, its transformations and the introduction of new metaphors can be charted. In addition, the modern story may preserve elements from the oldest version that interim versions do not. In addition to ancient associations, post-Conquest influences also are present in our modern story. In essence, what we have is an abridged version of the *Popol Vuh*, revealing alternate thematic metaphors that enhance our understanding of the Maya use of symbol. The modern redaction will add to our ability to cross-compare different metaphors, identify their common meanings, and clarify the astronomical content of Maya myth.

Santa Catarina Ixtahuacán, where our story was recorded, is about seven kilometers south of the Pan-American highway in the western highlands of Guatemala. As the crow flies, it is about fourteen kilometers northwest of Lake Atitlan. The town and the text are Quiché Maya. I have decided to retell the story in my own words, following William Norman's translation. The central events in the story are as follows:

- a man goes to another world
- he meets hostile strangers
- he tricks them, injures them, and escapes
- he returns home with something new

Already we see similarities to the *Popol Vuh*, where the Hero Twins travel to the Underworld, meet with the bizarre Xibalban Lords, trick them, kill them, and return home. The new thing they bring back or bring about is the dawn of the next World Age. Our folktale is filled with humor, so typical of Quiché narratives. Though entertaining and amusing, the story contains important information about ancient shamanism and the practice of undertaking vision journeys to "the other side."

A man goes to another world. They say that there once was a man who left this world and traveled to another one. The man was walking by the ocean, along the edge of the ocean, when suddenly an alligator jumped out and swallowed him.[2] The alligator returned to the ocean and went deep down to the bottom. Inside the alligator, the man saw it was dark and said, "Where am I?" After several days, maybe three, the alligator emerged onto a beach on the other side of the ocean. He lay there, sunning himself by the edge of the ocean. Inside the alligator, the man saw light coming through between the alligator's ribs and said, "Where am I, where have I come to?" The sun was shining inside the alligator. The man had a pocket knife with him, so he slowly lowered his hand into his pocket to retrieve it. Then he slit open the ribs of the alligator at the spot where the light was shining through. From that spot, he climbed out of the alligator. Immediately he knew he was in another world, on the other side of the ocean. The man had crossed over to the other side of the ocean. When he emerged from the alligator he said, "Where have I come to, where am I?" He found himself in another world. And there he began to walk alongside the ocean.

He meets hostile strangers. The man was quite hungry, since he had been inside the alligator for a long time. The alligator had been several days underneath the ocean. It had been several days since the man had eaten so he was very hungry.

As he walked along the edge of the ocean he saw a cornfield. He was so hungry he ran into the cornfield to pick an ear of corn, but it started yelling and screaming. So the owners of the cornfield came running out to the field. The owners were Moors; they say that the people who live in the other world are Moors. They came running to see what was going on in their cornfield. When they arrived, they found the man in their field. The Moors demanded, "What are you doing there, what are you doing to our corn?"

The man said to the Moors, "I'm very hungry because I haven't eaten for several days."

The Moors replied, "Why have you come here, and where are you from?"

So the man explained what had happened to him. "I am from another world. I was walking by the edge of the ocean. An alligator came out and swallowed me up, went back into the ocean and came out here. When he sunned himself on the shore, I saw the light inside the alligator, so I slit open his ribs with my knife. That's how I got out of the alligator, that's how I got here to this world. And so I am now very hungry, I haven't eaten."

And the Moors replied, "But what do you want with our cornfield? Why do you want to hurt our corn?"

"As I said, I am very hungry. In our town we eat. We make food from the dried ears of corn, or we roast the green ears of corn, and we eat them."

The Moors were very astonished, and asked, "Why do you eat?"

The man said, "We, we eat corn."

"So is the corn good for eating?" the Moors asked.

"Yes, yes, it's good to eat, that's why we eat it. Don't you eat it?"

The Moors said, "No, we don't eat the corn, we just smell it and get full that way."

The man replied, "It's not like that with us. We eat corn, we eat food, we eat all kinds of edible things: bread, meat, fruit, and all sorts of things."

And the Moors say,[3] "Why do you eat? We don't eat like that, we don't eat corn, it's the smell of the corn that makes us full. That's how we get full. How do you manage it? Is there then someplace for it to come out?"

He tricks them, injures them, and escapes. And the man thought and said,

"Well, yes there is, because we had our anuses perforated. First it's slit with a knife, and then it's pierced with a poker. Then when we squat, out of the hole comes our excrement. We can eat all types of things."

The Moors say, "Oh, okay. But we aren't like that, we don't eat, we can just smell the food and get full, always."

So the Moors gave permission to the man to pick some of the corn. He roasted it over a fire and ate it right in front of them. The Moors were amazed. After the man had finished eating the corn, he squatted in front of them. They were quite amazed at the man when he squatted. The man said, "See, I eat things and they come out. If we could find a way, you could eat too. Haven't you done anything to your anuses? If you want, we could find a way to perforate yours like we do in my town. There, we have all been perforated. Then you could do like us, you could eat all kinds of foods."

"Yes, we want to eat," said the Moors, "but we don't have anuses, there's no place for it to come out."

"Well," the man said, "You saw me eating and it came out. I'm not just lying to you." "Oh, yes," the Moors replied, and they were completely fooled by the man. "Could you perforate us?"

And the man said, "Well . . . maybe, if . . ."

"Please," exclaimed the Moors, "please, do us the favor, perforate ours."

"All right," said the man. "Do you have a poker I could use to perforate your anuses?"

"Yes, we do," the Moors replied, and they found a poker and gave it to him. The man sharpened the poker and then put it in the fire to make it hot. "Bend over," he said to the Moors. And since they wanted to eat all kinds of food, they said, "All right." So the man began to perforate the Moors, inserting the hot poker between their buttocks. He perforated one of the important Moors, the Moors' Father. The man thought of something while he did this. "Oh no," said the man, "I didn't bring any medicine." The important Moor whom he had just perforated said, "Oh! I'm dying of pain! What am I going to do?"

"I have some medicine at home," the man said, "but I didn't bring it. You know how I got here, inside an alligator, so I couldn't bring any medicine, it's in my home town."

The Moors say, "If only there were some way we could get your medicine back here from your town."

"If only someone would go get it," said the man.

"If only there were something we could use to stop the pain," say the Moors.

One Moor wonders, "Who could we find to go with you to bring back the medicine?"

"I don't know," said the man. "My medicine at home doesn't even make a scar, it just stops the pain once and for all, and forms a hole."

And they all say to him, "Then we better find you a horse right away, because we need the medicine now. Please hurry. There is the Ma'ts, and he'll be a good horse for you, you can ride on his back."

The horse they call Ma'ts is really a deer. The Moors went and asked the Ma'ts for the favor. They said, "If you are willing, please do us a big favor. Go on a trip." The horse asked, "Where?"

"Across the ocean to another world; carry the man to get his medicine. He perforated several men and they are dying of pain. We need the medicine now."

"Oh, of course," said the Ma'ts, "certainly I'll go, that's fine."

So the Ma'ts went with them. The Moors said to the man, "This is Ma'ts. He will be your horse, you can ride on his back." The man said, "Fine," and mounted Ma'ts. Then they went out on top of the ocean. They were well out over the ocean when the Moors started yelling to Ma'ts, saying, "Ma'ts, come back, our Father is dying! Come back right away, we say! Ma'ts! Our Father is dying." But Ma'ts couldn't hear them, since he was running at top speed on top of the ocean. He asked the man what the Moors were saying. The man said, "They say, hurry up, go faster!" "All right," said Ma'ts, and he ran on top of the ocean. He hurried along on his way on top of the ocean. They crossed over the ocean, they crossed over into this world. If Ma'ts had heard them yelling for him to come back, he would have gone back right away. Since he couldn't hear them clearly, he asked the man he carried what they were saying. But the man didn't tell the truth, since he knew that the men he had perforated were dying. So he just told Ma'ts that they said to hurry up. If Ma'ts knew, he would have gone back and the man would be killed. The man knew what was really going on, so he didn't tell Ma'ts. He didn't have any medicine, he had just tricked them. That is why he didn't want to return.

He returns home with something new. The man and Ma'ts crossed over. The man said, "Thank you for carrying me across the ocean, you brought me all the way back to my town. I am home. Whether or not you go back, it doesn't matter. I've won. I crossed back over to this side. Thank you. I'm not going." If the man returned among the Moors, he would be killed immediately. Because he had perforated the Moors but didn't return, they must have all died of pain. That's all that happened. He didn't return with any medicine, he just fooled them. And he definitely came back to his home town.

Now, as for Ma'ts, if he returned he would certainly be killed too. He decided he would not go back, and stayed here for good. That is how the deer arrived in this world long ago. They say that there used to be no deer here, that they were with the Moors in another world. The man rode the deer here when he came back over the ocean; that was how he crossed over.

This is how it happened. First, the man was swallowed by an alligator. Then he was spewn up by the alligator.[4] Next, he perforated the Moors, and finally, he used a deer to ride back over the ocean. According to our Mother-Fathers, that is what happened to the man, a long time ago.

METAPHORS AND MEANINGS

This story contains metaphors found in other world myths. For example, a man traveling to another world recalls the shamanic journey to the Underworld. The belly of the sea monster (the Jonas/whale motif) is a common symbol of the center of the cosmos, and partakes of universal or archetypal themes in the hero's quest. In Siberian shamanistic vision rites, the goal was to enter another realm through the Pole Star. In many mythic narratives, the sky is likened to the ocean; the mirroring of sky and Earth is thus emphasized through this parallel between opposite categories.

In our folktale, the alligator is the vehicle of travel to the Underworld. To Mesoamerican shamans, the caiman was a totemic spirit companion aiding in divination and Otherworld journeys. After going to "the bottom of the sea" (i.e., the top of the sky) and being gone for about three days, seeker and vehicle arrive in the Otherworld. There, the seeker cuts open his vehicle, meaning that he cannot return by the same way. Two other meanings are present here: Emerging from inside the alligator is a symbolic rebirth, and cutting the alligator open with a knife recalls the deity sacrifice necessary for Mesoamerican cosmogenesis. A new world is found (or manifests) and the cause or vehicle of that manifestation (the alligator) must be sacrificed to complete the world's "birth". This is similar to the Western philosophical concept of Emanationism, wherein the One God must fragment Itself to manifest in the multiplicity of beings which comprise Its creation. Significantly, just prior to the man's "birth," the sun shines in the alligator's stomach. The inference here is that the sun is in the alligator. But the man is really what is inside of the alligator, suggesting that he is really a solar hero, representing the sun. We should recall here that the alligator (the "cosmic monster") is the Milky Way, and its mouth is the dark-rift. If this astronomical symbolism is accurate, the meaning is that the sun (the solar hero) is "in" the dark-rift (the alligator's mouth) at the moment of cosmogenesis, which describes the Galactic Alignment on the Long Count end-date in A.D. 2012.

Now the real adventure begins. The man asks "Where am I?" but this is not just a casual question. This, I believe, is really intended as a hint for the audience. The sense is that one must consider this event very carefully, for perhaps something more profound is hidden here. Where is this "other world"? Is it the Xibalban Underworld of the ancient Maya? Is it the strange homeland of the Spaniards (the Moors), across the ocean? Or both at the same time? This multilayered technique of storytelling makes the listener perk up and think more deeply. And the statement is repeated three times even before the strange aliens are encountered. In this inevitable encounter, the question is answered. Yes, he has arrived in the ancient Maya Underworld. However, the Lords of Xibalba are now the Spanish foreigners who follow strange customs. Likewise, in the *Popol Vuh*, the Hero Twins journey to Xibalba and confront the Dark Lords of the Underworld. The Twins were summoned because of their loud ballplaying, which disturbed the Lords. The Mesoamerican ballgame is replete with corn-god symbolism, and in our folktale the yelling of the corn arouses the "Moors". And initially they are hostile.

The wily man thinks of a way he can trick these strangers when he discovers that they do not eat food. They do not eat the way humans do; they get full by just smelling the corn. In Maya ceremonies, incense is burned as offerings to the ancestors who live in Xibalba and to "feed" the beings living in other realms. And this practice is of great interest to the modern Tzutujil and Quiché, who maintain the world by feeding deities with incense offerings, a sacred fragrance and a subtle food. The point here is that the ancestors and other denizens of the Underworld live on the fragrance of incense offerings. Thus, the Moors, on one level, are quite clearly equated with the denizens of the ancient Maya Underworld, the Lords of Xibalba. At the same time, they are in fact called Moors, which is a diplomatically indirect way that Indians have of referring to their Spanish overlords. And, like the Lords of Xibalba, the Spaniards/Moors are strange and, quite frankly, evil. They follow strange customs—they don't even have anuses!

Here the story takes on a kind of reverse moralism, tempered with a mocking bit of vengeance. With veiled symbolism, the Quiché story offers to teach a lesson by giving the Moors a dose of their own medicine. The Indian experience in Guatemala has been one of torture and genocide, Janus-faced social policies in the name of good intentions. A foreign world with strange customs was foisted upon them, and there was no follow-up by the Moors when things did not turn out as promised. The "hot poker" evokes metal rods and Spanish branding tools (tools of torture), as well as the pre-Hispanic stingray spines used in bloodletting. But overall, with characteristic mocking humor, the anus-perforating episode simply means, "Well, up yours too!" As in the mocking Dance of the Conquistadors performed every year by indigenous people in Guatemala, the roles are reversed to safely express the real story. The lesson is: Do not force your evil ways on us without taking responsibility for the effects of your actions—a sobering message indeed.

The man is clever, and pulls a fast one on the alien beings. In shamanic journeys, the journeyer must often deal quickly and effectively with entities met, and the truly heroic sage not only comes back in one piece, but brings something back with him. In the *Popol Vuh*, the Hero Twins encounter the bizarre Dark Lords, overcome all their trials, and ultimately trick them with their clever magic. And the metaphors are violent. The Hero Twins end up sacrificing the Lords of Xibalba and do not revive them as promised. They did this to avenge the death of their father, One Hunahpu. Their father was killed in Xibalba, and they tried to bring him back after defeating the Lords. The *Popol Vuh* is strangely garbled at this point, and does not match the successful resurrection of One Hunahpu as portrayed on Classic-period ceramics and at Izapa. Again, the reason for this is that we are dealing with many versions of the *Popol Vuh* Creation myth, occurring through a two thousand year history. Nevertheless, what we have preserved in our modern folktale is the motif of reviving the ailing or dead father.

In the folktale, the theme of the dying father also is present, but strangely reversed in that it is the Moors' Father whom they want to revive or save. They sense that the deer is going for good, and it was believed that when the spirit companion (the *nagual*) departed, the person was sure to die. The Moors' Father was probably thought of as a Mother-Father, that is, a head shaman.[5] The totem spirit of the head chief was stolen, a cause for great anxiety. Shamanic curing often involved calling back the ill person's lost *nagual*, an animal spirit-companion that one is attached to at birth. Likewise, an evil shaman could steal another person's *nagual*, which would result in death.

Finally, the man of the folktale escapes back home, but not in the same way as he came, for his earlier vehicle of transport was sacrificed. This represents a total commitment to the journey. With his own wits, he must find a way back from the alien realm. In other words, he must bring something back with him, a new knowledge symbolized by the deer. The deer is a sacred being to the Maya. Like the caiman, the deer was a spirit ally of the shaman. Amazingly, this is also true for Siberian shamans and their reindeer, a partnership that involves the visionary use of *Amanita muscaria*, a psychoactive mushroom. The deer was used like a horse to ride over the ocean. Earlier, the alligator went "to the bottom of the ocean"; now, the deer takes the man "over the top" of the ocean. This suggests a cyclic process of some kind—of going and returning on the journey.

While the deer is indigenous to the Americas, the horse is not, but the two are matched in the folktale. "They say that there used to be no deer here, that they were with the Moors in another world." And it is true that the Spanish introduced horses to the New World, which the Maya probably perceived as the Spaniard's animal spirit companions. Indians adopted these as their own animal companions, but the deer is the archetypal and shamanic basis of the relationship.

In the *Popol Vuh*, the Hero Twins "bring back" the dawn. Among some Maya, the morning star apparition of Venus just before dawn is called the Deer Star.[6] Furthermore, the day-sign Manik (Deer) is one of the four year-bearers of the 260-day tzolkin calendar followed by the Quiché. The deer was and is very much a part of Maya religion, calendrics, and cosmology.[7]

Archaeologist William Fash uncovered a Middle Classic tomb at Copán during his excavation work. This elite burial contained a shaman who was treated with great honor. His tomb contained many artifacts, including stingray spines, a hopelessly deteriorated bark-paper codex, quartz stones, magnets, and the bones of his animal spirit companions—*a deer and a caiman*. As related by Fash, the circumstances of his discovery were bizarre. Several days after finding this amazing cache of artifacts, including the bones of the shaman himself, Fash suffered a serious injury that required surgery. The local people in the village of Copán were convinced it was caused by the shaman, and dubbed him El Brujo, The Warlock.[8]

The shaman's tomb at Copán demonstrates that the deer and the caiman had a specific meaning for the shaman. Perhaps one was used on the outgoing journey (the caiman), while the other was used to return (the deer). This is what the folktale suggests. One of the artifacts found in this prestigious shaman's burial was a bowl with a lifelike face carved on the handle, which Fash muses might be the shaman himself.

The Quiché Maya people who preserved "The Man Who Was Swallowed by an Alligator" may have come from Copán.[9] Quiché migration accounts in the *Popol Vuh* relate that they came from a "great eastern city" that used a bat as its emblem. A bat is contained in the glyphic placename for Copán. As such, we might even imagine that this Copán shaman is the man of our folktale. The heroic rider of otherworldly deer and passenger in cosmic caiman, he and his story might have been preserved for centuries. Overall, his life adventures were probably seen to fit the pattern of the Hero Twins.

ASTRONOMICAL SYMBOLISM IN OUR FOLKTALE

This short but rich folktale provides many metaphors that we can compare to similar motifs found elsewhere in Mesoamerica. In general, it seems that this folktale creatively maps the events of the Conquest onto the ancient Hero Twin myth, and preserves a very ancient context involving shamanic journeys. Shamanism is still a central feature of Maya religion, clearly present in Quiché divination and ritual. One metaphor present in the folktale is the alligator, and perhaps the single most important metaphor in the folktale is the alligator's mouth, which is portrayed as a portal, or vehicle of transport, to the Otherworld. The Quiché, as frequently noted, equate the Underworld road with the dark-rift in the Milky Way. The same is true of the mouth of the jaguar, which is another Earth deity, and jaguar-mouth symbolism is found on the oldest Mesoamerican carvings going back to the Olmec. As such, I do not believe that the presence of the alligator-mouth metaphor in the modern folktale is a recent innovation. Even though it is not present in the *Popol Vuh* version, it is clearly ancient.[10] On the other hand, one passage in the *Popol Vuh* relates that the Black Road "spoke" to the Hero Twins, indicating that the dark-rift was, in fact, thought of as a mouth.

Alligators' mouths and toads' mouths were important symbols at Izapa, where the first representations of the *Popol Vuh*/Hero Twin myth are found. In the *Popol*

Vuh, the method of going to the Underworld is via the Black Road, the *xibalba be*. I feel that the Black Road motif was a later replacement of the original mouth symbol, perhaps appealing more to the Quiché mentality. However, the alligator mouth and the Black Road both refer to the dark-rift in the Milky Way, which was understood as a cosmic portal to the Underworld at the center of the celestial Crossroads—the top and/or bottom of the "ocean." Considering the nature of the alignment that occurs on the Long Count end-date, anything that elucidates the mythical transformations of the dark-rift contributes to our understanding of Maya cosmogenesis. "The Man Who Was Swallowed by an Alligator" is about the shaman's journey into another world and his quest for new knowledge. As we know, Maya kings undertook these arduous journeys themselves, often with the aid of vision-producing plants and elixirs. They sat on their thrones, deep within the ceremonial temple, and passed through dimensions of time and space known to only a few. Mushrooms were a common plant used to alter consciousness, and archaeological evidence demonstrates that a vigorous and widespread mushroom cult existed in southern Mesoamerica when the Long Count and the Hero Twin myth were being formulated. Consequently, shamanic tools of vision are keys to understanding the context in which the Long Count was discovered. How did these sacred plants contribute to the Mesoamerican worldview? And how many different types of vision-producing substances were there? It is time to enter deeper into the world of the ancient shaman-astronomers, those intrepid cosmonauts who devised the Galactic Cosmology of the Long Count end-date.

CHAPTER 16

SHAMANIC TOOLS, THRONES, AND BIRTH PORTALS

The use of visionary substances in shamanistic rituals has a long history in Mesoamerica. The archaeological record highlights a period between 600 B.C. and A.D. 100, which corresponds to the development of Maya culture and calendrics, during which visionary substances were used and revered on a large scale. The development of the Long Count calendar took place during this Pre-Classic period, and it just so happens that a vigorous mushroom cult existed in southern Mesoamerica at this time.

MUSHROOMS IN THE MIST: AN ANCIENT PRESENCE

In the 1950s, pioneer mycologist Gordon Wasson discovered a surviving mushroom cult among the Mazatec Indians in Central Mexico.[1] Evidence for pre-Conquest use of mushrooms among the Mixtec and Mazatec comes from the *Codex Vindobonensis* and other Central Mexican picture books, where mushroom rites are depicted.[2] The Mazatec Indians of Oaxaca still use psilocybin-containing mushrooms, as well as other mind-altering substances such as *Salvia divinorum* and *Datura*, commonly called Jimsonweed. Many other groups in Oaxaca, Veracruz, and other areas of Mexico continue to use visionary plants. In southern Mesoamerica, hundreds of miles southeast of the Mixtec domain, there is little evidence that the Indians currently use entheogenic plants. Still, it is apparent

that a widespread mushroom religion once existed throughout the highlands of Chiapas and Guatemala and their Pacific coastal regions. For example, more than two hundred ceremonial "mushroom stones" and pottery effigies have been found throughout the Izapa region.[3]

At Kaminaljuyu, Guatemala, a ceremonial cache of nine mushroom stones was found in an elite tomb dated to roughly 750 B.C. They may represent the nine Lords of the Underworld, and suggest that mushrooms were used by the elite ruling class. This is not surprising, because kings were also high shamans, who had the responsibility of communicating with the ancestors by undertaking visionary journeys. In general, psychoactive mushrooms clearly played

Diagram 96. A mushroom stone from Guatemala, circa 300 B.C.

an important role in the religion and cosmology of the pre-Maya people of highland Guatemala and surrounding areas.

Diagram 97. Mushroom stones that resemble psilocybin-containing mushrooms

Mycologists (fungi specialists) recognize a distinct difference between two psychoactive mushroom species: *Amanita muscaria* and the psilocybin-containing mushrooms. The former contains muscimole as a psychoactive compound, whereas the latter contains psilocybin, which is considered to be the more powerful psychoactive. The *Amanita muscaria* mushroom (also known as the fly agaric) is distinctive in that its red caps usually open wide and are topped with prominent white spots. Psilocybin mushrooms are more rounded or bell-shaped and have smooth cap surfaces. The mushroom stones in the diagram above most closely resemble the psilocybin-containing mushrooms.

In his translation of the *Popol Vuh*, Dennis Tedlock discusses references to mushrooms, addressing an academic debate over whether *Amanita* or psilocybin mushrooms were the ones used by Maya shamans.[4] The reference to a mushroom in the *Popol Vuh* may be a memory of the ancient mushroom religion in the highlands, but was the religion based in psilocybe mushroom use or *Amanita* use? Maya shamans were no doubt aware of both, as *Amanita* is still widely used today as an inebriant by shamans in Asia, Siberia, and North America. None of the mushroom stones resemble *Amanita*,[5] but what appears to be an *Amanita muscaria* mushroom appears in a page from a Maya codex, shown below.

Although this evidence is persuasive, *Amanita* was probably not a favorite among shamans because it is unreliable as a powerful entheogen and the quality of its effects vary widely from region to region and from season to season.

An argument against the presence, let alone the use, of psilocybin mushrooms in pre-Conquest Mesoamerica hinges upon an important requirement that psilocybin mushrooms need in order to germinate. They are coprophilic, that is, they prefer to grow on the dung of ruminant animals such as cattle. The problem is that cattle were brought to the New World by the Spaniards. Anthropologist Peter Furst addressed this problem, and offered a solution: "The only animal that would seem to fit this probable requirement is also one that played an extraordinarily prominent role in Mesoamerican belief—the deer."[6] Many species of deer, of course, are indigenous to the New World. Symbolic and mythic associations between deer, the Underworld, and death are present in Maya religion. In fact, the shaman in the Quiché Maya folktale "The Man Who

Diagram 98. A possible Amanita muscaria *mushroom in the Maya* Madrid Codex

Was Swallowed by an Alligator" used a sacred deer to transport himself back home, over the cosmic ocean. The association between deer and the otherworldly journey inspired by mushroom use is significant. The deer is one of the most popular *naguales* (animal spirit companions) claimed by Maya shamans. As Furst wrote, the deer was probably seen "as the magical progenitor of the vision-producing mushroom."[7] Based upon these ideas, we can surmise that to "ride the deer" was a Mesoamerican metaphor for mushroom intoxication, which in fact is the case among Siberian shamans today. Overall, the argument that *Amanita* must have been the only psychoactive mushroom used in ancient Mesoamerica because psilocybin species could not have survived there prior to the arrival of Old World cattle is not well-founded.

BEYOND PSILOCYBIN

In addition to mushrooms, many other mind-altering plant substances were included in the ancient Mesoamerican pharmacopoeia of shamanic tools. Modern Quiché diviners use the seeds of the coralbean *palo de pita*, which is of the species *erythrina*,[8] as divining tools when they count the days for clients, and bone setters use the leaves of this plant to facilitate healing.[9] Infusions prepared from the coralbean are said to provide an effective sedative. It is not clear whether large doses of infusions from this plant are psychoactive, or if special methods of preparation would render it so. Bright red in color, the Maya call the coralbean seeds *tz'ite* seeds, and, interestingly, they also served as markers in the Aztec board game called *Patolli*. The coralbean's prominent standing in Quiché divination, being the very markers with which the days are ritually counted, suggests a long association with shamanism and magic.

Other shamanic vision techniques are quite bizarre, as evidenced by the tradition of "vision quest through enema."[10] By taking infusions of psychoactive substances directly into the rectum, shamans could avoid the turbulence that these brews sometimes inflict on the stomach.[11] Depictions of enema jugs and the procedure itself are found on Mesoamerican ceramics and sculpture.

Diagram 99. The enema jug and the procedure

The enema ingredients included Balche (mead fermented with the bark of the *Lonchocarpus* tree), maguey, *Datura*, and tobacco, and alcohol-based infusions may have been mixed with hallucinogenic substances. It is interesting to note that imagery associated with the vision-enema includes a facial expression dubbed "the howl." On one level, this may be the expected reaction when gourds are shoved in unaccustomed places, but it also suggests the singing and chanting performed by South American shamans to induce specific states and experiences, much like the overtone singing used by Siberian shamans to create unusual auditory and visionary phenomena.[12] The "howl" expression also resembles the Ahau day-sign glyph.

An endless array of psychoactive plants has been identified recently by independent ethnobotanists doing serious work in the field. Marlene Dobkin de Rios records other psychoactive plants that Mesoamerican shamans

Diagram 100. Ahau glyph and a "howl"

may have used to enter altered states of consciousness.[13] For example, the ubiquitous waterlily. An African representative of the waterlily genus is used as a narcotic among African tribes. The waterlily is often associated with death symbols in Maya art, and the complex of beliefs associated with this motif is similar to those connected with maize symbology. Many different types of entheogenic plants have been found in modern-day Mesoamerica, but our interest is, again, on the context in which the Long Count was invented. For this, we must focus again on the area of Izapa, and its monuments. There, we find a preoccupation with toads and frogs. Toads were sacred animal guides used by Mesoamerican shamans, and at Izapa both frogs and toads were carved on altars. Not surprisingly, like the magical relationship between deer and mushrooms, certain toads are the source of a vision-producing substance—5-MeODMT, a derivative of dimethyltryptamine (DMT), the most powerful hallucinogenic currently known.

THE PSYCHEDELIC BUFO MARINES TOAD

5-MeODMT is found in the "venom" of the North American toad species *Bufo marines*. Underground literature by Albert Most explains how the venom can easily be squeezed from this toad's parotid glands, dried, and smoked. However, this is not to be confused with the foolish practice of "toad licking"—a very dangerous thing to do. DMT also is present in the South American plant *Psychotria viridis*, which, when mixed with the monoamine oxidase (MAO) inhibiter found in the jungle vine *Banisteriopsis caapi*, yields the South American hallucinogen ayahuasca. There are probably many plant sources of DMT in Mexico and Central America but it needs to be combined with an MAO inhibiter to be orally active. Otherwise, DMT from a plant source would need to be extracted and distilled so that it could be smoked. The venom of *Bufo marines* provides a smokable form of DMT-derived 5-MeODMT that does not require much preparation apart from drying. Ethnologist Timothy Knab received information from a curandero in Veracruz on how to prepare venom extracted from the *Bufo* toad to neutralize its more toxic effects.[14] DMT and 5-MeODMT are close chemical cousins, but the subjective effects and response profiles are somewhat different. However, ethnographic and archaeological evidence indicates that Mesoamerican shamans were very interested in the 5-MeODMT they could extract from the *Bufo marines* toad, and depicted it as a vision-producing substance.

As mentioned, toads, like deer, were important totemic animals to ancient Mesoamerican shamans. Peter Furst discusses the symbolism associated with toads among the Olmec, specifically identifying the *Bufo marines* species as one the Olmec found interesting. This toad species goes through an annual molting during which the toad's skin is sucked into its mouth and eaten. As with skin-shedding snakes, the ancient Mesoamericans perceived this process as a symbolic rebirth and renewal. *Bufo* toads also have a distinct cleft in their foreheads, which Furst associates with the cleft heads in Olmec art. By way of the shared cleft motif, the Sacred Toad and the Mother Goddess are related. In fact, on one level of meaning, toads in Izapan art represent the Milky Way Mother Goddess. Furst explored the relationship between the psychedelic properties of toad venom and the mythology of the Hero Twins and the Toad-Jaguar-Grandmother.[15] He also writes that "it is presumably the conceptualization of the Earth Mother as a devouring-regenerative monstrous toad with jaguar characteristics that accounts for the monolithic toadlike Zoomorph B at Quirigua, Altar A at Copán, and the toad altar at Izapa. . . ."[16] For the Olmec, the prominent ritualistic and symbolic place occupied by the *Bufo marines* toad suggests more than a casual admiration. Large quantities of *Bufo* bones were found at San Lorenzo. Tobacco and smoking paraphernalia have been used by New World Indians for thousands of years. If the Olmec knew how to extract the magic venom from their toads, which they most certainly did, then they had the most powerful psychoactive substance at their disposal. This tradition was no doubt shared at Izapa. In fact, certain monuments at Izapa (for example, Stela 6) prove that Izapan shamans used the Sacred Toad as a vehicle for otherworldly journeys into the cosmic center. These toad monuments will provide a piece of the cosmic puzzle as we explore, in Part IV, the Galactic Cosmology developed at Izapa.

NEW DIRECTIONS

Psychoactive mushrooms and other powerful mind-altering substances were being used in the area of Mesoamerica that gave birth to the Long Count calendar. This is an important factor to consider in explaining the rapid transformation from the Olmec to the Maya culture, the rapid birth of a new cultural paradigm. A new version of the old mythology sprang up at the same time—the *Popol Vuh*/Hero Twin myth—and was first recorded on the monuments of Izapa. As discussed earlier, the Hero Twin myth is an esoteric World Age doctrine designed to describe and explain, in mythic terms, the astronomical process by which the December solstice sun converges with the dark-rift in the Milky Way. The Long Count and the *Popol Vuh* arose within a context in which powerful consciousness-enhancing substances were being used. And the Long Count, we will remember, is designed to end during a unique era of astronomical alignment pointing right at the Galactic Center. Could the use of hallucinogens explain how the ancient skywatchers became aware of the Galactic Center? Is it just a coincidence that the Galactic Center is near the crossroads believed by the Maya to be the place of World Age Creation? Could the use of consciousness-enhancing drugs facilitate such awareness? Even though our understanding of altered states of consciousness has improved in the last thirty years, we still have no idea what the limits of knowledge gathered with these visionary tools might be.

And, we must ask, what mysteries does the Galactic Center contain? Did the Maya somehow access information or energies resident there? Does their cosmology reflect information obtained shamanically, intimations of a complexly interweaving multidimensional cosmos? The sheer profundity and nearly impenetrable insights that are clearly present in Maya cosmology suggest this is so. Maya cosmology is based in experiential insights derived from using shamanic tools of vision, and to get an idea of the kind of worldviews that arise in cultures that use these substances as viable sources of information about the nature of reality, we can look to the cosmic models devised by hallucinogen-using Indians in South America—the Desana, Warao, and Kogi.

PSYCHEDELIC COSMOLOGIES

The Desana, who live on the equator in the Vaupés Territory of the Northwest Amazon, developed a complex geometrical cosmology. The founding myth of the tribe, which explains how their equatorial homeland was chosen, involves a supernatural hero who searched for a place where his staff, when held upright, would not cast a shadow. This is true for the equator on the equinoxes. The shamanic image of this event is that of the staff as a ray of sunlight, a divine sperm, which fertilized the earth. The guiding principle of the Desana thus is, as explained by ethnographer Gerardo Reichel-Dolmatoff, a "search for the center," the "Center of Day."[17]

The Desana envision space as a great hexagon bounded by six stars centered upon Epsilon Orionis, the middle star in Orion's belt. Desana shamans also perceive this six-sided shape in the structure of rock crystals and honeycombs. The Milky Way is an important celestial dividing line for the Desana, and the entire celestial vault is envisioned as a cosmic brain, divided into two lobes by the great fissure of the Milky Way. According to Reichel-Dolmatoff, "The Desana believe that both brains, the cosmic and the human, pulsate in synchrony with the rhythm of the human heartbeat, linking Man inextricably to the Cosmos."[18] Here we glimpse profound cosmological concepts developed by the ayahuasca-using Desana. Despite living simple lives as hunter-gatherers in the ever-dwindling jungles of the upper Amazon, the Desana utilize shamanic tools of insight and vision to arrive at a profound multidimensional model of the cosmos.

For the Warao Indians of Venezuela, the Earth is a flat disk floating in the cosmic ocean. A "Snake of Being" resides in the outer sea encircling the earth. The horizon thus serves as the outer rim of the Warao cosmos. The sky is conceived of as a canopy, supported at the zenith by the cosmic axis.

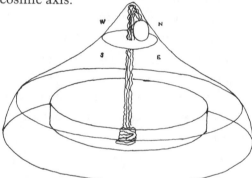

At the base of the cosmic axis lies a knotted snake—the Goddess of the Nadir—that has four heads, each facing one of the cardinal directions. At the highest level of the Warao cosmos, up where the bell-shaped canopy narrows, there is an egg-shaped place of shamanic power. Warao shaman journey to this supernatural zenith by ascending "ropes" of tobacco smoke. Tobacco is the only mind-altering substance Warao shamans use, but the strength and amount they use carry them into the lofty regions of hallucinatory trance. Thus, like the Desana, the Warao shamans' complex multilayered cosmology is informed by drug-induced journeys through the inner planes.

Diagram 101. Warao cosmos. After Krupp (1983:320)

The Kogi, descendants of a spiritual and secretive group in Columbia, also created an astounding and complex cosmology whose religion, philosophy, and cultural traditions are comparable to the high cultures of Mesoamerica.[19] The Kogi utilize horizon observations of the sun as well as solar zenith-passage dates. Like the Desana, the entire Sierra Nevada in which the Kogi live is imagined to follow a hexagonal plan. The corners of this huge rock crystal correspond to six sacred geographical sites, while their counterparts in the sky correspond to six first-magnitude stars centered on Epsilon Orionis. The Kogi retain complex initiation rites involving multitiered levels of a shamanic priesthood, and place special emphasis on astronomical record keeping, which sets them apart from nearby tribes. Although the Kogi place less of an emphasis on the relationship between astronomy and hallucinogenic drugs, the use of vision-producing substances was certainly a factor in the creation of their cosmovision.

These examples clearly illustrate the kind of complex multidimensional cosmologies that arise as a result of using vision plants to induce shamanic states of mind. The exploration of time and space is an eminently human drive. Mapping space gives rise to highly geometrized mandalic systems, a cosmology incorporating the multidimensional ecology of beings living in our world. Charting time is somewhat trickier, and involves very closely watching and recording the changing position of stars. I feel that this temporal aspect of cosmology building was also influenced and, indeed, facilitated by the use of powerful vision plants.

Though the Kogi Indians of South America have a knack for keeping records of sky observations, the scientific endeavor of measuring time seems to have fallen to the pre-Maya people of southern Mesoamerica. Their visionary and scientific skills should not be seen as incompatible. As it says in the *Popol Vuh*, "by sheer genius, by sheer acuity, they got it done." What they "got done," I believe, was the calculation of precession. In accomplishing this, the use of the sacred toad and psychoactive mushrooms apparently played a large role. The vision and dedication required had to be driven by a deep cosmological insight, the focus of which seems to have been events to occur during the anticipated alignment. The Galactic Center is a major player in the end-date alignment, but what is it about the Galactic Center that is so mysterious? Why was it the goal of vision journeys, and what is so "magical" about it?

A BLACK HOLE IN THE SKY

In Joel Davis' fascinating book *Journey to the Center of Our Galaxy*, we learn that we are 26,000 light-years from the Galactic Center.[20] Recalling that the full cycle of precession is 26,000 years, this means that the light, or "energy," reaching us now from the Galactic Center began its journey toward us during the last era in which the December solstice sun conjuncted the Galactic Center—in 24,000 B.C.

We can only wonder what this strange coincidence of numbers might mean. Are we currently experiencing some kind of time resonance with the Earth of 24,000 B.C.? Are we receiving archaic messages through the 2012 time-doorway, knowledge to help us evolve? What is it about the Galactic Center that might make this possible?

The primary message of Davis' book is that astrophysicists now believe there is a Black Hole at the center of our Galaxy, a hyper-dense object in which space and time collapse inward. Black holes were previously thought to be only theoretical constructs, super-large "wormholes" in space from which even light cannot escape. Now, cosmologists are actually finding evidence for the existence of Black Holes, along with other strange stellar beings like quasars and pulsars.[21]

Incredibly, when we look at Maya texts discussing the Creation event, we find mention of the concept of a hole in sky. And the evidence is quite specific. David Stuart and Stephen Houston, epigraphers concerned with deciphering the Maya hieroglyphic script, wrote a monograph on Maya placenames with a special interest in identifying the glyphs denoting specific sites. (For example, the glyph name for Copán consists of a bat.) Some "locations" in hieroglyphic texts, however, do not appear to be geographical—they refer to mythological places. Although it was not recognized in the study, since mythology and astronomy go together, these mythological placenames *refer to astronomical locations*. As I carefully read the chapter on mythological placenames, I found intriguing references to astronomical features associated with the 2012 end-date. Most amazingly, a glyph translated to mean "black hole" plays an important part in Creation events and king-accession rites.

A frequently occurring mythic placename in the Classic-period inscriptions is linked with Creation events, and the glyphic passage in which it is found consists of the elements "glyph-T-128" (which means "sky"), Yax (first or green), and the NAL superfix. NAL is related to the Mayan word *na*, which means both mother and house. Thus, the location of Maya Creation events is something like the First Sky-Mother House. This concept indicates that Creation events happen in the First House of the Mother Sky, the First Era of some great astronomical time cycle involving the Great Sky Mother, the Milky Way. In every case, the text refers to the location of events that happen on the date 13.0.0.0.0.[22] Here I must point out that the Long Count date 13.0.0.0.0 refers, literally, to the end of the current era in A.D. 2012 rather than to its beginning in 3114 B.C.

Now, this is where it gets really interesting. As mentioned, a place-glyph frequently associated with mythological events of the Zero Time is translated as "black hole." Remember, the dark-rift is called the entrance to the Underworld or the Black Road by the Maya,[23] and it appears as a "hole" in the sky. The "black hole" of the Creation text is associated with the Mesoamerican ballgame and its ballcourts, understandable because, in the *Popol Vuh*, there is a strong connection between ballcourts and the Underworld.[24] The "black hole" glyphic designation and its affinity with ballcourts and "entrance to the Underworld" contexts strongly associate it with the dark-rift in the Milky Way.

Furthermore, the black hole placename "when coupled with the Ahau title . . . can also appear in the name glyph of Classic Period Lords."[25] One example from Lacanha appears after an *ut-i* (it happened) expression "in inexplicable association with a 'birth' event that we presume to be mythological in character."[26] In other words, a mytho-astronomical "birth" happened at the "black hole." Interestingly, the Ahau title of rulership (the "king") is intimately associated with the dark-rift "black hole" and this "birth" event.

Another mythological placename is *ma-ta-wi-la* or *matawil*. Matawil, like the black hole, can refer to either a title (i.e., "king") or a location.[27] So, where is the king located? The idea of a throne comes to mind, because a throne in the cosmic center is reserved for kings upon their accession to rulership. In these texts, the celestial throne appears to be identical with the black hole "birthplace"—the dark-rift in the Milky Way near the Galactic Center that, according to modern astrophysicists, contains a Black Hole.

To state these findings unequivocally, we can say that Ahau rulers, in emulation of the mytho-astronomical Creation scenario, claim for their symbolic throne the Black Hole birth canal in the sky. This is why there is an association between title and location attributed to *matawil* and *the black hole*. The king becomes king when he enters the location of his kingship. His accession is likened to a birth, because at that moment a new being—the king—comes into manifestation.

The fact that astrophysicists are now saying that a Black Hole exists at the center of our Galaxy makes us wonder about the real knowledge behind the ancient Maya concepts of Creation and cosmogenesis. They believed that birth/creation (cosmogenesis) happens at the *black hole*. Something very profound and mysterious is going on here. Is it just a coincidence that lurking deep within the dark-rift "black hole" is the very real Black Hole at the center of our Galaxy? If not a coincidence, the dark-rift itself might indeed be the surface signifier of deeper cosmic mysteries, ones that the Maya were well aware of. My novel interpretation is not without additional support from Maya art and literature. Let us look more closely at how the Maya understood the "black hole in the sky."

SKY CLEFTS, SERPENT ROPES, AND TRANSDIMENSIONAL WORMHOLES

The "hole in the sky" is portrayed in Mesoamerican art as a Creation Place or birthplace. It is also called a "sky cleft" and is considered to be a portal to the Otherworld. A "sky cleft" is located in the highest point in the sky, in the center of the cosmic crossroads. (Remember, the Underworld is the night sky.) In terms of actual astronomy, we are talking about the dark-rift near the Milky Way/ecliptic crossroads. Maya concepts of birthing involve deities descending along "serpent ropes" from the sky cleft. In diagram 102, for example, the deity Nine Wind descends out of a sky cleft. In fact, sky clefts are extremely abundant in Central Mexican codices, the symbolism of which can be traced back to Toltec Teotihuacan and, ultimately, to the Olmec cleft-head motif.

Diagram 102. The Deity Nine Wind, from the **Codex Vindobonensis**

Various forms of sky clefts are also found in the Maya codices, demonstrating the widespread use of this very basic Mesoamerican concept. These sky conduits are portals to other realms through which deities are "birthed" and descend to Earth on serpent ropes, bringing with them otherworldly knowledge.

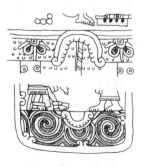

Diagram 103. Cleft-earth and cleft-sky images

In Mesoamerican ideas about world Creation, cosmogenesis takes place via a kind of weaving process. Reality is thus undergirded by a system of threadlike links. In other words, space-time itself is woven together in ways that human beings, stuck within the three-dimensional space-time "fabric" of observable reality, cannot readily perceive. This philosophical model developed by Mesoamerican thinkers is actually extremely progressive, for modern physicists also describe a network of threadlike links between distant places, "wormholes" in space-time that tunnel through a higher dimension. Physicists even joke about making faster-than-lightspeed journeys to distant stars by accessing these holes in space.

Did the Maya access these "wormholes" in their conjuring ceremonies? Did they "birth" into local space-time beings from other realms? Did they travel to distant worlds through these "serpent ropes?" If we may indulge in a little science fiction or, perhaps, metaphysical fact, then we may propose a complex Maya science of shamanically invoking a "wormhole" in local space-time, an opening to the transdimensional realm that ultimately gets its power from the Black Hole within the Galactic Center, and traveling through it to other worlds. The focus of this shamanic

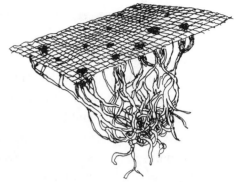

Diagram 104. Wormhole connections in spacetime. After Klein (1982:12)

invocation is the Galactic Center, signified by the visible dark-rift; serpent cords descend and open, providing local space-time access to the Cosmic Source and its eternal riches. In the deepest sense, Maya philosophers conceived of this "evocation of Creation" or "ritual summoning" as a type of birth.[28]

But what does it mean for a serpent cord to descend and open? Who was traveling through the hole in space-time? Is such a scenario just a fanciful fairy tale, or could it have involved the actual activities of Maya kings and shamans? To begin answering such questions, we can consult Maya iconography, which frequently portrays ancestors who have been conjured through shamanic vision rites peering out from the mouths of serpents. These serpents are often shown descending from a sky cleft, and gods and ancestors also are born (or appear) into this world through these sky clefts. As Karl Taube wrote, "It is likely that this cleft is a prehispanic form of the Glory Hole—a celestial conduit. . . ."[29] The Glory Hole, you may recall, is the hole at the top of the cosmic house. So, the sky cleft is a hole in the center of the sky, at the center of the crossroads designating the celestial throne. Since the center of the crossroads is the location of the sky hole as well as of the celestial throne of Maya kings, ascending to the cosmic throne must have a lot to do with vision journeys, conjuring, and magical birthing. However, birthing is the province of the Mother Goddess—what does she have to do with Maya kings?

COSMOS-MOTHER

Archaeologists have found hundreds of beautiful ceramic vases from the Classic Period, many painted with hieroglyphs and mythological scenes. Most of those found are cylinder shaped, except one, which is rectangular. It depicts birth imagery, and was thus dubbed the "Birth Vase".

Mesoamerican scholar Karl Taube examined this unusual rectangular vase and identified "wonderfully detailed views into Classic Maya ritual and mythology pertaining to birth."[30] A young goddess sporting a jaguar ear appears on Side I of the Birth Vase. A sash wrapped around her waist resembles the ropes or sashes used by midwives to facilitate birthing. She is surrounded by several old goddesses, who are midwives. Iconography on the vase suggests they are aspects of Goddess O, Ix Chel. Taube explains that Ix Chel is commonly, and wrongly, associated with the youthful and beautiful goddess when she is actually the old Goddess O, patron of midwives. She appears to have seven or nine aspects. According to Bishop Diego de Landa, Ix Chel is "the goddess of making children."[31] Ix Chel /Goddess O is thus the Great Mother, patroness of all birthing processes.

Diagram 105. Goddess O and birth ritual on Side I of the rectangular Birth Vase

The hieroglyphic text on the Birth Vase refers twice to a birth event and spans a large period of time, suggesting a mythological context. What this reveals is that mythological and biological birthing share the same imagery. On Side I, apart from the birth sash that is wrapped around the pregnant woman's stomach, there also is a rope that she grasps and that is fastened somewhere above her head. In modern Maya birthing practices, the woman giving birth holds onto a "birth rope," which is hung from the central roof beams of the house. Taube writes that "the birth rope is essentially the umbilicus of the house . . . [and] the house constitutes a basic metaphor for the cosmos."[32] We saw this imagery in the ceremonial houses constructed by the Chortí and Yucatec Maya, where the crossbeams symbolize the four directions and the top joint symbolizes the center of the sky. Even the Classic-period city-builders apparently conceived of the cosmos as a great house because the central buildings of large Mesoamerican cities were aligned with the larger cosmos.

In the Yucatec Maya language and elsewhere, the term *na* means both house and mother. (Grandmother is *nan* in Quiché Maya.) For the Tzotzil Maya, the universe was like a house or a table. Furthermore, in social life the house is the domain of the woman, who owns the hearth and tends the fire. Rather than being some kind of domestic drudgery, this position holds great authority. The woman especially adopts this role when she becomes a mother. Thus we see that "house," "mother," and "cosmos" are conceptually related. In other words, cosmos = mother.

This equation between cosmos and mother helps us understand the role of the Milky Way and the dark-rift in the 2012 end-date cosmology. The Milky Way is the arched sky of the cosmos-mother, and the dark-rift is her birth portal. When the December solstice sun aligns with her birth cleft, Cosmic Mother gives birth to the next World Age, the next "Sun." The *xibalba be*, as the mythic birth-canal, is the visible marker of the nearby Galactic Center, the de facto Cosmic Womb.

THE BIRTHING THRONE IN THE HEART OF SKY

Amazingly, in analyzing certain scenes on the birth vase, Taube concludes that the main figure seated on the "birth throne" can be either a Maya king or a pregnant woman.[33] This symbology clearly reveals the conceptual parallel between the king's throne-sitting and the Mother Goddess's throne-birthing. To dispense kingly authority from the rulership throne (the cosmic center) is equivalent to delivering new life from the birth throne (also the cosmic center). The human womb, not surprisingly, is likened to the Cosmic Source in the sky. The source of new beings and the source of the king's authority-to-rule is the same. Apparently, the Old Goddess O (Ix Chel) wields sovereignty over both. Interestingly, Goddess O imagery overlaps with that of the Jaguar God of the Underworld.[34] This makes sense when we recognize the Old Goddess O as a symbol of the Great Mother. The jaguar's mouth corresponds to the dark-rift, as does the Great Mother's birth canal. Her body represents the Milky Way, as does the jaguar's, whose spotted pelt was perceived as the starry sky. Furthermore, the monster/jaguar mouth and the birth canal both represent the throne of the king.

Several thrones from the Pre-Classic era of Kaminaljuyu (now Guatemala City) reveal additional details about Maya cosmology and the king's journey into the cosmic center. These thrones share motifs and physical characteristics such as short, sturdy legs and beveled edges.[35] The "Incienso Throne" (diagram 106) was found recently within Guatemala City, near the ruins of ancient Kaminaljuyu.

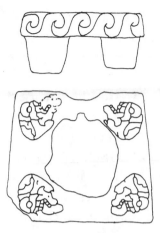

Diagram 106. The Incienso Throne, side and top, from Pre-Classic Kaminaljuyu

The edges of this throne depict wave-scrolls, suggesting that the enthroned king sits on top of the ocean (or, alternately, on top of the sky). More clearly revealing is the crossroads design on the seat itself, showing the chac-skulls of the four directions, with the ruler seated in the fifth, or central, zenith direction. Clearly, this ruler is enthroned at the center of the crossroads, the meeting point of the four directions—in the center of the cosmos. This throne symbology seems to have been universal in Mesoamerica, and in Part IV we will examine important thrones and throne imagery from Izapa that pertain directly to the alignment of the 13-baktun cycle end-date.

Given the meaning of Maya birthing symbols decoded thus far, we may summarize the core of the throne cosmology as follows: *King-shaman is born from the Jaguar Mother and, enthroned upon the lap of the Galactic Center, forever dispenses authority while communing with the sacred source—the Great Mother Goddess.* Furthermore, not to neglect the intimate relationship of all this to the alignment of the Long Count end-date: *The throne of the Jaguar Mother manifests when the First Solar King (the December solstice sun) joins with the Cosmic Mother (the Galactic Center).*

Underlying these activities and interests of Maya king-shamans is the role played by mushrooms and other psychoactive substances in the formulation of the Long Count and the Hero Twin myth around 300 B.C.—indeed, in the formulation of Mesoamerican cosmology as a whole. Given that these tools of vision were in use at that time, we should not be too quick to draw limits on what these king-shamans and astronomer-priests could or could not have accomplished. The Long Count calendar—a Galactic Cosmology—is the unique result of a shamanistic experiment seemingly conducted in secret, over perhaps three hundred years in the dimly understood Pre-Classic era. The tools of cosmic knowledge used by the ancient visionary cosmologists of Mesoamerica to discover and fine-tune their Galaxy-centered cosmovision were the same ones used by seekers of gnosis in other times and places—vision plants. The knowledge encoded in the Galactic Long Count calendar, after being lost for centuries, is now reemerging. Apparently, just in time.

CHAPTER 17

CONJURING CREATION

As we discussed in the previous chapter, both kings and pregnant women can occupy the Maya throne, which symbolically represents the cosmic center and source of life. In the sky, the source of life is the Galactic Center. On Earth, the source of life is Mother. Ideally, the design of Mesoamerican cities reflected the cosmos: The sacred central precinct was the inner zone of the cosmic center from which divine authority emanated. The great central temple was built directly on the sacred center and within it the throne was like the inner nucleus of power, the hot seat and hotline of communion with the cosmic center and source. Despite the astounding sophistication of these metaphors, this all appears to be quaint myth until we understand that shamanic journeys (to the center of the sky) were designed to *truly* invoke and channel the power resident in the cosmic center, which would then be dispersed throughout the city and kingdom. On a visionary or metaphysical level, the communion effected by king-shamans, in their effort to tap the source, was a real event, a spirit-journey to the heart and source in the sky. If this contention seems without precedent, we have only to consider the magical technique, or *siddhi*, practiced by Hindu and Buddhist mystics that involves projecting their consciousness into distant places. As with all successful shamanic journeys, the vision-seeker returns with newly acquired power and knowledge. In Maya thought, this journey was equated with the incredible magic present at the birth of a child, and thus Maya birthing symbolism rightfully overlaps. So the throne was the birthplace of world and child, of king and kingdom, and active on that spot were all the magic forces of birth and death.

Maya kings sat on their thrones, symbols of the cosmic center, and conjured forth the creative inspiration around which the Maya empire congealed, as if from nothing. This conjuring power sustained Maya civilization while it lasted; it was the spiritual conduit to the Heart of Heaven and a connection to the source of life, cosmic knowledge, and political power. Conjuring was an evocation of deity into this realm, a kind of birth, a channeling of beings and energies through the "Grand Central Station" of the cosmic center. How else do transdimensional influences emerge into our world unless they have been brought through the central nexus via a type of conjuring? Creation (the world) manifests, is organized, and is defined through such an act.

The Maya king's throne was the literal hot seat from which he dispensed the power and organizational energy conjured during his journey to the cosmic center. However, the connection could be lost. A story of the Yucatec Maya tells that a celestial conduit "filled with blood" used to connect different Maya cities, and when it broke, communications failed and cosmic order disintegrated. The Maya believed that sacrifices were necessary to keep the transdimensional communication channels open, and these sacrifices were usually performed by the throne-sitting king. Some thrones have small depressions on their sides where blood let from the penis could drip into sacrifice bowls placed below the throne. The parallel between the king's conjuring and the mother's birthing indicates that thrones were conjuring stations, portals of transformation, as well as birthing altars. Conjuring and birthing both took place on what was considered to be a throne, in relation to the Otherworld portal (the cosmic birth canal), and required sacrifices to be successful. In Maya thought, throne-birthing and throne-conjuring were two facets of the same reality.

Imagine the Maya king-shaman seated in contemplation on his stone throne. He has just ingested a large quantity of the sacred mushroom beverage, mixed with cacao (chocolate). Incense burns and he begins to swoon as the ancestors appear. In his mushroom-induced trance he lies back and closes his eyes. In his mind's eye, he journeys into the inner domains of the cosmic house, and is bathed and renewed in the nourishing life-force of the Cosmic Mother's womb. He communes with the spirit beings, receives the sacred teachings, and, hours later, revives and reawakens on his throne. Upon reentry, he delivers or "births" his new vision into local mani-

Diagram 107. Maya king enthroned in the Galactic Center

festation, to vivify and reorganize his realm. As a magician—a symbolic birther—he has successfully conjured Creation, having brought a new being and new knowledge into manifestation.

NEO-SHAMANS UNITE

The question remains, however, did the ancient Maya visionaries actually *travel* into the Galactic Center in heightened states of consciousness? How can we know for sure? The only way to test this theory, of course, would be to repeat the experiment. What would be possible if a team of neo-shamans opened their minds to the Galactic Center? Their shamanistic goal would be not only to find the cosmic center, but to *go into it*. Visionaries today claim to be doing such courageous consciousness calisthenics, and we should look carefully at what they tell us. One such modern cosmonaut is Barbara Hand Clow, who writes of visionary journeys into the Galactic Center in her book *The Pleiadian Agenda*. In Chapter 7, she takes readers on a cosmic journey into the nine-dimensional Galactic Center, where they meet the "Keepers of Time." The universe is revealed as a multidimensionally interwoven ecology of evolving intelligences, set to make their presence known by A.D. 2012. Other inner voyagers have developed shamanic techniques that could be applied to this Galactic task. For example, Michael Harner has identified a distinct state of consciousness he calls the Shamanic State of Consciousness, and teaches how to "journey" while in this state to other dimensions and times.[1] Channelers also claim to be contacting transdimensional beings, and UFO enthusiasts have their own angle on the opening doorway to come. Our culture, with its growing appreciation for the reality of nonmaterial worlds and inner experience, is opening to vast storehouses of universal knowledge that the Maya were very familiar with. If modern neo-shamans were to focus on the Galactic Center as a destination for their next knowledge-gathering journey, they would probably encounter the same insights into time and human becoming that echo, like an inviting laughter, in the crumbling temples of Mesoamerica. But the shamanic quest for knowledge is perennial, universal, and unstoppable. Shamans journey to other worlds with the intent of returning with secret knowledge not otherwise obtainable, and the place they must travel through to get there is the end of time and space. Only in that numinous nowhere can they contact beings from other worlds and times. It is the center and source that, in fact, is found in the religious ideas of all cultures—it is the "Grand Central Station" of Being, Heaven, the Huichol Wirikuta, the Well of All Souls, Tir Na Nog, Xibalba, Mictlan, and the Great Lake of Life.

A GOOD TIME TO CONJURE

What *is* going on? What is the metaphysical meaning of the end-date alignment? My interpretation is derived as much as possible from Maya iconography and calendar tradition. According to Maya calendar cosmology, the end of time and space is 13.0.0.0.0, December 21, 2012.[2] However, rather than it being the end of time and space, we might better speak of it as the *center* of time and space, which reflects the indigenous idea of periodic outflow and inflow around the cosmic center—the Maypole dance of cosmic time and human becoming. The source of space-time takes us back into itself during periods of transformation and renewal, and cosmic time is cyclic rather than linear.

Distinct points in history resonate with the end-date, by way of the harmonics of the Long Count calendar. These "little" period endings were treated by the Maya as rehearsals for "the big one," when monuments were smashed, new kings acceded to the throne, and vision ceremonies were performed. These conjuring activities were most effective when performed at katun and baktun endings of the Long Count, because of the natural resonance these dates have with the 2012 end-date. The miniperiod endings were understood to be resonation points with the far future 13.0.0.0.0 date, for it was believed that the future alignment of baktun 13 signified an open door to the cosmic center, in a sense the arrival of the cosmic source into local space-time, or, in other words, a renewal by returning into the central fire. The local and Galactic planes would then be aligned, opening the way, as the Aztecs said about the end of the Fifth Sun, for the *tzitzimime* (celestial demons) to pour down out of the sky to devour mankind. I will have more to say about the *tzitzimime* in a moment.

Conjuring ceremonies were planned for harmonic katun endings because, although the "door" was not fully open on these dates, at least a time-harmonic to the end-date doorway briefly appeared, which facilitated the channeling of trans-dimensional beings at that time. On the 13.0.0.0.0 date itself, the door will be open—and at that time some people may be more interested in figuring out how to close it. In fact, the current proliferation of fundamentalist closed-mindedness in political and religious discourse is already on the upswing. This may be a reactionary and regressive response to the alignment, which, properly understood, is the opening door to our multidimensional birthright as we approach the Galactic Zero Time of the Maya.

Major resonances to the 13.0.0.0.0 date include the Great Cycle's midpoint, 6.10.0.0.0: April 17, 551 B.C. This date divides the cycle of precession into ten periods of 2,600 tuns (2,563 years) each, rather than five periods of 5,125 years each. Other time shifts are defined by each baktun ending:

6.0.0.0.0	748 B.C.
7.0.0.0.0	354 B.C.
8.0.0.0.0	41 A.D.
9.0.0.0.0	435 A.D.
10.0.0.0.0	830 A.D.
11.0.0.0.0	1224 A.D.
12.0.0.0.0	1618 A.D.
13.0.0.0.0	2012 A.D.

The Long Count is the Galactic Calendar, and the sub-periods of the 13-baktun Great Cycle represent eras of resonance with the end-date. The 2012 end-date heralds a global transformation, and Maya history reveals that each baktun ending was attended by cultural change. European history does not conform as well to the model, probably because European values and goals have been antagonistic to the rhythms of nature. Western philosophy as a whole, as it comes down to us and survives today in the values of materialism, is notorious for battling the natural flow of time and change rather than embracing it to ride the wave of opportunity that transformation offers. Now, with the baktun-13 shift approaching, the forces of change are inescapable, and the entire Earth is unavoidably feeling the effects of global transformation.

THE MONSTERS OF THE END-TIMES

The Aztec myth mentioned above, in which monsters from the sky, the *tzitzimime*, descend to devour mankind at the end of the Fifth Sun, may be a metaphor for a natural process in the evolution of civilizations.

At the pinnacle of any epoch of growth, a society will begin to manifest its shadow aspects, aspects that have been driven into the unconscious. It then becomes a collective challenge to embrace our projections and seek unity through union with what we fear. As such, we should not confuse the projections of the ancient Mesoamerican unconscious (the *tzitzimime*) with our own shadows. Another interpretation is that this myth is not a metaphor, but actually foretells the arrival of autonomous transdimensional entities, ready to pursue their own agendas. Within the New Age movement, channeling strikes me as a warning of this possibility, and we must be careful not to be duped. We should thus challenge and question, in an intelligent, open, and conscious way, people who claim to be conduits for beings from other realms. A friend of mine whose father has been channeling entities for decades told me of a warning his father gave him. He said to be aware that beings contacted through inner doorways are attracted to human energy and desire to extract a unique kind of energy that living, conscious beings have. In the interest of remaining connected for as long as possible, some of these entities will say many things, much of which does not make sense. My friend's words reinforced my feeling that within some of the recent New Age rhetoric it does not even matter if what

Diagram 108. An Aztec Tzitzimitl sky demon, from the Codex Magliabecchiano

is said makes no sense—the very idea that it is the spoken gospel of some transdimensional being or dead Maya king is enough to warrant reverence and loyalty. The danger is that any lapse in our discrimination or good judgment could lull us into an unconscious spell, rather than stimulate our awakening.

The Galactic Alignment may, in fact, be giving us greater access to transdimensional communication with alien intelligences, but the implications of this cannot be simple. Our challenge, it seems to me, is to align ourselves with a selfless desire to understand our place in the greater picture and to cultivate a willingness to work for the benefit of the entire multidimensional ecology of beings of which we are a part.

MAYA COSMOGENESIS: COSMIC MOTHER GIVES BIRTH

In Part III we have explored the nature of the Hero Twin Creation myth, the folklore and traditions associated with it, and its esoteric function as a road map into the Galactic Cosmology of the 2012 end-date. We explored the nature of the vision journeys undertaken by Maya king-shamans and learned that they, like the solstice sun, journey into the cosmic center, where they are anointed and crowned in the raging fires of eternity. In this way, *precession* revealed the solar king's *procession* toward initiation within the Great Mother's cosmic body.[3] The underlying doctrine of Maya cosmogenesis and the 2012 end-date thus involves the rebirth of the world, when the Maya king takes his throne in the birth canal of the Great Mother. This is mythic language for the end-date astronomy: the convergence of the December solstice sun with the Galactic Center.

Understanding these aspects of Maya cosmogenesis may also help us understand our own impending millennial milestone. The precession of the equinoxes is, after all, primarily an *Earth rhythm*, suggesting that internal Earth dynamics could contribute to 2012 being a trigger for the evolution of Earth's lifeforms. At any rate, whether we call it Maya or millennial, we are living today in the shadows of a rare celestial conjunction that parallels, and perhaps explains, our increasing interest in "New World Orders," "post-historic" thinking, and a major shift in what it means to be human. Maya cosmovision, for all its complexity, reminds us of something very simple, that all life springs from the Great Mother. And for the Maya, the Great Mother is located in the womb of the Milky Way, in the nuclear forge of time, space, and the elements that we call the Galactic Center. Perhaps we should look closely at our impending alignment with our cosmic source, fathom its meanings, listen to what the Maya will tell us, and determine what this transformational shift means for future humanity. For the ancient Maya, on the far-future Creation Day, which for us is soon to arrive, Cosmic Mother and First Father join forces to engender a new World Age. The ancient Maya understood that the future alignment would have apocalyptic effects, and designed their World Age mythology to remind us of what is essential, and of what can help us through the transformation. Myth, legend, or ancient message, whatever it is, clearly the Galactic Alignment means we must all remember where we come from, where everything comes from: Mother.

PART IV:
IZAPA COSMOS

Izapan iconography is too important to be left to the iconographers.

— John Major Jenkins

CHAPTER 18

CEREMONIAL CITY OF THE ANCIENT SKYWATCHERS

Everything presented in this book up until now leads inescapably to the conclusion that a profound, sophisticated cosmic knowledge existed in ancient America. We have reconstructed and explored this ancient knowledge in detail, yielding a forgotten history of Mesoamerica's ambitious cosmological endeavors. But where did that cosmic knowledge come from? This too, we can trace and reconstruct. What I call the forgotten Galactic Paradigm seems to have been forged in the minds of brilliant stargazers from a humble ceremonial site at the foot of a monstrous volcano called Tacana. That ancient, sacred place, now crumbling in ruins, is the source of all this Galactic insight. It is called Izapa.

The Pre-Classic ruins of Izapa are located in southern Mexico near the Guatemalan border. Situated at the foot of the Sierra Madre along the narrow Pacific coastal zone, the fertile land of Izapa receives abundant rainfall and is the center of age-old cacao production. Chocolate is made from cacao, and in ancient times the Maya used cacao pods as money. The coastal bioregion in which the ancient city of Izapa is located, known as Soconusco, stretches north through the state of Chiapas and south into Guatemala.

Since the 1930s, archaeologists have identified over fifty carved monuments at Izapa, along with many thrones, altars, and miscellaneous monuments. It is clear that Izapa was primarily a ceremonial site, a place where rituals were performed as scheduled by the sacred 260-day calendar. Most astonishing, and a fact that is very valuable for reconstructing Izapa's cosmological beliefs, is that almost all of Izapa's monuments were found exactly as they were left some 1,900 years ago. Some had toppled, and some were buried underneath layers of soil eroded down from the high volcanic peaks to the north. A few were still exposed to the moist tropical air of coastal Chiapas, shadowed by thick jungle growth. These carved

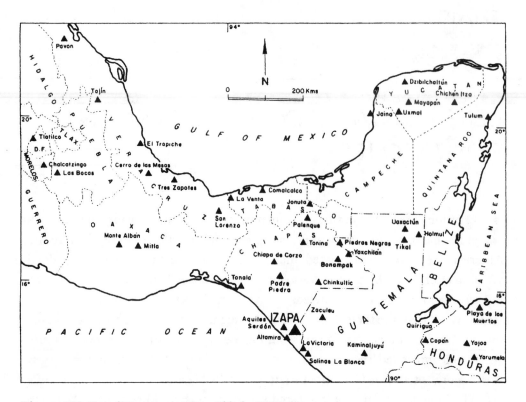

Diagram 109. Map of Mesoamerica. From Ekholm (1969:xii)

monuments contain amazingly complex scenes depicting characters from Maya Creation mythology, and it appears they were intentionally oriented toward important geographical and astronomical features along the horizon, such as Tacana volcano to the north. Tajumulco volcano, home of the ancient Fire God, looms to the northeast, where the June solstice sun rises. Most importantly, a main sight line from Izapa points to the December solstice sunrise, where, as I will show, Izapan skywatchers observed and calibrated the convergence of the solstice sun with the Milky Way.

There are many unanswered questions about Izapa. Why was Izapa located where it is? Who carved its monuments? Were the Izapan people Maya or Olmec? Izapan culture arose in a region that bordered several cultural areas. It participated in the Olmec expansion during the second and first millennia B.C., yet also played into the later rise of the Maya to the north. Scholars have noted similarities in art styles between Izapa and the Zapotec culture of Monte Alban (in Oaxaca), which is not surprising since Izapa is situated along ancient trade routes that connect Central Mexico with lower Central America. In addition, a nearby mountain pass gave Izapans access to central Chiapas and the Guatemala highlands. As a result of this fortuitous combination of geographical circumstances, Izapa had the great fortune of being in the middle of everything. In fact, in more ways than one, Izapa was the center of the early Mesoamerican world.

Early evidence of human occupation at Izapa dates to 1500 B.C. By 400 B.C., the Olmecs had faded, and Izapa was quickly entering the forefront of Mesoamerican history. The Maya civilization would not be in full swing until six hundred years later, and by then Izapa was a fading memory. Izapa experienced its heyday between the Olmec and the Maya—it was a transitional culture in time, drawing upon Olmec traditions and feeding the emerging Maya.

Poised in the center of Mesoamerican time and space, the Izapan civilization clearly had access to great Mesoamerican traditions and ideas. The Izapans had the opportunity to extract a wide range of ideas and knowledge that passed through their front yard with traders, traveling calendar-priests, and large-scale ethnic migrations. In fact, as I will show, Izapa itself was a skywatcher's mecca, a pilgrimage site visited by high-level shamans and calendar-priests from far-off corners of Mesoamerica. By 200 B.C., Izapa was already informed by 1,300 years of Mesoamerican history and cosmology. It is this scenario in which Izapa arose, and it was Izapa's destiny to formulate an advanced understanding of the cosmos. Most tellingly, two great traditions arose with Izapa, strongly suggesting that Izapa was responsible for their creation: the Long Count calendar and the Hero Twin Creation myth. Although we have already explored how these two systems are related, as Izapa's story unfolds it will become even more clear how these two traditions—one calendrical-astronomical and the other mythological—are two sides of the same coin, and point right to the 2012 end-date.

EXPLORATIONS AT IZAPA

In 1924, explorer Robert Burkitt wrote of mounds and carvings he visited in the vicinity of Tuxtla Chico, Chiapas. Since the village of Tuxtla Chico is less than two kilometers from the ruins of Izapa, it appears that Burkitt had stumbled upon the ceremonial city of the ancient skywatchers.[1] Back then, Izapa was in remote backlands, rarely visited by outsiders. Today, the closest large city is Tapachula, some fifteen miles to the north.

By the late 1930s, Izapa was turning the heads of archaeologists, though it was clearly not as spectacular as Tikal, Chichén Itzá, or Palenque. In 1938, archaeologist Karl Ruppert of the Carnegie Institute visited Izapa. Mexican writer C.A. Culebro published some observations regarding Izapa in 1939, including crude drawings of Stelae 1 and 5. Working under a joint grant from the Smithsonian Institution and the National Geographic Society, Matthew Stirling spent a week at Izapa in 1941, and published his findings in 1943. Stirling is the archaeologist who discovered the early Long Count monument at Tres Zapotes, in Olmec country. Mayanists J. Eric S. Thompson and Tatiana Proskouriakoff mention the "Izapan style" of carvings,[2] and in the 1950s a Brigham Young University archaeologist named M. Wells Jakeman published his interpretations of the amazing Stela 5 (see diagram 156).

In four papers on the subject, Jakeman developed his theory that the scene on Stela 5 illustrates events recorded in the Book of Mormon, in which one of the lost tribes of Israel came to the Americas in ancient times. In Jakeman's final analysis of Stela 5, he identified a total of fifteen Old World elements in the scene, providing evidence for the "Old World origin of an influence upon the ancient American civilization."[3]

Jakeman's essays were published between 1953 and 1958, all of them through Brigham Young University (where he was a senior archaeologist). Brigham Young University was founded by the Mormons, who believe in ancient connections between the Middle East and the Americas. Interestingly, an archaeological program to explore Izapa was begun by Brigham Young University in 1960—two years after Jakeman's final paper was published. One wonders if Jakeman really believed his own theory, or if it was just politics to get BYU to sponsor the dig. An interest in finding a Middle Eastern origin of the site to prove Mormon history might have been a motivation. In fact, Matthew Stirling's wife, Marion, who accompanied him on his excavations in the early 1940s, wrote that Stela 5 led Brigham Young University to begin the archaeological dig at Izapa.[4] An interest in a possible Middle Eastern presence at Izapa occurs from time to time in the writings of both Gareth Lowe (the archaeologist who excavated the site) and V. Garth Norman (who analyzed the carvings).

In 1962, almost 2,000 years after Izapa's demise, Brigham Young University embarked upon an extensive four-year scientific excavation of the site. Thirty-six years later, Izapa's role in the development of Mesoamerican civilization and calendar science remains largely unexplored, despite the academic studies of the Izapan monuments that began to emerge in the 1970s. For example, in 1973, BYU scholar V. Garth Norman published his line drawings of the Izapan monuments. Izapa's carvings are in the form of pictures; there are few hieroglyphs. As such, interpretation of Izapa's symbology and cosmovision is approached through iconography (symbol studies) rather than epigraphy (hieroglyphic decipherment). In 1976, Norman's lengthy analysis of Izapan iconography was published, revealing his rare sensitivity to using local topography and astronomy as interpretive aids. In 1980, Norman wrote his Master's dissertation on the astronomical orientations of Izapa, which provided the best information to date on Izapan astrono-

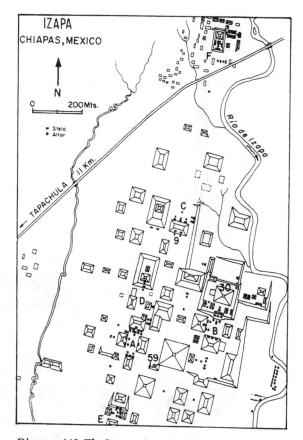

Diagram 110. The Izapan Ceremonial Center. From Ekholm (1969:5)

my. However, his was only a preliminary study that, apparently, was never expanded upon.[5] Although other academic studies also help to clarify the meaning of Izapan symbols and their relationships to other art traditions, those studies were limited to looking at the symbolic or iconographic content of Izapa's monuments.[6] My approach to understanding Izapa's monumental message begins with examining the local topography and astronomy as a basis for iconographic interpretation. Most of the iconographic studies completely ignore the orientation of the monuments within each plaza, their directional relevance to horizon astronomy, and their spacial relationships.[7] As Mayanist J. Eric S. Thompson once said, "Mayan astronomy is too important to be left to the astronomers."[8] In the same spirit, I feel that Izapan iconography is too important to be left to the iconographers.

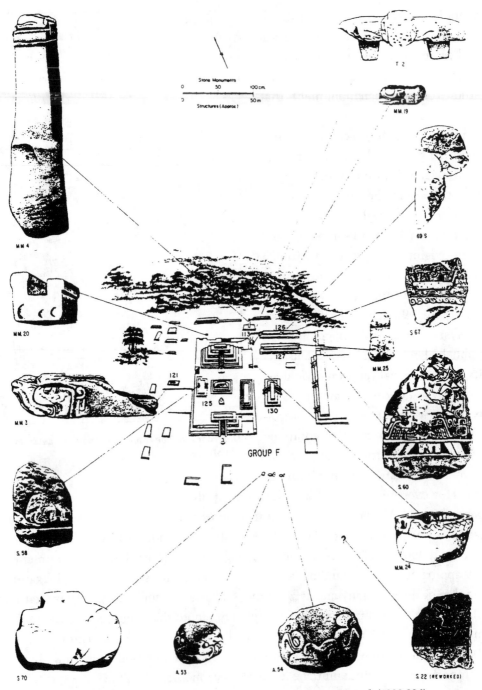

Diagram 111. Monument locations in Group F. From Lowe et al. (1982:224)

IZAPA SITE LAYOUT

In studying Izapa, I closely examined precise site maps and larger topographical maps to understand how Izapa is oriented to the larger environment. I noticed that the site contains a combination of important orientations. For one, the northward orientation is to Tacana volcano. To the northeast, the June solstice sun rises over Tajumulco volcano, the highest volcanic peak in Central America. Possibly the most significant orientation, at right angles to the northward "baseline," is to the rise point of the December solstice sun. Many of the carved monuments face this horizon, and thus the content of the monuments probably has something to do with the December solstice astronomy.

As mentioned earlier, Izapa offers us a unique opportunity for understanding Izapan cosmovision because its monuments were, for the most part, found undisturbed. In this century, their original placements as well as their orientations were identified, especially those of Groups A and B, which were in use between 300 B.C. and 50 B.C. A slightly later occupation was discovered for Group F, about one mile north of the main groups, which may extend into the Post-Classic period. The primary ritual feature of Group F is a ballcourt, aligned to the December solstice sunrise. The monuments in Group F (see diagram 111) apparently were selectively taken from other areas and arranged according to a ritual pattern that we will decode in Chapter 22.

Although the stelae, altars, and miscellaneous monuments in Group F are in poor condition, the carved symbols surrounding the ballcourt are particularly revealing of the deeper symbolism of the Mesoamerican ballgame. The main Izapan stelae groups are close together a short distance south of Group F.

Diagram 112. Map of main groups, central Izapa, primary orientations added. From Lowe et al. (1982:32)

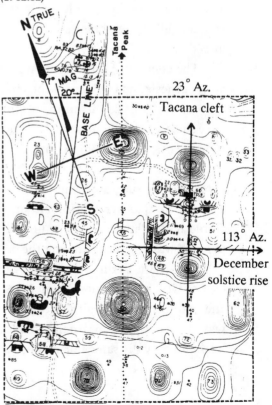

Here we have the orientation data to construct a picture of Izapa's primary cosmological interests. A few important points deserve immediate attention. The Group H "main" baseline points to the peak of Tacana volcano. It is 21° east of true north, and thus, in geodetic terms, it has a horizon azimuth of 21°. The azimuth value of any particular point on the horizon is determined by true north being designated 0°, and, moving eastward or clockwise, dividing the circular horizon into 360 degrees. Since true north is given an azimuth of 0°, true east has a 90° azimuth, true south has a 180° azimuth, and so on. The North Celestial Pole is located along a meridian extending vertically from the 0° azimuth (true north). Thus, the Group H axis points to the peak of Tacana volcano at an azimuth of 21°, that is, 21° east of the North Celestial Pole. The Group B axis, however, points 2° east of the Tacana peak, to a 23° azimuth. Never assuming that these kinds of aberrations are accidental, I looked closely at pictures of Tacana and discovered a shallow cleft a short distance down the eastern slope of Tacana, in fact, roughly 2°. The orientation of Group B, an important monument group, points directly at the cleft.

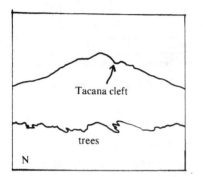

Diagram 113. The Creation cleft in Tacana volcano

The concept of the "mountain cleft" is central to Mesoamerican ideas about cosmogenesis and the birth of the First Father Solar/Maize God. The perpendicular (90° angle) to this 23° azimuth baseline points to azimuth 113°, the December solstice sunrise. Although Group H, which points to Tacana's peak, contains no carved monuments, Mound 60 in Group H is the largest mound at Izapa, and Tacana can be sighted over Mound 25 from Mound 60. In fact, the archaeologists who excavated the site suggested that Mound 25 was intended to conform to the shape of Tacana.[9] Similar pyramid/mountain relationships have been suggested for Cerro Gordo at Teotihuacan, at Cuicuilco, and at La Venta. In other words, the manmade pyramid was designed to mirror the deified volcano or mountain in the background.

Group A is to the west of the main Group H plaza, whereas Group B is to the east of Group H. Groups A and B are Izapa's primary central monument groups, and both contain a wealth of carved monuments, placed and oriented in specific ways to encode Izapan ritual, calendrics, and cosmology. Groups C, D, A, E, and F lie on roughly the same north-south axis. I will restrict my examination of Izapa's monuments to Groups A, B, and F, and only briefly mention, when pertinent, the remaining monuments from other locations. Detailed maps (similar to the one given above for Group F) will be shown later for Groups A and B, and the specific placement of each stela will be clear.

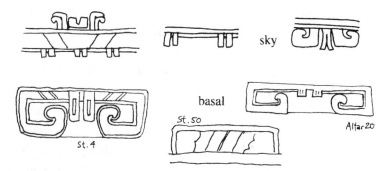

Diagram 114. Jaguar-snout sky panels and basal panels

Izapa's surroundings give us a clue as to how the Izapans thought about the cosmos. Their basic cosmovision reflects two extremes of nature: volcanoes to the north and ocean to the south. Volcanoes are the lofty sentinels of the sky and house the ancient Fire God. The ocean is the deep, watery abode of the cosmic caiman and serpent gods. If we look carefully at the structure of the pictures on Izapan stelae, we can verify this up-down polarity. Izapan stelae often contain a standardized basal panel, and the top of most stelae usually contain a sky panel featuring a cleft.

Many scholars agree that the cleft in the sky panel represents a stylized jaguar snout, indicating that the ritual scene below is within the jaguar's mouth, that is, in the Underworld. (The jaguar's mouth symbolizes the portal to the Underworld.) This means that the Izapan message is primarily ritual, mythological, abstract, and cosmological in nature rather than mundanely historical. In comparison, later Maya monuments usually portray historical events, such as captive sacrifices or king accessions, rather than cosmological or mythical ones.

The overall up-down frame of presentation in Izapan stelae suggests a polar or dualistic awareness. Within Izapan thought, the highest heaven in the lofty regions

Diagram 115. Three levels of Izapan cosmovision: Volcano, Izapa, Ocean

of the Fire God's dwelling place was somehow reflective of the deepest, watery home of the cosmic serpent below the sea. Furthermore, Izapa itself, as symbol of the unifying middle, is situated right between the two cosmic extremes, and thus there are three levels present in Izapan cosmovision (see diagram 115).

In general, the Izapan worldview, as revealed by its monuments, conforms to a north-south model. The terrestrial reference is to the northward volcanoes and the southward ocean. However, we will see that the primary interest of the Izapan calendar-priests was with the *astronomical* events that occurred to the north and south. In this kind of thinking, up-down, north-south, and sky-Underworld are complementary opposites, and events that occur in the two opposed realms reflect each other. For example, the deepest center of the Underworld ocean was conceived of as being equivalent to the highest point of the night sky. This derives from the Mesoamerican idea that the night sky *is* the Underworld.[10] Said another way, the night sky is the cosmic ocean. The up-down (or north-south) framework helps us interpret Izapan cosmovision and suggests the profound intellect employed by Izapan astronomers in their shamanic-scientific efforts to understand the cosmos. Ultimately, as we will see, the Izapan dualistic, or dialogical,[11] framework explains the formulation of the Long Count, with its 13.0.0.0.0 date placed on a rare alignment in the cycle of precession.

CHAPTER 19

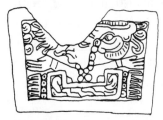

SOUTHERN MESOAMERICA, 200 B.C.: THE IZAPAN CIVILIZATION

Before examining Izapan calendrics, cosmology, and astronomy in detail, we will take a look at the wider context in which Izapa arose. This will help us understand the place occupied by Izapa in the flow of Mesoamerican history, and the practices, beliefs, and traditions that contributed to its development.

THE INVENTION OF THE LONG COUNT

The Long Count calendar was a system of time-keeping used primarily by the Classic-period Maya (A.D. 200–A.D. 900). Many Maya carvings are dated with the baktuns, katuns, tuns, and uinals of the Long Count. As sketched earlier, the 13-baktun cycle of the Long Count began in 3114 B.C. However, contrary to misconceptions in the literature,[1] this does not mean that the Maya invented it that far back—a rather absurd idea. The real barometer of when the Long Count system was invented is found by looking at the archaeological record. The earliest monuments dated in the Long Count date to the first century B.C., before the Classic-period Maya arose. There are only a few Long Count monuments dating prior to A.D. 41, and these are called Cycle 7 monuments because they were carved during baktun 7 (354 B.C.–A.D. 41). Monuments dating to Cycle 7 and early Cycle 8 were found over a limited geographical area of southern Mesoamerica, with Izapa near the center of the distribution (see diagram 116).

Since Izapa was one of the most prominent ritual centers active during the first century B.C., I believe that it played a major role in the formulation of the

229

1. Tres Zapotes
2. Chiapa de Corzo
3. Polol
4. Abaj Takalik
5. El Baúl

Diagram 116. Distribution of Cycle 7 Long Count dates around Izapa

Long Count. In fact, as mentioned earlier, Mayanist Michael Coe credits the Izapan civilization with the invention of the Long Count. The earliest known Cycle 7 date (37 B.C.) was found at Chiapa de Corzo in Chiapas, Mexico.

Archaeologist Matthew Stirling unearthed and identified Tres Zapotes Stela C as a Cycle 7 Long Count date. However, when he found it in 1941, the top half with the baktun glyph was broken off and missing. Based

Diagram 117. Cycle 7 date from Chiapa de Corzo

upon archaeological context and the remaining glyphs, he dated it as 7.16.6.16.18. Many scholars ridiculed Stirling's belief that Stela C contained such an early date. Incredibly, decades later the baktun section was found at the site, and it indeed turned out to be baktun 7.

Diagram 118. Stela C, front and back, Tres Zapotes

East of Izapa, along the Pacific Coast in Guatemala, an early center known as El Baúl sports a Cycle 7 date (see diagram 119).

Michael Coe wrote that this stela, dated to A.D. 37, "conforms to the Izapan style."[2] The early people of El Baúl were contemporaneous with Izapa. Furthermore, Abaj Takalik, a sister city to Izapa located just sixty-five kilometers to the east, contains a Cycle 7 Long Count date. Many other undated monuments at Abaj Takalik are similar to the Izapan style, and we will examine these later.

Baktun 7 ended in A.D. 41, which marked 8/13ths completion of the Great Cycle of thirteen baktuns. One wonders if this apocalyptic baktun-shift preoccupied Izapan cosmonauts. It is unfortunate that no Long Count dates have yet been found within Izapa. But given the presence of Long Count dates at several contemporaneous sites with which Izapa no doubt had contact, the esoteric understanding of the Long Count end-date must have been known to Izapan astronomer-priests. I suspect they were probably the ones who made the astronomical discovery of precession and did the calculations, since Izapa appears to have been the dominant site in the sphere of Cycle 7 Long Count dates. In addition, the astronomical information encoded in the Izapan monuments points right at the alignment of baktun 13— the end of the 13-baktun cycle of the Long Count. Around the end of baktun 7 in A.D. 41, the Izapan astronomer-priests may have been thinking, "exactly five more baktuns to go."

Diagram 119. Cycle 7 date, Stela 1, El Baúl

Support for my belief that the Long Count was invented as a result of astronomical calculations made at Izapa is provided by archaeologist Gareth Lowe, who identified fish symbols on Stelae 1 and 5 as prototypal tun and katun glyphs.[3] He proposes that the twenty or so carved monuments in Groups A, B, and D represent the seating of the twenty katuns of the Long Count baktun cycle.

Despite the fact that the appearance of the Long Count, in time and place, is well-established, controversy among different academic camps still simmers. I feel that the pictographic evidence supplied by the Izapan monuments settles the matter. We know that the earliest Long Count dates in the archaeological record go back to the first century B.C. Accepting that the Long Count was a calendar for tracking precession, and precession is a phenomenon that might take two hundred years to calibrate, the Long Count calendar was probably being perfected between 250 B.C. and 50 B.C. Other scholars have proposed that the invention of the Long Count goes further back, to 355 B.C., 550 B.C., or 236 B.C.[4] Perhaps there are more

Long Count dates to be found, but at this point it is safe to say that the Izapan culture was instrumental in the invention of the Long Count calendar. As Michael Coe put it: ". . . the priority of Izapa in the very important adoption of the Long Count is quite clear cut. . . ."[5]

THE IZAPAN DOMAIN: IZAPA AND ITS NEIGHBORS

The bioregion in which Izapa is situated includes the entire Pacific Coast strip running from the Isthmus of Tehuantepec in the north into Guatemala and El Salvador in the south. This area was known in ancient times as Soconusco. It provided an easily traversed trade route between northern and southern Mesoamerica. The major trade route through the Sierra Madre and into the Chiapan basin of the upper Grijalva River passed through Huixtla via the Motozintla pass, just northwest of Izapa.

A minor trade route, which was also a pilgrimage trail to Tacana volcano, led into the Guatemalan highlands via Union Juarez north of Izapa. This gave the traveler access to what is now Mam territory and the ancient sites of Tajumulco and Zaculeu. Highland-lowland trade interaction must have been significant, as the cacao grown around Izapa in ancient (and modern) times was valued throughout

Diagram 120. Depiction of Ahau canoe from Zaculeu, Guatemala

Mesoamerica. A design on a ceramic vessel found at Zaculeu, though dated later than Izapa, resembles the motif on Izapa Stelae 67 and 22.

In the 1940s, archaeologists Bertha Dutton and Hulda Hobbs excavated Post-Classic mounds at Tajumulco and suggested occupation of this site going back to the Pre-Classic.[6] Although most of their findings were Post-Classic and related to the Pipil culture, the authors considered Tajumulco as belonging to Soconusco, given its proximity to Izapa (forty kilometers) and the ancient trails through border-region Sibinal down to Izapa. They even suggested that intensive trade occurred between Izapa and Tajumulco, and that Izapa's role as a ritual center may have passed to Tajumulco after its decline around A.D. 100. After all, Tajumulco is situated on the slopes of the highest volcanic deity in Central America, which is the June solstice marker viewed from Izapa. Clearly, a full pilgrimage cycle outward from Izapa would have included Tajumulco as well as Tacana. Many of the motifs in Izapan and Tajumulcan art are shared. Compare Izapa Monument 53 with Tajumulco's stone sculptures J and O.

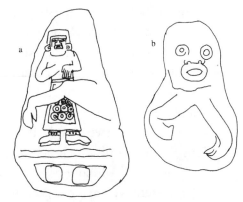

The ancient relationship between Izapa and Tajumulco unfortunately is muddied by the continuous occupation of Tajumulco into the Post-Classic, which effectively destroyed most of its earlier artifacts. Most likely, some kind of connection can be postulated for pilgrimage reasons, because Izapan calendar-priests would have been interested in making regular ritual offerings to the Fire God resident in Tajumulco.

Diagram 121. a) Tajumulco sculptures J and O; b) Izapa Monument 53

Diagram 122. Izapan-style Stela 1 from El Jobo, Guatemala

To the southeast of Izapa, just across the border into Guatemala, a broken Izapan-style stela was found at a small site called El Jobo. Notice the Izapan-style sky-cleft panel at the top.

Abaj Takalik, a site that thrived at the same time as Izapa, contains many fascinating sculptures and monuments, including a Cycle 7 monument, Stela 2.

The central column serves as the baktun tree in which the Long Count date is recorded, flanked by ceremonial attendants on the left and right. A cosmic bird is depicted at the top of the Stela 2 scene, out of whose mouth emerges a deity. Another interesting carving from Abaj Takalik was examined by Mesoamerican scholar Lee Allen Parsons (see diagram 124).[7]

In this image, a warrior ascends a snake-con-

Diagram 123. Abaj Takalik Stela 2

duit and emerges from its mouth at the top of the stela. This is a common motif found throughout Mesoamerica, especially noted at Chichén Itzá. In the center of the snake's birthplace, two U-shaped "mouths" face each other and bracket the lower portion of the carving. Between these two mouths flow water scrolls, in the center of which is a four-cornered U glyph out of which emerges the vision serpent. Here we have recognizable motifs: the

Diagram 124. Abaj Takalik Stela 4

quadrated symbol of the crossroads and the U-shape of the cosmic birth canal out of which is born a deity-ruler with his serpentine "spirit companion." Unusual flower motifs adorn the stela, and the basal panel resembles the cleft-like jaguar-snout sky panels of Izapan stelae.

Monument 27

Further east, El Baúl, where the Cycle 7 monument Stela 1 was found (see diagram 119), contains many impressive Pre-Classic and Classic-period monuments.

The two carvings shown to the left are from a later occupation of El Baúl, after a Classic-period migration from Central Mexico. However, the Monument 7 motif of a solar deity emerging from the mouth of an Underworld deity (a crab) compares to Izapa Stela 11, which depicts a solar deity emerging from the mouth of a frog. Despite later invasions of foreigners, El Baúl had an early occupation that was contemporaneous with Izapa.

Kaminaljuyu, present-day Guatemala City, rose to prominence during Izapa's decline. Kaminaljuyu was a bustling trade center during the late Pre-Classic and retained trade alliances with places as far

Monument 7

Diagram 125. El Baúl monuments 7 and 27

flung as Toltec Teotihuacan in Central Mexico. Trade items between these great Pre-Classic cities must have passed through Izapa. Unfortunately, very little remains of Kaminaljuyu, though more and more artifacts are coming to light. The ruins of Kaminaljuyu have, lamentably, been largely obliterated by the mindless growth of Guatemala City in recent decades. The thrones and stelae that bulldoz-

ers accidentally plowed up were sold to collectors or placed in local private museums. Fortunately, many of them were photographed and documented, so there is a growing record of Kaminaljuyu sculpture.

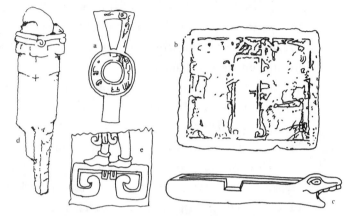

The Kaminaljuyu ballgame marker, a symbolic goalring, shown in Relief 2 here, resembles an Aztec stone marker illustrated in Laurette Séjourné's book *Burning Water*, where it is called a "hiero-

Diagram 126. Kaminaljuyu. a) Relief 2 (ballgame marker); b) Altar 2; c) Monument 47 (serpent canoe); d) Pedestal Sculpture 6; e) Stela 11, with Izapan-style basal panel

glyph for a cycle of time."[8] This connection between the ballgame goalring and time cycles reinforces my interpretation of the ballgame as a metaphor for the 2012 alignment. The goalring (representing the dark-rift in the Milky Way) symbolizes the place where time begins and ends. After all, when the ball goes into the goalring, the game (of time) is over.

The central glyph column on Kaminaljuyu Altar 2 probably originally contained a Long Count date. The axis mundi in this carving, flanked by two attendants, is a conventional arrangment that partakes of what I call "the fire-drill symbol,"[9] and also can be seen on Izapa Stela 2, Abaj Takalik Stela 2, El Baúl Stela 1 (a Cycle 7 date), and elsewhere. The meanings of Mesoamerican "fire-drill" rituals survive among the modern Tzutujil Maya of Guatemala, and involve weaving, birthing, and male-female intercourse.[10] Fire-drill symbolism is present in the New Fire ceremony of the Toltecs, which involved the drilling of the New Fire in the chest cavity of a sacrificial victim. Significantly, this occurred at the end of each fifty-two-haab time period, the Toltec unit of World Age measure. The drilling of the New Fire inaugurated a new cycle of time, and the portrayal of the figures on Kaminaljuyu Altar 2 and elsewhere as "fire drillers" is probably an intentional metaphor. The fire-drill symbol is especially relevant to the placement of early Long Count dates along the vertical axis of the fire-drill "shaft." In Old World cosmo-conception, the fire-drill symbol is very ancient. As discussed in Part I, the cosmic fire drill was thought to be fixed upon the Pole Star, and it determined the end of the world when it finally wore out its "hinge." Similar meanings must have existed in Izapan cosmology, which involved, as we will see, a total of three cosmic centers (polar, zenith, and Galactic).

Continuing with the Kaminaljuyu carvings shown above, Stela 11 has an Izapan-style basal panel. Monument 47 may represent a "serpent canoe," similar to the "Ahau boat" depicted on Izapa Stelae 6, 22, and 67. Pedestal Sculpture 6 resembles Izapa Miscellaneous Monument 4 and may be a form of zenith gnomon.

Most of these various examples are contemporaneous with the Pre-Classic Izapan context. We could examine many more Pre-Classic sculptures from the Pacific coasts of Chiapas and Guatemala, at the sites of Santa Lucia Cotzumalhuapa, Bilbao, Tonala, Chiapa de Corzo, and elsewhere, but the point is clear. Izapa and its related highland contact areas embraced a rich archaeological zone not very extensively studied. A lot was going on in this overlooked corner of Mesoamerica even before the Maya began their ascent to civilization in the Petén lowlands to the north. Izapa was the major ritual center in this time and place, defining the art styles and cosmological ideas for other sites within its large sphere of influence. With its Olmec antecedents and pre-Maya flowering, it truly did occupy the transitional era between the Olmec and the Maya. Between 500 B.C. and A.D. 50, Izapan skywatchers were engaged in an important ongoing endeavor that must have influenced the worldview of other regional sites such as Abaj Takalik, El Baúl, and Chiapa de Corzo, all of which contain Cycle 7 dates. In addition, Kaminaljuyu, the major Pre-Classic site rivaling Teotihuacan, probably adopted many of the cosmological ideas pioneered at Izapa.

IZAPA: BIRTHPLACE OF THE HERO TWIN CREATION MYTH

The mythic message on Izapan monuments describes distinct episodes in the Quiché Creation story, the *Popol Vuh*. As you will remember, the Quiché *Popol Vuh* was recorded in the 1550s, and was probably derived from an actual hieroglyphic book. The Hero Twins and their *Popol Vuh* adventures have been identified at Classic sites and on Classic-period ceramics. Going back further, we can identify Hero Twin actions and *Popol Vuh* episodes on the monuments of Izapa. Clearly, Izapa contains the first manifestation of the Hero Twin story in the archaeological record. This version of the Maya Creation myth, being some 1,800 years older than the Quiché *Popol Vuh*, is better referred to as the Hero Twin story, to avoid confusion over semantics. No, the Quiché were not hanging around Izapa 2,000 years ago. But the Quiché legend called the *Popol Vuh*, like most epics, belongs to a wider cultural context, and some form of it goes back thousands of years. The Hero Twins' adventures and their battles with Seven Macaw (the Big Dipper) comprise a Creation myth filled with astronomical symbolism that first appears at Izapa. Apparently, the Izapans were the ones who created it. They no doubt adopted older motifs into their new cosmology, such as the concept of the cleft mountain as an emergence place. However, some shift in cosmological understanding must have stimulated the formulation of the new Creation myth.

Beatriz Barba de Piña Chan interpreted over a dozen Izapan stelae as representing aspects of the *Popol Vuh* (or Hero Twin story).[11] The fantastic Stela 5 is thought to be the primordial Creation scene. V. Garth Norman and Gareth Lowe both characterize Stela 5 as an ancient Mesoamerican migration story involving the Maya creator couple Xpiyacoc and Xmucane, and call it an early version of the Quiché *Popol Vuh*.[12] The central tree in Stela 5 is the Tree of Life and the sitting figures include Hunahpu and Xbalanque. Other Izapan stelae depicting motifs from the Hero Twin myth are shown in diagram 127.

According to Piña Chan, Stela 21 is one of the Xibalban lords cutting off the head of the Hero Twins' father, One Hunahpu. Stela 2 represents the head of One Hunahpu being hung in the crook of the calabash tree in Xibalba. Stela 27 depicts a gameball (or a corn seed) being delivered to Blood Moon, which may symbolize her impregnation with the Hero Twins. Stela 10 depicts Blood Moon sitting by the Milky Way tree, in which One Hunahpu's head hangs, preparing to impregnate Blood Moon. She is depicted umbilically connected to the Hero Twins, that is, pregnant with them. On Stela 4, a new head is being made for Hunahpu, an event that takes place during the Twins' ballgame with the Lords of Xibalba. According to Piña Chan, Stelae 22 and 67 are scenes of the Hero Twins' self-sacrifice, death, transformation, and resurrection. Stela 60 shows the final defeat and sacrifice of the Xibalbans at the hands of the Hero Twins. Stela 9, according to Piña Chan, is

Stela 21

Stela 2

Stela 27

Stela 4

Stela 22

Stela 67

Stela 10

Stela 9

Stela 50

Hunahpu and Xbalanque being transformed into the sun and moon at the end of the story. Other Izapan scenes interpreted by Piña Chan in terms of Hero Twin mythology include Stelae 6, 14, 19 and 20, 50, and 11. Although some of Piña Chan's identifications are not convincing, she is correct in emphasizing that the Hero Twin Creation myth is the primary concern of Izapa's monuments. As we have seen, this myth ultimately describes the resurrection of the Hero Twins' father, One Hunahpu, which is a mythic metaphor for the rebirth of the solstice sun through the Milky Way cleft.

Finally, on Stela 25, we find an important depiction of the

Popol Vuh episode in which Hunahpu's arm is torn off by Seven Macaw (see diagram 128).

Luckily for us, Brigham Young University archaeologists recovered this stela from looters in the town of Tapachula as it was being prepared for the black market. It shows Hunahpu dealing with the Seven Macaw/Big Dipper deity, the false sun of a previous World Age.[13] The inverted caiman on the left is the Milky Way. Its head and mouth (where the dark-rift is located) are under-

Diagram 127. Izapan stelae depicting motifs and episodes from the Quiché Popol Vuh

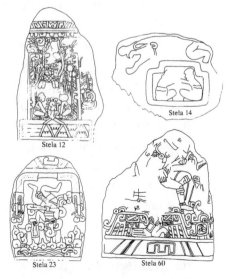

Stela 12

Stela 14

Stela 23

Stela 60

neath the basal panel, that is, under the Earth, indicating that it is not above the horizon at the moment depicted. Notice the up-down polarity between the Big Dipper and the dark-rift, united via the artificial vertical pole held by Hunahpu, clearly portraying the basic structure of the Izapan worldview, which operates via a dialogue between astronomical events in the north and analogous events in the south. As such, the polar center occupied by Seven Macaw counterposes the Galactic Center hidden within the mouth of the Cosmic Caiman (the Milky Way).

We have seen that the Izapan civilization, the transitional culture between the Olmecs and the Maya, occupied the center of an innovative phase of Pre-Classic ritual activity in southern Mesoamerica. Furthermore, because so many of Izapa's monuments contain Mesoamerica's earliest depictions of the Maya Creation story—even specific episodes that survive in the latter-day Quiché *Popol Vuh*—Izapa was clearly the place where the *Popol Vuh*/Hero Twin Creation myth was formulated.

Diagram 128. Izapa Stela 25. Hunahpu, the Milky Way crocodile-tree, and Seven Macaw

Understanding the wider context in which Izapa arose clarifies for us the traditions and ideas that informed Izapan cosmovision. As a result of our careful look at iconography and calendar dates found at related sites, we have reconstructed Izapa as the center of Pre-Classic thought in southern Mesoamerica. Now, before embarking upon our exploration of Izapan astronomy, cosmology, and the astronomical information encoded in Izapa's mytho-astronomical monuments, we must first explore some important facets of the Izapan calendars.

CHAPTER 20

IZAPAN CALENDRICS

I t is already clear that the Long Count calendar was invented by the Izapan
skywatchers. As such, the Long Count is an Izapan calendar. But what about the
260-day tzolkin calendar? The earliest known occupation of Izapa began around
1500 B.C., which places the origin of Izapan culture prior to when many scholars
feel the 260-day calendar was invented. Izapa is therefore a candidate in the quest
to locate the origin place of the 260-day sacred calendar, and one scholar in particular has looked closely at this possibility. By tracing the evolution of the calendar
systems of Mesoamerica through temporal and geographical distribution, Vincent
Malmström argued that Izapa was, in fact, the origin site of the 260-day calendar.
His reason is astounding in its simplicity and involves the intervals between the
two solar zenith passages at the 15°N latitude of Izapa.[1]

ZENITH INTERVALS: LATITUDE AS CALENDAR

Earlier in this book, we discovered that the sun passes through the zenith at
high noon twice a year within the Tropics. However, the dates of the solar zenith
passage change with latitude, and the further south one goes, the larger the interval
between the two zenith passages becomes. The zenith-passage dates at Izapa are
August 12 and May 1.[2] The significance of the zenith-passage intervals at Izapa lies
in the resulting division of the year into 105- and 260-day sections.

Izapa's identity as origin place of the tzolkin calendar is supported by the 260-
day interval between its August and May zenith passages. In the Izapan mind, this
represented the sacred interval between the sun's two passings through the Heart of

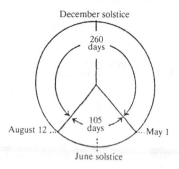

Heaven, from its birth to its rebirth. And you may remember that Maya shamans also equated the 260-day period with the nine-month period of human gestation, from conception to birth. The Izapan zenith passages were observed with vertical gnomons, upright pillars that cast no shadows at high noon on the zenith-passage days. Several zenith gnomons have been found at Izapa, notably the three pillar-and-ball

Diagram 129. Zenith intervals within the solar year at Izapa

monuments in Group B and Monument 4 in Group F. But there is more. The Long Count calendar also is indicated by the 15°N latitude of Izapa, for two reasons:

- The first zenith passage at Izapa, August 12, was the *first* day of the Great Cycle of 13 baktuns (0.0.0.0.1 = August 12, 3114 B.C.).[3]
- December 21, the December solstice, lies halfway between the August and May zenith passages at Izapa, and is the *last* day of the Great Cycle of 13 baktuns (13.0.0.0.0 = December 21, 2012 A.D.).

Notice in the diagram above how the solstice axis divides the zenith-passage intervals into equal halves. The June solstice divides the lesser interval into two periods of 52½ days each, and the December solstice divides the 260-day interval into two 130-day periods. The solstice axis is thus a kind of temporal axis mundi, suggesting a meaning for the December solstice as "center point" or Zero Point. And, of course, the 13-baktun cycle end-date (the December solstice of 2012) points to a temporal Zero Point (in precession) as well as to the center of the cosmic crossroads (in space)—the Galactic Center.

Diagram 130. A four-cornered solstice cosmogram

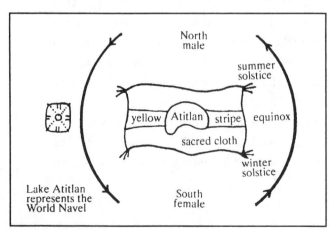

The solstices were very important in the early calendar systems of Mesoamerica. A common and very ancient concept in Maya thinking involved a four-cornered image of the cosmos, based on the rise and set points of the sun on the solstices.

This cosmo-conception, used to model time as well as space, is found among the Tzutujil, Chamula, and Quiché Maya, the Mixe-Zoque Indians of Santa Clara, in the alignments of Uaxactun in the Petén, and at Izapa.[4] The four corners simultaneously represent the four calendric year-bearers, the pillars of the sky, and the arms and legs of a human being. Most importantly, the solstice cosmogram employed by the Izapans represents the four places along the horizon where the sun rises and sets on the solstices. At Izapa, the two solstice points along the eastern horizon were very important.

The June solstice sunrise took place over Tajumulco volcano. The December solstice horizon is where the Milky Way and the dark-rift near the Galactic Center rose before the sun in the era of Izapa's heyday. In other words, the December solstice horizon is where the convergence of the Milky Way and the solstice sun was observed and calibrated by Izapan astronomers.

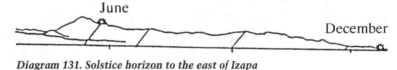

Diagram 131. Solstice horizon to the east of Izapa

A fact that helps us understand Izapan cosmovision is that the sun rises furthest south (i.e., the "lowest") on the December solstice. In comparison, 130 days later, on the May 1 zenith passage, the sun passes through the zenith (i.e., reaches its "highest"). Thus, to reiterate, the 130-day interval between the solstice and the zenith passage reveals a solar movement from lowest to highest. It may seem like this interpretation utilizes mixed metaphors, in that the "lowest" criterion applies to the southernmost rise point of the sun whereas the "highest" criterion applies to the sun's passage through the zenith. If we keep our metaphor categories straight, the opposite of the zenith passage should be the nadir, not the southernmost solar-rise azimuth. However, we will see that this kind of analogy-based thinking, in which different categories of experience are perceived to operate in parallel, is intrinsic to the multidimensional consciousness of Izapan skywatchers.

The primary players in the Izapan calendar thus appear to be the solstice dates and the zenith-passage dates. This explains the importance of these key dates, and encourages us to look at the astronomical movements on these dates. We will examine the details of these astronomical movements later, but we can pause here to propose a general model of how the solstices relate to the zenith passages.

THE SOLAR-LUNAR DIVISIONS OF THE IZAPAN ZENITH CALENDAR

The information sketched thus far suggests that the key dates of the Izapan calendar were used to structure solar and lunar processes. As just mentioned, between the December solstice and the May 1 zenith passage (130 days) the sun goes from "lowest" to "highest." Significantly, during this same period of time, the moon goes from new to full.[5] If the moon was new on the December solstice, it would be full on the May 1 zenith passage. These two processes, though different in nature, were probably understood to mirror each other. The sun mimics the moon in its new-to-full process because, at the December solstice, the sun is furthest south (i.e., just born or "new"), whereas on the May zenith passage it reaches the highest heaven in the north (i.e., completed or "full"). This solar-lunar model emerges from looking at the key dates derived from Izapa's latitude.

The overall point here is to identify the most likely days that played a role in Izapan seasonal festivals. The May zenith passage is particularly relevant because at Izapa, as in other areas of Mesoamerica, it signals the beginning of the rainy season. In fact, the May zenith-passage observation survives today as a syncretic blend of indigenous and Christian concepts in the Festival of the Holy Cross, celebrated on May 3 in many Mesoamerican communities. The June solstice is clearly significant because of its orientation to Tajumulco volcano, the highest volcano in Central America (4,220 meters). The December solstice remains significant because of its importance in being the perpendicular to the Group B Izapan baseline, and for the astronomical convergence that occurs in that direction. In addition, the December solstice divides the 260-day interval between solar zenith passages in half. The northward Group B baseline, as mentioned, points to the "cleft of Creation" along the eastern slope of Tacana volcano. As we will see, this northern horizon also is the location of important astronomical events. To summarize the most noteworthy dates in the Izapan seasonal calendar:

- the December solstice
- the May 1 zenith passage
- the June solstice
- the August 12 zenith passage

We now have four days, probably the most significant days in the Izapan calendar, that we can use to examine the changing Izapan skies over a year. The details of this examination are covered in the next section, but I can say at this time that the astronomy on these dates implicates the three cosmic centers that were of interest to the Izapan skywatchers—the North Celestial Pole, the zenith, and the Galactic Center.

THE IZAPAN CALENDAR ROUND RECONSTRUCTED

We have already seen that the Long Count was a calendar created by the Izapans. In addition, the 260-day tzolkin calendar itself also may have been invented by them. But what about the other traits of the Izapan calendar? What year-bearers did they use in their tzolkin calendar? When was their New Year's Day? In my book *The Center of Mayan Time*, I reconstructed the Izapan tzolkin-haab calendar. The combination of the 260-day tzolkin cycle with the 365-day haab results in a 52-year cycle known as the Calendar Round. The motive behind my reconstruction was a glaring conceptual error in the academic literature. Scholars assume that the 4 Ahau 3 Kankin tzolkin-haab combo usually given for the Long Count end-date represents the haab used by the people who first devised the Long Count. In fact, this tzolkin-haab combo is from the Tikal calendar, which arrived on the scene several hundred years after the Long Count was invented.[6] By the time the Tikal calendar was instated, the earlier haab placement of the Izapan calendar had probably shifted several times.

The transformations of calendar systems throughout Mesoamerican history are complex. The best source on this question is Munro Edmonson's *Book of the Year*. Possible changes to Mesoamerican calendar systems include the year-bearer system used (of five possible ones) and the haab date. It should be emphasized that the tzolkin calendar was never altered. The 260-day cycle has been followed unbroken for almost 3,000 years, and the same placement survives today. The haab date changes when different year-bearers are adopted or when haab-month counting shifts between 0-19 and 1-20 (this shift involves the choice of whether to begin counting the haab month from 0 or from 1).

My assumption in reconstructing the Izapan Calendar Round is that the Izapan calendar, as an expression of a very early calendar, used Type V year-bearers. These year-bearers are Ahau, Chicchan, Oc, and Men (Yucatec Maya day-names are used here). Their polarities are obvious (see diagram 132).

The meanings of these opposed day-signs are perhaps the most time-resistant

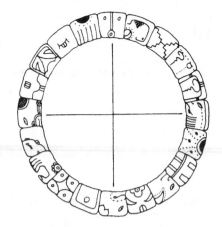

and compelling of all the day-signs. Chicchan-Men (Serpent-Eagle) recalls the ubiquitous Mesoamerican Quetzalcoatl deity (Quetzal = Bird; Coatl = Serpent). As Munro Edmonson explained, the four calendric year-bearers were associated with the four seasonal quarters—the two equinoxes and the two solstices.[7] One of the year-bearers was always thought of as primary, and each 52-year Calendar Round began when this senior year-bearer coincided with the coefficient 1 to initiate a new year. The senior

Diagram 132. Day-sign wheel showing polarities of the Type V year-bearers

year-bearer in the Type V system was probably Ahau, given the important meanings and uses of this day-sign and its potent mythological associations. Earlier, I showed how the seasonal quarter corresponding to Ahau in the archaic Mesoamerican calendar was the December solstice.[8] The reasoning behind this belief is quite simple: The December solstice is the first day of the year, thus its association with Ahau, the primary or senior day-sign. What follows is the clear-cut connotation of 1 Ahau with the First Sun and the deity First Father/One Hunahpu, a significant identification because 1 Ahau (One Hunahpu) is the name of the Hero Twins' father in the *Popol Vuh*. The related concept chain suggests that the December solstice sun is to be understood as "First Father," the Solar Lord who is reborn as the new World Age ruler at the end of the *Popol Vuh* Creation myth. Elsewhere, First Father/One Hunahpu has a second identity as the Maize Deity because maize, like the sun, is a source of life. The Mesoamerican association between maize, the sun, and deity resurrection is understandable, partly because maize is reborn every year at harvest time and the sun is reborn every year at the December solstice.[9]

As mentioned, Munro Edmonson reconstructed the earliest Olmec calendar and he identified the June solstice as the primary start point. For the Izapans, the primacy of the December solstice over the June solstice is apparent from considerations already sketched. Historically, the December solstice was considered to be the New Year's Day by several Maya groups. In the interest of condensing a lot of my previous research and arguments into the essential conclusions, my reconstruction of the Izapan Calendar Round is as follows:

- The Izapan Calendar consisted of Type V year-bearers and counted haab months from 1 to 20: 1 Ahau 1 Pop began the Calendar Round every 52 years.

- An Izapan Calendar Round cycle thus began in 32 B.C. on 1 Ahau 1 Pop, which fell on August 14.
- The projected Izapan New Year's Day in A.D. 2012 equals April 5 (4 Ahau 1 Pop), exactly 260 days before 13.0.0.0.0. However, this is just a New Year's Day; it is not the beginning of a Calendar Round.
- Most importantly, the Izapan haab date for December 21, 2012 A.D. is thus 1 Kankin.

My reconstruction is derived from a probable three-day haab shift from the older Izapan calendar to the later Tikal calendar.[10] Several compelling considerations emerge from my reconstruction. First, the Calendar Round beginning in 32 B.C. fell on August 14, very close to the second zenith passage at Izapa. In fact, it is within the three-day range of zenith-passage observations at the latitude of Izapa. That the New Calendar Round began on a zenith passage reminds us of the practice among the pre-Conquest Yucatec Maya of using July 26 (a zenith-passage date at their latitude) as their New Year's Day.

Projecting the Izapan calendar forward to 13.0.0.0.0 yields a haab date of 1 Kankin (rather than 3 Kankin in the later Tikal system). In that the haab number is now 1, we can suspect that we have, in fact, found the original tzolkin-haab placement of the culture that created the Long Count—the Izapans. Following well-known linguistic meanings, my reading of this kan-kin month is broken down into:

- *kan* (or *chan*) = four, snake, sky, and cross (as in the "kan" cross)
- *kin* = day and sun

The meanings of these two words bring to mind the four directions or four World Ages, the Milky Way snake, the celestial cross, and the sun—the key players in the 13-baktun cycle end-date cosmology. Thus, appropriately, we can say that *the solstice sun enters the crossroads in the center of the sky, in the belly of the Milky Way snake, on the haab day 1 Kankin: One "cross-day-sun."* My reconstruction is based upon the principles of calendar transformations identified by Munro Edmonson. At the very least, one important fact is exposed by this line of questioning: Contrary to conventional academic wisdom, 3 Kankin was not the haab date used by the creators of the Long Count for the end-date in 2012. And, if my reconstruction of the Izapan Calendar Round is correct, the meaning of 1 Kankin is very suggestive of the astronomical alignment that takes place on the end-date: 4 Ahau 1 Kankin, 13.0.0.0.0.

THE IZAPAN CALENDARS:
THE LONG COUNT AND THE TZOLKIN

The zenith intervals at Izapa define a kind of geodetic seasonal calendar in which the solstices provide a primary axis. The implied intervals and zenith-passage dates draw attention to the 260-day tzolkin cycle and the first and last days of the 13-baktun cycle of the Long Count. My reconstruction of the Izapan Calendar Round (the August 14 Calendar Round beginning in 32 B.C.) points to a key date in the Long Count (its "first" day), which is also a zenith-passage date at Izapa. Finally, the meaning of "1 Kankin" is very suggestive of the astronomical alignment of the 2012 end-date.

In general, Izapa is clearly the origin place of the Long Count calendar, and probably of the tzolkin calendar as well. Izapa was an incredible place of innovation, skywatching, visionary shamanism, and ingenious myth-making. The monumental legacy of Izapa comes down to us today as a reminder that we are approaching a critical World Age rebirth.

Michael Coe was of the opinion that "the Long Count itself might have been the invention of one person."[11] This is an astounding suggestion, but is mitigated against when we consider that the Long Count must have been formulated over centuries of tracking precessional motion. However, like Hipparchus in the Old World, perhaps the final pieces of the puzzle were assembled by one intrepid Izapan skywatcher. In his book *Cycles of the Sun, Mysteries of the Moon*, Vincent Malmström argues for just such a scenario—that the Long Count was invented at Izapa during the first millennium B.C. by one person, whom, ironically, he calls the "New World Hipparchus."[12] Despite Malmström's search for the astronomical underpinnings of the Izapan calendars, no mention was made in Malmström's book of precession and its role in the Long Count end-date. We may never know if the Long Count was the creation of one person or of a lineage of dedicated skywatchers engaged in calibrating precession over several centuries. However, Malmström's use of the name Hipparchus, the name of the astronomer who discovered precession in the ancient Greek world, is perfectly appropriate.

CHAPTER 21

IZAPAN ASTRONOMY AND COSMOLOGY

The Izapan skywatchers were astronomers and calendar-priests. They also were shamans, adept visionaries who undertook journeys into the cosmic center. This specific concern of shamanism goes back thousands of years, to the Asian forebears of the human beings who migrated into the Americas. The Neolithic shamans of Asia believed that the Pole Star was the cosmic center, and the Pole Star was of great interest to them because, at northern latitudes, it is almost straight overhead. Within the Tropics at Izapa, the ancient shamanistic concern with finding the center embraced more complex considerations, ones that forced New World skywatchers to search for other possible cosmic centers, and determine which one was true.

The monument orientations and alignments at Izapa reveal that Izapa's shaman-astronomers recognized three cosmic centers. Viewed from Izapa, the North Celestial Pole lies in the direction of Tacana volcano to the north, and since Izapa is at a southerly latitude, the North Celestial Pole appears to be low in the sky. In fact, the altitude of the North Celestial Pole is always equivalent to one's latitude of observation. As such, at Izapa the North Celestial Pole is viewed 15° above the northern horizon. The peak of Tacana is actually to the east of the North Celestial Pole, but serves as a general indicator for the polar center (diagram 133).[1]

As viewed from Izapa, the circumpolar stars spin counterclockwise around the

249

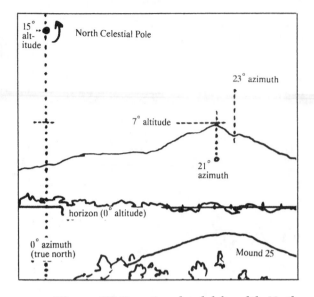

Diagram 133. *Tacana's peak and cleft, and the North Celestial Pole*

polar center. As such, we can imagine the circumpolar constellations, such as the Big Dipper, rising behind Tacana, and we can understand the importance of Tacana within Izapan astronomy. Earlier, we saw how the shallow cleft on Tacana's eastern slope was mythologized as the primordial "cleft" of Creation, which is spoken of in the *Popol Vuh* and other Mesoamerican Creation myths.[2] In the *Popol Vuh*, it is "the split place, the broken water place" from which maize and the Maize God were born. As a birthplace, something is "born" or emerges from the cleft. Clearly, the Big Dipper, which we already know corresponds to the Seven Macaw deity in the *Popol Vuh*, fits the bill. Thus, the polar region, as marked by Tacana, was one cosmic center that the Izapans recognized and incorporated into their cosmological ideas.

Another cosmic center implicit in Izapa's cosmology is the zenith center, which draws from the Mesoamerican interest in the center of the sky directly overhead. As described earlier, Izapa's latitude demarcates a 260-day interval between solar zenith-passage dates. Solar zenith passages were observed with vertical pillars such as those found in Group B. Twice a year, rituals of ascension took place in which the Izapan astronomer or shaman-priest journeyed into the cosmic center at the moment the sun passed into the zenith. This no-shadow moment occurred at high noon, 130 days before and after the December solstice. The zenith was thus another significant cosmic center recognized at Izapa.

A primary orientational axis at Izapa lies on a perpendicular to the north-south baseline of the site. This is the southeast-northwest axis that corresponds to the December solstice sunrise and the June solstice sunset (azimuth 114° vs. azimuth 294°). This axis points to the most mysterious and intriguing cosmic center indicated by Izapan alignments. Many monuments face the December solstice horizon, and the pictographs on those stelae portray what occurs in that direction.

Imagine standing in the center of Izapa, perhaps on the top of the large temple-mound in Group H, in the predawn hours of a December solstice 2,100 years ago. You look to the southeast. You see the sky begin to lighten, but it is not from the rising sun. It is the shimmering stars of the Milky Way rising above the solstice horizon, the bright central bulge of the Milky Way, the Womb of Creation. It is the Great Mother and Creator of All. This, truly, is the birthplace of the sky-Earth; it is the cosmic center from which everything is born. Soon after the Galaxy rises, the solstice sun begins to make its presence known. The sky brightens, the cosmic womb/center fades into light, and the New Year begins. Given the astronomical fact that a main axis at Izapa points directly at the Galactic Center as it rises on the December solstice, the Galactic Center within the crossroads formed by the Milky Way and the ecliptic was, undeniably, another cosmic center recognized by Izapan cosmonauts.

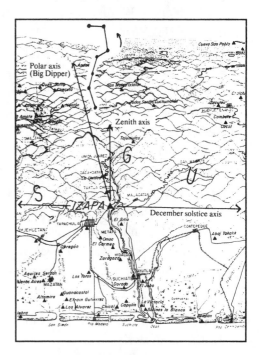

Diagram 134. 3-D Izapan axes: Zenith-Polar-Galactic. Adapted from Lowe et al. (1982: Fig. 4.11)

The polar center, the zenith center, and the Galactic Center: We must incorporate all three of these cosmic centers into our exploration of Izapan cosmology. As such, we must deal with a complex cosmic map system involving three axes and three centers.

A monument from Kaminaljuyu supports the idea that the ancient skywatchers of southern Mesoamerica recognized three levels of cosmic centers. We have seen the close relationship between the art motifs of Izapa and Kaminaljuyu. In addition, these two Pre-Classic sites were the largest cities of their day, both playing an important role in long-distance trade and regional ceremonies. Kaminaljuyu Monument 65 is an astounding confirmation of the three-tiered cosmological model. Accepting that the missing part contained an attendant, the monument shows three levels of enthroned cosmic rulers, each flanked by two attendants (see diagram 135).

As we saw earlier, thrones were symbols of the cosmic center, and here we have three. I interpret this image as proof of a Mesoamerican interest in three interfacing cosmic centers: polar, zenith and Galactic. Seven ball-courts at Kaminaljuyu are oriented roughly to the December solstice sunrise azimuth; three other ballcourts are perpendicular to this azimuth and therefore reflect the Tacana orientation at Izapa. Because of these shared orientations, I believe that the builders of Kaminaljuyu attempted to adopt the complex cosmovision formalized earlier at Izapa. At Izapa, Groups B and F both have promi-nently placed thrones; only Group A lacks a throne. However, a corner fragment of a third throne was, in fact, found at Izapa.[3] It was recov-ered from a refuse dump near Group F, and may or

Diagram 135. Kaminaljuyu Monu-ment 65

may not have originally been located in Group A. This throne's original location remains unsolved, but the thrones in Groups B and F suggest that the three main monument groups, as ceremonial representatives of their respective cosmic axes and centers, each contained a throne. The Kaminaljuyu image of three tiers of thrones is compelling and lends credence to my thesis of a three-level Izapan cosmovision, but a clearer validation of Izapa's interest in three cosmic centers comes from ex-amining the astronomy associated with its three primary monument groups.

THE THREE COSMIC CENTERS IN A NORTH-SOUTH FRAMEWORK

When we look at the timing of astronomical cycles that surrounded Izapa dur-ing its heyday (500 B.C.–A.D. 100), we will understand the importance of the three cosmic centers. First, we can simplify this three-level model by considering how the Izapans thought about space and geography. Fortunately, Izapan cosmology can be boiled down into a generalized north-south framework.

Tacana lies to the north of Izapa, and symbolized the polar region. However, with its peak ascending into the highest regions of the sky, Tacana also symbolized the zenith. One wonders how Tacana could have represented both polar north and the zenith. The answer to this dilemma is evident when we look carefully at recent breakthroughs in understanding Mesoamerican mapping systems. We find that the northern cardinal direction (i.e., "north") was equivalent to "up" (the zenith direction). In other words, the Mesoamericans did not view directions in the same way that Europeans do, as abstract absolute concepts of north-south-east-west separated by 90° around the horizon. Mayanist Clemency Coggins wrote an interesting article called "The Zenith, the Mountain, the Center, and the Tree"[4] that provides a dualist framework for understanding Izapan cosmovision. She summarized the recent breakthroughs in understanding Mesoamerican directional concepts, reminding us that the vertical axis of zenith-nadir was associated in the minds of Mesoamerican thinkers with the topographical axis of north-south: North is equivalent to "up" (the sky) whereas south is equivalent to "down" (the direction of the Underworld). In Mesoamerican thought, the zenith is the fifth, central direction, and is thus also "up." As such, both polar north and the zenith belong to the conceptual category of "north." At Izapa, the December solstice direction to the south occupies the conceptual category "south"—north is the sky and south is the Underworld. Remember, too, that the Galactic Center, which rises along the December solstice horizon to the south, is near the Road to the Underworld, and, again, south is the direction of the Underworld. Here we see how the three cosmic centers fit into a basic north-south framework.[5]

In the *Popol Vuh*/Hero Twin Creation myth that appears on Izapan stelae, the primordial world prior to the first World Age consisted solely of sky above and Earth below. In other words, the underlying framework of space and time was conceived as an up-down or north-south polarity. The *Popol Vuh* goes on to state that the world began with a dialogue between the sky above and the ocean below, a basic doctrine clearly present at Izapa. In support of this notion of a dialogue between opposed conceptual categories, Izapa Stela 25 reveals a north-south polarity between the Big Dipper (polar center) and the Milky Way's dark-rift (Galactic Center).

The manmade pole Hunahpu holds serves to identify the conceptual north-south axis. I believe Stela 25 portrays the sky at midnight on the December solstice in era 100 B.C. The bird at the top is the Big Dip-

Diagram 136. Izapa Stela 25, a north-south polarity

per (in the "north"). The inverted caiman monster on the left is the Milky Way, whose head represents the Galactic Bulge, far below the Earth at midnight (farthest "south"). Thus, Stela 25 depicts the opposition between sky (north) and ocean (south), and we can deduce that Izapan cosmologists were interested in the dialogue that occurs between the astronomical movements of the Big Dipper and the Milky Way. As we will see, this dialogue is nothing less than the Creation myth dialogue between the old Polar God (Seven Macaw/Big Dipper) and the new Galactic God (One Hunahpu/December solstice sun). In sum, Izapa's north-south cosmovision manifests in the dialogue between the northern "centers" (polar and zenith) versus the southern "center" (the Galactic Center, located by the dark-rift and the cross formed by the Milky Way and the ecliptic in Sagittarius).[6]

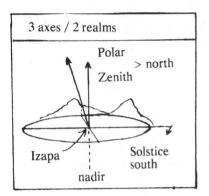

Diagram 137. North-south centers in Izapan cosmovision

One more consideration: The zenith has no horizon. As such, when looking for astronomical rise events along the horizon, as we must do to understand Izapan horizon astronomy, we are limited to the polar north and the solstice south. What is actually going on, astronomically, in these directions? First, let us look at the astronomy to the polar north.

As sketched earlier, the 23° azimuth baseline of Izapa Group B points not to the Tacana peak, but to a place 2° down the eastern flank, where we find a shallow cleft. As previously mentioned, this feature in the silhouette of Tacana is highly significant, and is related to the Olmec motif of a cleft-head deity. For the Olmec, the sacred volcano of the north was San Martín Pajapan, and artifacts and sculptures found in this volcano's crater demonstrate that offerings were made there to the Fire God (a very ancient First Father deity). Furthermore, the crater on top of San Martín was probably understood to represent the Creation cleft, the origin place of corn mentioned in the *Popol Vuh* as "the broken place, the bitter water place," which is an apt description of a volcanic crater.[7] The Solar/Maize Deity was thought to have been born from this place. The Maya Witznal deity often has a stepped or cleft forehead, and was probably derived from the older Olmec symbology. Furthermore, a cleft-head motif is very common in Olmec art, and corn is usually shown sprouting from it.

The Tacana cleft likely partook of Olmec Creation symbology, and thus the Izapan alignments to it are not surprising. This particular cleft also is near a mountain pass (a minor trade route into the highlands) and thus symbolizes a literal portal from one zone to another, recalling the symbolic associations involving caves and Otherworld portals. Emergence motifs surround this cave-cleft symbol-complex,[8] and it is certainly no coincidence that, around era 300 B.C., the Big Dipper rose along the eastern flank of Tacana where this cleft is located.[9]

My discovery of the Big Dipper's emergence through the Tacana cleft, though critical to understanding the message of Izapa's monuments, has yet to be recognized in studies of Izapa. After exploring the Big Dipper's movements with astronomy software, I recognized a pattern that highlights solstice dates as being significant in the Big Dipper's "cycle of emergence." On the December solstice during era 100 B.C., the sun set in the southwest (its

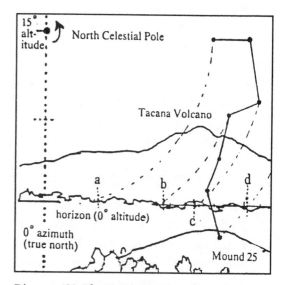

Diagram 138. The Big Dipper rising through the Tacana cleft after sundown on the December solstice of 100 B.C., viewed from Izapa

furthest southward set), and as the rays of the setting sun dissipated, attention turned to the north, where the Big Dipper's star, Dubhe, was seen rising over Tacana peak. Next, the Big Dipper's star Merak rose near the Tacana cleft, followed by the other stars in the Big Dipper.

In the diagram, we can see how the Big Dipper appeared to rise through the Tacana cleft more than 2,100 years ago, which is exactly what the Izapan skywatchers would have seen. The Big Dipper rose at sunset and set at sunrise on the December solstice, which means that it was visible for the entire night. The December solstice was thus a time when the Big Dipper was in a strong, ascending, and fully present place. In comparison, the sun on the December solstice was conceived of as weak and on the verge of death and rebirth. Six months later, the tables were turned. During the June solstice, the sun was "strongest," most fully present. At this time, the Big Dipper rose at dawn and thus was not visible at all throughout the night.[10]

Clearly, some kind of mythic story—or dialogue—was woven around these astronomical movements.

Next, let us look at the astronomy to the south, along the December solstice horizon. As a result of Group B's 23° azimuth baseline to the Tacana cleft, the perpendicular southeastward orientation of Izapa points to the December solstice sunrise, meaning that many of Izapa's carved monuments face the December solstice horizon, as if paying homage to it. The astronomical players on that horizon are the Galactic Center, the Milky Way, the crossroads, the dark-rift, and the December solstice sun. This place and time is, like the Big Dipper's emergence through the "cleft" in the north, also meaningful as a "birth" place. For one, the December solstice is when the sun dies and is reborn from the Underworld, to begin its phase of increasing daylight. Secondly, as I have explored throughout this book and in previous publications,[11] the dark-rift "cleft" in the Milky Way rose two hours before the December solstice sun in era 100 B.C. The dark-rift is the portal to the Otherworld, the celestial cave leading into the Heart of Sky, and the birth canal of the Great Mother (the Milky Way). The Milky Way's cleft in the south is, as mentioned earlier, conceptually analogous to the Tacana cleft in the north. Both are emergence places, and both involve competing deities or cosmic centers: polar versus Galactic; north versus south.

I feel it was a primary interest of Izapan skywatchers to compare the north and south emergence places, to derive a mythological dialogue between the two deities involved—the Big Dipper (Seven Macaw) versus the December solstice sun (One Hunahpu/First Father). This mythic dialogue plays itself out in the *Popol Vuh* battle between the avenging sons of the Solstice Deity and Seven Macaw (the Big Dipper Polar Deity). Ultimately, what we find encoded in this epic story, if we read between the lines, is the demise of the old Polar God of the Olmec, who is replaced by the Galactic God and the associated end-date cosmology. Here we catch another glimpse of the true meaning of the Hero Twin story.

To recap, the astronomical process in the north is twofold: The ascent of the sun into the zenith, occurring twice a year, signaled key events in the Izapan calendar and agricultural year. However, the zenith center is unique in that it has no associated horizon along which astronomical events occur. The other cosmic center of the north—the North Celestial Pole—is where significant mythic astronomy occurs. The Big Dipper rose through the Tacana cleft at sundown on the December solstice. This northern emergence was mirrored by rise events in the south. The cleft of Creation in the south is the dark-rift in the Milky Way, and the Milky Way itself was thought of, on one level, as the great fount of Creation, conceptually identical to the Tacana volcano as a Creation place. In this way, the astronomical "emergences" in the north and south reflect each other. The astronomical players are different, but were understood to symbolize similar functions. The Big Dipper rose through (or was born from) the Tacana cleft. In comparison, the December solstice sun was projected to rise through (or be born from) the dark-rift cleft of the Milky Way. These astronomical facts will be the keys to interpreting Izapa's monuments and cosmology.

Notice that the convergence of the solstice sun with its rebirth place (the dark-rift) is not an annual event. It takes place over thousands of years because it is caused by precession. If the north-south model is to hold true, precession also must be involved in the north and somehow impart effects on the Big Dipper. And it does. Here we enter into profound esoteric territory. The Izapan calendar-priests now appear as incredibly advanced astronomers and cosmologists, human beings who were far beyond what we have so far imagined. They were innovative visionaries who, as we will see in Chapter 23, also were very interested in initiating seekers into their profound discoveries.

THE NORTH-SOUTH DIALOGUE AT THE LEVEL OF PRECESSION

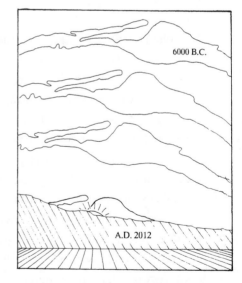

There is something else going on with the astronomy of the northern direction, and it involves precession. Here we must look at Izapan astronomy as it manifests on the level of World Ages. The Izapan skywatchers were tuned into vast cycles of time, and so were interested in the effects of precession. In this book, I have explored the meaning of the astronomical alignment that culminates on the Long Count end-date, which involves the December solstice sun converging with the Galactic Center near the dark-rift in the Milky Way. To the Izapan astronomers who calibrated the process, the convergence looked like this diagram.

Diagram 139. The Milky Way's movement or "fall" toward the December solstice sun between 6000 B.C. and A.D. 2012

The ancient skywatchers of Mesoamerica must have been very interested in the astronomy of this event and in calibrating its precession-caused convergence. Within the Izapan dialogical cosmovision, this event happened in "the south" and was somehow opposed to the Big Dipper's movement in the north. The slow approach of the solstice sun occurred at a consistent rate, because it occurred along the ecliptic. Precessional change along the ecliptic underwent a steady rate of slippage amounting to one degree every 71.5 years. However, the stars around the North Celestial Pole experienced variable rates of precession-caused change.[12] The reason can be understood by examining this diagram.

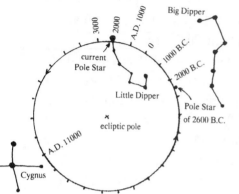

Diagram 140. Polar Circle inscribed during a full precessional cycle

The circle indicates the changing position of the North Celestial Pole over its 26,000-year precessional cycle. The years shown around the circle indicate where the North Celestial Pole was located during the epoch given. Picture the Big Dipper revolving around the North Celestial Pole of 3000 B.C.; then in 1000 B.C.; and A.D. 2000—and notice how the precession of the North Celestial Pole changes the orientation of the Big Dipper.

Take note of something else, too. Between 3000 B.C. and 1000 B.C. the Big Dipper, as a unit, remained uniformly close to the North Celestial Pole. For almost 2,000 years the Big Dipper hung close to the polar region.[13] After 1000 B.C., and increasingly after 600 B.C., the body of the Big Dipper began appearing to move away from the North Celestial Pole faster and faster. The effect is that of the Big Dipper hightailing it away from his polar roost *after* 1000 B.C.! This phenomenon was undoubtably tracked through a continuity of star lore collected and passed down by the earliest inhabitants of Izapa. But what might the Izapans have thought about this movement? Given that it involved the region in which the ancient Polar God resided, they must have been rather alarmed. Could this be the astronomical basis of the *Popol Vuh* myth of Seven Macaw falling out of his roost—being evicted rather abruptly from his ancient perch in the Heart of Heaven? This is a perfect example of how precessional astronomy and Izapan mythology were merged, and our attention is drawn to examine Izapa's monuments. An altar from Izapa shows Seven Macaw, the Big Dipper Polar God, sitting on his polar perch (see diagram 141).

Notice that his wings are not outstretched. He is not flying, or carrying a seed or the sun. He is just sitting on his perch, supplicated by the priest below. The "fall" of Seven Macaw, a key event in the closing of the previous World Age as testified to in the Maya Creation myth, involved his separation and increasing distance from his ancient polar home. Clearly, the astronomical divergence that began occurring around 1000 B.C. explains the disqualification and falsity of Seven Macaw/Big Dipper—he literally had a falling out from his status as the true avatar of the cosmic center. Accordingly, the Izapans must have concluded that the

Diagram 141. Izapa Altar 20: Seven Macaw on his polar perch

entire polar center was "false." In terms of astronomy, this is absolutely true. Though the sky is observed to revolve around the North Celestial Pole, it is not really the center of the sky. Or rather, it appears to be, but only from a limited perspective. Nor is it the cosmic source from which everything springs, although its diehard followers may falsely proclaim it to be. In fact, the cult of the Polar God may have survived in Mesoamerica for many centuries, its proponents irrationally holding on to erroneous half-truths. This unfortunate development, what we might call the evolution of Mesoamerican religious movements, mirrors the megalomania attributed to Seven Macaw/Big Dipper in the *Popol Vuh*. He believed that everything revolved around him; he was the vain and false ruler of the previous World Age, and the bearers of the new cosmology had to eject him from his high office to make room for the Galactic God of Precession, One Hunahpu. The *Popol Vuh* muses that the wooden people who lived during Seven Macaw's reign were so stiff and unfeeling (stuck as they were on the pole) that their tools rose up and destroyed them. It appears, then, that the *Popol Vuh* encodes hidden dimensions of the evolution of Mesoamerican cosmology, and warns us against believing in false gods. The Izapans were on to something.

The process by which the Big Dipper falls away from the North Celestial Pole continues for many millennia. Ultimately, the Big Dipper will be some 65° away from the North Celestial Pole in era A.D. 11,400. This means that 9,400 years from now the Big Dipper will share the same rise azimuth as the June solstice sun! The Big Dipper's changing rise azimuths during this journey through one-half of a precession cycle look like the following diagram:[14]

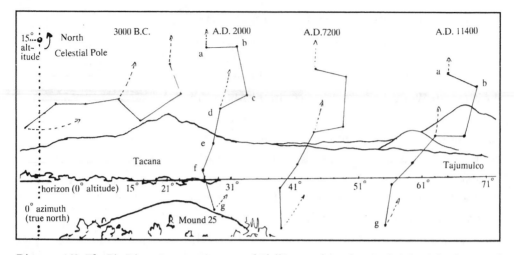

Diagram 142. The Big Dipper's precession-caused "fall" away from the North Celestial Pole toward Tajumulco and the June solstice sunrise

The ultimate twelfth-millennium rise place of the Big Dipper is made even more significant when we consider the topography surrounding Izapa. By A.D. 11,400 the Big Dipper will rise almost directly over Tajumulco. On the June solstice, the sun will still rise over Tajumulco, but some twelve hours after the Big Dipper, resulting in a beautiful counterpoint effect. The Big Dipper will have achieved an opposed synchronization with the June solstice sun—they will share the same rising azimuth, but will rise twelve hours apart. After era A.D. 11,400, the Big Dipper will begin to close distance with the North Celestial Pole once again.

The Big Dipper was closest to the North Celestial Pole between 3000 B.C. and 1000 B.C. Afterward, the Big Dipper's time as regent of the cosmic center came to an end, and its "descent" began. The slow advance of the Big Dipper through eons of time is pictured in diagram 143.

Notice the changing declination of the Big Dipper as precession moves it further away from the North Celestial Pole. Ultimately, the Big Dipper's southernmost declination in era A.D. 11,400 will coincide with the sun's declination on the June solstice—the day of the sun's northernmost declination. Whether or not the Izapans were aware of this particular far-future event, the convergence suggests a cosmic meeting of ancient deities.

Clearly, precession affects the Big Dipper and its relation to the polar center of the north. And the astronomy fits precisely into the Creation story preserved at

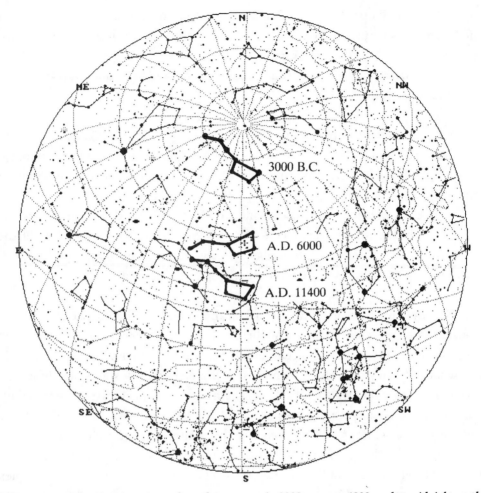

Diagram 143. The Big Dipper's southward movement in 3000 B.C., A.D. 6000, and at midnight on the June solstice of A.D. 11,400

Izapa, that which later became the Quiché *Popol Vuh*. Historically and mythologically, Seven Macaw started rapidly falling away from his polar perch beginning around 1000 B.C. Translating this back into astronomy, the Big Dipper's distance from the North Celestial Pole did, in fact, start to increase rapidly at this time. This era of rapidly increasing change also fits perfectly into the transformative period in Mesoamerican history during which the Olmec faded and the Maya began to emerge, armed with a new cosmological knowledge. But their new knowledge came only after the Izapans looked in the other direction, the south, where the future installation of the next World Age ruler, One Hunahpu, was observed and calibrated over the December solstice horizon. Given that the new cosmic center of the new cosmology was the Galactic Center, the Izapans, truly, were on to something big.

The amazing precessional cosmology discovered and fine-tuned at Izapa can be summed up as follows:

- **North:** The Big Dipper's flight or "fall" away from North Celestial Pole toward the June solstice, beginning around 1000 B.C. In terms of horizon topography, the movement is from one sacred volcano (Tacana) toward another (Tajumulco).
- **South:** The December solstice sun's flight or "birth" through the dark-rift cave in the Milky Way. Or, from a different perspective, the "fall" of the Milky Way toward the December solstice horizon. This convergence culminates in A.D. 2012, 13.0.0.0.0 in the Long Count calendar.

To summarize our exploration of Izapan astronomy, a complex three-directional model has been identified. The three directions or axes of Izapan cosmovision each points to its own cosmic center, and these three domains belong to a basic north-south framework. The zenith-passage dates are clearly significant in Izapan astronomy, as are the two solstice dates, and the astronomical features that make a hard-to-ignore appearance on these dates include the Milky Way, the dark-rift, the Big Dipper, the solstice sun, and, of course, the zenith sun. These clues are what we need to confidently approach the Izapan monuments with some hope of correct interpretation. We should be prepared to meet the challenge set by the complex multilevel cosmovision we have already decoded.

In this book, especially in Part II, I explored a precession-caused alignment in both the zenith center and the Galactic Center. And now we see that a similar precession-caused movement occurs in relation to that other cosmic center, the North Celestial Pole. In the same way that Quetzalcoatl was identified as the deity of the Zenith Cosmology and One Hunahpu was identified as the deity of the Galactic Cosmology, we can identify Seven Macaw as the deity of the Polar Cosmology. Each deity moves toward (or, in the case of Seven Macaw, away) from a cosmic throne, which Mesoamerican philosophers recognized as a cosmic center. I feel that the most important of the three cosmic centers, and the one best represented in Izapan cosmology, is the one identified by the 13-baktun cycle end-date: the

Galactic Center. Given that the new cosmology formulated at Izapa was oriented toward this cosmic center, I suggest that we consider this the ultimate secret of the Izapan Mysteries as we examine the monuments. It will be the key to interpreting the fascinating but nearly inscrutible monument arrangements in Group F. Now we have ventured into completely unknown cosmological territory, discovering nothing less than a lost Galactic paradigm. The profound cosmic understanding that gave rise to the Long Count calendar is, after lying buried for almost three baktuns, finally yielding its secrets.

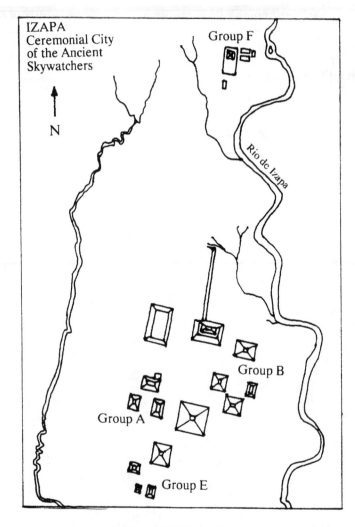

Diagram 144. Map of Izapa

CHAPTER 22

THE MONUMENTAL MESSAGE

The Izapan monuments contain mythic dramas, tantalizing adventures recognizable as the Hero Twin Creation story. Given the astronomical interests of the Izapans, it is no surprise that the Hero Twin story is a metaphor for astronomical events, and that the key to understanding it involves recognizing that the monuments of Izapa, upon which the Hero Twin myth is preserved, reflect astronomical events occurring along the horizons toward which they are oriented. Here we recover the lost half of the Hero Twin myth, the astronomical events that up until now have been obscure.

The primary Izapan monument groups can be located in diagram 144.

Since Izapan cosmology involves three cosmic centers and axes, I have chosen to simply identify monument meanings based on their relationship to these three axes: polar north, zenith, and solstice south. (Since the December solstice horizon is where the Milky Way/ecliptic crossroads rose during the Izapan era, the solstice axis points to the great central bulge in the Galaxy and thus can be considered to be the Galactic Center indicator.) As such, we can categorize the symbolic content of Izapa's monuments under the following three cosmic centers:

- The Polar Center. The monuments of Group A contain the message of the ascent and descent of Seven Macaw to the north—the rise and fall of the Big Dipper around Tacana and the North Celestial Pole.
- The Zenith Center. Group B, with its zenith gnomons, Throne 1, and Stela 9,

was clearly the ceremonial section of Izapa in which the zenith center was worshiped. Throne 1 contains complex astronomical information demarcating zenith-passage days, with the zenith at the center.

- The Galactic Center. The Group F ballcourt, oriented to the December solstice horizon, contains thrones and monuments that describe the astronomical convergence occurring in that direction—the convergence of the Milky Way and the solstice sun that will culminate on 13.0.0.0.0. Stela 11 from Group B and the two stelae from Group E face the same horizon and reinforce this message.

Each of the three monument groups refers to a specific cosmic center. However, certain monuments in a given group may refer to a different cosmic center, because the different centers were interrelated in Izapan thought. In other words, though each group has its primary reference to a specific cosmic center, the other two cosmic centers also were incorporated into each group's message because the centers mirror each other. The mythology encoded in the monuments was concerned with a dialogue between the centers. For example, Group A primarily contains information about the Big Dipper (Seven Macaw) to the north. However, Stela 27, on the eastern side of Group A, is the only monument in that group that faces the December solstice horizon.

Diagram 145. Stela 27, a depiction of the solstice horizon astronomy

It portrays an inverted caiman-tree, a symbol identified by Maya scholars as the Milky Way. As such, though Group A's primary concern is with the polar center, Stela 27 is a reminder of the Galactic Center that rises to the southeast.

Likewise, Group F primarily describes the solar convergence with the Galactic Center along the December solstice horizon. The Group F ballcourt itself, pointing to the Milky Way and the dark-rift, symbolizes the Milky Way. And yet Stela 60 is placed prominently in the Group F ballcourt, and it shows a victorious ballplayer standing over a fallen Seven Macaw. This seems to be a reminder that the Galactic convergence cannot occur unless the Polar God has been defeated. In general then, we should be aware that all of the monuments in a given group do not exclusively portray the same cosmic center. Having said that, it remains clear that each group has a primary association with one of the three cosmic centers.

GROUP B: HOMAGE TO THE ZENITH GOD

Group B contains a large northward-facing temple, called Mound 30a, in which archaeologists found many offering caches. Like other Mesoamerican temples, its very form encodes the quadrated cosmogram with the zenith in the center. The northward-facing platform in Group B is the primary focus of the plaza's monuments. Although there are platforms to the east, west, and south, only the northern and western platforms contain carved monuments. The western platform contains Stelae 11, 12, and 50, which face the December solstice sunrise and the Galactic Center; they appear to make a separate statement about that cosmic center, and we will look at them in detail later. The primary ritual focus of Group B is along the line formed by Throne 1, the pillar-and-ball monument directly in front of Throne 1, the large Stela 9 (flanked by Stelae 8 and 10), and the Stela 24/Altar 20 combo on the main platform.

Diagram 146. Group B: The Zenith Group. From Lowe et al. (1982:178)

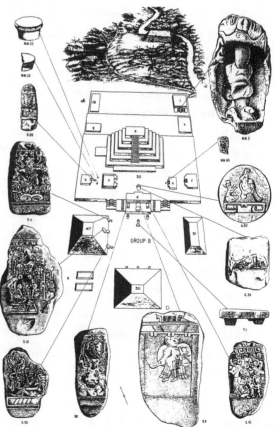

The three pillar-and-ball monuments most likely were used to identify the date of the solar zenith passage. These are vertical gnomons that cast no shadows at high noon on the zenith-passage days, and the ball on top symbolizes the sun on top of the cosmic zenith axis.[1] Throne 1 is incredibly interesting, as it has five glyphs along its edges and a crossband on its flat upper throne surface:

Notice in diagram 147 that the

five glyphs are all basically the same. They are deity faces, used as directional placemarkers similar to the directional chacs of the Yucatec Maya. The cross-bands that are found on most Mesoamer-ican thrones symbolize the cosmic center from which the king-shaman rules, and Izapa Throne 1 is no exception. Re-member, Mesoamerican king-shamans were enthroned upon the cosmic center and cultivated their power by periodically

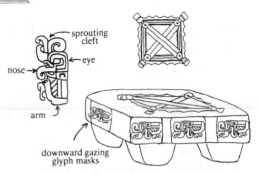

Diagram 147. Throne 1: Glyph arrangements, crossbands, and deity mask details

journeying into it. The specific cosmic center represented by the crossbands de-pends upon the context. Here, the crossband design represents the Mesoamerican zenith cosmogram: The corners are the four solstice rise and set positions, and the center represents the zenith. Thus, Throne 1 is the king-shaman's seat in the ze-nith center.

Throne 1 provides another clue that Group B represents the zenith center: Only three of the five glyphs around the edge of Throne 1 accurately correspond to the quadrated scheme. The two glyphs on the south corners refer to the December solstice sunrise and sun-set positions—the solstice south di-rection. The center glyph on the south edge refers to the center di-rection—the zenith direction also

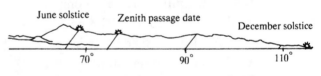
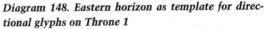

Diagram 148. Eastern horizon as template for direc-tional glyphs on Throne 1

indicated by the crossbands on the upper surface.[2] Significantly, the two glyphs along the east and west edges are not quite on the back corners; they are only about four-fifths of the way back. If we look at the eastern horizon sunrise in diagram 148, we get a clue as to what these two glyphs probably represent.

In the diagram, notice where the zenith sun rises in relation to the two solstice sunrises—about four-fifths of the way in between. As a result, it is fairly clear that the two glyphs on the east and west edges of Throne 1 represent sunrise and sunset on the solar zenith-passage dates. (The horizon positions for both the May and Au-gust zenith-passage dates are the same.) So, Throne 1 actually encodes a great deal of cosmological information.

Throne 1's encoded information:

a) December solstice sunrise
b) December solstice sunset
c) Zenith-passage date sunrise
d) The zenith (noon on zenith-passage date)
e) Zenith-passage date sunset
f) June solstice sunrise
g) June solstice sunset
h) Sight line to Tacana cleft (north)
i) Center glyph meaning zenith and north
j) Equinox axis (rise and set)

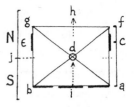

Diagram 149. Izapa Throne 1's encoded astronomical information (N = North; S = South)

The crossband on Throne 1 reinforces the notion of a quadrated universe based upon the solstice axes, a cosmo-conception that we first encountered in Izapa's solstice orientation. The crossbands conform to the rectangular shape of the throne-stone itself. The five glyphs around the edge, however, provide additional information by way of their offset positions. Two of them are at the corners, and therefore represent the December solstice rise-set, which occurs in the south. Three of them refer to zenith events (one to sunrise on the zenith-passage date, one to noon on the zenith-passage date, and one to sunset on the zenith-passage date). This glyph-triplet is replicated by the three nearby pillar-and-ball gnomons, closely associated with Throne 1.

Diagram 150. Throne 1 and associated zenith gnomons, with Stelae 8, 9, and 10

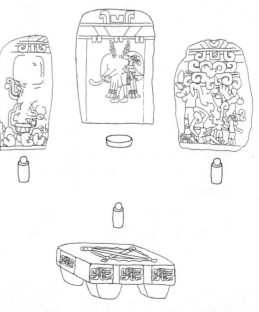

In all probability, the center-front pillar-and-ball zenith gnomon corresponds to the center-front glyph on the south edge of Throne 1 (both symbolize the sun in the zenith). The glyph on the left or west edge of Throne 1, together with the western pillar-and-ball gnomon, refers to sunset on the zenith-passage days. The glyph on the east edge of Throne 1, together with the eastward pillar-and-ball gnomon, refers to sunrise on the zenith-passage days.

Stelae 8, 9, and 10 are directly in front of the pillar-and-ball throne-glyph triad, and the center stela in this group is Stela 9. This stela depicts a solar deity carrying a human figure up into the zenith, symbolizing the vision quest undertaken by the priest-ruler who sits on Throne 1. He has successfully invoked his celestial *naguales* (spirit helpers), who now carry him into the cosmic center, in this case, the zenith.

Stela 9 is flanked by Stelae 8 and 10, both of which contain a vertical polarity. The general up-down polarity is most clear on Stela 8, in which the upper and lower frames are enclosed within squarish or quadrated boxes. Some kind of frog or caiman beast unites the upper and

Diagram 151. Stela 9. A solar shaman's ascent to the zenith

lower scenes, and the lower scene shows a human figure sitting on a throne, framed in the quadrated Underworld symbol.[3] This cross-marked throne-spot is in the belly of the Stela 8 beast, reinforcing the idea that the throne-sitting ruler is in the cosmic center (in Maya thought, the belly of a cosmic monster represents the center of the Underworld). Because of the solar connotation of the zenith passage, the throne-sitting figure on Stela 8 must be a solar ruler or earthly representative of the sun. Unfortunately, most of the upper scene on Stela 8 has chipped off. What remains is a squared scene near the upturned mouth of the Stela 8 frog-caiman monster. The serrated edge within the squared frame is

Diagram 152. Stelae 8 and 10 compared

similar to the serrated pattern around the Throne 1 crossbands, suggesting the Otherworld and sacred center concepts. Some kind of up-down parallelism seems intended on Stela 8, which confirms the north-south model adopted by Izapan cosmologists.

According to V. Garth Norman, the upper frame of Stela 8 contains a strange creature, possibly a bee. Interestingly, bees can signal the zenith-passage day because when they leave their hives at high noon on zenith-passage days, they are directionally disoriented. They navigate by orienting themselves to the sun, and when it is in the zenith they are confused. Finally, the surviving serration device on Stela 8 also resembles the design surrounding the Solar Lord on Stela 67 in Group F, which portrays the sun in the center of the Milky Way canoe. As such, its usage on Stela 8 probably reflects the same meaning as the quadrated cartouche below it, saying, in effect, "this is happening in a cosmic center."

In general, Stela 8 embodies a dialogue between womb and mouth, each representing a cosmic center, and the two competing centers share the implied mythic reading of both "womb" and "mouth." Why? The conjuring or "womb-birthing" that occurs on Throne 1 refers to the zenith center. The upturned frog-caiman (with its mouth open) means "to be born" or "date initiation." Thus, the upper frame of Stela 8 suggests both birthing and swallowing, womb and mouth. The lower frame is in the belly or stomach of the beast. The throne within the belly seems to imply that this is the location of another cosmic center, one in the south, one in the belly of the beast (the Milky Way's central bulge or womb). This cosmic womb is the caldron of Creation, observed as the "fat" part of the Milky Way near the dark-rift. And the dark-rift is the birth canal of the Great Mother. Thus, our examination so far yields a dialogue between two cosmic centers, one in the north (the zenith) and one in the south (Galactic).

Moving to Stela 10, to the right of Stela 9, we see a caiman-tree deity uniting the upper and lower scenes. The entire scene, as previously mentioned, depicts the pregnancy of Blood Moon, mother of the Hero Twins. Connected to her womb via an umbilical rope, we see the Hero Twins, Hunahpu and Xbalanque. She rests against the caiman-tree, and a similar caiman-tree on Stela 27 in Group A has a quadrated cartouche in its midsection, much like the one we just saw on lower Stela 8. The upper branches of the caiman-tree on Stela 10 billow into cloud scrolls, similar to the ones used to portray the Central Mexican Milky Way deity, Mixcoatl. The human figure caught up in these star clouds of the Milky Way is One Hunahpu, father of the Hero Twins. In the *Popol Vuh*, he hangs in a crook in the sacred calabash tree and impregnates Blood Moon below with the Hero Twins. Recalling that the crook of the calabash tree that stands by the road is the dark-rift in the Milky Way, we have a statement here of a cosmic center—the Galactic Center. Like the ascending figure on Stela 9, on Stela 10 First Father is in a cosmic center—the big, fat, fertile part of the Milky Way that marks the Galactic Center.

Earlier, in the zenith symbology of Throne 1 and its related pillar-and-ball gnomons, we identified the zenith as Group B's preferred cosmic center. This identification was confirmed on Stela 9, where a deity figure is being carried into the zenith. However, here on the neighboring Stela 10, a similar deity figure has ascended into the billowing clouds of the Milky Way's center. The center of the Milky Way is, in fact, located near the place where One Hunahpu's head was hung, at the cosmic crossroads formed by the Milky Way and the ecliptic near Sagittarius, where the dark-rift "crook of the calabash tree" is located. This is where the billows of the Milky Way are brightest and thickest. Recalling that the Milky Way was sometimes viewed as a snake, the image evokes a pregnancy. Furthermore, the snake metaphor suggests a deeper interpretation of this symbology. Snakes are clearly bloated right after ingesting a meal, suggesting devouring, and the idea arises that birth and death are related processes. A conceptual similarity between snakes' mouths and human birthing is evident when we understand that a woman's cervix "unhinges" while she is giving birth, just like a snake's mouth can while it is devouring something. The Maya were no doubt aware of these parallels that are also evident, as sketched above, in the womb-mouth polarity of Stela 8. A sophisticated philosophy of creation and destruction as being two sides of the same coin is nicely merged in this Izapan snake metaphor for the Milky Way.

The stelae we just examined all contain a vertical duality, confirming the north-south framework already identified as a fundamental tenet of Izapan cosmology. Stela 11, on the west platform, also contains an up-down polarity. Stelae 11 and 8 both depict an up-ended caiman-frog with a quadrated form in their "stomachs." On Stela 11 it is a crossband, symbolizing the cross of the Milky Way and ecliptic towards which it faces; on Stela 8 it is the quadrated cartouche. Both stelae appear to have an important upper scene in which something (a solar deity on Stela 11) is being born from the deity's mouth. We will explore Stela 11 in more detail in a later section of this chapter.

These comparisons demonstrate the interweaving nature of Izapan mythology. Some motifs are almost interchangeable, because they refer to the same cosmological concept—the cosmic center. We cannot leave Group B without mentioning Altar 20, which lies on the main north-south axis with Throne 1 and Stela 9.

The stela associated with Altar 20 is almost completely obliterated, but seems to show a standing human figure. The bird deity on Altar 20 resembles the one on Stela 25, who, as we saw, is Seven Macaw, the Big Dipper. The Altar 20 image often has been mistakenly interpreted as a bird carrying a fruit to a beckoning person. But this bird is not in flight; its wings are not outstretched. Instead, Seven Macaw is depicted here perched upon the North Celestial Pole around which he revolves. The human figure on Altar 20 is worshiping or making an offering to Seven Macaw, as would happen on this northward-facing altar. In other words, it appears that offerings were made to a specific constellation, what we call today the Big Dipper. In addition, basal panels like the one on this altar portray a bar-and-two-dots "7", reinforcing the identification of this bird deity as Seven Macaw because there are seven stars in the Big Dipper. As mentioned earlier, proof of the identification of Seven Macaw with the Big Dipper comes from solid ethnographic data.[4]

We should remember that the Big Dipper rose out of the cleft on Tacana's eastern flank, most notably after sundown on the December solstice in era 100 B.C. This opposed the sun's "rising" or "birth" through the cleft of the Milky Way in the south. So, it is not surprising that the third cosmic center portrayed in Group B is the polar center. Altar 20 depicts the polar center as Seven Macaw sitting on his polar perch. However, the pole and the zenith both belong to the same category of

Diagram 153. Altar 20's bar-and-two-dots "7" on its basal panel

"north" whereas the Milky Way/ecliptic cross near the Galactic Center is in the "south." Overall, the various stelae in Group B attempt to demonstrate, by way of complementary analogy, the reversible unity of the north-south Izapan cosmology.

Though Izapan cosmovision boils down to a north-south opposition, we should remember that three cosmic centers are involved. These different centers were synthesized into one mythic whole in the multilevel cosmic consciousness attained at Izapa. However, because of the centrality and prominence of Throne 1, Stela 9, and related pillar-and-ball monuments, Group B was primarily arranged to celebrate the zenith axis and the zenith center as a destination of Izapan astronomer-priests.

GROUP A: THE POLAR GOD'S DEMISE

Group A, to the west of the main Group H baseline, contains many of Izapa's most iconographically compelling stelae. This group is comprised of four platforms, oriented north-south or toward the December solstice. All of the carved monuments in Group A, except one, are at the north or south platforms. The exception, Stela 27, is in front of the east platform and is oriented to the December solstice horizon.

Stela 27 is clearly in league with the Group B references to the December solstice end-date alignment. On this stela, we see an inverted caiman-tree that contains a quadrated cartouche symbolizing the Sacred Tree "crossroads" of the Milky Way and the ecliptic. If Izapa was a center of learning and initiation, as I will argue later, then Stela 27 may have served to introduce the Izapan initiate to the idea that there was more than one cosmic center. As such, Group A may have been the first group visited during initiation into the ancient Izapan Mysteries.

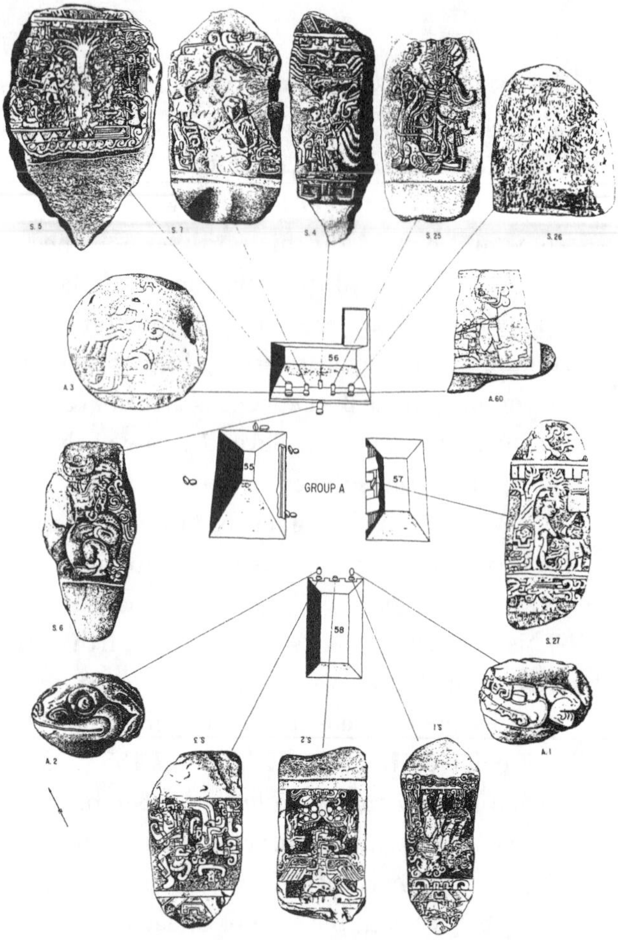

Diagram 154. Group A monuments. From Lowe et al. (1982:158)

The primary north-south monuments of Group A tell of the circumpolar adventures of the Big Dipper bird deity, Seven Macaw. The north platform contains a row of five stelae, including Stela 25 and Stela 5. The altar associated with Stela 7 depicts Seven Macaw in upward flight.

Diagram 155. Altar 3. Seven Macaw in upward flight

Stela 5 is probably one of the oldest monuments at Izapa, dating to about 300 B.C., and was called a "supernarrative" by V. Garth Norman in his compendious 1976 analysis of Izapan stelae. Volumes could be written about this carving, but I will limit our exploration to a few basic themes.

There is a sky panel at the top, water scrolls at the bottom, and a central Sacred Tree (probably representing Tacana and/or the Milky Way) connecting the two. On the extreme right we see downflowing rain and on the extreme left evaporation scrolls, indicating that the narrative of the scene moves in a clockwise direction. At the base of the tree, at ground level, seven figures are involved in various activities. I will number these figures 1 through 7 from right to left. Figure 1 on the far right is holding an umbrella, and appears to be assisting Figure 2. Figure 2, probably Hunahpu, holds a writing utensil and is teaching Figures 3 and 4. Figure 3 is probably a small child. On the left side of the tree, Figure 5

Diagram 156. Izapa Stela 5. The Mesoamerican Creation myth

appears to be taking instruction from the imposing Figure 6. Norman and Lowe believe that Figures 6 and 7 are Xpiyacoc and Xmucane, one of the Creator couples from the *Popol Vuh*.

In the background of the entire scene, visible on the extreme left and right of the stela, a U symbol with a gaping tooth-filled jaw can be identified. This U symbol is a common component of many Izapan stelae, and is thought to represent the moon or an Earth deity. In general, however, this symbol of the tooth-filled jaw represents the mouth of the Underworld. As such, Stela 5 is intended to portray mytho-astronomical events rather than mundane, historical ones. The narrative in complex scenes like this is read by following the symbolic connections between the figures. For example, it is probably no accident that the feet of the small figure directly above Figure 2 touch the "Ahau" cap of that figure. On the left and right of the tree, there are two main human figures suspended in midair. They are wearing bird deity masks, and the beak of one of them seems to be inserted into the tree. Stela 5 probably depicts events from different World Ages, and thus the narrative sequence can be temporal as well as spacial. Norman goes a long way toward clarifying what is going on in this incredible monument, and concludes that it is some form of a prototypal Mesoamerican Creation drama, clearly related to the *Popol Vuh*.[5]

The so-called "roots" of the tree in Stela 5 are strange, and look like beard scrolls or a deluge of water. In fact, they look a lot like the flood scene from the

Dresden Codex, in which water spews downward from the mouth of a sky deity attached to zodiac panels. The *Dresden Codex* scene illustrates the end of a previous World Age, and, significantly, the flood comes out of a mouth (see diagram 91 in Part III). In the

Diagram 157. Flood-glyphs designating Hurakan and Ahau rulers

Popol Vuh, the high god Hurakan destroys a previous World Age by flood, and we should not rule out that this flood was sent out of Hurakan's mouth, as that is a common flood motif. In addition, Hurakan was the Heart of Sky, a primary Creator God of the *Popol Vuh.* If Hurakan or his earthly Ahau servants are portrayed anywhere in the monumental art, they should be identifiable by some kind of glyphic insignia, such as those shown above.

Diagram 158. Stela 2. Cleft Creation tree, Seven Macaw, and the Hero Twins

In these prototypal Ahau glyphs, notice the beard-like extensions from the mouths. These are not song-scrolls, as some scholars suggest. I propose that these are glyphic designations for the mighty flood-bringer Hurakan himself, signatures for his earthly Ahau representatives. Other "flood-beards" are found on Stelae 11 and 67, and a "flood from the mouth" image appears on Stela 12. When these appear in a monument, a calendric period-ending event is probably being portrayed. Stela 5 may in part portray such an event—the end of one age and the beginning of another. After all, Stela 5 is generally acknowledged as a complex depiction of the Maya Creation myth.

Moving on to other Group A monuments, Stela 2 is in the middle of the south platform. It is flanked by Stelae 1 and 3. Instead of an upturned serpent as on Stela 3, Stela 2 portrays a tree with branches spread wide, above which is the Seven Macaw/Big Dipper deity.

The cleft tree here, because of the north-south orientation of Stela 2, is probably a metaphor for Tacana and its cleft. (The cosmic axis concept was mythologized variously as a mountain/volcano, a tree, or a caiman-frog deity.) As we have seen, the Big Dipper emerges from this cleft in era 300 B.C. But, on Stela 2, the Big

Dipper appears to be falling, head down. How can the Big Dipper rise and fall at the same time? Stela 2 contains a profound paradox. As shown earlier, the Big Dipper's precessional journey away from Tacana accelerated and moved southeastward along the Tacana-Tajumulco horizon beginning around 1000 B.C. According to my reconstruction, the entire "fall of Seven Macaw" myth actually refers to a larger World Age context involving precession. Stela 2 depicts the Hero Twins doing something, most likely facilitating the demise of Seven Macaw. As such, Stela 2, along with other monuments in Group A, participates in the message that Seven Macaw, the Polar God, is no longer valid. However, the Izapan initiate could still make the nightly observation that Seven Macaw continued to rise through the cleft. The paradoxical message of Stela 2 is that Seven Macaw rises nightly but, in the long run, he falls.

Diagram 159. Stela 4. The sacrifice of Seven Macaw

Across the plaza, opposite Stela 2, Stela 4 also depicts the descent of Seven Macaw. The figure holds a sacrifice club, reminding us that deity sacrifice must take place before world renewal. Seven Macaw must be done away with before the new World Age ruler can arrive. It should be emphasized that Stelae 2 and 4 are located in the center position of their respective north and south platforms, along Group A's main axis. Because of the Seven Macaw/Big Dipper themes on these monuments and their position on the north-south "polar" axis, I feel that Group A was primarily intended to represent the polar center.

Just to the east of Stela 4, Stela 25 depicts a scene from the *Popol Vuh* and, as discussed earlier, the sky at midnight on the December solstice:

Diagram 160. Stela 25. Midnight on the December solstice, era 300 B.C.

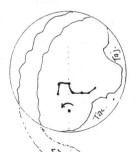

The inverted alligator is the Milky Way, with its dark-rift mouth closed and "beneath" the Earth, that is, below the horizon. Seven Macaw

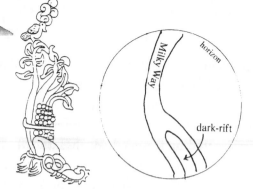

is standing firm on his polar perch, striking a victory over Hunahpu by snatching his arm. The Big Dipper has not quite reached its meridian transit to begin its fall in the west. There are other times of the year when this Big Dipper-Milky Way configuration is equivalent, though it occurs at different times of the night. In general, Stela 25 shows the Big Dipper bird deity in a strong, ascended place, while other Group A scenes

Diagram 161. Milky Way as Cosmic Tree compared with caiman-tree on Stela 25

show him falling. Clearly, the rise and fall of Seven Macaw is a primary story that Izapan cosmologists wanted to tell their initiates. They wanted to convey the cosmological discovery that, despite his apparent glory, Seven Macaw was a false god and the polar center was no longer a valid cosmic center.

Maya scholars Linda Schele and David Kelley identified the caiman on Stela 25 as the Milky Way.[6] Kelley's diagram (161) of the Milky Way serpent-caiman reveals why the tail end is flowering. The "mouth" side of the Milky Way is near the December solstice, the time of year when the rains fail and things become dry and infertile, when, in a sense, life is devoured by the mouth of the death monster. The tail end is in the rainy, fertile months of May and June, and thus is depicted as flowering. We have a clear statement here that caiman and snake-beings refer to the Milky Way on Izapan stelae. However, as seen on Stelae 27 and 10, the caiman transforms into a tree (note the caiman masks at the base of these trees). The mouth, or dark-rift, is inactive in these depictions, but on Stelae 6 and 11 the caiman-frog deity is pointing upward with its mouth open. This upturned mouth symbol means "to be born."

Diagram 162. Stela 1. A paradox circle

Stela 1, on the south platform, contains a clockwise rain-cycle motion. It accurately reflects the sky motion occurring behind someone who faces the stela.

The circular motion on Stela 1 may have been a teaching device, similar to the reversible paradox of simultaneous "rising and falling" on Stela 2. The intitiate stood in front of the Stela 1 rain invocation, facing south. Looking at the stela, the rain cycle is clockwise. Turning around, the initiate observed the stars spinning *counterclockwise* around the North Celestial Pole. But if the initiate faced the stela and imagined the stars spinning behind his head, he might "get it" and realize that the polar sky's rotation is directly imaged on Stela 1.[7]

ANOTHER GROUP A MESSAGE: TOOLS OF VISION AND THE GALACTIC TOAD

During the first century B.C., Izapa was contemporary with Tres Zapotes, a latter-day Olmec town near the Gulf Coast, and it is clear that Izapa retained connections with the Olmec heartland to the north. Some Izapan monuments are distinctly Olmec, and we can expect that important shamanistic institutions were shared. In Part III, I elaborated on the use of psychoactive substances (such as psilocybe mushrooms and toad venom), and, at Izapa, there are many depictions of frogs, toads, and alligators. For example, in front of Group A's south platform, both Stela 3 and Stela 1 have toad altars in front of them. The other important toad image in Group A is on Stela 6, located on the main north-south axis. In the same way that the three pillar-and-ball monuments in Group B triangulate, the three toad depictions in Group A also form a triangle.

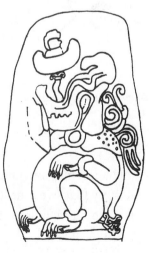

Diagram 163. Stela 6. Triptamine vision scrolls

Izapan shamans perceived toads—especially their mouths—as vehicles or doorways to the Otherworld, capable of birthing and/or swallowing deities who are often seated in little boats. Stela 6 shows this kind of scene, as well as something else.

Notice the strange dotted shoulder area, right where the *Bufo* toad's triptamine-containing parotid glands are located. (Toad Altar 2, in front of Stela 3, also has dotted parotid glands.) The curling vision clouds emerge from this area, indicating that the toad's gland secretions are a source of vision. The mythic meaning seems to be that the Sacred Toad can carry one into the mouth of the Otherworld, into the cosmic center! Though there are toad altars and many other carvings of toads and

Diagram 164. The three-spot toad-gland motif

crocodiles at Izapa, the Stela 6 depiction is unusual among Izapan sculpture. And it says a great deal about one important facet of Izapan cosmology: It was informed by the use not only of psychoactive mushrooms, but also of 5-MeODMT, a powerful hallucinogen. As such, we can probably apply the same knowledge to other towns within the Izapan sphere, such as Abaj Takalik and El Baúl, places where very early Long Count monuments were found. But precision in equating toad habitats with early Long Count monuments is not even necessary. These substances were definitely used, and were probably traded throughout large areas of Mesoamerica. The insights and knowledge afforded by such progressive evolutionary tools were clearly part of the shamanistic and cosmological mindset of the people who created the Long Count. Using these tools wisely, in the development of an advanced cosmology we are just beginning to understand, implies a type of sophistication on the part of Izapans not to be equated with their level of technological achievement. The advanced paradigm forged by the ancient skywatchers, orienting themselves to the greater Galaxy, was achieved by recognizing and using the powerful tools of consciousness, offered by nature herself, lurking within deer dung and warty toads.

Evidence of this kind also is found elsewhere. For example, there is a toad glyph on the Tablet of the Palace at Palenque, dated to A.D. 645.[8] The mundane reference of this glyph is to the haab month "Uo" (frog), but the primary attribute of this toad glyph are the three spots on the back of its head—the parotid glands of *Bufo marines.*

Diagram 165. Crocodile deity from the murals of Bonampak

This three-spot toad motif is found elsewhere in Maya art, for example, on a "crocodile" being from the murals of Bonampak. The deteriorated Bonampak murals were recently reconstructed with high-tech computer equipment.[9] In Room One, there are human beings (deity impersonators engaged in a Mystery Play) wearing deity masks. The one of interest is the caiman or crocodile mask, which includes a three-spot motif on its shoulder, out of which sprouts a waterlily vision plant.[10]

Of course, this is a crocodile rather than a frog, illustrating the crossover in the representation of different animal species that scholars recognize as common in Maya art. In other words, snakes, frogs, and caimans are in the same mythic category as all water deities—beings of the watery Underworld beneath the cosmic ocean.

These depictions suggest that the toad was a shamanic spirit guide and also served as the "vehicle" of vision. Stela 6, like the similar jaguar-toad deity on Stela 11, is the Milky Way, and the upturned mouth is thus the dark-rift. In this alternate reading, the boat floating above the toad's mouth may depict the solar hero sailing over the Milky Way or into the Otherworld. Or, the boat may simply indicate that a journey is being made, a vision journey into the mouth of the Milky Way. In any case, Stela 6 is very important, for it suggests that the Izapan shamans knew how to use the *Bufo marines* toad to facilitate vision journeys into outer space.

THE LESSON OF THE POLAR GOD

The primary concern of Group A's message is with the north-south polar axis, and the movement of the Big Dipper around Tacana to the north. This seasonally changing movement was keyed to the rain cycle, and thus involved the birth of corn and the Maize Deity. Group A's reminders that the northern polar events were opposed to the southern December solstice events are provided by Stela 27, Stela 25, as well as Stelae 6 and 3.

The symbolism on each Izapan monument, regardless of which group it is in, refers to its respective cosmic center in consistent ways. The stelae associated with the December solstice horizon (27, 11, 50, and 10) involve impregnation, umbilical connection, and birth or rebirth. Scenes oriented north-south (Altars 20 and 3, Stelae 4, 25, and 2) consistently portray the cyclical rise and fall of the Seven Macaw/Big Dipper deity around the pole. Apparently, the Izapan astronomer-priests considered the cyclical ascent-descent motion (of the north) to be equivalent to the cyclical death-rebirth process (of the south), a notion supported by the *Popol Vuh* metaphor that equates dawning with birthing. In Maya thought, the rising or "dawning" of celestial bodies is likened to birth and growth, whereas stellar descent is equivalent to dying and death. This concept is found throughout Mesoamerica and is certainly true for the modern Quiché Maya.[11] The descent of the stars of the Big Dipper symbolizes the death of the old Polar God, Seven Macaw. He was a vain and false ruler, follower of lies. His lesson to humanity is that deception is fueled by self-interest and ultimately results in exposure and self-destruction.

Izapan thinkers mythologized the December solstice astronomy primarily with birth and resurrection metaphors. However, it also involves death motifs. The dark-rift Otherworld doorway that rose heliacally on the December solstice as the Big Dipper set is a birthplace *and* a deathplace. Why? It is a birthplace because it is the birth canal of the cosmic Milky Way Creatrix, where the solstice sun gets reborn in A.D. 2012. It is a deathplace because it is the portal to the land of the dead and unborn. The cosmic birthplace also is the sacrificial altar, the *chilate* hole of offering. World renewal does not just happen, the day does not automatically dawn, the rains do not always fall on time—these things require ongoing sacrifices to facilitate and ensure their recurrence. As we saw earlier, ritual sacrifice played a prominent role in the Mesoamerican ballgame. It was ritual sacrifice performed as a form of sympathetic magic to ensure that the cosmic gameball went into the cosmic goalring. The cosmic meaning of the ritual ballgame—that the game is over in A.D. 2012—is clearly present in Izapa's ballcourt.

IZAPA'S COSMIC MESSAGE: GALACTIC CENTER CONVERGENCE

Each of the three main Izapan monument groups each point to one of the three cosmic centers recognized in Mesoamerican cosmology. Group A refers to the polar center, and portrays the mythic rise and demise of the ancient Polar God. Only Stela 27 in Group A clearly refers to another cosmic center, almost as if to answer the question: If Seven Macaw is a false god, defeated by the Hero Twins, where then is the true cosmic center? Stela 27 provides a clue, leading us over to the Group B monuments. As we saw, Group B refers to the zenith center, and Throne 1 in particular encodes a large amount of relevant astronomical information. Several stelae in Group B clearly portray the astronomy in the December solstice direction, as if the esoteric message was slowly being revealed to the Izapan initiate. Yes, there is more than one cosmic center. The Group B monuments tell us that the cosmic center is the zenith, and one may ascend into it, but only on certain days of the year. Knowing that the latitude of observation is critical for measuring solar zenith-passage dates, Izapan astronomers must have realized that the zenith center could be accessed, but the timing of its manifestation varied. So, our attention is drawn to the three stelae on the west platform of Group B, which includes Stela 11, where a solution to the zenith dilemma is offered. It was probably here that the Izapan cosmonauts-in-training first learned of the vast cycle of precession, and it was here, in front of Stela 11, that they were initiated into the mysteries that would lead them to Group F and its ballcourt. The ultimate revelation of the Izapan Mysteries is the Galactic Convergence on 13.0.0.0.0, but they *first* glimpsed this incredible knowledge when they saw Stela 11 in Group B. Group F, as we will see, encodes the Galactic Center synchronization of 13.0.0.0.0 via its ballcourt monuments. Before we move to explore Group F, we must pause at certain exceptional monuments from areas outside Group F that face the December solstice and make important statements about the future Galactic Alignment that occurs there.

Stela 11 is one of the most symbolically striking monuments in Group B. In my book *The Center of Mayan Time*, I emphasized this stela as the best Izapan monument representative of the World Age astronomy of the 13-baktun cycle end-date. It faces the December solstice sunrise, where the dark-rift rose shortly before the solstice sun during Izapa's heyday. I still feel that Stela 11 tells a simple and straightforward story about the sky toward which it faces—its message concerns the rebirth of the world.

Is Stela 11 only telling us about the sun's rebirth at dawn? Is it only portraying the sun's annual rebirth on the December solstice? No, for it is shortsighted to limit the metaphor to the daily and annual levels. It does not take a great leap of insight to understand Stela 11 for all it is worth. If we accept that the toad-jaguar's mouth symbolizes the dark-rift, Stela 11 says "the sun is reborn when it is in the dark-rift—the place of transformation, the portal to the Otherworld, the birth canal of the Milky Way Great Mother."

Diagram 166. Stela 11. The December solstice sun in the dark-rift, a visual portrayal of the astronomical alignment of December 21, 2012

In Stela 11 we can clearly see the true meaning of the dark-rift "mouth" of the Milky Way as a birthplace. Gareth Lowe, one of the archaeologists who excavated Izapa in the 1960s, associates Stela 11 with the day-sign Ix (Jaguar).[12] The toad-jaguar's mouth has symbolized the portal to the Otherworld since Olmec times, and the modern Quiché Maya call the dark-rift the *xibalba be*, the Road to the Otherworld. Commonly, Underworld portals were visualized as caves. In the Tzotzil Maya language of highland Chiapas, the word for "cave" is *ch'en*, which also means "vagina."[13] Lowe also associates Stela 11 with the Yucatec Maya haab month Chen ("cave").[14] Here we have meaningful connections implicit in the work of Maya scholars that associate Stela 11 with jaguar mouths, caves, portals to the Otherworld, and birthplaces.

And what of the solar deity emerging from the toad-jaguar's mouth? The outstretched hands on Stela 11 represent completion or measurement—a typical period-ending concept. In the *Popol Vuh*, First Father measured the cosmos at the beginning of time by stretching a measuring cord to the four cosmic corners. On Stela 11 we see a frog or toad (the Milky Way) birthing the solar First Father deity. In the calendar glyphs, the frog or toad glyph stands for the 20-day uinal period of the Long Count. As such, again we encounter the concept of time-period completion (and commencement).

In Maya hieroglyphs, when the frog's mouth is upright and open, the meaning is "to be born" and "date initiation."[15] This identification is basic and very important, and confirms that Stela 11 represents the alignment of the December solstice sun with the dark-rift in the Milky Way that occurs on the 13-baktun cycle end-date in A.D. 2012. Furthermore, given the "to be born" meaning of the upturned frog's mouth, the way the future alignment was thought of in Izapan/Maya Creation myth involved the solar First Father hero being reborn, or emerging, from the dark-rift portal to the Otherworld, which was symbolized by the mouth of a toad.

My emphasis on the fact that the upturned frog-glyph means both "date initiation" (as in a new Creation) and "to be born" (as in the sun in the dark-rift) challenges Maya scholars Nikolai Grube and Linda Schele's identification of the celestial Creation Place of the Maya. They focused exclusively on the "Ak" or turtle glyph as a reference to the three hearthstones of Creation (three stars in the Orion constellation). On certain Classic-period ceramics, the First Father/Maize Deity is depicted being reborn from the back of a turtle. Thus, they argue that the celestial location of his rebirth is in Orion. However, the Classic-period representations of the cosmic turtle's back (Orion) as a birthplace probably do not reflect the original Izapan Creation myth. Ultimately, the frog-mouth birthing glyph is just as compelling as Schele's interpretation of Maya Creation that was based on the Ak turtle glyph and that focused only on the Milky Way/ecliptic Creation crossroads near Gemini.[16] In terms of astronomical exactness, the scenario near

Sagittarius is much more precise than the one proposed for Gemini-Orion. (The three hearthstones in Orion are quite far from both the Milky Way and the ecliptic.) Given my extensive work on the true meaning of the 13-baktun cycle end-date, an important and central aspect of Maya Creation astronomy definitely appears to have gone unrecognized by scholars. *If the turtle or "Ak" glyph was hailed as the key to Grube and Schele's interpretation of Maya Creation occurring near Gemini-Orion, then the "to be born" frog glyph is the epigraphic and iconographic key to my reading of Creation at the Milky Way dark-rift near Sagittarius.*

Diagram 167. a) Creation via the dark-rift near Sagittarius: the upturned frog's mouth means "to be born"; b) Creation via the three belt stars in Orion: the Ak turtle's cracked back

Ultimately, as I argued in Chapter 10, both Creation locations are probably valid, each being a dialectical inflection of the same underlying Creation complex. In other words, the birth of the Maize Deity from the Ak turtle (in Orion) represents the annual rebirth of the Solar/Maize God around the June solstice (when the sun passes through Gemini). On the other side of the sky, the December solstice sun's rebirth through the dark-rift in the Milky Way is the rebirth of the First Father Solar/Maize Deity on the level of World Ages.

The sun-in-mouth image is found elsewhere at Izapa, and throughout Mesoamerica. Stela 11 remains an outstanding example, complete unto itself, of the future astronomical alignment toward which it faces. It portrays the future conjunction as a joining of deities—the First Father/Solar Deity joins with the Jaguar-Toad Deity, who is the cosmic birther and therefore an avatar of the Great Mother (the Milky Way). In fact, the jaguar-toad on Stela 11 is equivalent to the caiman-tree on Stela 25, which has already been identified with the Milky Way. The real identity of the Milky Way as a Cosmic Birther lurks behind these multiple metaphors. As such, the future alignment was mythologized as the union of First Father and Cosmic Mother. Amazingly, stelae representing these mother-father principles are found in Group E, where we will briefly pause on our journey to the Group F ballcourt.

GROUP E: THE MOTHER-FATHER UNION

Group E is the southernmost group of monuments along Izapa's main north-south axis. In Group E, Stelae 19 and 20 are oriented to the rising December solstice sun, and presumably tell us something about what happens there. We can imagine Izapan priests standing at the altars in front of Stelae 19 and 20, making offerings as they watched the dark-rift in the Milky Way rise in the predawn December solstice sky. The dark-rift was understood to be the birth canal of the Milky Way Great Goddess. It was the portal to other dimensions, the cave in the sky into the Heart of Creation, the mouth of the snake or frog or jaguar, all of whom were animal totems of the Milky Way Mother, vehicles of travel into the Underworld Womb of All. Frogs croak wildly before the Mother Goddess's water blessing of rain. Snakes, tadpoles, and other amphibians shed their skins and transform. Likewise, the Cosmic Mother principle is the Great Transformer.

Diagram 168. Stela 19, the cosmic female principle, and Stela 20, the cosmic male principle

Stela 19 is an abstract representation of the female creation principle. The V-shaped cleft and the vertical slot within the circular diadem symbolize the female birth cleft.

Stela 20, on the other hand, with its phallic "breechcloth" of Ahau rulership, is an abstract representation of the male creation principle. Together, Stelae 19 and 20 symbolize the cosmic male and female principles.

The ancient astronomer-priest that we imagined performing offerings in front of Group E's mother-father stelae would have been observing a profound event with a knowing eye. As dawn drew near, the December solstice Ahau or solar deity, who only appears once a year, began to show his face. The sky brightened and the penetrating, fertilizing power of the solar rays announced the rebirth of the year. The magic of watching the December solstice sunrise at Izapa 2,300 years ago lay in the knowledge that the cosmic male and female principles were slowly approaching each other, revealing an exquisitely extended foreplay that will culminate in the engendering of a new World Age when they join—an event projected by Izapan calendar-priests, quite accurately, to occur on 13.0.0.0.0: December 21, 2012 A.D.

Diagram 169. Stela 88 sky panel as a seed-in-cleft motif

Stelae 19 and 20 emphasize the ritual importance of the December solstice, cosmic creation via a union of opposites, and world renewal. They are the only abstractions of their type at Izapa, and share Group E with just one other poorly carved boulder. They embody the dialogical ideal of mutual complementarity, or oppositional union, and that union is achieved only after an excruciatingly long period of time. My reading of the Group E monuments is quite simple: They state that 2012 is an era of cosmic insemination, the union of the highest male and female principles of Creation manifest in the solstice sun and the Galactic Center. It is an event that impregnates the next World Age with new growth.

Stela 88 is a fragmented sky panel found near Group B a few years after the

Diagram 170. Cleft-like "jaguar snout" sky panels

Brigham Young University archaeological project at Izapa was completed (diagram 169). This sky panel symbolizes the fertilization of the female cleft. The round element is the solar male seed and the V-shaped cleft with spiral scrolls on either side is the female birth cleft. As such, this stelae speaks the same message as Stelae 19 and 20 in Group E. In fact, many sky panels at Izapa are cleftlike.

On one level of interpretation, these sky-panel motifs represent the stylized snout of a jaguar. Thus, the mythic scenes that unfold on each stela occur in the mouth of the jaguar, that is, in the Otherworld. For my reading of Stela 88, this makes perfect sense, as the female birth canal is also the portal to (and from) the Otherworld.[17] In general, Izapan stelae depict principles of mythic astronomy or abstract concepts rather than local historical events. Together, Stelae 19, 20, and 88 clue us in to how the Izapan skywatchers thought about the astronomy along the

December solstice horizon, and mother-father union appears to have been a central metaphor. If they were unaware of precession and the future alignment of 13.0.0.0.0, how do we adequately account for the mytho-astronomical symbolism so clearly portrayed on these monuments? And beyond this evidence, the Group F ballcourt provides a profound and clear confirmation of my reconstruction of the esoteric mysteries of Izapan cosmology.

Importantly, the cleft sky-panel symbol is structurally similar to the glyph for a ballcourt, reinforcing the well-known association between ballcourts and the Underworld. Ballcourts were theaters of Mystery Play, and the dramatic Creation events enacted on their fields symbolically occurred in the Otherworld—the dimension that underlies material manifestation—where humans and deities dance together and cocreate the cosmos.

GALACTIC COSMOLOGY IN THE IZAPAN BALLCOURT

As we have seen, Group B is primarily concerned with the zenith axis, whereas Group A depicts events around Tacana on the north-south "polar" axis. It is not surprising then that the Group F ballcourt is oriented toward the southward December solstice axis and the Galactic Center, and tells us with its symbolic monuments about the astronomical events viewed in that direction.[18] The Group F message is read in the following monuments:

- Throne 2 and associated monuments on the west end of the ballcourt
- Stela 60 and associated monuments on the east end of the ballcourt
- Stela 67 along the north edge of the ballcourt, comparable to Stela 22, found a short distance south of Group F
- Monument 25, a Sky Mover Deity on the south edge of the ballcourt, across from Stela 67
- Feature 12 (recovered from a burial cache in nearby mound 125a)

The astronomical message of Group F and its ballcourt is strong and clear. While Group A is thought by archaeologists to have been in use early in the Guillen Phase (300 B.C.–50 B.C.) and Group B was used simultaneously and a short time later, Group F was used up through the Classic period, and even into the Post-Classic. This suggests that the Izapan Mysteries, with Galactic synchronization as the most coveted and highest degree of initiation, were taught for a thousand years. All of the Izapan monument groups were ritual in nature, and Izapa as a whole was a sacred ground where warfare did not take place and where few, if any, people lived. It was a place where the Galactic Cosmology was revealed as the most profound spiritual mystery human beings could embrace.

Roughly 2,100 years ago, certain monuments from other parts of Izapa were brought to Group F and reset according to a specific message.

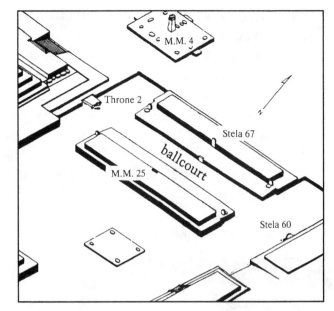

Diagram 171. Group F ballcourt area. From Lowe et al. (1982:237)

The main platform is oriented north-south but only a few scattered and broken monuments were found there. However, many offerings were excavated inside Temple 125a, including a throne-sitting king-shaman, which tells us something important about the throne in the ballcourt. Two frog altars and a T-shaped stone were found south of the main platform. The primary monumental message of Group F, however, revolves around the ballcourt (see diagram 171).

Diagram 172. Stela 60. Victorious Hero Twin as ballplayer standing over Seven Macaw

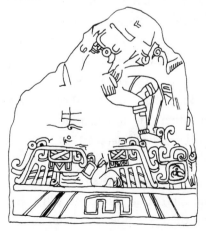

Note Miscellaneous Monument 4 to the northwest of the ballcourt. This is a zenith gnomon, apparently the only nod to the zenith center in Group F. Stone balls and rings were found in specific placements at both ends of the ballcourt, and they clearly represent the gameball and the goalring. Throne 2 is at the west end of the ballcourt, and the visual field offered to one who sat on this throne sights down the lengthwise axis of the ballcourt to the December solstice horizon, where the solar "gameball" and the dark-rift "goalring" rose on the morning of the December solstice. During Izapa's heyday, they were separated by roughly 30°, and were not set to join for another 2,100 years.

Throne 2 and Stela 60 oppose each other on the southeast-northwest axis of the ballcourt. Stela 60, though fragmented, shows one of the Hero Twins as a victorious ballplayer standing over a completely defeated Seven Macaw (see diagram 172).

This stela portrays the final victory over the Lord of the Polar Region. As we have already explored, in the Quiché *Popol Vuh*, the Hero Twins defeat Seven Macaw by shooting him out of his tree before they begin their attempts to resurrect their father, One Hunahpu. The final defeat of all the Xibalban Lords prior to One Hunahpu's resurrection occurs in the Underworld Ballcourt, place of mythic battle and victory over the powers of darkness. In front of Stela 60 we find Monuments 33 and 35, a stone ball inside a doughnut-shaped "goalring." Together, all of these monuments say, "The gameball is in the goal, the game is over, Seven Macaw is dead, the solstice sun can be reborn." Clearly, Stela 60 and its ball-and-ring stones express part of this statement, while the dawn astronomy on the December solstice, viewed directly over this group of monuments, supplies the rest. Those who viewed the skies over Stela 60 were the ballplayers themselves and the king-shaman who sat on Throne 2 on the other side of the ballcourt. This is what they saw (diagram 173).

Diagram 173. Viewing the rising December solstice sun "gameball" and the dark-rift "goalring" from the Izapan ballcourt: Victorious ballplayer defeats the Polar God, and the cosmic gameball goes into the cosmic goalring

We already explored the cosmic symbolism of the Mesoamerican ball-game in Chapter 11. However, to briefly review, the gameball symbolizes the sun. Its movement into the dark-rift "goalring" represents solar rebirth on the highest of three temporal levels: daily at dawn, yearly (at dawn on the December solstice), and in terms of World Ages (at dawn on the December solstice of 13.0.0.0.0). At Chichén Itzá, the ballcourt was oriented to the Milky Way at midnight on the June solstice in era A.D. 865.[19] Thus, the ballcourt itself was understood to be the Milky Way. But it had other mythological identities too. For example, Stela 67, in the center of the ballcourt's north wall, shows a victorious solar hero inside a long canoe.

Diagram 174. Stela 67. First Father in the center of the Milky Way canoe

His arms are outstretched, like the First Father figure on Stela 11. This arm-span measuring gesture symbolizes a period-ending event, and brings to mind the great period-ending of 13.0.0.0.0. But why is this Solar Ahau sitting in the middle of a canoe? Could it be that the world ends when the Solar Lord (First Father) comes to sit in the middle of the Milky Way "canoe"? Mayanist Linda Schele identified the sky canoe on incised bones from Burial 116 at Tikal as the Milky Way.[20] The Paddler Gods, including the First Father Solar/Maize Deity, are among the occupants of this Milky Way sky canoe. Izapa Stela 67 seems to portray the same meaning, and indicates that the Milky Way could be a ballcourt or a canoe.[21] Given that Stela 67 is along the lengthwise edge of the ballcourt, halfway between the east and west ends, the placement of the canoe portrayed on it parallels the ballcourt itself. The Group F ballcourt, then, represents the Milky Way, and its orientation physically points to the Milky Way's rising central bulge on the December solstice. But the Milky Way was also seen to be a canoe, because it sails through the oceanic night sky, rising and setting. The dark-rift, in this canoe metaphor, is likened to the depression in which the First Father/Paddler God sits. Because the Milky Way canoe's movement involves precession, the Paddler God is the Mover of the Sky, the architecton who controls the shifting of the celestial vault. In short, the Paddler

Diagram 175. Stelae 6 and 3. Vision boats and the Underworld portal

God is another manifestation of the First Father/One Hunahpu deity.

Solar Lords inside canoes are found on other Izapan monuments. Stela 6 and its opposed partner Stela 3 both show serpent-toad deities with upturned gaping mouths (see diagram 175). Both have manned "U-boats" balancing just outside their mouths. Since serpent-toad mouths were thought of as Underworld portals, this image may symbolize the shaman-astronomer's vision journey through the Underworld (the night sky). It appears that

Diagram 176. a) Danzante from Izapa-Tuxtla Chico; b) Monument 25 from Izapa Group F

the First Father Solar/Maize Deity sits in the "center" of the Milky Way canoe, in the cleft, and journeys through the night sky (into the *xibalba be*, Underworld portal). The serpent-toad mouths upon which the canoe floats reinforce the Underworld context, as well as the meaning of "to be born." When the astronomer-priest returns from his otherworldly journey, he experiences a reentry or rebirth. In addition, the psychoactive substance extracted from the *Bufo marines* toad portrayed on these monuments was, literally, the vehicle of travel into the Otherworld.

In general, then, Stela 67, placed in the "middle" of the northern wall of the Group F ballcourt, shows the First Father deity in the middle of the Milky Way. In other words, it shows One Hunahpu in the Galactic Center. Remembering that One Hunahpu represents the December solstice sun, the mythic astronomy encoded on Stela 67 points right at the end-date in 2012.

The monument on the wall opposite Stela 67 adds to this interpretation. Monument 25 was found along the south wall of the Group F ballcourt, but it was in very poor condition. However, archaeologist V. Garth Norman compares it to a well-preserved "Danzante" figure found in the Izapa-Tuxtla Chico area (see diagram 176).[22] The Danzante figure represents what Monument 25 probably originally looked like. It broadly resembles the Olmec figure found in

Diagram 177. Olmec Sky Mover deity from San Martín volcano

the cleft crater atop San Martín Pajapan, the sacred volcano of the Olmec (see diagram 177).

Linda Schele interpreted the San Martín God as the ancient Creation God who "raised the sky", the Milky Way.[23] The Izapa-Tuxtla Chico Danzante is a form of the Sky Mover deity. Could the deity on the eroded Monument 25 also be a Sky Mover? Having been placed along the southern edge of the Milky Way ballcourt, he could have been the Creation Being intended to push the Milky Way through the sky. As such, his function was similar to the Stela 67 Solar Lord on the opposite wall, who rides in the Milky Way canoe. Imagine the original Monument 25: The Sky Mover kneels, preparing to lift the Cosmic Axis, the Milky Way. It is as if he pushes the celestial frame along—he shifts the Milky Way's position, eventually bringing it to a place where First Father can sit in its center.

Diagram 178. Dresden Codex *Paddler God*

This scenario suggests the precessional "movement" of the Milky Way into conjunction with the dawning December solstice sun at the horizon (to occur on 13.0.0.0.0). Stela 67, opposite Monument 25, reflects this sky-moving activity by depicting a solar hero in the "center" of the Milky Way ballcourt/canoe. Furthermore, the "Chac paddling a boat" illustration from the *Dresden Codex* resembles the San Martín Sky Mover via its squatting position and handling of the paddle (the paddle "moves" the Milky Way canoe). This later Maya God probably combines attributes from Stela 67 with the interpretation of Monument 25 as a Sky Mover.

Diagram 179. Galactic Cosmology in the Izapan ballcourt. a) Throne 2, Miscellaneous Monuments 17, 18, and 19; b) Head-in-mouth ballcourt marker example from Patzun

In general, Stela 67 and Monument 25 both state that the Milky Way ballcourt moves through the sky, that a period-ending occurs when the Solar Lord/Paddler God arrives in the center of the Milky Way, and that the Sky Mover atop the sacred volcano resides in a cosmic center and is responsible for the sky's slow shifting. What we have so far is astounding confirmation of the end-date cosmology at Izapa. But there is more.

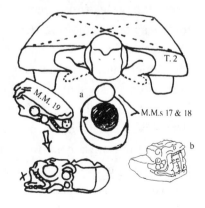

The most incredible and amazing mythic message of Group F, consistent with ballgame astronomy and the end-date cosmology, revolves around Throne 2 and its associated monuments on the west end of the ballcourt.

Take a careful look at this convocation of symbols, for they encode a profound message. The drawing above shows how these monuments were originally found. Because of the throne, we can guess that this place and this arrangement were of primary significance in the cosmic meaning of the Izapan ballgame. An astronomer-priest or perhaps an initiate sat here and performed rituals and vision-journeys while the ballgame Creation myth was being played out on the galactic ballcourt in front of him or her. Before dawn on the December solstice, looking along the eastward axis of the ballcourt (over Stela 60), the shaman-skywatcher sees the dark-rift in the Milky Way—the goalring of the cosmic ballcourt—rising ahead of the solstice sun (the cosmic gameball).

Unlike Throne 1 in Group B, Throne 2 does not have a crossbands carved on it. However, thrones were always thought of as four-cornered seats in the cosmic center. While Throne 1 represents the zenith center implicit in Group B, Throne 2 represents the cosmic center within the cross formed by the Milky Way and ecliptic. This cosmic center is none other than the Galactic Center, identified by the observable "nuclear bulge." That the Galactic Center was the supreme orientational principle for Izapan cosmonauts is reinforced by the ballcourt's orientation to the Milky Way/ecliptic crossroad and the Milky Way's "nuclear bulge" as it rose heliacally on the December solstice.

The only carved feature on Throne 2 is in the middle of its eastward edge, facing the December solstice horizon.[24] It depicts a squatting frog or toad, feet broken off, with a large eroded human head emerging from between its open legs. This is a birth image, called the "hocker" position, and is widely represented in Mesoamerican art.[25] One may be tempted to see a diving god here, after the style of Tulum in Quintana Roo, but the splayed limbs are definitely legs, and, furthermore, their form resembles the splayed jaguar-toad beast on Stela 11 and Stela 8. We also have a clue from a ceramic figurine found in a burial offering from the mound located just behind Throne 2.

Diagram 180. Feature 12. Birth or "hocker" posture on Izapan throne

Here we see a human figure sitting on a throne. It sports an

"Ahau" cap of rulership, and sits in the birth posture, reminding us that Maya king-shamans were conjurers, adepts who could travel into the Heart of Heaven and channel or "birth" into local space-time the organizational patterns of the cosmic center. The shaman on Feature 12 in diagram 180 above is squatting rather than cross-legged, in a manner similar to the splayed legs on Throne 2. The role of the person who sat on Throne 2 was to facilitate the birth of the Solar Godhead through the birth canal between the legs, which is a metaphor for the future alignment projected to occur along the December solstice horizon. The human head, like emerging heads on sculpture elsewhere in Mesoamerica, represents a solar hero or warrior, but, in general, the head symbolizes the sun. In Mesoamerican belief, each *kin* (day or sun) has its own "face." In the *Popol Vuh*, One Hunahpu's severed head was hung in the crook of the calabash tree (the dark-rift in the Milky Way). The head of his son, Hunahpu, also was cut off, and at one point it was substituted for the gameball. One Hunahpu's head, as explained earlier, represents both the December solstice sun and the gameball. When he goes into the goalring, he is reborn from the cosmic birth canal. In fact, the heads of the father and son together may represent the same symbolic function via lineage continuity, a kind of reincarnation of spiritual essense through procreation.[26]

Because the birth canal of the splay-legged being on Throne 2 symbolizes the dark-rift in the Milky Way, observed rising to the southeast on the December solstice down the lengthwise axis of the ballcourt, the priest-king, or whoever sat on Throne 2, engaged in a kind of visionary ritual magic to facilitate the future rebirth of the world—the movement of the December solstice sun into birth-union with the cosmic vagina (the dark-rift). In addition to this ceremonial magic, kicking the game-ball into the goalring through athletic prowess provided a parallel set of symbols and another form of sympathetic magic. The ball-and-ring symbol of the underlying astronomical meaning of the 13-baktun cycle end-date occurs in front of Stela 60 on the eastern end of the ballcourt, as well as in front of Throne 2 on the western end. In front of Throne 2, we see the familiar ball and basin, directly underneath the emerging solar head. This basin, ritual in function and symbolizing the goalring, also may have served to collect the priest's blood during ceremonial bloodletting rites.

The third symbol associated with Throne 2 is an inverted serpent-head marker, which probably was brought from somewhere else in the ballcourt. Labeled Miscellaneous Monument 19, it had something in its mouth which is now broken off.

Similar serpent-headed wall adornments were found in other ballcourts in southern Mesoamerica (e.g., at Guaytan), many of which originally had little "solar" heads placed in their mouths.[27] Archaeologist V. Garth Norman suggests this monument, too, originally held such a head—a little solar Ahau—in its mouth, depicting the ubiquitous motif of a solar deity emerging from a serpent's mouth. I believe the Izapan ceremonialists intentionally placed this serpent-head monument next to Throne 2 as a reiteration of the two other symbolic messages: The serpent's mouth is analogous to the goalring as well as to the deity-ruler's vagina or birthplace.[28] The shared astronomical reference is, of course, to the dark-rift in the Milky Way. So, here we find three symbol complexes that actually refer to the same mythic astronomy—the celestial convergence viewed along the ballcourt's axis over the eastern horizon:

- Miscellaneous Monument 19. Inverted serpent (Milky Way) with a head in its mouth (sun in dark-rift).
- Throne 2. Solar head emerging from birth canal (sun in dark-rift). This throne-birthing was enacted by a shaman-priest or king-shaman impersonating the Milky Way as a Great Creatrix deity. In this case, the throne symbolizes the crossroads formed by the Milky Way and the ecliptic in Sagittarius rather than the zenith as on Throne 1 in Group B.
- Miscellaneous Monuments 17 and 18. A stone ball and a stone ring. When the gameball (the sun) enters the goalring (the dark-rift), a new World Age is born and Seven Macaw (the old Polar God) is defeated; Stela 60 and its ball-and-basin on the other side of the ballcourt reinforce this reading.

Everything in the Group F ballcourt cries out that the December solstice horizon is where the sun converges with the cosmic birth canal. This cosmological event, pinpointed via the 13-baktun cycle end-date of the Long Count calendar, and encoded into the ancient Hero Twin story that later became the Quiché *Popol Vuh*, is intimately tied into the socio-political meaning of Mesoamerican king-shamans as throne-sitting conjurers and birthers, and was facilitated through the sympathetic magic of the ritual ballgame. It is quite astounding that these Group F monuments yield such a consistent, complex, and meaningful message. The key to unlocking these multilevel symbols is accepting that the ancient Izapan astronomers were tracking the precessional movement of the astronomical features over the solstice sunrise horizon.

When I started this course of research many years ago, I saw Stela 11 as the only likely candidate at Izapa to symbolize the World Age convergence over the solstice horizon. Now, with these other revelations resulting from a close scrutiny of Izapan iconography and astronomy, I am convinced that Izapan skywatchers were tracking precession, played an important role in the formulation of the Long Count calendar, created the Hero Twin story, and were informed by the use of psychoactive substances. There are multiple levels of meaning within Izapan cosmology, but all levels are interwoven. The interpretive continuity I offer for a formerly inscrutable iconographic code strongly suggests, in and of itself, that the underlying cosmological meaning I propose is correct.

The profound cosmology hidden within Izapa's pictographic code represents a great flowering of knowledge, an era of great visionary openness and achievement that may have eroded into bland secular dogmas by the time the Classic Maya appeared on the scene. The Classic Maya did adopt the Long Count calendar, already in use for hundreds of years, and should have retained the profound Galactic Cosmology of the Izapans in some form. But how much do we, denizens of the most technologically advanced civilization, retain of the ancient Greek art of sacred geometry? How much do Euro-Americans even care about the ancient traditions of their own forebears—the lyrical bards, ley-line geomancers, me-

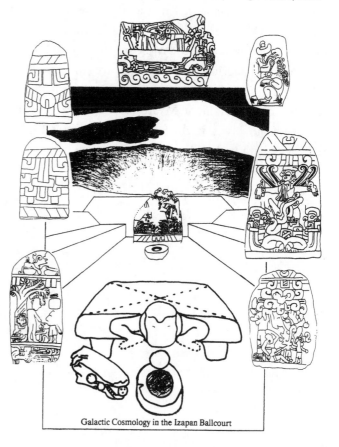

Diagram 181. Izapa's monumental message, sighting down the Group F ballcourt toward the future Galactic Alignment of 2012

Galactic Cosmology in the Izapan Ballcourt

dieval herbalists and alchemists? In looking closely at Izapan monuments, orientations, topography, calendrics, and astronomy, we encounter a profound multidimensional cosmovision that may have been history to the Maya. However, when we look deeper into Mesoamerican precessional mysteries, as we did in Part II, the Galactic Cosmology does appear to have been present as late as ninth-century Chichén Itzá, where it was synthesized with the Zenith Cosmology.

The Galactic Cosmology that was formulated by the ancient Izapans is relevant today because the jewel in the crown of their cosmic science was the identification of the era of World Age transformation to be experienced not just at Izapa, but around the globe. We are living right now in this rare era of transformation. And this is not just a vague, visionary prophecy—it is based on the empirical fact of Galactic synchronization. I believe that one goal of the Izapan cosmonauts was to spread their discoveries throughout the Mesoamerican world, and I believe they did this by offering initiatory teachings at the site, using the monuments as visual aids. For hundreds of years, Izapa was the home of esoteric Mystery Teachings and initiation rites into Galactic Knowledge. Dare we imagine what these rites might have been like? Our journey into the ancient Maya mysteries has taken us down long-overgrown pathways of the Mesoamerican psyche, and now we stand at the Izapan gateway of Galactic Initiation. Shall we turn and flee at the profound majesty of it all, and deny its promise of greater cosmological insight? Or shall we take a step forward into the Galactic Mysteries that have been dormant for centuries and experience for ourselves, in the final days of baktun 13, the deepest Maya mystery? Let us take a walk around Izapa.

CHAPTER 23

INITIATION INTO THE IZAPAN MYSTERIES

Picture life in southern Mesoamerica, along the fertile slopes of the Pacific littoral. Volcan Tajumulco, the highest volcanic deity in a long chain of coastal mountains, rises to the northeast. Volcan Tacaná rises to the north, and from Izapa the very heavens seem to revolve around this ancient sentinel's peak. Imagine groups of dedicated Izapan stargazers in the little understood period between 700 B.C. and 300 B.C. embarked upon a journey of discovery, to fix the rate of the sky's slippage. Data is gathered, is compared with that of other groups of skywatchers, and the resulting knowledge is passed down through elite dynasties of specialized shaman-astronomers. For a hundred, two hundred years, the goal is constantly kept in mind. Life is simple. Cacao is grown. Corn is grown. Temples are built. Trade improves, rituals are performed. Shrines are swept, ancestors are called. And all along, the sacred tools of vision are harvested and consumed, to commune with the inner reflection of a place in the night sky, the deep cosmic center within—and without. Knowledge and insights are gathered, calculations are fine-tuned. The Galactic Calendar is formulated, tried and tested, and finally set in stone. It is now several tuns before the arrival of the Savior in the Old World, and the countdown to the Galactic dawn begins. The birth of the next World is over five baktuns into the future, and it will occur only through the efforts of king-shamans, midwives, and ballplayers. When Cosmic Mother and First Father join, then the doors will open and human beings will truly be born.

Imagine you are an initiate, a truth seeker, come to Izapa to understand a new knowledge. Your home is Tres Zapotes, and you are descended from the Olmec people. You were taught that Seven Macaw is the highest god, that your people have worshiped him as the ruler of the cosmic center for thousands of years, since before the legendary migrations from the Far North took place.

But something is astir. Rumors abound that a new understanding of the cosmos has surfaced, that skywatchers and calendar priests at a ceremonial site to the south have decoded a profound insight into the cosmic order. They offer initiation into their knowledge, the Izapan Mysteries, and you determine to find out what it is all about. You have been told that you must wait until the time of the solstice, when the Solar God is reborn. The time approaches. For twenty days you travel along well-worn trade routes until you arrive at the controversial city.

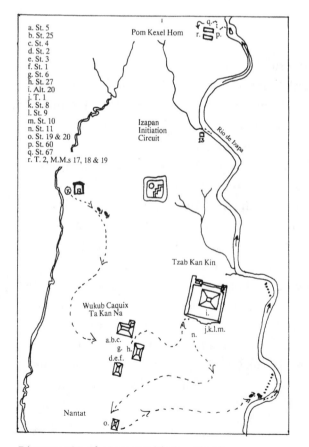

a. St. 5
b. St. 25
c. St. 4
d. St. 2
e. St. 3
f. St. 1
g. St. 6
h. St. 27
i. Alt. 20
j. T. 1
k. St. 8
l. St. 9
m. St. 10
n. St. 11
o. St. 19 & 20
p. St. 60
q. St. 67
r. T. 2, M.M.s 17, 18 & 19

Pom Kexel Hom

Izapan
Initiation
Circuit

Rio de Izapa

Tzab Kan Kin

Wukub Caquix
Ta Kan Na

Nantat

Diagram 182. The Izapan Initiation Circuit

At first, you are not impressed. There are no large pyramids like those found in your homeland. But an energy stirs, a bright, new, and mysterious energy. Three days before the solstice, the Izapan astronomer-priests bring you, along with twelve other initiates, to the first group of monuments. You are told that a story and a new understanding of things will be revealed to you over the next three days as you ceremonially journey around the site. You will see things you have never seen before, and you are told you should spread the word of what you learn to all your people and all your descendants. For what you will see is the revelation of the True God, the highest cosmic center and source.

At sundown three days before the solstice, before the birth of the New Year, you enter Seven Macaw's Group (Group A). First, you view Stela 5 and are told of the ancient migrations to Izapa.

STELA 5

You then see Stela 25 and are shown how Seven Macaw rules from his throne in the polar regions. The sun sets, and to the north you see Seven Macaw rising through the Creation Cleft of the volcano they call Ta Can Na—the Place of the Fourfold Mother-House.

STELA 25

At midnight Seven Macaw passes through his highest arc and begins his descent. The priests now point out Stela 4, right next to Stela 25, which shows your ancient god falling and being sacrificed. Looking at the pictures, looking at the sky, you see how Seven Macaw falls.

STELA 4

And you are told that he will fall away from the cosmic center of the north for thousands of years to come. You do not understand, but are told that you soon will. You will see how he falls from his perch, how he abandons his throne in the polar center.

You resist being told that the Polar God is false. Still, you observe the descent scene on Stela 4 and across the plaza on Stela 2. Walking across the plaza, you notice that they both lie on the main axis of Seven Macaw's Group, an axis that points to the polar throne above Ta Can Na.

STELA 2

Here you see the Hero Twins. They are Solar Gods, sons of the December Solstice Lord. They shot Seven Macaw out of his perch in the cosmic tree; they dethroned the false god to make way for the rebirth of their father, who will take over as the new World Age ruler.

The priests compare the cleft tree on Stela 2 to the cleft volcano to the north. Near Stela 2 you see Stela 3, and are told that there exists another Cleft of Creation, and it is like a snake's mouth.

STELA 3

You are now facing south, away from the Creation Cleft of the Fourfold Mother-House volcano. At first you do not understand how there can be two Creation Places. But, using the pictures on the monuments, the priests illustrate for you a profound truth that disperses your confusion. They show you the rain cycle on Stela 1. Wordlessly, with hand gestures only, they show you how the rain cycle spins to the right.

STELA 1

They tell you to turn around and watch the sky. You look and see that the sky spins around the Creation Cleft of the north, spinning to the left. You look again at the rain cycle on Stela 1, and begin to understand. The direction of the cycle, when facing the southern ocean, reflects the direction of the sky's movement going on behind you. You understand a profound truth: North and south, backward and forward, up and down—these processes, though opposed, actually reflect each other, like a pyrite mirror reflects the gaze, but in reverse.

Facing south, dawn approaches, and you see the Creation Cleft of the south rising. It is the mouth of the great serpent, as shown on Stela 3. It is the Road to the Underworld in the Milky Way stream of stars. It is the birth canal of the Cosmic Mother. Yes, this is another Creation Place; it is opposite Seven Macaw, and you begin to wonder what this new knowledge means. They tell you straight out: There, in the mother sky, is the true Fourfold Mother-House. Contemplating these new thoughts, these introductory teachings, your mind opens slightly to the possibility of truths higher than those you were taught back home. Day breaks, and the priests usher you away to a thatched-roof hut where you are sequestered for meditation, fasting, and sleep.

That evening you awaken, ready for more. It is now two days before the December solstice. Once again, the initiation rites begin at dusk. You are shown Stelae 1 and 3 again, which introduced the snake's mouth as the other Creation Place.

You understood why the snake's mouth is a birth canal, the Road to the Underworld that devours and births. It is the cosmic Black Road leading into the depths of the Fourfold Mother-House. Having reflected on what you were shown the previous night, you see with your inner knowing that the cosmic Mother-House is fourfold because of the four roads that emanate from her birth canal. You remember what appeared to you yesterday, that what happens in the north is mirrored by what happens in the south. Standing there, in comprehension of secret truths, the priests step forward and whisper that, to fully understand the Izapan Mysteries, you must journey into the mouth of the Cosmic Mother's *nagual*, or spirit companion. You see that Stela 3 depicts the serpent form of the Great Mother's spirit companion. In front of Stelae 1 and 3 are the toad altars upon which you must sacrifice your old beliefs. They portray the vision toad, which you recognize as the same sacred toad coveted by your own shamans back home. You grow fearful, unsure of what the new knowledge might entail, but determine to continue with the initiatory revelation. The priests show you how the two toad altars make a triangle with Stela 6 on the other side of the plaza. Walking across the plaza, you glance at the darkening sky and see the gleaming stars, each like an eye, watching your movements. On Stela 6, you see the Galactic Toad, spirit companion of the Milky Way Mother, and you are told you must now journey to the Otherworld, into the dark-rift Creation Place. Yes, your sacrifice involves being devoured by the Galactic Toad.

STELA 6

By now the sun has fully set. In the darkness, you see Seven Macaw waxing to its height over Ta Can Na, as portrayed on Stela 25. For a long time you contemplate what awaits you. As midnight approaches, you watch Seven Macaw going over the top of his pole, and then he begins to fall, to die in the west. The priests explain you will now see how Seven Macaw really falls, and they give you the smoke of the Galactic Toad. Inhaling the smoke deeply three times, you fall back upon the grass, gazing into the spinning stars of the polar zone. The sky strangely shifts, time opens up, and the stars spin faster. The days and nights begin to speed by. Years fly by in a whir; you watch Seven Macaw spinning and rising, rising and falling, rising and falling. As the katuns fly by, he rises further and further away from the center of the sky—he is falling away from his throne, his perch in the ancient polar center. See how he moves! He rises further east along the slope of the volcano, no longer passing through the Creation Cleft. After what seems an eternity, you stand abruptly to gaze deeply into your own inner realization, and you now understand that the Polar God is false. Immediately, you are whisked over to Stela 27, the only monument truly facing the December solstice horizon—the rebirth place of the Hero Twins' father.

STELA 27

You see the dark-rift rising, along with the bright, sparkling stars of the widest part of the Milky Way—the area the Izapans call the Womb of All, the womb of the Milky Way Mother. The priests show you how to project yourself into the cosmic mouth. They tell you to gaze at the carving, then at the sky, and to dive in. Your head still swimming with the vision toad's smoke, you look at the cosmic caiman-tree in the picture, and the cross in its center. Then, raising your gaze to the sky behind the carving, you let go of yourself and fly upward through the interwoven celestial realms of many dimensions, into the raging fury of the Creator-Destroyer. You see the Hero Twins being conceived, and the Sacred Fount of Creation that is a tree, a volcano, a river of stars, a churning hurricane of being. You journey into the heart and source of all Creation, and understand the nature of human beings, time, and the role of Earth in universal spiritual evolution. You forget about the old Polar God, recognize him as the antiquated idea of a lesser understanding, and, in a flash, you see the True Deity of All. She is the Cosmic Birther of all time and all space, of all beings and all worlds.

You descend back into your body, feeling disoriented. With the aid of your Izapan guides, you stand. They lead you to the nearby river, where you are ceremonially immersed three times. They lead you to a fire, where you are warmed, fed, and carefully observed. Daybreak soon comes, you stand up and stretch, and the initiation process moves to the next level.

After sleeping for only a short while, during the next day you are told the meaning of Seven Macaw's Group. The Polar God is no longer valid, for higher truths have been discovered. You saw them the previous night with the aid of the Great Mother and the Galactic Toad. You had a firsthand glimpse of the True Deity and the true cosmic center and source. Hearing this, and knowing what you saw, you feel you must let go of the old god, and embrace greater truth. Strolling around the Polar God's group, you reflect upon what you have seen. You look, once again, at Stela 27, and see how it portrays the events in the south, as a reflection of Seven Macaw's movement in the north. Yes, you understand that there are two different cosmic centers, and you begin to wonder if there are even more. As if reading your mind, the priests lead you to Group B, a short walk through a grove of trees. You are told that this is the Group of Tzab-Kan-Kin, the Zenith God, otherwise known as the feathered serpent.

In Group A you realized that the Polar God was false, and other centers of the sky could be viewed. Stela 27, your yantric doorway into the Cosmic Mother, introduced a new place of Creation and the importance of the Sacred Tree Cross. Now, Group B introduces the zenith center, another center of the north, for, as you know, "up" and "north" lie in the same zone of the sky.

ALTAR 20

This altar faces north and lies along the main axis of Group B, reminding you that Seven Macaw sits on his perch in the north, and you used to worship him. The priests show you how the three pillars near the throne measure the passage of the sun through the center of the sky, and they point out that the throne represents the zenith center.

THRONE 1

Next to the throne is Stela 8. You see, in the lower section, a priest sitting on a throne. In the upper portion the priest is traveling into the mouth of the zenith center.

STELA 8

Your teachers explain the complicated astronomical symbolism encoded onto Throne 1 and Stela 8, and then instruct you to sit on the throne and contemplate Stela 9. You sit for hours, studying the image that stands before you. It is a very simple picture, a human figure being carried into the zenith by a winged spirit companion.

STELA 9

You remember the Seven Macaw altar facing the north, and how Seven Macaw is false, and realize that the zenith center, since it also belongs to the north, must also be a limited cosmic center. The deity ascending into the sky on Stela 9, carrying an initiate such as you, has wings like Seven Macaw. The Zenith God is in league with the false Polar God. Suddenly, you understand how to recognize false truths and misleading doctrines. You understand the message of the Zenith God's group: Some cosmic centers are illusions. Quickly now the priests turn your attention to another part of the sky, as depicted on the monument to your right.

STELA 10

Here you see the birth of the Hero Twins, with One Hunahpu—the First Father/December Solstice God—in the fat, billowing center of the Womb of All. The priests told you of these new gods yesterday, and you see how they participate in the new thought. In the image, First Father, the Solstice God, has ascended into the many-layered realms of the sky, into the cosmic Mother-House of Creation, and from there he impregnates the moon with Hunahpu and Xbalanque, so that they may facilitate his future rebirth.

Again the priests direct your attention, this time to the three solstice-facing monuments on the western platform. Most striking is Stela 11, and as dawn begins to arrive, you look to the horizon it faces and see the Womb of All rising.

STELA 11

Soon, the Solstice Sun Deity makes his presence known, and you understand the meaning of Stela 11. At some time in the remote future, the Solar Lord and the Womb of All will join. In a reverse process to Seven Macaw's "fall" away from the cosmic center in the north, which occurs over many baktuns, One Hunahpu ascends toward the cosmic center of the south, the Womb of the Milky Way Great Mother. You do not see it in a vision as you did with Seven Macaw's fall the other day; nevertheless you sense that this is part of the new truth. But you wonder, *when* will the resurrection of the Solar Lord occur?

The night is not yet fully over, and your teachers lead you to the group of Cosmic Mother-Father Union (Group E). Here you observe priests making offerings on the altars in front of two stelae. You look closely at the two stelae and intuit that they represent the cosmic mother and father principles, which are now beginning to rise in the east.

STELAE 19 AND 20

The priests tell you more about the Hero Twins and their father, who is symbolized on Stela 20. He is the December Solstice Sun (First Father/One Hunahpu), father of the Hero Twins. They also tell you about Cosmic Mother, who is symbolized by Stela 19. She is the Milky Way, the Womb and Birther of All—and her birth canal lies in the center of the crossroads rising to the east. Observing the priests making offerings and chanting ancient songs, you understand that their offerings are intended to ensure the future union. Yes, we must make offerings to facilitate the sky-Earth union, to bring renewed life and harmony to the world. Dwelling upon the implications of all you are witnessing, you deduce that the world that will experience the mother-father union exists in the remote future, and you cannot imagine who will be around then. Will anyone still be worshiping at these altars? Will seekers still be initiated into the Izapan Mysteries, the Galactic Cosmology? Will anything even remain of Izapa itself? Or will the Galactic Knowledge be lost to humans? The priests sense your confusion and questions, and explain that the day will come when the knowledge of the True Deity will be lost to humans. But you are also told that as the day of union approaches, the seeding of the Womb of All by the penetrating rays of First Father will prepare the humans alive during the end-times to self-initiate and revive the lost knowledge. You are told that the message of the Izapan Mysteries will survive intact under the jungle canopy, while a dark chapter in human history unfolds. Forgotten and decaying for a thousand years, the ceremonial carvings that preserve the Cosmic Wisdom will eventually be recovered, just in time for the New World to dawn. The shaman-priests have spoken, opening their wisdom to you, and you respect their words, for they are not only priests but visionary prophets. They are the *nik wakinel*, those who have gazed into the center and have peered through the veils of time. And so another day of initiation comes to a close as you watch the mother-father principles rise in the east as the new day dawns.

Finally, the day before the solstice deity shows his face arrives. It is the final day and night of your initiation into the new Galactic Cosmology. The priests continue their lessons, and teach you the intricacies of the new calendar, designed to calibrate the countdown to the future union of First Father and Cosmic Mother. It has five number places, and works alongside the tzolkin calendar that your people have followed for ages. You learn that a date of 7.18.0.0.0 is approaching, and are told to take the new long-range calendar back with you to your homeland and to teach it to others. They also tell you that the end-date, when the sky and Earth join, is called 13.0.0.0.0. Working with the numbers on bark paper, you realize that the resurrection of the True God will not occur until over 2,000 years have elapsed. The teachings on this day have educated you in the tangible dynamics of the new science, but your initiation is not over. You still must journey into the center of time, into the Heart of Heaven and the end-beginning caldron of eternity. You have yet to see the most profound message of the New Thought, and so you are brought to an outlying group with a ballcourt—the group of the Sacred Ballgame.

The priests call this place Pom Kexel Hom, which means "Offerings and Resurrection in the Ballcourt Graveyard." Offerings are made here, to ensure that time will continue rolling forward and that the future union of First Father and Cosmic Mother will occur. Resurrection, or rebirth, occurs when the shaman-initiate returns from an incredible journey into the Galactic Center, reborn after being bathed in the Galactic Knowledge of the cosmic Mother Womb. Such a rebirth will also occur for the entire world when it is renewed upon the future union of the December solstice Solar Lord with the Great Mother's Galactic Heart. The word for ballcourt is *hom*, which also means graveyard, and your teachers explain that new life comes through death; sacrifice must be made in the ballcourt's "graveyard" to ensure future rebirth. At first you fear being put to death, but are told that the sacrifice is not literal. For the initiate into the Izapan Mysteries, what must be sacrificed is the ancient Polar Paradigm and all the vain illusions associated with it. Only then can new life within a larger galactic consciousness be possible.

You, the initiate, are brought for rebirth into the ballcourt graveyard. It is after midnight, the night before the December solstice deity arrives. After processing with other initiates along the sacred path that links the main groups with the Galactic ballcourt, you stand on the temple and view the entire area. The ballcourt stretches below you, and you wonder what mysteries you will behold this night. Solemnly, cacao and the sacred mushrooms are passed around. You drink, chew, assimilate, and sit in meditation.

The stars turn . . . As the veils of your vision begin to lift, a sense of the sacred bestows you with courage. At that moment you are brought to the eastern entrance to the ballcourt. There you are shown the death of Seven Macaw, killed by the victorious ballplayer. Yes, your old god is dead, exposed as false.

STELA 60

You, the initiate, are that ballplayer, and you must travel through the goalring. Like One Hunahpu of the Creation myth, your head—your consciousness—will separate from your body, and travel along the Milky Way ballcourt until you find your way into the goalring, the dark-rift rising to the east. There, you will sit in the middle of heaven, pass through the spacetime portal, and fly upward into the many-tiered cosmic layers, as depicted on Stela 67.

STELA 67

Slowly, the priests guide you in your increasing dreamlike trance to the west end of the ballcourt, where they seat you on the Birth Throne. Straddling the God Head on the front of the throne, you gaze into the eastern sky and see the Galaxy— the Great Mother—majestically rising.

THRONE 2, MONUMENTS 17, 18, AND 19

You look down and see the stone gameball at your feet, tottering on the abyss of the goalring, and you envision it slowly, slowly, falling down into the hole. You look up, head swimming with ecstasy, and fall forward. No, you are flying forward, into the dark-rift hole in the sky rising over the distant horizon. Sailing upward and outward, you are drawn magnetically into a spinning vortex of memory and feeling, a hurricane of Creation forces pulling at every cell of your being. For what seems like an eternity you sail through alien worlds and ancient vistas, dream clouds sailing past you, and then you break through to a place of serenity filled with pres-ence—the presence of consciousness and life. It is a dark realm; it is Xibalba. But, strangely, although dark, it seems filled with a subtle light, the light of knowledge. Emerging from between the shadows, the dim outline of a vast jeweled cavern be-gins to take shape. It seems like a huge, many-faceted eye, extending out to see all times and places, and you are floating in its center. Bathed now in this numinous nowhere, you feel the heartbeat of the Cosmic Mother surrounding you, welling up inside you, enveloping you with love. Replenishing, rejoicing—a feeling of pure consciousness cascades over you with a glowing urgency. Gratefully, in awe of the gift, you wordlessly breathe in life and recognize that to live within this greater domain is truly your Galactic birthright. All your illusions begin to melt, vanishing in the sheer beauty of truth revealed. And then you begin to vanish, becoming so subtle as to slip into the light, like a drop of water into the ocean. Everything stops, and you cease to exist.

Diagram 183. The Maya jewel in the Galactic lotus

The next thing you know, you are suddenly startled with a shock of deceleration. Feeling your mind stretching across alien landscapes, searching for its home, you experience waves of energy and sound that seem to realign your entire being, imbuing it with new life. You feel yourself being constricted, pushed backward into the warm, moist, steambath of your flesh. You slowly begin to remember who you are, why you are here, and where you come from. A world of form begins to congeal, as if materializing in front of you. The walls of the ballcourt appear to your left and right, and the shadows begin to lighten. Your eyes refocus, Xibalba fades back into the shadows, and the world takes form again. Gazing deep into the distant horizon, in complete astonishment you see that the Great Mother has risen higher in the east and realize that you were there, just now. A tear streams down your left cheek as it dawns upon you that, yes, you journeyed into the sky, into the Cosmic Womb of Creation at the center of the cosmic crossroads. Along with the lightening shadows that illuminate the ballcourt walls comes a dawning light of knowledge within yourself. And at the very moment in which your face brightens with the new inner knowing, and your heart pounds, the dawning Solstice Sun Lord, whom the priests call One Hunahpu, dramatically breaks free from the horizon, his own face shining in the east.

The life-affirming light of truth has dawned, and you begin to sing a gentle song of worship, one you just made up, a wordless vibration of thanks to the cosmos and life. You know that your journey into the cosmic center fed a process of cosmic union that will culminate in the distant future. Your consciousness, your heart, ascended into the Womb of All, the throne of all space and time, and returned reborn. Now you understand that One Hunahpu makes this journey too, but much more slowly. One Hunahpu travels in the royal procession of cosmic time, each ascending step a katun, to his ultimate enthronement within his Cosmic Mother's heart. He will arrive there intact only with the help of humans.

On your journey, you let go of disbelief and widened One Hunahpu's path, bringing the cosmos one step closer to completion. You perceive that, like a magical magnet, the Great Lake of Life draws all souls back into it, back to the center, for rejuvenation and replenishment.

The more who make the journey, the bigger the spirit-magnet gets, until we have all been drawn back into the cosmic heart. Returning to our daily lives renewed and realigned with the Creation Place, we bring the Galactic wisdom and a little bit of eternity down to Earth.

PART V:
GAZING INTO THE GALAXY

WINTER SOLSTICE

Here is the place of fear

for four days

no greasy foods are eaten

there is no coffee

no trade

all places of business are closed

for ten days

no sweepings

no garbage is taken out of the house

not even cigarettes are lighted outside

people shouldn't use their cars

the street lights are all turned out

This is the middle of time

— Dennis Tedlock, *alcheringa*

CHAPTER 24

THE FORGOTTEN GALACTIC PARADIGM

zapa was the center of initiation rites into Galactic Cosmology. It was an innovative ceremonial center where initiates were led around the monument groups, slowly revealing that the ancient Polar God was false and that there were several cosmic centers. In Group E, abstract cosmic principles were unveiled and their future union was introduced. The ultimate revelation of the Izapan Mysteries came in Group F, where pageantry and Mystery Play—a new Creation myth, a throne-sitting shaman-king, and a ritual ballgame—all came together to facilitate and celebrate the future rebirth of the world. This would come through the center of the Sacred Tree, through the Underworld Portal, by seeding the Cosmic Womb with the fertilizing power of the highest day-sign and year-bearer, One Hunahpu, the Galactic God of Precession. High initiates sat on the ballcourt throne, inhaled the sacred smoke of the Galactic Toad, watched the ballgame Creation myth unfold in front of them, and, finally, to their amazement, received the revelation of the meaning of the mysteries presented to them. They saw it and understood: The Cosmic Womb began rising over the distant horizon, followed by the glorious appearance of the solstice sun. That is when they got it. That is when they began to count the days to the Zero Point of 13.0.0.0.0. That is when they saw First Father and Cosmic Mother slowly embracing, and when they recognized the Galactic Center as the true cosmic center and source. That is when Mesoamerica graduated from the limitations imposed by the ancient Polar God and reached the highest expression of shamanistic cosmology.

After these December solstice initiations were over, the awestruck pilgrims returned to their various corners of Mesoamerica and began to build a world that would barely survive to see the cosmic dawning. The Izapans oriented Mesoamerican civilization to the Galactic Center as a supreme organizing principle, and the rest is history. The esoteric message of the Hero Twin story was eventually forgotten, the Galactic Cosmology of the Long Count was lost. But the story was preserved on Izapa's monuments. Now, in the final days of the Great Cycle of thirteen baktuns, the fragments of this lost knowledge have been assembled and decoded. Izapa was a unique astronomical center and innovative ceremonial origin-place of Mesoamerican cosmic wisdom. With its monuments now dug up and reset in their upright positions, the Galactic Ballcourt recobbled and swept clean of debris, it beckons us to initiation into a forgotten Galactic Cosmology, the culmination of which happens in less than a katun.

The implications of the lost Galactic paradigm formulated at Izapa are profound. It is a way of looking at the cosmos that seems strange to modern values and assumptions, yet answers so many nagging and unresolved questions. Who are we? What is our role in the greater scheme of things? An ancient style of relating to the world is resurfacing, one that was followed by our Neolithic ancestors and that survives in increasingly small populations of indigenous peoples. This new-old paradigm values a way of being that is at odds with our own paradigm. For example, the value of *partnership* as a basis for relating to others was one held in high regard by the ancient cultures who worshiped the Mother Goddess, yet this position counters the *dominator* mode of Western civilization that sets up hierarchies of subordination.[1] In the ancient paradigm, the value of direct connection between oneself and deity is taken for granted, yet a fundamental concept in the Judeo-Christian tradition is the necessity of going through the Church and a secondary deity to get to the primary one. Could it be that something is fundamentally wrong with the basic tenets of our own paradigm, and that ancient Maya cosmology offers an alternative, one that is more appropriate for surviving the impending transformation?

The ancient skywatchers "engaged in the study of nature and its limits."[2] Considering that the Long Count cosmology is one that can, like other indigenous knowledge systems sketched in Part III, be termed "psychedelic" or "multidimensional," the limits of "nature" are the limits of the human mind. The knowledge-seeking visionary journeys undertaken by New World shaman-astronomers provided the data with which they crafted deeply profound cosmologies. In addition, as anthropologist Billie Jean Isbell wrote, "the native philosophers, who are usually astronomers or astronomer-priests, use methods and metaphorical language that are unfamiliar to us."[3] Some writers have even suggested that indigenous peoples are more right-brained than their logical, left-brained cousins. In Maya thinking, as with Amazonian tribes, "there exists a close relationship between astronomical observations, cosmological speculations, and drug-induced trance states."[4] The Indian cosmologists engaged in questing inward for knowledge, into "the many layered dimensions of the human mind."[5] And in so doing, they encountered insights into the fundamental principles of life, time, and spiritual evolution. By looking into the human brain and mind, Maya cosmonauts discovered that the inner and outer realities reflect each other, and that nature constantly engages in a dialogue between apparently unrelated categories of experience. In other words, the evolutionary heartbeat of humankind beats in rhythm with a higher, Galactic heartbeat, and it is our inner dialogue with our cosmic source that weaves the future. As Gerardo Reichel-Dolmatoff wrote, shamans understand that the human brain "is modeled after the celestial vault and the human mind functions according to the stars, which are the ventricles and sensoria of the cosmic brain."[6]

The cosmological understanding that emerges from shamanistic knowledge-gathering journeys into inner space results in a worldview that is deep, profound, and right on target. These worldviews, though developed among materially impoverished jungle tribes, embody the implicit order of the larger cosmos as reflected and experienced within the human microcosm. This is a gnostic or experiential knowledge quest, an approach to gaining an understanding of the cosmos that is completely different from that of Western science. As a result of these considerations, to correctly interpret the data offered by an interdisciplinary study of Mesoamerican cosmologies and cultures, we must at some point go beyond the confines of Western science. We must put ourselves into the mind-set of the ancient skywatchers to understand the deep insights they had found, and the ingenious ways they worked those insights into their calendric cosmology and their other shamanistic rituals. We might even adopt their exploratory methods and their tools of vision. Such an endeavor is not outside the scope of what is available to the average person: Modern ethnobotanists report that *teonanacatl* (psilocybin mushrooms), San Pedro cactus, ayahuasca analogues, and other sacred plant medicines are fairly easy to cultivate.[7] However, many modern cosmonauts emphasize that the way these sacred vision plants are used (preparation, motivation, setting, and expectations) determines the substance and quality of the knowledge and understanding gained.

The considerations just sketched may explain why Mesoamerican scholars have failed to identify the Galactic Cosmology so blatantly present in Mesoamerica's basic institutions. Science (based on the rational, linear, scrutinizing intellect) suffers from a limited perspective. Mesoamerican cosmology, on the other hand, is derived from accessing the multidimensional capacity of the human mind and soul, the multidimensional nature of reality. The academic model typically skirts around the most profound, fundamental concepts of shamanistic cosmology, because they simply do not fit into preconceived ideas of what is possible. The closest thing to the insights of Maya cosmology to be found in Western science involves quantum physics, with its concepts of Black Holes, wormholes, quasars, and other strange space-time anomalies.[8] As I demonstrated in Part III, these concepts are common in Maya Creation imagery. Ironically, the progressive theories of quantum mechanics are hailed as advanced, recent discoveries. The Maya, however, not only knew about quantum anomalies, they were able to conjure them up at will and travel into them. They gazed deeply into the cosmic center, the Black Hole in the center of our Galaxy, and to them the work of modern physics would probably seem like child's play.

POLAR TO GALACTIC: THE EVOLUTION OF MESOAMERICAN COSMOLOGY

We have traced the development of cosmology in Mesoamerica by understanding the primary interests of the peoples who migrated into the New World tens of thousands of years ago. These cultures came from the Far North of the Asian continent, from Mongolia, northern China, and Siberia. Ultimately, these transcontinental ethnic migrations can be traced back to Central Asia, the traditional "cradle of civilization."[9] As we have seen, Neolithic cultures belonged to a common substrate of humanity that practiced shamanism. Shamans today living in China, Central Asia, and Siberia attest to an ancient cosmological and ritual paradigm that understood the polar region to be the highest level of the celestial vault. They think of it as a cosmic center, a natural conclusion because in the Far North the North Celestial Pole is almost straight overhead.

Shamans undertook vision journeys into this cosmic center to retrieve otherworldly knowledge and powers. The people who migrated east and south into the Americas—forty-, twenty-, and ten-thousand years ago—probably all nurtured this basic cosmological belief. As these groups eventually found themselves crossing into the tropical zone, into Mesoamerica and ultimately across the equator into South America, their ancient polar paradigm must have undergone a transformation. The further south they traveled toward the equator, the lower the North Celestial Pole appeared to be in the sky. Being interested in the stars and a cosmic center they could journey to, these cultures started to slowly revise their ancient ideas. Mesoamerican cultures in particular probably noticed that another cosmic center, the zenith, presented itself twice a year, at noon on the solar zenith-passage dates. The solar zenith-passage dates suggested an alternative cosmic center, especially relevant in the tropical zone, to which astronomer-priests could undertake vision journeys twice a year. This center probably seemed ambiguous, however, because the solar zenith-passage dates changed with their latitude of observation.

Meanwhile, at places like La Venta, early astronomers observed that the rise times of circumpolar stars were slowly shifting. In other words, they became aware of the slow shifting of the heavens; they discovered precession. Based upon activity at La Venta, I place this discovery at roughly 1200 B.C., after which the race was on to accurately calculate the rate of precession. In order to calibrate precession, the early skywatchers focused on the solstice sun's future entry into the Milky Way's heart through the Underworld Road—the dark-rift near the cosmic crossroads. They realized that precession exerts erratic effects on circumpolar stars, and that astronomical locations along the ecliptic exhibited the most consistent rate of shifting. The Milky Way was chosen as the best background marker, for the Great Central Bulge in the Milky Way, which lies along the ecliptic, was seen as a Creation Place, the cosmic womb of the Great Mother. They had, in fact, discovered the Galactic Center, which truly is our cosmic center and source, or, as the Maya would say, the Heart of Sky.

The story of the evolution of cosmology in the Americas is the story of the search for the ultimate cosmic center. The early cosmologists of Mesoamerica understood that this was not only a place, but a time. And so they tracked the movement of the December solstice sun toward the Milky Way's womb, determined the rate of precession, and revealed 13.0.0.0.0 as a unique moment of alignment be-tween human beings living on Earth and their cosmic heart and source. Thus, our opening to the Galactic Center through the solstice doorway occurs in A.D. 2012.

As revealed by the Hero Twin Creation myth, the ancient Izapan shaman-astronomers recognized the polar region as false, as belonging to a previous World Age during which a less comprehensive cosmological understanding prevailed. The regents of the polar center, Seven Macaw (the Big Dipper) and his wife, Chimalmat (the Little Dipper), reside in the polar region around which all the stars appear to revolve. Seven Macaw, as a vain and false ruler, had to be done away with before the true World Age ruler could be instated. This task fell to the Hero Twins. Once they accomplished this deed, their father, One Hunahpu, was resurrected and recog-nized as the true cosmic ruler. Given the astronomical identification of One Hunahpu as the December solstice sun, and the other clues decoded throughout this book, his cosmic throne is the Galactic Center. That is where, after an eons-long proces-sion through the night sky, he finally takes his throne in the Heart of Sky. Mythol-ogy thus cryptically describes the astronomical alignment that culminates on the 2012 end-date, when the December solstice sun conjuncts the Galactic Center.

And so, Mesoamerican cosmology shifted from a polar orientation to a Galac-tic orientation. Appropriately enough, this ideological transformation occurred during the transitional era between the Olmec and the Maya, during the height of the Izapan civilization roughly 2,200 years ago. At the same time, the Long Count calendar appeared, which is a Galactic Calendar because its end-date was anchored to our impending alignment with the Galactic Center. The Hero Twin myth also appeared at this time, carved on Izapa's monuments. We can regard the simulta-neous appearance of the Long Count and the Hero Twin myth as evidence for a shift in cosmological perspective, an enhancement of knowledge, and a profound development in the understanding of reality, time, and consciousness. In short, the Izapan skywatchers dispensed with the false polar paradigm and formulated a Galactic Cosmology that stimulated and informed the beginnings of Maya civili-zation.

ECSTATIC COMMUNION AS SOCIO-POLITICAL ORGANIZING PRINCIPLE

Maya kings were shamans, and they embarked upon visionary journeys by ingesting psychoactive plants. In fact, the highest Maya political office *required* taking hallucinogens! The point of their endeavor was to travel to the outer limits of the cosmos and return with an understanding of the "big picture." Like a Hindu yogi, shamans could project their consciousness wherever they wished—into other realities, other planes of being, other planets and dimensions. They could journey back to the dawn of time, to the center and source of all life and being, and return with power and wisdom. The Galactic Center was the goal of their journey, for there the portal to infinity—the Grand Central Station of all beings and times— was located. Upon returning, the organizational reintegration that these adept kings experienced had the effect of reorganizing their kingdoms. In other words, the kingdom responded empathetically with the king's own experience of reintegration after having been blown out into eternity, and, like the order that emerges the moment that temperature drops far enough for water to crystallize into ice, the king effected a renewal of social order through his own "coming down." Thus, his royal ecstatic communion with the cosmic source was essentially a socio-political act.

But how different this sensibility is from that of modern civilization. Imagine the president of the United States taking psilocybin mushrooms ten hours before giving the State of the Union Address! Scholars know that Maya rulers took mind-expanding plants, undertook vision journeys, and were glorified as great shamans, but they have not explored the implications of this kind of socio-political system. The reasons are many, not the least of which are fear of the unknown and the current institutionalized anathema toward hallucinogens. And yet, looked at objectively, the Mayas' use of such knowledge-bestowing tools is completely understandable, even desirable. The leaders of society *should* be able to journey into the deep psyche, to access the fount of all creativity and genius, to commune with the ancestors and beings from other realms and times, and to deliver into their country the organizational frequencies emanating from the cosmic source. Maya kings were diviners, journeyers, channelers, and magicians, and they were the respected designers and leaders of a great civilization.

This situation, in which one worldview is incapable of appreciating the other, clearly indicates an intractable problem. Something very basic to the Western mindset prevents it from understanding the full profundity of Mesoamerican cosmovision. Scholars can label Maya beliefs and practices, yet they completely evade *seeing* what those beliefs actually mean. For example, scholars do not accept that Maya shamans could *actually* journey to distant times and places. Scholars phrase this as "Maya kings *believed* they could journey to distant locations." In fact, the mental/spiritual capacity for consciousness projection is well-known in the Hindu and Buddhist religions, as well as in most animistic worldviews. Why should the Maya be exempt from such achievements? One begins to suspect that the scientific mindset is really far behind the ancient multidimensional paradigms of mysticism and shamanism, where the full potential of the human mind is allowed to manifest. To fully understand Maya culture and cosmology, we must admit that the Maya king journeyed to distant places, communed with transcendental wisdom, and periodically conjured his kingdom into being, sustaining it by renewing it at specific nexus-points in the Long Count calendar.

THE GALACTIC COSMOLOGY IN MESOAMERICAN INSTITUTIONS

I call the precession-caused astronomical convergence of the solstice sun with the Galactic Center the "Galactic Cosmology." In the ancient Pre-Classic period, the discovery of this World Age–ending celestial convergence engendered an entire cosmology, as evidenced by its ubiquitous presence in several important Mesoamerican institutions. It is not surprising that the cosmological discovery that was encoded into the Long Count calendar and the Hero Twin myth served as a foundation-template for many Mesoamerican concepts. Keeping in mind the association of these mythic symbols with the solstice sun, the dark-rift, the crossroads, and the Milky Way, let us review the most important manifestations of the Galactic Cosmology in Mesoamerican institutions:

- kingship rites of accession to the cosmic throne
- birthing symbols and concepts, both mythological and biological
- the conception and birth of the Hero Twins
- the cosmic symbolism of the Mesoamerican ballgame
- the resurrection of One Hunahpu
- the origin of maize and the birth of the Maize Deity
- monster mouth imagery as a "to be born" place
- the Milky Way as the Great Mother

Kingship symbology partakes of the end-date cosmology because the king was enthroned upon the quadripartite crossroads, the celestial Creation Place signified by the crossing point of the Milky Way and the ecliptic in Sagittarius. Birthing symbology relates to the king's role as conjurer, and the cosmic birth canal was the nearby dark-rift. The king's journey into the cosmic center was equivalent to re-birth within the Great Mother (the Milky Way). His *procession* to rulership up the red carpet of the ecliptic reflected the solstice sun's slow *precessional* journey into the throne-lap of the Galactic Center.

By now, we have already thoroughly explored the connections between the traditions outlined here and the end-date astronomy, and there is no need to sum-marize. However, the cosmic symbolism of the ballgame is probably the most com-pelling manifestation of the Galactic Cosmology within an important Mesoamerican institution, and I would like to muse on this connection a little further.

The Mesoamerican ballgame was not just a sport. It was a ceremonial replica-tion of Creation events in Maya cosmology. The ball symbolized the head of First Father, One Hunahpu in the *Popol Vuh*, who represented the December solstice sun. The ballcourt represented the Milky Way, and the dark-rift was the doorway to the Underworld ballcourt. The goalring of the Mesoamerican ballgame symbolized this doorway, which also was understood to be the birth canal of the Great Mother, who was the Milky Way. Most importantly, the ballgame was performed as a ritual form of sympathetic magic to aid the solstice sun's movement into rebirth within the body of the Great Mother.

Although scholars interpret the ballgame to symbolize the *annual* rebirth of the sun, the mythology and shamanistic rituals attending ballgame ceremonies clearly reveal that the gameball and the goalring correspond to astronomical fea-tures involved in the World Age level of solar rebirth—the Galactic Alignment of 13.0.0.0.0. When the ball/sun finally went through the goalring, a sacrifice took place. This is in keeping with the Mesoamerican idea that deity sacrifice must take place before world renewal. In the ballgame myth, One Hunahpu is decapitated, his head becomes the gameball, and, after the Hero Twins defeat the Lords of Dark-ness, he is resurrected in "the ballcourt graveyard" as the true World Age ruler. But his anointing in the crown of heaven comes only upon the blessing of the Great Milky Way Mother, for it is initiation into life within her cosmic body that bestows the power of rulership.

Often, Maya kings themselves would play the ballgame, playing the role of a Hero Twin or even One Hunahpu. Maya kings might even have offered to be sacri-ficed as a necessary measure to keep the convergence rolling. They wanted to facilitate the future dawning, and they strove to feed the deities of time so that a future epoch of transformation could bathe the world in new life, enhanced to a new level of being. They knew this was part of a cosmic plan, but also understood that they must willingly and consciously participate in this celestial drama. And it was understood to be a game, a play of yin and yang, a dance of ball and hoop, a deity dance jumping over the Underworld Abyss to arrive in a new cycle of cosmic Creation. The Maya kings were willing to die for the benefit of future generations, and we are blessed to live during the era in which the cosmic gameball reaches its goal.

The Galactic Cosmology that centers on the events of 13.0.0.0.0 provides the archetypal foundation-template for many important Mesoamerican institutions, rituals, and concepts. Emerging as a profound cosmological discovery in the Izapan era before the Maya arose, its exposition of the Galactic Center as a supreme sociopolitical organizing principle was adopted as a basic tenet by an entire civilization, and it cast its influence over all of Mesoamerica.

13.0.0.0.0: THE ZERO TIME OF PRECESSION

On 13.0.0.0.0 in the Long Count calendar—what we call December 21, 2012—the Maya expected nothing short of the rebirth of the world. With great insight, the Maya cosmologists anticipated this cosmogenesis event to be caused by the movement of the solstice sun into alignment with the Milky Way, a movement determined by the precession of the equinoxes. In Western astrology, the movement of the vernal (spring) equinox through the twelve zodiacal constellations defines precessional ages, each of which lasts some 2,160 years. However, the method of tracking precession in Western astrology is rather ambiguous because the twelve zodiacal constellations are of different sizes, though each is given an abstract conceptual span of 30°. In fact, the timing of our passage into the next zodiacal age is subject to debate. Some writers have looked at this question very closely and report that, in terms of precise astronomy, the Age of Aquarius will not dawn for several centuries.

So, just when is the Zero Point of Western astrology? This question is important, for if precession is understood as a collective gestation of the human spirit, it requires a birth moment in which the cumulative achievements of a 26,000-year growth cycle come to fruition.[10] Traditionally, Pisces is the last sign of the Western zodiac, so might the Zero Time occur at the end of the Piscean Age? From one perspective, the answer is no. Precessional motion, as we know, moves backward through the zodiac, and a problem arises when we consider that the end of the Age of Pisces occurs when the vernal point is actually at 0° Pisces, preparing to enter 29° Aquarius, rather than at the "last" degree of Pisces. However, perhaps we should acknowledge a hidden intention within Western astrological tradition and take the notion of Pisces as the last zodiacal age at face value. Doing so, Western astrology proclaims that the Zero Time of precession is when the Age of Pisces—the "last" zodiacal sign—ends, which would be sometime in the next two centuries. From this perspective the Zero Time of Western astrology appears to be in general accord with the Maya end-times.

However, Maya cosmology, because of its use of the Milky Way as a more precise Zero Time target, gets us straight to the heart of the matter. Furthermore, the dark-rift in the Milky Way provides an even more precise target. For the Maya, it is the movement of one of the seasonal quarters into conjunction with this marker that defines eras of transformation in human civilization. (The last time this occurred was 6,400 years ago, the dawn of Old World civilization, and it involved the fall equinox.) For the Maya Galactic Cosmology, the precise astronomical "finish line" is, as we will explore in the next chapter, the Galactic equator—the field-effect dividing line of the Milky Way. Overall, the Maya recognized the precessional cycle as the origin of Galactic Seasons that periodically bring us into alignment with the Galactic Center, thereby catalyzing evolution on Earth.

As the seasonal anchor-point, the Maya chose the December solstice rather than the March equinox of Western astrology. The reasoning behind this is understandable. The December solstice is the "turnabout" time in the solar year, when the year is reborn from darkness. It is thus the "Zero Point" of our solar season. It is a time of direction change, renewal, rebirth, and increasing light and life. The equinox, on the other hand, is when the sun rises halfway between the solstice extremes. Whereas the solstices are rest points, the equinox sun moves very quickly along the horizon from day to day. Technically speaking, the sun's rate of declination change is very rapid around the equinoxes (see Appendix 3). This makes for a fast-paced energy dynamic in human affairs, a "gotta get there" syndrome. It thus may be misleading to think of the March equinox as New Year's Day, because at that time the sun is racing along, halfway through its journey from one extreme to the other. Equinoxes are times of balance in activity, momentum, and mediation whereas solstices are times of rest, renewal, and new beginnings. The December solstice sun appeals to common sense as the time of renewal, the date of New Year's Day. In fact, the creators of the Long Count regarded it as the beginning of the next World Age, since 13.0.0.0.0 is a December solstice.

The end-date of the 13-baktun cycle of the Long Count calendar is an artifact of an advanced and forgotten cosmology. It may represent the most advanced paradigm yet created by human beings. In this light, human civilization as a whole has regressed, or, in other terminology, Western philosophy has yet to catch up with the ancient Maya. Clearly, the Maya were advanced in ways that we in the West are just beginning to understand. However, based upon the fact that the ancient Long Count calendar pinpoints a rare alignment in the 26,000-year cycle of precession, we can at least say that the Maya were correct in suggesting that 13.0.0.0.0, December 21, 2012, is the appropriate Zero Time nexus of the Great Year of precession. Being the culmination of an ages-long quest for understanding the nature of time, Maya cosmological insights are reminding us that the Zero Time is upon us.

CHAPTER 25

BACK TO THE CENTER:
THE MESSAGE OF THE MAYA END-DATE

B ased upon insights gathered while in altered states of consciousness, the an-
cient skywatchers wove an amazing calendric cosmology around the Galactic
Center, a cosmology encoded into the Long Count calendar. This is why I call the
Long Count calendar a Galactic calendar, and the resultant philosophical model a
Galactic Cosmology. But what does the 2012 alignment mean for human beings on
Earth? In general, the solstice sun will be in conjunction with the great bulge of the
Galactic Center, which we can understand as a rare conjunction of Earth, the local
sun, and the Galactic heart. More importantly, however, in A.D. 2012 the solstice
meridian will cross over the Galactic equator.[1]

The Galactic equator is the astronomical term for the dividing line of the Milky
Way band, separating the left and right "lobes" of the sky, similar to how the Earth's
equator divides the Earth into two hemispheres. On Earth, we experience distinct
field-effect properties on the two sides of the equator. For example, water spins
down the drain counterclockwise north of the equator, and clockwise south of the
equator. Likewise, hurricanes and tornadoes in the Southern Hemisphere spin in
the opposite direction of those in the Northern Hemisphere. These effects involve
gyroscopic conservation of angular momentum, what we might call field-dynamic
reversals. Any spinning body will exhibit these properties, and there is no reason to
deny that the same phenomenon holds true for the Milky Way. On the Galactic
level, the Milky Way's equator, like the Earth's equator, is the field-effect dividing

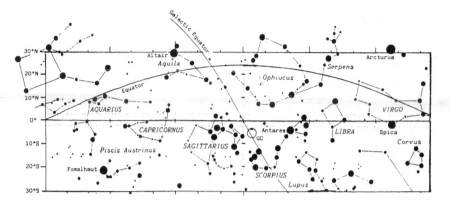

Diagram 184. Galactic Center and Crossroads. From Palden Jenkins (1987)

line. As with a spinning magnetic top, the field effects on one side are different from those on the other, and Maya insights offer us the notion that a field-effect reversal occurs when the solstice meridian crosses over this line. In other words, in 2012 the Earth's orientation, as defined by the solstice meridian, passes through a paradoxical null-point, much like the calm eye of a hurricane balances the surrounding chaos.

The "energy" field emanates from the Galactic Center and includes the entire electromagnetic/photon field in which our planet exists. There are dimensions of subtlety within this field—the telluric or astral realms—extending beyond the physical forces of science to include spiritual planes of being. If we imagine this field as being similar to the lines of force surrounding a magnet, we can understand that our changing orientation to this field has immediate consequences, and has little to do with cause-and-effect transmission of energy between us and the Galactic Center. We are, instead, in a relationship of *resonance* with our source, one that connects us deeply within to each other, and, in fact, to all other beings in this Galaxy. Based upon these considerations, I would like to emphasize that the Galactic equator—the precise edge of our spiraling Galaxy—is the Zero Point location of the turnabout moment in the cycle of precession. This World Age shift occurs when the solstice sun crosses over the Galactic equator, and thus the Galactic Alignment in 2012 is about a field-effect energy reversal.

But what does this mean for life on Earth? What kind of field effects will be present on Earth during the 2012 alignment? And what occurs when the solstice meridian transitions to the other side? As suggested by the spinning-hurricane metaphor, our basic orientations will be inverted. On the level of human civilization, our basic assumptions and foundational values will be exposed, and we will have the opportunity to embrace values long since driven under the surface of our collective consciousness. When a given set of rules and assumptions has run its course, and has led civilization to the end of a particular road, the opposite orientation begins to appear. The full manifestation of one style of human expression thus gives way, like the old year gives way to the new, to a fresh style based upon a completely opposite set of values and assumptions. This polarization is beautifully symbolized by the Chinese Tai-Chi symbol, which is very similar to a Mesoamerican design commonly referred to as Hunab Ku, from the *Nuttall Codex*.

Both of these symbols portray a process-oriented transformation from one extreme to the other that occurs on many levels of reality, from night changing into day to the evolution of values in a civilization. In terms of the spiritual evolution of human beings, this metaphor evokes eras of darkness giving way to eras of light, the eternal battle between igno-

Diagram 185. Polar reversal symbols: Tai Chi and Hunab Ku

rance and consciousness, and we can thus begin to understand the 2012 field-reversal as a moment in which the human spirit can emerge from unconscious patterns and blossom. The Swiss psychologist Carl Jung called this process of reversal *enantiodromia*. On the level of civilization, enantiodromia occurs over relatively brief periods of cultural chaos, and cultural transformation affects peoples' spiritual values, as well as the scientific and philosophical underpinnings of society's thinkers and policy makers. During these eras of social change, a polarization of values occurs, opposite camps define themselves and pull apart, each forming a new set of values, belief systems, and philosophies.

These are complex evolutionary processes ruled by the universal principles of birth, growth, and death, but we can imagine what this process of polarization is moving toward if we draw from a cellular metaphor. During cell mitosis, one cell pulls itself apart and divides into two cells; a previous cellular "oneness" is breached, and breached again, and yet again, as the cells continuously divide to form new, whole cells. At first, cellular splitting may appear degenerative because stability is lost and wholeness is constantly breached. However, this "breaking apart" of cell mitosis inaugurates embryogenesis, the most miraculous and transformative growth process of human becoming. In other words, cell mitosis is a splitting process that results in the seemingly blind generation of more cells that, however, is driven by an inner ordering program designed to create one unified being, on a higher level— a level beyond the dimension of the cell. If we apply this cellular metaphor to the level of human civilization and the evolution of human consciousness, periods of historical transformation during which polarization occurs signal the germination of a higher being, and the possible union of polarized camps on a higher level.

The Maya understood the principle of enantiodromia and believed it was driven by our changing orientation to the field-effects of the Galaxy. The 260-day tzolkin calendar is based upon the 260-day period of human embryogenesis, and, on a higher level, the 260-day tzolkin symbolizes, or structures, the 26,000-year period of precession, what we might call human spiritual embryogenesis. The Maya believed that the 26,000-year Great Year of precession is a spiritual gestation period for humanity, and that the 2012 alignment will catalyze the birth of what has been growing on this planet for 26,000 years. For the Maya, Father Sun's movement into union with Cosmic Mother's heart also signified the insemination, or seeding, of what will come to fruition in 26,000 years. The 2012 era is about the birth of something new on this planet, but it is also a death, the rupture of the womb-world that held us comfortably warm for millennia, unaware of the larger world outside of our limited sights.

On small or local levels of manifestation—in cultural revivals and in religious movements for example—the historical process of polarization has occurred before, but the 2012 era represents a global reversal. On a literal level of interpretation, one supported by many popular writers, the field-effect reversal that mystics and futurists intuitively feel occurring on this planet bodes an impending pole shift, a literal shift in the position of the Earth's North Celestial Pole, an event that would have disastrous effects around the globe. According to geologists, pole shifts indeed have occurred in the past; and if we are due for one now, I suppose there is not much we can do about it. Visions of apocalypse, however, may originate more in erroneous notions of linear time combined with fears implanted by our own Judeo-Christian conditioning than in reality. As a result of my studies of Maya end-date cosmology, I prefer to emphasize what might be termed a pole shift in our collective psyche. This places the possibility of successful, positive transformation squarely in our own hands. What I suspect this is about is already underway—a shift from the dominator mode so characteristic of our civilization to a partnership style. Social historian Riane Eisler emphasizes that these terms—dominator and partnership—refer to an opposed orientation in terms of cultural values, rather than qualities intrinsic to patriarchy (males) and matriarchy (females).[2] Her distinction is important, for if patriarchy upholds the values of hierarchical dominance and territorialism, matriarchy is the exact same style of organization except with women, rather than men, at the top of the hierarchy. Both are dominator modes of social orientation. According to Eisler, the partnership mode, on the other hand, upholds the values of relationship, cocreation, and life-affirmation through partnership with nature and other human beings. The partnership mode does not "belong" to the female principle any more than the dominator mode belongs to the male.

Western or Euro-American civilization currently rules the globe through dominator forms of coercion and resource control. This style of being-in-the-world can be traced back to the early city-states of Sumer, the very beginnings of the current chapter in Earth's history. Before Sumer, however, early ceremonial sites such as Çatal Hüyük in Central Turkey reveal that a very different social style prevailed in late Neolithic times, one that worshiped the Great Mother as the supreme life-principle and that honored relationship over status, partnership rather than domination. The Anatolian culture of the seventh millennium B.C. represented a partnership ideal with roots extending far back into the Paleolithic. Research by archaeologist Marija Gimbutas demonstrated that the Magdalenian culture of ancient Europe, which thrived more than 19,000 years ago, was linked with distant trade centers, worshiped the Great Mother, and may have had a form of glyphic writing.[3]

Clearly, our distant ancestors participated in a style of culture that is fundamentally antithetical to our own. And the pendulum of enantiodromia is swinging, pulling us out of ingrained habits, and stimulating a renaissance of an ancient paradigm that may be our only salvation. Western civilization is now confronting its own shadow in the form of global pollution, institutionalized corporate greed, and political instability. Fortunately, social upheavals and changes in the last thirty years indicate that we already appear to be moving in a direction that celebrates cocreation, relationship, and working together rather than violence, conquest, and force. In this emerging paradigm, we are indispensable cocreators of the post-shift world. The real pole shift may thus be about a shift in our fundamental orientation to each other and to the world, stimulated by our recommitment to life-affirming values. To go forward on our journey to collective wholeness, we must abandon our illusions and return to the center, back to rejuvenation within the Great Mother, our cosmic heart and source.

This book ends with a departure, for, having been led through the gate of Galactic initiation to the threshold of a new world, a new beginning opens to us, filled with its own challenges and joys. The Maya understood that human civilization cycles from one extreme form of social organization to the other. Out of this process of polarization, or spiritual mitosis, arises a new, greater being. Every time the cosmic cell divides, every 26,000 years, we are one step closer to the birth of that vast higher being of which we are just cells. Our committed, willing participation in the galactic processes of Maya cosmogenesis, recognizing our place in the great chain of creation, is what enobles our souls and elevates our spirits to a plane infused with unity and relationship. The opening doorway of baktun thirteen offers us conscious relationship with each other and a creative participation with the Earth-process that gives birth to our higher selves.

APPENDICES

APPENDIX 1

A BRIEF HISTORY OF AN IDEA

I do not claim to have made the initial discovery that an alignment of the solstice meridian with the Galaxy looms before us, but I do feel I have provided original insights into how it is connected with Maya calendar tradition and have elucidated its many manifestations in Mesoamerican cosmology quite clearly. The Galactic Alignment is an important astronomical event that, I believe, will be talked about a great deal in the upcoming years. As with the simultaneous invention of the telephone in distant areas, unrelated by cause and effect, the cosmologically potent concept of Galactic Alignment is an idea whose time has come, or, shall we say, has reemerged. Many people may lay claim to prior discovery of this phenomenon, which I feel is besides the point, because it was the early Maya who discovered it more than 2,000 years ago. My early contribution to elucidating the Mayas' discovery of a future Galactic Alignment was recognizing that the *xibalba be*, the Sacred Tree, and One Hunahpu/First Father were mythological keys to understanding the astronomy of the 13-baktun cycle end-date. Beyond this, my research unraveled large amounts of additional evidence, resulting in the reconstruction of a lost paradigm that I term the Galactic Cosmology. In the interest of clarity, I will reconstruct as thoroughly as possible how my encounter with the Maya Galactic Cosmology unfolded.

The earliest source that recognized (indirectly) the alignment of the solstice "colure" with the era of A.D. 2000 was *Hamlet's Mill*. This is not surprising, seeing how the authors, Giorgio de Santillana and Hertha von Dechend, were very interested in precession. However, they do not connect this with the Maya Long Count end-date. They speak frequently of the last time, some 6,400 years ago, when the Milky Way coincided with one of the seasonal quarters (the fall equinox). Frank Waters' book *Mexico Mystique* sourced material from *Hamlet's Mill*, and was concerned with exploring the "astrological" nature of the end-date, but failed to mention the era-2000 A.D. alignment suggested in *Hamlet's Mill*. As a result, no connection was made with the Maya. This is unfortunate, because if Waters had put this on the table for examination in 1975, we might be a lot further along in understanding how this key idea operated in Mesoamerican cosmology. (Waters used an erroneous end-date of December 24, 2011 A.D., sourced from an early edition of Michael Coe's book *The Maya*.) Next, the authors of the 1975 edition of *The Invisible Landscape*, Dennis McKenna and Terence McKenna, quoted from *Hamlet's Mill* and placed the end of the posited timewave in the year A.D. 2012 (174). A brief discussion of the Galactic Center, precession, and the alignment circa 2012 is on pages 189-190. However, at this point, the Maya were not mentioned, though they were in the 1993 edition. The McKennas became aware of a possible connection between the solstice-Galaxy alignment and the Maya calendar end-date in the mid-1970s.

During the 1980s there were only indirect or partial references to this idea. *Norton's 2000.0* star atlas clearly shows the alignment of the solstice meridian with the Galactic equator (the centerline of the Milky Way band) and astronomers must encounter this fact as a matter of course. However, connecting it to the Maya end-date in 2012 is another thing altogether. Major discoveries can stare you in the face for years before they flower. Basing his finding on the *Norton's 2000.0* star atlas, Nick Kollerstrom wrote a short "article particle" in *Mountain Astrologer* (August-September 1993) mentioning the solstice axis alignment with the Milky Way "in A.D. 2000." Futurist Moira Timms mentioned the solstice/Galaxy alignment "in 1999" in her book *Beyond Prophecies and Predictions*, but not in relation to the Maya calendar.

In my correspondence with Terence McKenna in mid-1993, the idea again came up regarding the solstice/Galaxy alignment being at the heart of the Maya calendar. Looking over some star charts that summer, I became convinced that something was definitely going on. In early 1994 I understood the importance of some incredibly provocative comments in Dennis Tedlock's *Popol Vuh* translation that indicated the crossing point of the Milky Way and the ecliptic in Sagittarius as a significant astronomical place recognized in Maya myth. I put two and two together and more pieces of a compelling cosmological puzzle started fitting into place. The dark-rift in the Milky Way, known to the Maya as the Road to the Underworld, was particularly relevant. In addition, something Tedlock said in the 1993 *Parabola* magazine interview had stuck with me: Maya Creation occurs at a celestial crossroads.

In May of 1994, I began to think this puzzle through, and located my astronomy software (EZCosmos 3.1) so I could model this thing. With *Norton's 2000.0* as a secondary reference guide (for precisely locating the Milky Way and its dark-rift), I was shocked to find the December solstice sun of A.D. 2012 directly in the dark-rift, at the precise junc-

tion of the Milky Way and the ecliptic! This was the first time anyone had identified Maya mythlore and cosmological concepts to argue for the Maya's intentional placement of 13.0.0.0.0 on the solstice/Galaxy alignment. The synchronization of calendar and astronomy, combined with meaningfully supportive Maya concepts, was probably not coincidental. So, who *did* create the Long Count? And when? These were the next questions I asked, and I knew that the answers were generally known within academia. In a flurry, I did research at the local university library and kept encountering more support for my suspicions. Surveying specialized studies in Maya myth and astronomy, I began to see Izapa as the likely birthplace of the cosmic knowledge encoded in the Long Count calendar.

In May, I completed an article describing this discovery and submitted it to *Mountain Astrologer* magazine, where it was accepted for publication in the December 1994 issue. Meanwhile, in August of 1994 astrologer R. Mardyks published a brief mention of the galactic astrology and the 2012 date in *Sedona* magazine. As an astrologer, Mardyks distinguishes an astrological difference between the precise solstice/Galaxy alignment "of 1999" and the 13-baktun cycle end-date of 2012, and, therefore, in personal correspondence with me (January 1998) he has disagreed with my interpretation that the Maya intended their 2012 end-date to mark the Galactic Alignment. My own interpretation follows common sense in allowing for *at least* a thirteen-year range for precessional calculations, and thus I emphasize that the Maya did, indeed, intend their 2012 end-date to mark the solstice-Galaxy alignment.

In late 1994 I noticed an article by astronomer Dawn Jenkins posted on a Maya astronomy website that mentioned the coincidence of the December solstice sun with the

Milky Way. Later, she told me that she had presented this same article to her astronomy club in Ohio in early 1994. So, the word was out while my article was in press. Since I do not claim intellectual ownership of this discovery, I do not think this is even a question of who "discovered" it first. The questions are: How can we understand this? What are the deeper implications? How does this cosmology manifest in other Maya traditions, such as the ballgame? What does it mean for us today? My initial interest was in clarifying how the ancient skywatchers of Mesoamerica figured it all out, and how they incorporated it into their mythology, cosmology, and culture. Having done that, more recently I have turned to exploring the philosophical implications of the alignment (see Chapters 24 and 25). Ultimately, I have come to realize that the cosmological discovery of a future alignment with the Galactic Center was the core insight and *primus motor* of Maya civilization.

My *Mountain Astrologer* article (1994) received recognition from widely diverse quarters. Astrologer Bruce Scofield mentioned it in his book *Signs of Time* (1994:203). (He had read an advance copy of it.) Barbara Hand Clow related my findings regarding the advanced details of the alignment in her book *The Pleiadian Agenda* (1995). Terence McKenna posted my 1994 *Mountain Astrologer* article on his Hyperborea website. Wolfram Oehler (1996a and 1996b), a researcher in Germany, translated some of my work into German and has written articles about the 2012 alignment based upon my research. Kenneth Johnson (1997:176) wrote of my article in his book *Jaguar Wisdom*. Mathematician and Maya scholar Stephen Eberhart at California State University, Riverside, mentioned my work in class workbooks devoted to ancient calendars, astronomy, and mathematics. Other scholars have also com-

mented on my research into Maya cosmology. For example, in personal correspondence Anthony Aveni wrote that he appreciated "new insights" in "A Hawk, a Cross, and a Mouth" (see Chapter 14).

In 1997, astrologer James A. Roylance wrote an interesting article called "Galactic Alignments" that appeared in *The Astrological Journal*. In it, Roylance discussed the precession of the equinoxes and the astronomy behind the impending alignment of the solstice meridian with the Galactic equator. He related the precessional movement of the vernal point away from the galactic plane as an alienation from attunement to the greater cosmic picture. In his interpretation, this explains the rise of Monotheism—the "worship of a disembodied God"—over the last 6,000 years. Consequently, the arrival of the Age of Aquarius, which Roylance measures with the impending Galactic Alignment, marks the beginning of the vernal point's return to the Galactic homebase (the Galactic plane), thus "calling forth a fundamental realignment of the human psyche." Interestingly, Roylance also notes that three constellations (of Western astrology) appear to point to the Galactic Center. He also provides a mathematical analysis of when the solstice meridian's alignment with the Galactic equator will be most precise. Given the necessary margin of error, precession will bring the "Galactic angles" onto the "seasonal (cardinal) cusps" between February 1998 and November 1999. The lunar mansions of ancient Vedic astrology also appear to indicate the Galactic Center as a "root" or starting point of time (Frawley 1991:343).

In April 1997, I discovered a book by Michio Kushi called *Visions of a New World: The Era of Humanity*. Two chapters, "The Ancient World" and "The Future World," presented ideas about the precession of the equinoxes and the way it changes our relationship to the Milky Way. Kushi wrote that the Earth's polar axis will be oriented toward the Milky Way in about A.D. 8500. The band of the Milky Way is understood to be a field of energy, and when our Earth's axis is so aligned, Kushi proposed that energy cascades through the vertical (north-south) axis and affects weather patterns and life on Earth. Kushi's ideas are fascinating and ahead of their time, presenting a compelling mechanism to explain how our precession-caused changing relationship with the Milky Way can affect life on Earth. He sees evidence for ancient knowledge of this cosmology in Revelations and in the Taoist I-Ching philosophy. In fact, he sees the epic ups and downs of human history to be intrinsically related to our changing relationship to the Milky Way. However, he does not mention the alignment of the solstice meridian with the Galactic equator circa A.D. 2012. Nevertheless, Kushi's ideas should be acknowledged as a very early foray into an amazing and very ancient Galactic Cosmology.

APPENDIX 2

MESOAMERICAN PRECESSIONAL KNOWLEDGE: IN THE LITERATURE

Did the Maya know about precession? What kind of mythological motifs characterize knowledge of precession? Where do we begin our search for precessional knowledge? Armed with the strong circumstantial evidence, supplied by the nature of the Long Count end-date, that the Maya tracked precession, we should expect to find concrete evidence uncovered by other researchers. In fact, there is a fair amount of discussion of this topic in the academic literature. Let us take a look at what several Maya scholars have said about this topic.

Gregory Severin published his analysis of the *Paris Codex* with The American Philosophical Society in 1981. The *Paris Codex*, one of four surviving Mayan books, contains a thirteen-sign zodiac. Herbert Spinden first pointed this out back in 1916, but the idea has not until recently generated a great deal of commentary. Now, many scholars, including David Kelley (1989), Meredith Paxton (1992), Linda Schele (in Freidel et al. 1993), and Victoria Bricker and Harvey Bricker (1992) are advancing hypotheses to explain the details of this Maya zodiac. Their work is supporting the concept that the Maya utilized spatial divisions of the ecliptic, and therefore had a type of sidereal astronomy. Gregory Severin's theory was quite different. The premise of his monograph is that the thirteen signs of the *Paris Codex* delineate zodiacal ages, each being a division of the 26,000-year precessional cycle. The entry from one zodiacal age to the next was marked by the vernal point (the spring equinox) mov-

ing into a new sign. The symbol for this equinox position is, according to Severin, one that was formerly thought to represent eclipses.

Severin's study is ambitious, insightful in certain respects, but ultimately flawed. Severin may have held too many Western astronomical assumptions in analyzing this data (for example, that the *vernal point* must be the marker), and the Maya may have conceived of things in a way quite alien to our expectations. Michael Closs, associate professor of mathematics at the University of Ottawa, reviewed Severin's monograph in an essay entitled "Were the Ancient Maya Aware of Precession?" (1983). It immediately seems unlikely that Closs will be able to answer the title question simply by refuting one researcher's work. In his concise seven-page review/essay, Closs pointed out flaws in Severin's analysis and therefore concludes, regarding the blanket question of precessional knowledge, that "After reviewing the evidence in Severin's work, this writer remains unconvinced and in his judgment the answer is no" (170). However, Closs's final statement may be a case of throwing the baby out with the bathwater, for he cannot possibly conclude the ancient Maya were ignorant of precession simply because a modern interpreter of one of their documents made errors.

The prolific researcher David Kelley (1983a) was less skeptical. In his review of Severin's study, he wrote that Severin adequately demonstrated that the *Paris Codex* could have been used to calculate precession, providing a "good but not overwhelming case" (S70). Despite pointing out several of Severin's errors, he concluded that "scholars will be led to new insights" by Severin's work "for years to come."

Other Maya scholars commenting on ancient precessional knowledge support it directly. Gordon Brotherston, Mesoamerican scholar and author of *The Book of the Fourth World*, considers the evidence to be clear. A very interesting discussion in this book begins with the topic "World Ages and Metamorphosis." The concept of "Suns" or World Ages is central to Maya as well as Aztec cosmology. In the *Popol Vuh*, a total of four ages are laid out, and the first three have already ended in destruction. The efforts of the Hero Twins are designed, in part, to facilitate the removal of the "false" world ruler Seven Macaw, and to install One Hunahpu/First Father as the true god. Aztec cosmology, the best representation of which is carved on the so-called Aztec Sunstone, describes five ages. The center of this monumental calendar stone is the "ollin" symbol of movement, the quincunx symbol that illustrates four ages at the four corners united in the center, the fifth age. According to Aztec cosmology, we live in the Fifth Age, the age of "movement"—symbolized by the seventeenth day-sign of the tzolkin—and our age will be destroyed by earthquake.

Brotherston considered the Creation myth in the *Popol Vuh* to be closely linked, via basic doctrinal content, to later stories that emerged in Central Mexico. Furthermore, Brotherston revealed how great cycles of time are evident in many native cosmologies. For example, there is the 60,000-year glacier cycle known to the Mapuche people; "millions of years" are said to have elapsed in the narrative of the Witoto Indians; a 73,000-year period in Chimalpahin's Seventh Revelation; and spans of 80,000 years are still counted out by the Tzotzil Maya. According

to Brotherston, the "indispensible concept" in these doctrines is the 26,000-year precession of the equinoxes. Brotherston acknowledged what should be self-evident in studies of any cultural history: Precessional knowledge leads to a doctrine of World Ages.

But Brotherston did not rely on vague generalities as proof of his belief that Mesoamerican astronomers were aware of precession. He pointed out the .242-day discrepancy between the 365-day haab and the synodic seasonal calendar (365.242 days). The .242-day difference amounts to a year every 1,507 years. (I corrected obvious numerical typos in Brotherston's book [1992: 298-299]. These errors have to do with his rounding off the values for the "synodic seasonal calendar" and the "sidereal year of the stars." His observation that the .014-day difference amounts to precession is still accurate and correct.) According to Brotherston, the .014-day precession formula also is found in the *Mexicanus Codex* of Central Mexico. The sidereal year of the stars is 365.256 days, and this .256-day difference measured, again, against the 365-day haab amounts to one day over 1,427 years, and this interval is marked in the *Tepexic Annals* of Central Mexico. As Brotherston explained, the .014-day difference between these two formulas corresponds to precession, and amounts to a year in just under 26,000 years, and this time span is indicated in the Aztec Sunstone as well as the *Rios Codex* from Tenochtitlan. Brotherston's analysis is rigorous, well informed, and it has the authority of respected scholarship behind it.

In an article entitled "The Year 3113 B.C. and the Fifth Sun of Mesoamerica: An Orthodox Reading of the Tepexic Annals," Brotherston analyzed the glyphic content of the Aztec Sunstone. He noticed that the length of the Four Ollin era is recorded on the rim of the Sunstone in ten lots of numbered Rounds.

The iconography and conventional style of recording "bundles" as time-periods indicates a total of 20,800 years for the first four eras, and 5,200 years for the present era. This totals 26,000 years for a complete Era Cycle. In the *Cauahtitlan Annals'* transcription of the Sunstone cosmology, four-fifths of the "Great Year" is noted as "CCCC Mixcoa," which is 400 cloud-snake rounds, or 20,800 years (400 x 52). The *Rios Codex* contains five World Ages that total, according to Brotherston, "a little less than 26,000 years." Implicit in these number systems is the final figure of 26,000 years, obviously indicating knowledge of precession. (See Brotherston 1992:298-302 for the full argument.)

Eva Hunt's book *The Transformation of the Hummingbird* contributed to defining the relationships between Mesoamerican myth and astronomy. Like scholars before her, she identified Tezcatlipoca with the North Celestial Pole, but Hunt added new insights to the discussion. Tezcatlipoca, it will be recalled, was a multifaceted god who had only one leg. Thus, he is envisioned spinning about the pole of the ecliptic. The four faces of Tezcatlipoca, according to Hunt, represent four eras or "Suns" defined by the changing Pole Stars that appear over long periods of time. Of course, the phenomenon that causes the Pole Star to move and, in fact, be replaced by other nearby stars is the precession of the equinoxes. Hunt writes, "The changing of the position of the celestial pole, due to the equinoctial precession that changes the polestar and the planetary orbitings, was expressed in the complicated myths of Tezcatlipoca's transformations" (152). She goes on to suggest that a careful reading of pre-Hispanic myths would "provide us with a series of prehispanic counts of dated events in the equinoctial precession" (152). She cites the different identities of Tezcatlipoca as evidence for this, finding that

"his divine 'movement' or 'change' (that is, the change of the position of the northern polar center from one star to another) was recorded in written form in the *Historia de los Mexicanos por sus Pinturas*, in the sixteenth century" (152-153). The myths analyzed all reveal four eras or Suns (changing Pole Stars), and the fifth Pole Star era is then thought to be the current one. These ideas are reiterated in another Central Mexican myth called the Legend of the Suns.

Hunt's ideas are startling, clearly providing an interpretive foundation for understanding precessional mythology in many Mesoamerican sources. Although her book was reviewed by several Mesoamerican scholars (e.g., Gossen 1982), they did not comment on this important information.

The Milky Way is an unambiguous partition of the ecliptic. If the thirteen-sign zodiac in the *Paris Codex* implies the use of a type of sidereal astronomy, we would expect that one of the constellation divisions would be right at the Milky Way. Three different placements are offered by three different researchers: Severin in his monograph, Schele in *Maya Cosmos*, and the Brickers in *The Sky in Mayan Literature*. One of the division points between zodiacal constellations in the *Paris Codex* is given by Victoria Bricker and Harvey Bricker as December 3 in the era A.D. 750 to A.D. 770. They call this the "second" constellation, and it begins within 1° of the Galactic equator in Sagittarius, on the *xibalba be*. In other words, according to the Brickers' model, the Galactic equator cuts right through one of the divisions of the thirteen-sign zodiac in the *Paris Codex*. The *Paris Codex* constellation in question is the rattlesnake, suggesting a polarity between Scorpio (dark-rift as snake mouth) and the Pleiades (rattlesnake's rattle) that is recognized in indigenous cosmologies of Mesoamerica and South America. This information is very suggestive, and Maya concepts of stellar mansions need to be examined more carefully to find evidence (in addition to Kelley 1989) that the Milky Way was thought of as an astronomical dividing line or beginning point for time. To this end, the *Madrid Codex* would probably be a useful source.

Calendar experts have identified the 13-baktun cycle's midpoint (April 17, 551 B.C., 6.10.0.0.1) as the most likely date on which the Long Count was officially installed. According to Mesoamerican scholar Robert Hall (1989-1993a), April 17 is close to the day, in era 551 B.C., when the sun conjuncted the Pleiades. As we know, this conjunction date changes with precession so that currently the sun conjuncts the Pleiades on May 20. Hall therefore suggested that among the ancient skywatchers there was "a concern for the day on which the sun was at the longitude of the Pleiades in each century, moving through April and into May one day each 71 years with the precession of the equinoxes. Mechanisms such as these certainly were in effect" (121). Hall clearly implies here that the Long Count was inaugurated in 551 B.C. to track the precession-caused changing dates of "sun conjunct Pleiades" through the centuries.

Hall's essay is well-argued and researched, but his use of the Pleiades as a background feature against which precession was tracked makes sense only if the date is measured against a seasonal quarter. In other words, as shown in my foreground-background model of precession tracking (Part I), one needs the "anchored" dates of the seasonal quarters (or the zenith-passage dates) to measure sidereal shifting. At any rate, counting the days to the nearest seasonal quarter is a simple affair. Apart from this, Hall's scenario is in effect very similar to the one I present in my Zenith Cosmology. If Hall's thesis is correct,

and it may be, then adjustments within the Calendar Round framework may have been used as a means of tracking precession. This probably became the New Fire institution (see Chapter 7).

The modern Yucatec Maya shaman Hunbatz Men stated that the sun travels around the Pleiades once every 26,000 years. On the surface this sounds absurd, but let us remember that the Maya often see things quite differently; when they look at the moon, and half of it is there, they call it a half moon. Modern astronomy calls that a quarter moon, because it is one-fourth of the way through its full cycle. Who is right? Both are. What I call observational astronomy is quite literal. Hunbatz Men's statement might make more sense if we add to it "the *spring equinox* sun travels around the Pleiades once every 26,000 years." Here we have a description of Hall's hypothesis, relayed to us by a "New Age" Maya shaman. It is true, the position of the spring equinox sun against the background of stars, in relation to the Pleiades, will slowly circle around the zodiac once every 26,000 years. We needed to anchor the sun to a position in the solar year—the spring equinox—for the statement to make sense. As for my end-date scenario, the answer to *which* sun approaches the *xibalba be* is *the December solstice sun* (the first day of the seasons) or, in mythological terms, One Hunahpu/First Father.

This brief survey of the academic literature on the precession question, as well as additional information contained in Part I, demonstrates that many Maya scholars believe the ancient Maya were tracking precession. Given the level of astronomical sophistication possessed by the ancient Mesoamerican astronomers, and the Mayas' well-known obsession with time, it would be surprising if Maya astronomers did not notice and then accurately calculate precession.

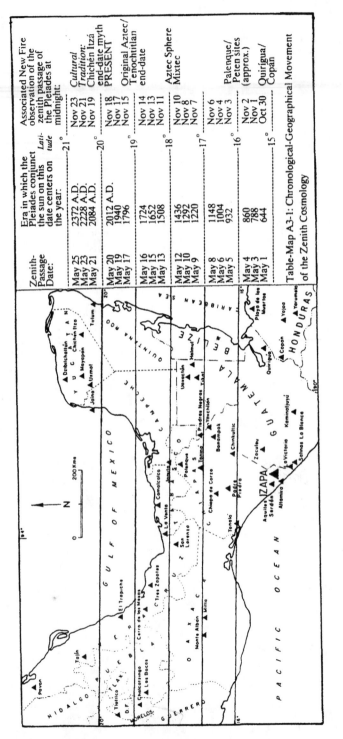

Zenith-Passage Date:	Era in which the Pleiades conjunct the sun on this date centers on the year:	Latitude	Associated New Fire observation of the zenith passage of the Pleiades at midnight:	
		—21°—		*Cultural Tradition:* Chichén Itzá end-date myth PRESENT
May 25	2372 A.D.		Nov 23	
May 23	2228 A.D.		Nov 21	
May 21	2084 A.D.		Nov 19	
		—20°—		Original Aztec/ Tenochtitlan end-date
May 20	2012 A.D.		Nov 18	
May 19	1940		Nov 17	
May 17	1796		Nov 15	
		—19°—		
May 16	1724		Nov 14	
May 15	1652		Nov 13	
May 13	1508		Nov 11	
		—18°—		Aztec Sphere Mixtec
May 12	1436		Nov 10	
May 10	1292		Nov 8	
May 9	1220		Nov 7	
		—17°—		
May 8	1148		Nov 6	
May 6	1004		Nov 4	
May 5	932		Nov 3	
		—16°—		Palenque/ Peten sites (approx.)
May 4	860		Nov 2	
May 3	788		Nov 1	Quirigua/ Copan
May 1	644		Oct 30	
		—15°—		

Table-Map A3-1: Chronological-Geographical Movement of the Zenith Cosmology

TABLE-MAP A3-1.

APPENDIX 3

SPACE-TIME MAPS OF THE SUN AND THE PLEIADES IN THE ZENITH

The Mesoamerican interest in the sun, the Pleiades, and zenith passages was explored in Part II, where I deciphered how the myth encoded into the Pyramid of Kukulcan at Chichén Itzá incorporates the compelling dynamics of these primary players. The phenomenon by which the sun, the Pleiades, and the zenith converge, what I termed the Zenith Cosmology, is complex, and is caused by the precession of the equinoxes. Some clarification is needed in regard to solar zenith-passage ranges, and I have devised a chronological-geographical map to concisely express the astronomical dynamics involved in the Zenith Cosmology. I wove together criteria of space (latitude) and time (eras determined by the precession of the equinoxes) to create a comprehensive space-time map (see Table-Map A3-1).

TABLE-MAP A3-1. CHRONOLOGICAL-GEOGRAPHICAL MOVEMENT OF THE ZENITH COSMOLOGY

Table-Map A3-1 encapsulates the movement and parameters of the Zenith Cosmology. The last column (on the right) associates a direct space-time dynamic between specific cultural traditions and the occurrence of the phenomenon in question (coincidence of solar zenith passage with sun-Pleiades conjunction). Cultures living at the correct latitude at the correct time (such as at Copán) would have experienced the sun-Pleiades-zenith convergence. Thus, Copán skywatchers were probably tracking this phenomenal convergence of two different celestial events "as it happened." For a cultural epoch in which the time and latitude factors do not converge very well, something else may have been going on. For example, activity at Chichén Itzá in the ninth century A.D. was concerned with the future synchronization that, for the 20°N latitude, occurs in the twenty-first century. As explained in Part II, Chichén's Zenith Cosmology encodes long-range precessional calculations and explains the hidden meaning of the architecture and orientation of the Pyramid of Kukulcan.

Table-Map A3-1 collapses a great deal of information into a deceptively simple presentation. The latitudes on the left of the table can be matched with the latitudes on the right side of the map. The astronomical synchronization illustrated involves dates of sun-Pleiades conjunctions (these change with the precession of the equinoxes) and dates of solar zenith passages (these change with latitude). This table-map serves as a guide to answer the question: When and where do sun-Pleiades-zenith conjunctions occur? The complex dynamics of the Zenith Cosmology define an ever-changing emphasis on different latitudes and different eras. The general flow of the "Zero Point" of the zenith alignment is from south to north, from past to future. Latitudinal bands are indicated in the map for ease in identifying cultural locations.

The table in Table-Map A3-1 is divided into five columns. The first column gives the solar zenith-passage date for the corresponding latitude. These are ideal mid-point dates; zenith observations (as we will see below) fulfilling the criterion of "no shadows at high noon" actually extend over several days. As can be seen, from the latitudes of 15°N to 21°N, all of the zenith-convocation dates fall in May. The second column gives the era in which the Pleiades were in conjunction with the sun on the corresponding date. Because of precession, these eras are 72 years long, with the dates given representing the midpoint of each era. The third column shows the latitude, with the dates given corresponding to one-third divisions of each degree. With the information in these first three columns, one can thus identify the era and latitude in which the solar zenith-passage date corresponds to the date of the sun-Pleiades conjunction. This means that at high noon on the given date, in the given era, at the latitude indicated, both the sun and the Pleiades, together, pass through the precise center of the sky. As proposed in Part II, this astronomical event was of great interest to Mesoamerican cosmologists, who perceived it as the apotheosis and manifestation of Quetzalcoatl-Kukulcan. The fourth column gives the date exactly one-half year after the date given in column 1, because I believe that the November New Fire ceremony of the Toltecs and Aztecs, during which the passage of the Pleiades through the zenith *at midnight* was carefully observed, was a method for tracking the precise date of a sun-Pleiades conjunction six months later. Again, these observations change with precession, whereas solar zenith-passage dates only change with the latitude of observation.

THE NO-SHADOW DATE-RANGE

I have made a distinction between the appearance of the phenomenon in question to the inhabitants of Chichén Itzá and to the inhabitants of Copán. Copán is at the latitude of 15°N, where the sun-Pleiades passed

through the zenith together in the era A.D. 644. At that latitude, the phenomenon occurred on May 1. For Chichén Itzá, which is much farther to the north, the phenomenon centers on May 23 (in the twenty-second century A.D.). However, I have made the case that latitude-dependent zenith observations are subject to a range of several days, making the Chichén event relevant to May 20 in our current era, with a negligable deviation. Why is this? Another space-time table is called for.

Since the visible marker of the zenith-passage phenomenon involves the criterion of "no shadows at high noon," the allowable range of days hinges upon how much the sun changes its declination from day to day. "Declination" is the angular distance measured from the celestial equator to an astronomical object at its highest arc (its passage through the meridian). If the rate of declination change is great, only a two- or three-day range can be accepted. If the declination change is slow, a range of up to fifteen days or more can be acceptable. The rate of the sun's change in declination from day to day is a function of how close the dates in question are to the solstice. Around the solstices, the sun's declination changes very little from day to day. Thus, shadows cast by the sun over a five- to ten-day period will show little variation. On the other hand, if the solar zenith-passage date falls near the equinox, the rate of declination change is very great. Consequently, the range of acceptable "no-shadow" days is limited. Dates progressing from the March equinox toward the June solstice show a gradual slowing of the sun's rate of declination change. In real terms, this means that for Copán, where the sun-Pleiades-zenith-passage days were closer to the spring equinox, the phenomenon came and passed more quickly than at latitudes farther to the north.

The solar zenith-passage dates applicable

in this appendix fall between April 28 and June 28. Table-Map A3-1 can be augmented by Table A3-2, which shows the rate of dec- lination change for each day from April 28 to June 28 (any year):

TABLE A3-2. RATE OF SOLAR DECLINATION CHANGE

Date	Rate of Declination Change Per Day	Latitude of Zenith Passage On This Date	Date	Rate of Declination Change Per Day	Latitude of Zenith Passage On This Date
April 28	00°19'05.4"	14°00'27.2"	May 29	00°09'38.5"	21°32'45.1"
April 29	00°18'51.5"	14°19'18.7"	May 30	00°09'16.1"	21°42'01.2"
April 30	00°18'37.5"	14°37'56.2"	May 31	00°08'53.5"	21°50'54.7"
May 1	00°18'23"	14°56'19.2"	June 1	00°08'30.7"	21°59'25.4"
May 2	00°18'08.3"	15°14'27.5"	June 2	00°08'07.8"	22°07'33.2"
May 3	00°17'53.3"	15°32'20.8"	June 3	00°07'44.6"	22°15'17.8"
May 4	00°17'37.8"	15°49'58.6"	June 4	00°07'21.2"	22°22'39"
May 5	00°17'22.2"	16°07'20.8"	June 5	00°06'57.8"	22°29'36.8"
May 6	00°17'06.1"	16°24'26.9"	June 6	00°06'34.1"	22°36'10.9"
May 7	00°16'49.8"	16°41'16.7"	June 7	00°06'10.4"	22°42'21.3"
May 8	00°16'33.1"	16°57'49.8"	June 8	00°05'46.5"	22°48'07.8"
May 9	00°16'16.1"	17°14'05.9"	June 9	00°05'22.5"	22°53'30.3"
May 10	00°15'58.9"	17°30'04.8"	June 10	00°04'58.3"	22°58'28.6"
May 11	00°15'41.3"	17°45'46.1"	June 11	00°04'34.1"	23°03'02.7"
May 12	00°15'23.5"	18°01'09.6"	June 12	00°04'09.7"	23°07'12.4"
May 13	00°15'05.3"	18°16'14.9"	June 13	00°03'45.3"	23°10'57.7"
May 14	00°14'46.8"	18°31'01.7"	June 14	00°03'20.8"	23°14'18.5"
May 15	00°14'28.1"	18°45'29.8"	June 15	00°02'56.2"	23°17'14.7"
May 16	00°14'09"	18°59'38.8"	June 16	00°02'31.5"	23°19'46.2"
May 17	00°13'49.7"	19°13'28.5"	June 17	00°02'06.9"	23°21'53.1"
May 18	00°13'30.1"	19°26'58.6"	June 18	00°01'42.1"	23°23'35.2"
May 19	00°13'10.3"	19°40'08.9"	June 19	00°01'17.4"	23°24'52.6"
May 20	00°12'50.1"	19°52'59"	June 20	00°00'52.5"	23°25'45.1"
May 21	00°12'29.7"	20°05'28.7"	June 21	00°00'27.8"	23°26'12.9"
May 22	00°12'09.1"	20°17'37.8"	June 22	00°00'03"	23°26'15.9"
May 23	00°11'48.2"	20°29'26"	June 23	00°00'21.8"	23°25'54.1"
May 24	00°11'27.2"	20°40'53.2"	June 24	00°00'46.5"	23°25'07.6"
May 25	00°11'05.9"	20°51'59.1"	June 25	00°01'11.3"	23°23'56.3"
May 26	00°10'44.3"	21°02'43.4"	June 26	00°01'35.9"	23°22'20.4"
May 27	00°10'22.6"	21°13'06"	June 27	00°02'00.7"	23°20'19.7"
May 28	00°10'00.6"	21°23'06.6"	June 28	00°02'25.3"	23°17'54.4"

In the left column, a bracket spanning May 2 to May 6 is marked "> 1°". In the right column, a bracket spanning June 5 to June 21 is marked "> 1°".

This table shows that I am justified in using at least a six-day range for solar zenith-passage observations at the latitude of Chichén Itzá, because between May 20 and May 25 the declination of the sun changes less than one degree. The sun itself spans one-half a degree in the sky, so shadow-casting observations will certainly support a six-day range as proposed in my theory about the Pyramid at Chichén Itzá (meaning that the "sun-Pleiades in the Zenith" event is currently within range over Chichén Itzá on May 20).

The two zenith-passage dates for any given latitude are bisected by the solstice axis; thus, the rate of change for both is identical. Notice in Table A3-2 how the rate of change in June is very small. This means that the day-to-day changes in the shadows cast by vertical poles will be hardly noticeable. Since late-May and June solar zenith-passages are associated with latitudes farther to the north, it might be said that the phenomenon "lingers" in those regions. In comparison, the early May zenith-passage dates farther to the south (e.g., at Copán or Izapa) are much more fleeting. We can thus say that the solar zenith-passage phenomenon had different "qualities" at different Maya cities. Although this is a complicated phenomenon, for us to take the time to familiarize ourselves with its dynamics gives us a glimpse of how sophisticated Mesoamerican skywatchers must have been. Since it is now accepted that skywatchers throughout Mesoamerica were making solar zenith-passage observations, this changeable nature of the phenomenon was probably recognized and incorporated into their evolving cosmological concepts.

Zenith-passage events were important facets of Mesoamerican cosmology. Archaeoastronomers should incorporate *the rate of declination change* into their examination of solar zenith passages at different Meso-american sites, for the reasons outlined above. Toward making this easier, one can consult the tables in this appendix. Finally, Table A3-3 shows the changing dates of sun-Pleiades conjunctions through the centuries.

TABLE A3-3.
DATES OF SUN-PLEIADES
CONJUNCTIONS (CHANGING WITH
PRECESSION)

Gregorian	Julian
5-20-2012	
5-19-1940	
5-18-1868	
5-17-1796	
5-16-1724	
5-15-1652	
5-14-1580	5-5
5-13-1508	5-5
5-12-1436	5-4
5-11-1364	5-4
5-10-1292	5-3
5-9-1220	5-3
5-8-1148	5-2
5-7-1076	5-2
5-6-1004	5-1
5-5-932	5-1
5-4-860	4-30
5-3-788	4-30
5-2-716	4-29
5-1-644	4-29
4-30-572	4-28
4-29-500	4-28
4-28-428	4-27
4-27-356	4-27
4-26-284	4-27
4-25-212	4-26
4-24-140	4-26
4-23-68	4-25
4-22-(-4)	4-25

In this table, I use May 20, 2012 A.D. as

the "Zero Point." Because of the space occupied by the Pleiades, the question of when the sun is exactly in conjunction with the Pleiades is difficult to pin down. The year A.D. 2012 serves as an ideal era marker. Back-calculations of sun-Pleiades conjunctions thus subtract one day per seventy-two years (I used seventy-two-year intervals as an approximation of one day/degree of precessional movement), resulting in this table of the dates for sun-Pleiades conjunctions that we can compare with Table-Map A3-1 and Table A3-2.

Table A3-3 also indirectly defines the day six months later when New Fire observations were made. David Drucker (1986) claims New Fire ceremonies took place at Teotihuacan in Central Mexico in A.D. 311-312. Interestingly, when we move forward from this date at fifty-two-year intervals, we find the baktun shift of A.D. 830 and the 1 Ahau 18 Kayab date of November, 934—the Sacred Day of Venus in the *Dresden Codex* identified by Floyd Lounsbury (1983). Another Maya researcher, Robert L. Hall (1989-1993a), stated that the sun conjuncted the Pleiades on April 27 (G), 411, which demonstrates the accuracy of this table.

Heliacal rises and sets of the Pleiades are still of interest to the Chortí Maya. Ethnologist Raphael Girard (1966:198) reported that the Chortí Maya (who live near the ancient site of Copán) carefully observe the Pleiades *on the dates of solar zenith passage.* This is very intriguing, and we know by consulting Table-Map A3-1 above that the sun and the Pleiades moved through the zenith together on May 1 during Copán's heyday (in roughly A.D. 644). Since then, the sun-Pleiades con-

junction date has moved forward nineteen days (because of precession). This means that today, on the May 1 solar zenith passage at the latitude of the Chortí, the Pleiades are rough-ly 19° east of the sun, and are making their last appearance as evening stars.

Anthony Aveni (in Closs et al. 1984) summarizes essential information about the northern extremes of Venus and a possible observation window in Structure 22 at Copán. Around the time of the building of Temple 22, in the year prior to a great Venus extreme, the day of Venus's first visibility fell within an eight-day period ranging from April 25 to May 3. Significantly, the A.D. 650 construction date for Temple 22 falls within range of the great alignment of the sun-Pleiades with the zenith at Copán. Since the heliacal rise of Venus occurs only four days after its inferior conjunction with the sun, this coincidence of astronomical phenomena suggests the seventh-century skywatchers of Copán intentionally tracked Venus-sun-Pleiades conjunctions in the zenith. An exploration of the iconography of Structure 22 with this in mind might yield interesting insights.

At the very least, the space-time maps provided in this appendix demonstrate the complexity of one astronomical phenomenon that occupied Mesoamerican skywatchers, a phenomenon that was encoded into the Zenith Cosmology. Rate of declination change, latitude-specific date-ranges of zenith passages, the movements of the Pleiades, Venus, and the zenith sun—these are the celestial dynamics that New World astronomers explored and that revealed to them the subtle and complex rhythms of heaven and Earth.

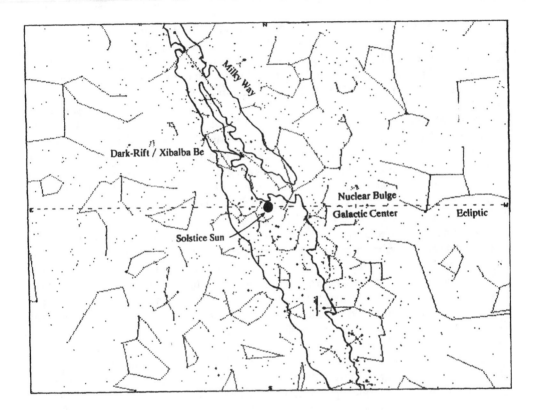

APPENDIX 4:

EVIDENCE FOR A BLACK HOLE IN MAYA CREATION TEXTS

The corpus of Maya hieroglyphic material contains information about the names of places. Some of these are actual Maya cities, whereas others are more enigmatic and are typically ascribed to "mythological" locations. Some of these mythological locations are where Creation events happened, and, knowing that myth describes astronomy, we can expect that these Creation narratives probably refer to specific celestial locations. In this appendix I will review academic material on Maya placenames that refer to mythological Creation events and will decode the astronomy. The academic material supports my thesis that the Maya believed Creation to occur in the Galactic Center (near the crossroads in Sagittarius), in the Black Hole that resides there, because Maya Creation narratives explicitly point to a celestial crossroads and a "black hole" that gives birth to deities. How are we to explain this parallel? Scholars are prone to dismiss this kind of association as a coincidence, but the fact is that it may point to the real knowledge that Maya cosmologists, through intuition and shamanistic technologies, gathered and formulated into their astounding cosmology.

Maya epigraphers David Stuart and Stephen Houston published a monograph on Maya placenames that included a chapter on mythological locations. Although no effort was made to associate these mythological locations with their corresponding astronomical locations, I will use this association as a key to identifying the actual astronomical location of Maya Creation and the astro-nomical features the Maya believed to be involved in cosmogenesis.

One of the mythological "sites" identified by Stuart and Houston was deciphered as meaning "black hole." When I read this, I immediately thought of the dark-rift in the Milky Way near the ecliptic in Sagittarius, as well as the Black Hole that astrophysicists now believe resides within the center of our Galaxy. My work with the Maya Long Count end-date and Maya *Popol Vuh*/Hero Twin Creation myth strongly suggests that the dark-rift was the Maya Creation Place, the cosmic birth canal of the Milky Way Great Mother.

The dark-rift can be thought of as a black hole in the sky and may be the visible pointer to deeper cosmological mysteries lurking nearby. Astrophysicists now recognize that a Black Hole, a hyper-dense object from which even light cannot escape, exists within the center of most galaxies, including ours. Black Holes are mysterious "singularities" in which space and time break down. In the academic and popular literature, they have been envisioned (and mathematically modeled) as transdimensional portals to other universes. The Black Hole in the center of our Galaxy is literally located where everything in our Galaxy, including us, originated. It represents a great mystery, resonating with the mysteries of being at the heart of the human soul. The deepest inner mystery of human origins corresponds with the deepest stellar mysteries, both traceable to the center and source of our world, the Black Hole in the Galactic Center. As I will outline below, there is clear evidence within Maya Creation narratives that the Maya were aware of the Black Hole in the Galactic Center and considered it to be intimately involved in cosmogenesis.

In Stuart and Houston's chapter on mythological placenames, a frequently occurring mythic placename in the Classic-period inscriptions is linked with events at the beginning of the current era, 4 Ahau 8 Cumku, 13.0.0.0.0 (1994:69). The glyphic passage consists of the elements glyph-T-128, "sky," Yax (first or green), and the NAL superfix. "In all cases, the text refers to the place of events that happened at 13.0.0.0.0" (71). Here I will point out that the Long Count date 13.0.0.0.0 refers, literally, to the end of the current era in A.D. 2012, rather than to the beginning. It does appear that Long Count, tzolkin, and haab dates on monuments such as Stela C from Quirigua are, in fact, referring to the "beginning" date of the current era, but it just may be that the Maya were looking at the astronomical event to happen on the end-date to describe what had happened on the "beginning" date. This is in accordance with the nature of cyclic time and the cyclic return implicit in the 13-baktun cycle. We might say that, conceptually, the beginning is the end. In fact, it is rather strange that the Maya recorded the "beginning" with a value of thirteen in the baktun register. Considering that the Maya recognized place values greater than the baktun, there might be something else going on here. In fact, one must make a leap to assume that the Maya just willy-nilly recorded the "beginning" of the current era as 13.0.0.0.0 (rather than 0.0.0.0.0). It may be just as much of a leap (in the other direction) to entertain that Maya Creation monuments actually describe astronomy to occur on the end-date. However, within modern Maya thinking, birth is thought to occur *at*

the end of a process, rather than at the beginning.

Importantly, prevalent "north" and "sky" glyphs point to the sky as the location of mythological Creation events. As many Maya scholars now concur, "north" can mean either "up" or "zenith" in Maya cosmography. Another prevalent place-glyph associated with the Creation setting was translated to mean "black hole" and is associated with the Mesoamerican ballgame and its ballcourts (71). In the *Popol Vuh*, there is a strong connection between ballcourts and the Underworld (D. Tedlock 1985:46). Hunahpu's severed head is used as a ball in a game between the Hero Twins and the Underworld deities. Linnea Wren (1995) showed how on the night of the June solstice in era A.D. 865, the Milky Way, with its dark-rift looming overhead, aligned with the Chichén Itzá ballcourt. Thus, the black hole glyphic designation and its affinity with ballcourts and "entrance to the Underworld" contexts strongly associates it with the dark-rift in the Milky Way. The dark-rift is called the *xibalba be* or "Black Road" by the Maya (D. Tedlock 1985:358).

Continuing with our examination of Stuart and Houston's monograph, the "black hole" compound "when coupled with the Ahau title . . . can also appear as a name glyph of Classic Period Lords" (71). And one example from Lacanha appears after an *ut-i* (it happened) expression "in inexplicable association with a 'birth' event that we presume to be mythological in character" (71-72).

So we have an association between the Ahau title of rulership (originally meaning "sun"), the dark-rift/Black Hole, and a birth event. The dark-rift is the place where One Hunahpu's head is hung (D. Tedlock 1985:39, 334); in other words, the crook in the tree is a metaphor for the rift in the Milky Way tree. From there, One Hunahpu's skull spits to impregnate Blood Moon with the Hero Twins. Thus, the rift is a place of conception, the celestial place of Creation and birth, if you will. Other Mesoamerican depictions, such as the inverted Goddess from the Tamoanchan emergence scene in the *Codex Fejervary-Mayer*, clearly imply that the dark-rift also was envisioned as the birth canal of the Great Mother, the Milky Way. A similar scene is found in the *Selden Codex*.

Next, the black hole compound is occasionally coupled with a glyph designating a watery environment. Water belongs to the feminine principle. Here we may have a reference to the Milky Way's other identity as a river, and Mesoamericans believed water to be a great rejuvenator, a nectar of life. Steam baths and community houses were sacred domains where purification rites took place. The black hole compound is associated with Copán Structure 22A, considered to be a *popol nah*, or community house, where vision ceremonies took place. The beautiful, carved imagery on Structure 22 depicts the Milky Way, the ecliptic, and the portal to the Underworld (the dark-rift).

Another mythological placename is ma-ta-wi-la or *matawil*. Matawil, like Black Hole, can refer to either a title (as in rulership) or a location: "Similar shifts between title and toponym mark the use of the "black hole" compound" (75). The idea of a throne comes to mind, in which a celestial location is reserved for people of special position. The Milky Way/Mother Goddess would probably be a good homebase for Ahau rulers, and the crossing point of Milky Way and ecliptic—the Creation Place—would certainly be a good throne for a ruler. This cross also is now known to be the center of the Maya Sacred Tree, such as we see on Pacal's sarcophagus lid. In Maya Creation myth, the Maize God (who is none other than One Hunahpu/First Father) sets up his house of rulership by

"stretching the cord" and marking the sides and corners of his domain, an act centered upon the cosmic crossroads (D. Tedlock 1985:334), which, again, is the crossing point of Milky Way and ecliptic (with the dark-rift nearby). The dark-rift in the Milky Way, being known as the *xibalba be* or the Road to the Underworld, is identical to the primordial cave of creation out of which came the first humans. It also is the place or cave of creation because it is the birth canal of the Milky Way Goddess-Mother. I also argue that One Hunahpu (First Father) is reborn from the dark-rift, because the December solstice sun (First Father) conjoins the dark-rift on 13.0.0.0.0. (In other words, Ahau rulers, in emulation of the mythological-astronomical Creation scenario, claim for their symbolic throne the Black Hole birth canal in the sky. This may be why there is an association between title and location attributed to *matawil* and *the black hole* in Stuart and Houston's analysis.)

A depiction in Stuart and Houston's monograph (76) from La Pasadita shows two men operating a fire drill. The lower portion shows a gaping skeletal mouth enclosing a box of glyphs, including the matawil compound. Matawil is associated with dead ancestors, and the gaping skeletal mouth (being a common mode for representing the Underworld) reiterates this Xibalban context (77).

Although it was not mentioned in Stuart and Houston's monograph, the black hole glyph depicted and discussed (75) looks like a miniature abbreviation of the gaping skeletal mouth in the carving mentioned above. The skeletal mouth serves the same symbolic purpose as other mouths; it is a passageway to the Underworld, the *xibalba be* or dark-rift.

According to Stuart and Houston, when placenames (mythological or otherwise) are attached to a verb, this indicates the location of an event (77). The matawil compound behaves like this, and in several texts describing the birth of certain deities, the matawil compound follows a birth event. Most likely then, "Matawil is where the deities are born" (77). In Maya thought, life comes from death: One is dead before being born. One comes into the Earth plane from Xibalba. One is born through the birth canal portal (the dark-rift/Black Hole) into this realm. Considering matawil's association with the dead ancestors of the Underworld, the way to get from the Underworld to being born on Earth is through the birthplace, through *the road which leads to/from the Underworld.*

"But where is this Matawil?" (77). Stuart and Houston's query is now answerable with a fair amount of certainty, but they veered down another path in looking for the answer. They even provided a set-up for the correct answer: There are hints "that Matawil corresponded to an area both enclosed and defined by skeletal jaws . . ." (77). At this juncture, they seem to miss some pretty obvious connections. For clarity, I will summarize the symbolic connections I have outlined so far: *skeletans refer to the dead, and jaws or mouths refer (as in the archaic symbol of the jaguar's mouth) to the entrance to the Underworld. The Road to the Underworld is called* xibalba be, *whose astronomical counterpart is the dark-rift in the Milky Way.* Perhaps Stuart and Houston were not on the wrong track in their explanation of Matawil's location, but were just being obscure. They do mention the early mythic history of Palenque and migration legends (which I should add are tied to Creation and emergence legends). A phrase they use reveals a conceptual assumption that, again, makes me think they err: ". . . in terms of movements over a landscape fusing real and mytho-

logical imagery" (77). The counterpointing of "real" and "mythological" suggests that mythological places are being thought of as purely imaginary, without any place in the real world. However, Maya mythology has been shown to be very concrete—it is observed in the sky—and this has been my guiding interpretive basis all along. That Stuart and Houston missed this interpretive key is clear in the final words of their discussion on mythological placenames—which I will get to momentarily.

In their chapter summation, Stuart and Houston say something profound: ". . . just as the deities acceded to high office or gave birth, so too did they live in specific places, ranging from the 'fifth sky' to the 'black hole'" (80). But then they feel the need to keep humans separate from deities, stating that ". . . the overlap between human and mythological geography would appear to be small . . ." (80). Their conclusion continues by thus saying that human beings did not perform rituals in the places where supernaturals were, nor did deities dwell among people. This belief has some truth, but when coupled with the previous quote in which their misconception of mythological geography as "not real" is stated, I think they are invoking a dualist framework where it is not appropriate. Terrestrial geography provided a parallel map to celestial geography, and astronomical events *are* the landscape of so-called mythological places and events. Sky and Earth are the duality here, but the Quiché Maya concept "skyearth" suggests that the Maya do not perceive these as separate realms, and probably never did. Therefore, I cannot accept that these two geographies— mythological and terrestrial—were "kept rigidly apart" (80). In that the entrance to the Underworld could be found in a nearby cave, in the body of a woman, as well as in the dark-rift in the sky, celestial and terrestrial geographies were clearly interwoven. Said another way, dead ancestors and other deities were immediately present; much of Maya ritual was concerned with feeding these ever-present beings.

If my own work is on the mark (Jenkins 1994d, 1995a and 1995b), the birth canal of the Great Mother is an extremely important "mythological" location that has, as is the convention, an astronomical counterpart. Stuart and Houston's identification of the mythological placename called "black hole," with attendant contexts relating to ball-courts, mythological "birth" events, Ahau rulership, Underworld doorways, and the beginning date of the current era (with likely reference to the astronomical events that actually occur on the end-date), strongly suggests that the Black Hole concept refers to the dark-rift in the Milky Way in Sagittarius. Furthermore, by extension, it may in fact refer to the Black Hole within the Galactic Center, which would seem to be the more likely astronomical feature responsible for these profound Creation mysteries of the Maya.

APPENDIX 5

RESPONSE TO COUNTERARGUMENTS

This appendix grew out of a need to respond to "Comments on the Creation Date," posted on the Mesoamerican Archaeology website by Linda Schele in April 1996. The so-called "end-date" of the 13-baktun cycle of the Maya Long Count in A.D. 2012 has been the subject of internet discussions, and in early 1996 Linda Schele responded to a question regarding the Long Count. She addressed the importance the Maya applied to the date in A.D. 2012, and reiterated her viewpoint as found in *A Forest of Kings*: "The Maya, however, did not conceive this to be the end of creation, as many have suggested" (82). This basically sums up her position on the meaning of the 13-baktun cycle end-date in 2012. The statement is essentially correct, because the Maya believed that time is cyclic, but continuing ambiguities demand that we clarify our terms and ask more pointed questions regarding this date. I have always made an effort to refer to this date more specifically as "the end-date of the 13-baktun cycle of the Maya Long Count calendar," and I do not concur with the Neo-Atlantean pole-shift cataclysmologists that the world will literally end in 2012. With this distinction in mind, I admit that I still occasionally write, as a shorthand note, "end-date" or "end-date in 2012." This does not mean that I believe the Maya calendar or the world will end in A.D. 2012. However, as I will show, it is clear that the 2012 date was singularly important for the people who created the Long Count calendar.

In comparison, the sense of Schele's position, as it has filtered out to become a kind of conventional wisdom, is that the date in A.D. 2012, though an important baktun shift, is just another somewhat ambiguous cycle ending, and is ultimately less important than a proposed 20-baktun cycle. Schele writes, "Pacal, the great king of Palenque, predicted in his inscriptions that the 80th Calendar Round anniversary of his accession will be celebrated eight days after the first 8000-year cycle [20 baktuns actually equal 7,885 years] in which the Mayan Calendar ends . . . A.D. October 15th, 4772" (1990:82).

Schele uses this as her primary argument that "the Maya did not conceive this [the 13-baktun cycle end-date in A.D. 2012] to be the end of creation." I submit that a 20-baktun cycle had little importance for those who created the Long Count, and that the 13-baktun cycle end-date in A.D. 2012 was, in fact, considered to be the end of a World Age, a large cycle of time. The important question to ask is: What were the intentions of the creators of Long Count? The latter-day political machinations of one Maya ruler (Pacal) are less important; neither Pacal nor his era developed the Long Count calendar. The first Long Count date appears in the archaeological record in the first century B.C. Edmonson (1988) and Hall (1989-1993a) have even argued that the inauguration of the Long Count actually goes much further back, to the fourth century B.C. or the sixth century B.C. The intended meaning of the Long Count and its subsequent baktun-endings must derive from those who placed it in real-time, not to a king who appeared on the scene some seven hundred years after the fact.

But what about Pacal's era? Was a cycle of thirteen baktuns recognized by Pacal's contemporaries? Yes, and there are three examples from three different Maya kingdoms: Coba, Quirigua, and Palenque. Dated inscriptions at these sites, erected during the Classic period, call the end of the previous era (in 3114 B.C.) 13.0.0.0.0, 4 Ahau 8 Cumku. These are the so-called "Creation monuments," and they reveal a lot about exactly when the Maya calendar clicks back to zero (i.e., at what interval the great World Age cycle repeats). The Creation monuments demonstrate that thirteen is the final baktun place value to be used when counting ages of Creation. The previous era ended after the completion of thirteen baktuns, after which the baktun place value reset. If that was not the case, then, for example, the Hauberg Stela, which contains the Long Count date 8.8.0.4.0, would really be dated 21.8.0.4.0. Since all Long Count dates ever found were recorded with the assumption that 13.0.0.0.0, 4 Ahau 8 Cumku (August 11, 3114 B.C. according to the 584283 correlation), equals zero, the early Maya clearly understood a cycle of thirteen baktuns to be *the* significant Creation cycle. We may presume that the current cycle was intended to follow the same pattern; after all, why should one Creation cycle be thirteen baktuns long and the next be twenty baktuns long? Pacal's 20-baktun period is an exception; it does not speak for how his contemporaries understood when the Creation cycle begins anew, nor does it reflect what the Long Count's inventors apparently had in mind (which we will get to shortly). A 13-baktun Creation cycle was clearly the consensus belief.

The questions that the end-date debate distract us from examining involve the astronomical nature of the 2012 end-date. The people who put the Long Count system in place, some seven hundred years prior to the birth of Pacal, were apparently targeting the date in A.D. 2012 as one they thought would be an appropriate "end" of a great time-cycle of Creation. On what grounds do I say this? Three reasons: thirteen baktuns = 260 katuns, 13.0.0.0.0 = an accurate winter solstice, and the astronomical alignment in A.D. 2012.

I will treat these points one by one. The first reason is a suggested rationale for thirteen baktuns being a valid period. As Hall (1989-1993a) proposed, katun periods were probably recognized prior to the full-scale development of the Long Count. Thirteen baktuns equal 260 katuns, and this mirrors (in the typical holistic cosmovision of the Maya) the 260 *days* of the tzolkin calendar.

Schele (1996) suggests that twenty baktuns is preferable to thirteen baktuns because it is in accordance with the vigesimal counting system used in Mesoamerican mathematics. The end-date of the 20-baktun cycle certainly has value as a benchmark in time, but there are exceptions to the strict use of multiples of twenty. As we know, the uinal period (of twenty days) is multiplied by eighteen (rather than twenty) to give us the 360-day tun. In addition, thirteen was just as important a number as twenty, so there is no reason to argue against a 13-baktun cycle. At any rate, I do not believe that the length of the so-called Great Cycle is as important to look at as is the date in 2012. There are unique astronomical qualities to this date that, for whatever reason, have not been acknowledged by most Maya scholars, which brings me to point two.

According to the 584283 correlation, the 13.0.0.0.0 end-date falls on December 21, the winter solstice. I will anticipate and address a common argument against this date and then return to my point. Following the work of Floyd Lounsbury (1983), Linda Schele and David Freidel report the end-date of the 13-baktun cycle in A.D. 2012 as December 23 (Schele and Freidel 1990; Freidel et al. 1993).

(By the way, many other people, including scholars such as Coe (1992) and popular writers such as Hancock (1995), have followed Schele's and Freidel's lead.) In my correspondence with professional academicians, some have argued, rather absurdly, that this is not "close enough" to be considered a December solstice, thus disqualifying my point. I offer the following clarification as a much needed and little acknowledged correction on a fine point of the correlation question. Erroneous "conventional wisdom" can delay advances in any field of study for decades, until someone eventually comes along to point out the obvious. I explored this problem in detail in my study of the Maya Venus Calendar (1994a:23-82). A rundown follows as briefly as possible, and then we will continue with point three.

Lounsbury (1983) argued for resurrecting the old 584285 correlation value (Thompson 1930) by way of his brilliant identification of a heliacal rise of Venus in the *Dresden Codex*. The date recorded in the *Dresden* was 1 Ahau 18 Kayab, which was November 18, 934 A.D. (Julian Calendar) according to the 584283 correlation, and November 20, 934 A.D. (J) according to the old 584285 correlation. Venus actually rose as morning star precisely on the latter date, supposedly "confirming" the old 584285 value. Using a "zero deviation" criterion, Lounsbury based his argument for the 584285 on this event. However, the requirement of "zero deviation" is erroneous; the synodical cycle of Venus in fact varies between 580 and 588 days *from cycle to cycle*. As Dennis Tedlock reported (1985:238), Lounsbury's astronomical argument for the 584285 value could, according to astronomer John B. Carlson, "easily be two days off." Bricker (1988) wrote that Lounsbury's theory is based on "a misinterpretation of the astronomical data" (82). And there is another reason why Lounsbury's position

points us to December 21, which I will address shortly.

Lounsbury's follow-up (1992) on the same argument uses a curious bit of circular logic to support his theory, but is not at all convincing when examined closely. This close examination was something that few did, and I direct the interested reader to my essays posted on my Four Ahau Press website for a complete and detailed analysis. Unfortunately, Lounsbury's position, though erroneous, was passed along to his students, causing confusion on this point of a two-day discrepancy on the "end" date.

The major challenge to Lounsbury's hypothesis (1983) that quickly emerged (D. Tedlock 1985:238) is the fact that the surviving day-counts followed by many different Maya groups in Guatemala all confirm the 584283 correlation (LaFarge 1947; Lincoln 1942; Oakes 1951; Sexton 1981; B. Tedlock 1982). Lounsbury explained this by proposing that there must have been a two-day shift in the day-count sometime between the time the *Dresden* Venus information was recorded and the Conquest. This would have had to have been a two-day shift orchestrated simultaneously throughout Mesoamerica, a scenario almost impossible to imagine. However, if we accept all of the explanations offered, including the two-day shift that in effect brings the 584285 into line with the 584283 correlation *after the Conquest*, then we still arrive at December 21, 2012 A.D. as the 13.0.0.0.0 date. So, even if we support Lounsbury's theory, we cannot use an "unshifted" 584285 correlation number to calculate any post-Conquest dates, including the end-date in A.D. 2012. The bottom line then, is that whether one follows the widely accepted 584283 correlation or Lounsbury's theory, the end of the 13-baktun cycle of the Maya Long Count calendar occurs on December 21, an accurate December solstice.

On February 19, 1994, I met my Quiché daykeeper friend Diego in Antigua, Guatemala. With great humor at the impending serendipity of it, we both pulled out our *Cholb'äl Q'ij* (1994) calendar books and pointed out to each other that the day of our first meeting was 1 Hunajpu (1 Ahau, the ancient Sacred Day of Venus). This is in accordance with the 584283 correlation, which, of course, is supported by the numerous ethnographic studies cited above.

In the True Count still being used by the highland Maya, February 19, 1994 equals 1 Ahau, and projecting forward from this date to December 21, 2012 A.D. yields, appropriately enough, 4 Ahau, the traditional tzolkin date on the 13-baktun cycle end-date. Although this whole clarification may seem petty or minor, it should be made because without it doubt may remain in the minds of those requiring absolute accuracy regarding the truth of calling the 13.0.0.0.0 end-date a December solstice.

So, having addressed the sources of conflict on this point, we can now, without suspicion, ask some appropriate questions about the end-date in A.D. 2012. First of all, the very fact that it is an accurate December solstice is quite striking. This means that the people who created the Long Count system of timekeeping and defined its placement in real time were able to calculate an accurate December solstice some 2,000 years into the future. It also suggests that the fixing of the 13-baktun cycle in "real" time was determined by its end-date. Why did the ancient Maya choose to highlight a December solstice, and how did they do it? To answer the last part of this question first, according to Edmonson (1988) this was accomplished with the "year-drift formula," in which 1,507 solar years (of 365.2422 days each) equals 1,508 haab (of 365 days each). This in itself reveals a level of scientific sophistication not commonly granted to cultures of this era (circa 200 B.C.). As to "why," it could be argued that a December solstice is an appropriate "end" or "beginning" marker because it basically has that meaning within the annual cycle of the seasons. This is certainly true, and can remain an adequate explanation until we ask the next question: "Why 2012?" By now we have learned to avoid answering these questions with such trite inconsequentials as "no particular reason" or "just a coincidence" and accept that Maya cosmology has much more intentionality lurking within it than previously thought. The 2012 date is not an arbitrary calculational artifact derived from fixing the "beginning" date back in 3114 B.C. Because the end-date is a December solstice, and for other reasons I will address shortly, it appears to have been the primary and intended "anchor" of the 13-baktun cycle. If anything, it is the "beginning" date in 3114 B.C. that we should consider an ambiguous back-calculation.

To state this simply, the 13-baktun cycle was fixed in real time for an astronomical reason (the December solstice), and the end-date was the anchor. As such, we might be willing to generate more questions by assuming that A.D. 2012, as well, was an intentional choice. This brings me to my third point, not really a surprise after all we have been discussing: the astronomy in A.D. 2012. As argued throughout this book, on 13.0.0.0.0 the December solstice sun will be in conjunction with the Milky Way. We can call this an alignment between the galactic plane and the solstice meridian. This is an event that has slowly converged over a period of thousands of years and is caused by the precession of the equinoxes. As such, December 21, 2012 A.D. identifies a rare alignment in the cycle of precession, using the Milky Way and the dark-rift "Road to the Underworld" as the markers. This alignment is perfectly evocative of the culmination (the "end") of a Great Cycle of creation. We really have two *facts* that occur at the same time, the 13-baktun cycle end-date and a rare alignment in the cycle of the precession of the equinoxes.

If we do not allow these ancient skywatchers to have been sophisticated enough to notice precession, we relegate the alignment of A.D. 2012 to the unexamined bin of "coincidence." To conclude that this is coincidence pushes our thoughts beyond credible bounds of reason. The alternative, as resistant as many will be, is that the creators of the Long Count calendar calculated the rate of precession over 2,000 years ago. Few Maya scholars are as qualified to comment on this point as archaeoastronomer Anthony Aveni, who wrote, "Ancient astronomers easily could detect the long-term precessional motion.... Through myth and legend the earliest skywatchers transmitted their consciousness of the passage of the vernal equinox along the zodiac from constellation to constellation" (1980:103). In the interest of clarity, I will mention that it would be more accurate to say that the alignment occurs in *the era* of A.D. 2012; because precession is such a slow phenomenon, fifty years on either side of 2012 might be appropriate. Of course, this wider timespan strengthens the position of the coincidentalists.

In summary, it is true that December 21, 2012 does not represent "the end of the Maya calendar." Such generic phraseology rarely results in clarity. Though I continue to occasionally use "end-date" as a casual convention, the more accurate identification, one that is perfectly true, is "the end-date of the 13-baktun cycle of the Maya Long Count." Schele's argument that a 20-baktun cycle had precedence over the 13-baktun cycle is not well-founded, as it confuses what one seventh-century Maya ruler said about the nature of the Long Count with what the original creators of it intended. A repeating 13-baktun cycle is implied wherever Creation monuments have been found—for example, at Coba and Quirigua. Rather than looking at Classic-period examples to define the nature of the Long Count, we need to look carefully at who created the Long Count system, and where and when it arose. This consideration sends us back to the little understood Middle Pre-Classic period of the Izapan civilization.

APPENDIX 6

RECENT BREAKTHROUGHS IN DECODING ANCIENT COSMOLOGIES

In doing my research into the Maya calendar's Galactic Alignment in A.D. 2012, I became convinced that precession was central to understanding the meaning of the end-date and Maya cosmology. Every time a book came out on the Maya, such as *The Mayan Prophecies*, I thought that other researchers might have independently explored the same thing. However, upon reading the new literature, I found that the fact that the December solstice of 2012 pinpoints a rare alignment in precession was not discussed or even mentioned as the reason why the Maya chose 2012. In addition, popular books on the millennium, often mentioning the 2012 end-date of the Maya, fail to recognize the solstice-Galaxy alignment. Despite this dearth of recognition, I have grown to understand that the Galactic Alignment is the underlying reason for the unprecedented transformation currently sweeping the globe, and therefore the Maya win the best prize for prophecy.

Recently, independent researchers have been reconstructing the esoteric secrets of Egyptian cosmology. A key to understanding this new perspective is the idea that the ancient Egyptians were well aware of the precession of the equinoxes. French researcher Schwaller de Lubicz ([1961] 1982) suggested this decades ago and *Hamlet's Mill* (1969) explored precessional myths world wide. Jane B. Sellers (1992) decoded precessional evidence in the ancient Egyptian texts. New ideas about the Great Pyramid emerged with Robert Bauval and Adrian Gilbert's amazing *The Orion Mystery*. Bauval had noticed that the three Giza pyramids mirrored, in relative size and spacing, the three stars of Orion's belt overhead. Moreover, the so-called air shafts of the main pyramid were understood to actually be sight tubes, designed to view Sirius and the stars in Orion during specific eras of precession. As a result of using the key of precession to unlock Egyptian astronomy, Bauval realized that the precession-caused movements of Orion were of central importance to the ancient Egyptian astronomer-priests. They proposed that a time over 12,500 years ago was the *Zep Tepi* or "First Time" of Egyptian myth and calendar. This was when Orion made its lowest passage through its meridian. (The altitude of Orion oscillates higher and lower with precession.)

After success with *The Orion Mystery*, Robert Bauval collaborated with Graham Hancock to write *The Message of the Sphinx*. Both authors relate their frustrations in dealing with closed-minded and intolerant Egyptologists who ignore new findings coming from independent quarters and delay the advance of knowledge. In the book, additional findings were discussed, along with Hancock's emphasis that the Sphinx faced the vernal equinox sunrise in Leo during the First Time of 10,500 B.C., and this precession-caused alignment may have motivated its construction.

In addition to discussing the First Time of Egyptian cosmology—roughly 10,500 B.C.—Bauval and Hancock also discuss a projected "Last Time" in A.D. 2450, which is one-half a precessional cycle later (1996: 283). Although the authors do not discuss the Maya end-date alignment of solstice and Galaxy, the Egyptian dates roughly bracket the two eras in which the solstice meridian aligns with the Galactic equator. Bauval and Hancock also provide astronomical charts showing the First Time of 10,500 B.C. and the Last Time of A.D. 2450 (1996:283). Both diagrams show the Milky Way where it runs by Orion, and the Last Time diagram shows the June solstice sun barely touching the west edge of the Milky Way. This is about as close as these authors come to recognizing the 2012 alignment. Apparently, a solstice-Milky Way synchronization was not a part of Egyptian cosmology. But if we were to subtract 438 years (6° of precessional motion) from the Last Time date and look at the opposite solstice, we would see the December solstice sun in the dark-rift near the Galactic Center.

Bauval and Hancock may be right in their reconstruction of the First and Last eras of Egyptian cosmology, in that they involve the highest and lowest meridian transits of Orion that are intimately related to precessional movement. However, it seems strangely coincidental to me that these two eras also define (roughly, for the Egyptian argument) the eras in which the Maya solstice-Galaxy alignment occurs. I am surprised that this was not the central doctrine that they found. Instead, the Maya were apparently the Ancients who were clued into the conjunction of the December solstice sun with the Milky Way and Galactic Center as a precession-defined era of transformation for humanity. Although the extreme meridian transits of Orion were most certainly interesting to ancient astronomers, the 2012 solstice-Galaxy alignment is a more compelling Zero Time of the precessional growth cycle. Why? Because of the role played by the Galactic Center in the astronomical alignment of 2012. Since this specific idea is not found in the Egyptian mate-

rial, yet is the highest expression of Maya cosmological science and universal precession wisdom, an Egyptian source of Maya knowledge, as some researchers believe, is not likely. In other words, the Maya were on to something the Egyptians missed. The Maya tapped into an understanding of the cosmos that is beyond what the Egyptians accomplished, and they did it independently.

Turning now to Mesoamerican cosmology, Graham Hancock's book *Fingerprints of the Gods* embarked on a global survey of ancient mythlore and astronomy and contains a lengthy section on Maya and Aztec calendrics, astronomy, and cosmology. However, Hancock's opinion of Maya culture and its accomplishments is not very well informed and his conclusions are unfair.

Hancock reports the end-date as December 23, 2012 A.D., sourced from Michael Coe's book *Breaking the Maya Code* (1992:275). Coe's information is based upon the erroneous arguments of Lounsbury (1983), repeated by his student Linda Schele (Schele and Freidel 1990). As I discussed in Appendix 5, this end-date is based upon an academic misconception. But most unfortunate is Hancock's emphasis that Maya calendar science was probably imported from elsewhere. He interprets Mesoamerican knowledge through Old World filters, and much gets lost in the process. He denigrates independent Maya genius by arguing that "the 'semi-civilized' Maya" (1995:161) would have no use for something as complex and sophisticated as the Long Count calendar (let alone might they have invented it). According to Hancock, apart from their use of zero and place numeration, the Maya were an "unremarkable Central American tribe" (1995:160). After summarizing information about the huge Long Count numbers recorded at Quirigua, extending, theoretically, to millions of years, he writes: "Isn't this all a bit *avante-garde* for a civilization that didn't otherwise distinguish itself in many ways? It's true that Mayan architecture was good within its limits. But there was precious little else that these jungle dwelling Indians did which suggested they might have had the capacity (or the need) to conceive of really *long* periods of time" (1995:162).

This odd bit of reasoning betrays Hancock's lack of understanding of Maya civilization and cosmology. Predictably, these words preface his proposition that Egyptians and, ultimately, the Atlanteans were the great mysterious geniuses behind Maya science. Unfortunately, Hancock's thesis of a foreign source for Maya astronomical and calendric science must be disregarded. After all, the tzolkin and the Long Count are unique and uncomparable to any calendric system developed elsewhere in the world. Hancock did not explore where or when the Long Count was invented or who created it, nor did he make a connection between the solstice-Galaxy alignment and the 2012 end-date. In general, Hancock's sources for supposedly cutting-edge ideas about Mesoamerican civilization are outdated and have little to contribute to current understanding. Furthermore, Hancock's view that the Maya were incapable of independently developing a complex calendar cosmology requires a disingenuous dismissal of independent Maya genius.

Adrian Gilbert and Maurice Cotterell's *The Mayan Prophecies* (1995) attempted to reveal the true meaning of the Maya end-date in A.D. 2012, but it contains many misunderstandings and errors. Despite their book's promise to supply an explanation for the end-date, the solstice-Galaxy alignment is neither recognized or mentioned. Gilbert and Cotterell both tried to answer the question of why 2012 was so important to the Maya, but they each took slightly different view-

points. Cotterell's theory about the transformative nature of 2012 is that sunspot cycles give rise to larger solar aberrations in which the sun's magnetic field periodically reverses, causing the Earth's poles to shift and thus resulting in cataclysm. According to Cotterell, the solar reversals come in groups of five, which together make a grand cycle of 18,139 years. The five "ages" are not all of the same length, due to complex solar rhythms that Cotterell modeled on a computer. Three of the ages last 3,553 years each, whereas two last 3,740 years each. These are supposed to correspond to the Maya/Aztec myth of four or five ages. A key number here is the number of days in 3,740 years, which Cotterell calculated (using 365.25 days per year) as 1366035. Cotterell noticed that this magic number is "close" to a number in the *Dresden Codex*, written in Long Count notation as 9.9.16.0.0. This corresponds to a date in A.D. 627, which is 1,366,560 days after the so-called Long Count "zero date" of 3114 B.C. The "closeness" of these numbers (500+ days) is supposed to demonstrate that the Maya were aware of sunspot cycles and solar magnetic field reversals, and that is why the Long Count pinpoints A.D. 2012 as a World Age cataclysm. Gilbert writes, ". . . Cotterell has concluded that the Maya prophecy for the end of the fifth age concerns a reversal of the earth's magnetic field—around A.D. 2012" (192). However, earlier in the book we are led through an interesting lesson in dendrochronology so we can understand how field reversals of the past can be charted. In this way, Cotterell identifies the dawn of the Long Count (3114 B.C.) as the location of one of these shifts. Consequently, a magic 1,366,035 days later, in A.D. 627, another shift occurs. "What really intrigued Cotterell is that they seemed to have anticipated the magnetic reversal [of A.D. 627] and consequential decline in fertility, for the magic number 1366560 corresponds to the magnetic shift period" (185). The obvious problem here is that the next magnetic shift should take place 3,553 years after A.D. 627, more than 2,000 years after A.D. 2012. Nowhere does the book address this discrepancy.

Cotterell also proposes that the Maya collapse (which historically began around A.D. 800) was caused by a decline in fertility attended by the field-reversal of A.D. 627. In Appendix 4, Cotterell shows that the field reversal does not happen overnight, but over a 374-year period. The year A.D. 627 is identified as the "mid-point" of the shift, which thus extended from A.D. 440 to A.D. 814. The problem here is that this time period does not correspond very well with the Maya decline; in fact, it corresponds better with the Classic-period florescence of Maya culture (A.D. 300 to A.D. 900).

Gilbert, for his part, emphasizes the idea that the beginning of the Long Count represents a so-called "Birth of Venus," based partly upon checking the date with his Skyglobe astronomy software and partly on the fact that the Maya supernumber 1366560 is divisible by 584. However, 584 is only an approximation of the true 583.92-day cycle of Venus, and, furthermore, 1366560 is also divisible by the Mars cycle, the Mercury cycle, the 365-day haab, the 360-day tun, the 18,980-day Calendar Round, and the 37,960-day Venus Round as well—this is why scholars call it the Maya supernumber. Gilbert punched up a sky chart for August 12, 3114 B.C., the beginning date of the 13-baktun cycle of the Long Count, and saw Venus just west of the sun (136). This means that it was rising in the morning just before the sun, technically, in the morning star position. However, this was not the first appearance of Venus as morning star at the time, the "Venus birth" scenario that concerned the Maya, because, in fact, Venus was *moving toward*

superior conjunction on August 12 of 3114 B.C. It was not making its first appearance nor was it even waxing toward its morning star maximum. In fact, according to two different sources I consulted (EZCosmos and Aztec Astro Report), Venus made its *last* appearance as morning star *almost two weeks before* the Long Count zero-date. Although minor variations are to be expected with computer modeling, Skyglobe provides the same data and Gilbert must not have double-checked his findings. Based upon this faulty observation, Gilbert begins referring to the Long Count zero-date as "the Birth of Venus."

Gilbert's summary toward the end of the book apparently is supposed to reveal one of the miraculous breakthroughs about the astronomical basis of the 2012 end-date promised by the book. But his observations are not very compelling and are purely speculative, with little basis in Maya cosmological concepts or traditions. In Gilbert's summational look at the end-date astronomy, Skyglobe revealed to him that "Venus sinks below the western horizon as the Pleiades rise over the eastern horizon. . . . [A]s the sun sets, Orion rises, perhaps signifying the start of a new precessional cycle" (211). And such is the final revelation. Clearly, these astronomical observations are not very illustrative of vast World Age shiftings. *The Mayan Prophecies*, though hailed as inventive in popular reviews, is in my view an unfortunate example of a good-risk marketing strategy based upon Gilbert's previous success with *The Orion Mystery*. For a detailed and complete review of *The Mayan Prophecies*, see Jenkins (1995f).

William Sullivan's *The Secret of the Incas* (1996) is a good example of solid independent research, asking the right questions and finding the right answers. Following the trail blazed by *Hamlet's Mill*, Sullivan examined Inca mythology with an eye toward decoding its astronomical underpinnings. The parts of the sky that drew his attention were the same ones that are involved in the Maya end-date of A.D. 2012. Sullivan drew from the important pioneering work of Gary Urton (1981) and explained the importance of the Milky Way and its "dark-cloud" constellations in Andean cosmology. In South America, the bright central bulge of the Milky Way is high in the sky, and the dark clouds in this area are much more visible than in North America. The dark-cloud forms recognized by Andean skywatchers as a mother llama and her baby suckling are located near the central bulge of the Galactic Center, confirming the idea that the central bulge of the Milky Way was conceived, in the indigenous mind, as a Creation Place or Cosmic Mother womb. Nearby, at the crossing point of the Milky Way and the ecliptic, Sullivan identified the dark-cloud constellation called *Atoq* —the Fox. This dark cloud is just south of the dark-rift that the Quiché Maya call the *xibalba be*. The two dark-cloud forms are close but not identical. Sullivan's thesis is that the precession-caused shiftings of the rise times of the Fox constellation were noticed by early Andean astronomers. Always carefully documenting his search, Sullivan explores fox-related myth and folklore and decodes a complex mythic-astronomy concerned with tracking precession. In general, Sullivan believed that it was *the last heliacal rise* of the Milky Way on the June solstice of A.D. 650 that marked a critical moment in Andean history. Notice that the same precession-caused convergence that resulted in the Milky Way no longer being visible at dawn on the June solstice of A.D. 650 is the same movement that causes the Maya solstice-Galaxy conjunction in A.D. 2012.

Sullivan went further in pointing out that a Saturn-Jupiter conjunction occurred on the June solstice of A.D. 650. This is significant, because *Hamlet's Mill* proposed that Saturn-Jupiter conjunctions (three of which equal roughly sixty years) were used in ancient times to track precession. Here I should mention that some Maya scholars believe the Long Count originally developed from, and is based upon, the twenty-year katun period. For example, Hall (1989-1993a) believed the katun period was designed to represent Saturn-Jupiter conjunctions; 260 katuns equal the Great Cycle of thirteen baktuns, which ends on the solstice-Galaxy alignment.

Overall, Sullivan's scholarship and insights are welcome in an era of scholastic intolerance for anything that goes beyond the limited one-dimensional conclusions of tenured academes. Sullivan has identified the precession paradigm as it manifested in South America. Technically speaking, the formulation of it is pre-Inca by a long shot; it highlights Tiahuanaco as its likely place of origin. Scholars and independent thinkers should look carefully at Sullivan's important work. I do not have the space here for a full review of its important insights, but can offer some comments regarding how it relates to Maya cosmology.

Andean precessional astronomy is directly related to my reconstruction of the precessional myth among the Maya, but an important difference drew Sullivan's attention away from the solstice-Galaxy alignment in era 2012. Sullivan focused on an Andean interest in the *last heliacal rise* concept, whereas the Maya were interested in *conjunction*. In terms of field effects and the role played by the Galactic Center in the Maya Galactic Cosmology, *conjunction* would seem to be a very important requirement for World Age transformation. Sullivan did venture into Maya myth and astronomy, looking for supportive data and other clues to aid his reconstruction work. Unfortunately, he relied heavily on Raphael Girard's interpretation of the *Popol Vuh* (1979), which offers some insights into *Popol Vuh* mythology, but is outdated and contains rather eccentric identifications of *Popol Vuh* deities. Girard's voluminous work on the Chortí and Quiché, obtained during ethnographic visits between the 1930s and the 1950s, is incredibly valuable to modern researchers. However, his *Popol Vuh* translation originally appeared in Spanish in 1948 and was finally translated into English in 1979. So, the *Popol Vuh* source used by Sullivan is a translation of a translation of a Conquest-era document that in turn was rendered from an ancient hieroglyphic book (D. Tedlock 1985). Unfortunately, Sullivan did not access the important translation by Dennis Tedlock (1985), which had a great sensitivity to astronomy in the *Popol Vuh*. In fact, Barbara Tedlock and Dennis Tedlock's prolific ethnographic work, which identifies the cosmic crossroads, the Black Road, the *xibalba be* dark-rift, and other important elements of Maya myth and symbology that have direct bearing on precessional astronomy in Mesoamerica, was not mentioned in Sullivan's book. Nevertheless, Sullivan has accomplished a great work and his book must be acknowledged as the first in-depth exploration of ancient precessional cosmology in the New World.

END NOTES

All notes in this book utilize the American Antiquity documentation style.

INTRODUCTION: FIXING OUR SIGHTS

1. The date Waters used was wrong by almost a year. His information came from an early work of Michael Coe, in which Coe states that the end-date was December 24, 2011.
2. Jenkins (1995f, 1995g). Also, see Appendix 6 for a detailed review of *The Mayan Prophecies*.
3. See Schele and Freidel (1990), and Freidel et al. (1993).
4. "The How and Why of the Mayan End-Date in 2012 A.D." In *Mountain Astrologer*, December 1994. The response to this article was overwhelming. Terence McKenna posted it on his Hyperborea Website (at http://www.levity.com/eschaton/why2012.html). Other sources of comment include Clow (1995:5, 39, 49); Johnson (1997:176); Scofield (1994:203); Reed (1996); and Oehler (1996a and 1996b).
5. After my presentation, Ray Stewart, the director of the Institute of Maya Studies, told me that he had sent my submission materials to archaeo-astronomer John B. Carlson, to solicit comment. Carlson told him that he was working on his own paper on the Maya end-date astronomy, but it was not yet ready. Apparently, Carlson's interest in the end-date validated the importance of my work and helped the I.M.S decide to bring me to Miami. A video recording of the presentation is available for $25 p.p. from Four Ahau Press, Box 635, Louisville, CO 80027.
6. J.L.E. Dreyer (1906:203).
7. D. McKenna and T. McKenna ([1975], 1993:196).
8. Santillana and von Dechend (1969:67).

PART I: PRECESSION ASTRONOMY

CHAPTER 1: A TIMELINE OF MESOAMERICAN CULTURE

1. Waters (1963:214).
2. Edmonson (1988).
3. The origin of Olmec civilization is still being debated. Soconusco, the Gulf Coast heartland itself, Guerrero, and South America are among the contestants. Malmström (1997) surveys the differing viewpoints.
4. See Evans and Meggars (1966); Opperman (1983).
5. Hatch (1971).
6. Seaman and Day (1994).
7. Schávelzon (1978).
8. D. Tedlock (1985); B. Tedlock (1982, 1985).
9. Fash and Kowalski (1991:66); Brundage (1979:10); Krickeberg (1966:248-249); Reilly (1995:31); Klein (1976a:30).
10. For example, Coe (1992); Carrasco (1990); Schele and Freidel (1990); Freidel et al. (1993).
11. In my book *Tzolkin: Visionary Perspectives and Calendar Studies* (1994), I examined natal charts for Pacal, Chan Bahlum, and other Maya rulers and found interesting astrological patterns in their dynastic lineages.
12. Carlson (1991).
13. Lamb (1980).
14. See Carmack (1973, 1981, 1995).
15. Lafarge (1947); Lincoln (1942); Sexton (1981); B. Tedlock (1982). All of these sources confirm the 584283 "GMT" correlation. See note 7 in Chapter 2 of this book and Jenkins (1994a). The 584283 correlation is what I call the True Count, because it is the one still followed today by many Maya groups in the highlands of Guatemala, and it is the same one that was followed at the great Classic-period cities of the Maya. The need to clarify this information came in response to books on the Maya proclaiming to provide an authentic count of days, when, in fact, what I termed Newly Created Counts or Variant Counts were being promoted. For clarifications on this point, see Jenkins (1996h). December 21, 2012 is, appropriately enough, 4 Ahau in the True Count.
16. See, for example, Nelson (1996).

CHAPTER 2: CALENDRICS: MAPPING METHODS

1. The word *tzolkin* is derived from the Maya phrase *chol qij*, meaning "count of days." See B. Tedlock (1982).

2. D. Tedlock (1993:233-234). I prefer Tedlock's English translation of the Quiché day-signs because the Quiché daykeeper tradition can claim an unbroken lineage back to the pre-Conquest period, and Dennis Tedlock is not only a Quiché language translator, having produced the definitive translation of the *Popol Vuh*, but is also a trained daykeeper (B. Tedlock 1982). Readers may be familiar with other day-sign lists, which are based on other Mesoamerican language groups. For example, the Yucatec day-signs, adapted from the records of Diego de Landa, equate Quiché *Imox* (Lefthanded) with *Imix* (Alligator). This day-sign in the Aztec calendar is *Cipactli*, which means Crocodile. Though linguistic variations exist, the inner order of the day-signs has a common genetic base. For example, the parallel day-sign order between the Quiché and the Yucatec day counts is apparent from similarities such as *Kawuq* and *Cauac*, *Imox* and *Imix*, *Iq'* and *Ik*, *Aq'ab'al* and *Akbal*. For a comparative list of day-signs from different groups, see Scofield (1994:39).

3. I have explored the philosophical, metaphysical, and spiritual dimensions of Maya time philosophy in previous publications. See Jenkins (1991, 1994a, 1994b, and 1994c).

4. Two Calendar Round periods equal one Venus Round (of just under 104 years). I do not discuss the Venus Round calendar separately here because it is based upon the Calendar Round. Surviving Maya books, such as the *Dresden Codex*, contain data about the astronomical movements of Venus, which alternately rises as eveningstar and morningstar in distinct, calculable intervals. In Jenkins (1994a), I reconstructed the Maya Venus calendar and determined that the next Venus Round cycle will begin when Venus rises as morningstar on April 3, 2001. This date in the tzolkin calendar is 1 Ahau, the traditional Sacred Day of Venus for the Classic Maya.

5. N'oj means *thought* in Quiché (D. Tedlock 1993);

it is equivalent to Caban in the Yucatec system.

6. Edmonson (1988:194).

7. To be more specific, this is called the end-date of the 13-baktun cycle of the Long Count calendar. It should be clarified here that the "zero" date of the 13-baktun cycle is August 11, while the "first" day is properly called August 12. A recurrent misconception in the academic literature results in an erroneous end-date of December 23, rather than December 21. I analyzed this problem very carefully in my book *Tzolkin: Visionary Perspectives and Calendar Studies*. From Jenkins (1994d:57, 100): "Linda Schele and David Freidel, unlike most Mayanists, continue to support the work of Floyd Lounsbury in promoting the 584285 correlation. This is two days off the Thompson correlation that I use. The decisive factor in supporting the Thompson correlation of 584283 is the fact that it corresponds with the tzolkin count still followed in the highlands of Guatemala...." See Appendix 5, "Response to Counterarguments," in this book, for a more detailed clarification.

8. See Puleston (1979).

9. Schele and Freidel (1990:66-70, 90, 425) and Freidel et al. (1993:75-106).

CHAPTER 3: COSMOLOGY: FINDING THE CENTER

1. This terminology is drawn from the work of Davíd Carrasco (1990).

2. Carrasco (1990:21).

3. Carrasco (1990:21).

4. In keeping with the Mesoamerican concept of sky-Earth unity, the biological or organic realm of Earth was also understood to generate time; the tzolkin models both of these realms. See Jenkins (1991, 1994a).

5. By "zenith," I here mean the exact center of the sky. Some sources confuse "meridian transit" with "zenith" transit. A star's meridian transit is the highest point it reaches during its nightly arch through the sky. For some stars, such as the Pleiades, this meridian transit can reach the zenith during certain times of the year.

6. I acknowledge the possibility of trans-Pacific contact from China (e.g., Martínez 1990), but

the point is that the majority of New World populations migrated through northern Asia (see Shao 1983).

7. Hatch (1971).

8. A monograph on Lakota star knowledge (Goodman 1992) reports that the Lakota believe there used to be a star located in the crosshairs of the four stars of the Big Dipper's bowl—the same "center point" that Hatch (1971) proposed the Olmec used for astronomical sighting.

9. A sidereal year is the time it takes Earth to make one revolution in its orbit around the sun as measured by its relation to the fixed stars.

10. Aveni and Linsley (1972).

11. Aveni and Linsley (1972).

12. See Dow (1967).

13. Hunt (1977) demonstrates the probable association of the four Tezcatlipocas with the polar area, suggesting that this deity's changing nature symbolizes the shifting of the North Celestial Pole with precession.

CHAPTER 4: PRECESSION: THE MYSTERY OF THE AGES

1. Santillana and von Dechend (1969:230-232).

2. This is its true sidereal position. Astrology asserts that by definition the December solstice point is at 0° Capricorn, which is currently some 27° off from the true sidereal position.

3. Sellers (1992); Schwaller de Lubicz (1982); Bauval and Gilbert (1994). From Dreyer (1906:203) we read: ". . . they [the Babylonians] seem to have been aware that earlier determinations of the equinoxes required some correction, as three tablets give different positions of the equinox, 10°, 8°15' and 8° 0' 30" of Aries."

4. Ulansey (1989).

5. See, for example, Closs (1983).

6. Brotherston (1982:129).

7. Brotherston (1982:129).

8. Aveni (1980:103).

CHAPTER 5: MYTHOLOGY AND ASTRONOMY

1. Miller and Taube (1993).

2. Kelley's model is important because it contrib-uted to Linda Schele's breakthrough reconstruction of Maya Creation mythology, which she presented at the Austin Hieroglyphic meeting in 1992. See Schele (1992b).

3. Kelley (1989).

4. Kelley anticipates the importance of his pioneering work: "Detailed analysis of related myths and study of other sequences will, I think, eventually allow us to reconstruct much of the underlying mythology and see how it is assigned to various parts of the sky" (1989:77). It thus seems that Kelley provided the key to understanding Maya cosmology: The dark-rift is a place where time begins and ends. Unfortunately, he did not follow up on the implications of his discovery, nor did he recognize the alignment in A.D. 2012. I feel that Linda Schele's later work (Schele 1992b, Freidel et al. 1993) is based upon Kelley's ideas, and her reconstruction of Maya Creation mythology does, in fact, utilize the belt stars of Orion as a critical key. However, the equally important placement of the dark-rift in Kelley's model did not, for some reason, enter into her reconstruction. This loophole in academia is where I picked up the thread, and my research has been driven by the realization that the dark-rift near the cosmic crossroads is the place of World Age Creation.

5. Urton (1981).

6. Wisdom (1940).

7. D. Tedlock (1985:358).

8. B. Tedlock (1982).

9. B. Tedlock and D. Tedlock (1993a:44).

10. B. Tedlock and D. Tedlock (1993a:44, 49-50); D. Tedlock (1985:39, 334, 358).

11. Scholars do not recognize the impact of external New Age influence on Maya people and tradition. The New Age Hunab Ku symbol comes from the *Nuttall Codex*, a Central Mexican rather than a Maya source. Hunab Ku is a term that was popularized in the books of José Argüelles and the Yucatecan daykeeper Hunbatz Men. It is currently used by thousands of Mexicans, Mayas, and fans of Maya culture. Rather than dismissing this term as invalid, scholars are obliged to recognize it, document its source, and include it in the inventory of ethnographic data on Maya culture.

12. Milbrath (1980a:298; 1980b:449).
13. Gossen (1974:39).
14. Milbrath (1980a:298).
15. D. Tedlock (1985:115; 1992:256-257).
16. D. Tedlock (1992:258).
17. D. Tedlock (1985). This myth of the 400 Boys ascending into the zenith as the Pleiades may have to do with the Pleiades at the top of another World Axis—the zenith axis. Moreover, considering the nature of the Zenith Cosmology, the implication is that the Pleiades and its ascent to the zenith may have been used to track precession.
18. D. Tedlock (1985).
19. Sosa (1986, 1989).
20. Prechtel (1993).
21. One potential problem with *Hamlet's Mill*'s focus on the polar area is the fact that the Pole Star is very low in the sky at tropical latitudes. Hunrakan may in some contexts refer to a different cosmic axis, perhaps the zenith axis or even the Galactic. My feeling is that he, like Tezcatlipoca, was *originally* the Polar God, but adopted variant meanings as cosmological understanding evolved in Mesoamerica. Ultimately, the question of where the true cosmic center is located was resolved with the Long Count's end-date marker on the Galactic Center.
22. Hunt (1977:152-153).

PART II: THE UNION OF CAPTAIN SERPENT AND CAPTAIN SUN DISK

CHAPTER 6: THE PYRAMID OF KUKULCAN: A COSMIC MYTH IN STONE

1. The terms Captain Sun Disk and Captain Serpent are the names for these Maya-Toltec deities preferred by epigrapher Linda Schele and archaeologist David Freidel in their book *Forest of Kings* (1990).
2. Diaz-Bolio (1988).
3. One source for this identification is Redfield and Villa Rojas (1971:206): "The Pleiades bear the name of the rattlesnake's rattle (tzab). . . ." An-

other source is Carlson (1990), where a diagram shows the Pleiades as a rattlesnake rattle. The Lacandon Maya share this identification of the Pleiades as a rattlesnake rattle (Bruce et al. 1971); Milbrath (1980a) summarizes additional data on this topic.

4. The latitude that defines the limits of the tropics (23°26') is directly related to *the obliquity of the ecliptic*—the tilt of the Earth in relation to its orbital plane.
5. Anthony Aveni, Horst Hartung, and Charles Kelley explored an amazing astronomical observatory situated on the tropic of Cancer in Zacatecas, Mexico. See Aveni et al. (1982). The context of this site suggests it was a remote outpost of Teotihuacan. As at Chichén Itzá, this town experienced a flood of refugees from Teotihuacan in the eighth and ninth centuries. The presence of Central Mexican astronomer-priests at this site suggests they were very interested in calibrating the different zenith-passage phenomena occurring at different latitudes.
6. Contrary to a popular misconception, the Pleiades do not rise heliacally on July 26. The term "heliacal" designates the date of the *first* appearance of a celestial feature in the pre-dawn skies. For the Pleiades, this currently occurs in early June. While it is true that the Pleiades can be found in the eastern pre-dawn sky on July 26, that date does not have any distinct significance in the cycle of the Pleiades.
7. Juan Pío Pérez's "Cronologia Antigua de Yucatán y Examen del Método con que los Indios Contaba el Tiempo; Sacada de Varios Documentos Antiguos" was reproduced in Stephens ([1843] 1963:278-303).
8. In astronomical terminology, from day to day the declination of the sun changes very little at this time of year. At the solstices, the sun's declination does not change at all, and then it reverses.
9. Aveni and Hartung (1981). In this essay, Aveni and Hartung note that ". . . a fundamental coördinate axis in the Mesoamerican celestial reference frame consisted of four lines connecting the world to the four cardinal points, a fifth axis being directed toward the zenith" (S51-S52).
10. In fact, the timing of zenith passages at a given

latitude does vary slightly as the obliquity of the ecliptic changes, but these effects are so minor, even over millennia, that they can be disregarded.

11. Milbrath (1980a:292); Brundage (1979:104-109); Dow (1967).

12. Coe (1992:275).

13. The sun-Pleiades-zenith alignment is latitude specific and thus it has special meaning for the modern Yucatec Maya. It may herald a cultural resurgence based upon a reclaiming of their ancient knowledge.

CHAPTER 7: THE TRUE MEANING OF THE NEW FIRE CEREMONY

1. See Drucker (1986). Drucker's contribution to reconstructing the origins of the New Fire ceremony at Toltec Teotihuacan is summarized in Coggins (1989). For a discussion of the New Fire ceremony at Chichén Itzá, see Coggins (1987).

2. Slightly revising the chronology offered by other scholars, Clemency Coggins (1989) argues convincingly for an early ninth-century building of the Caracol and Pyramid of Kukulcan at Chichén Itzá. According to Coggins, their construction as astronomical and mythological knowledge-capsules was completed around the conclusion of baktun 10 (A.D. 830). This Long Count baktun shift was an important event in itself, probably fraught with the same anxiety that all cycle endings brought to Mesoamerican people. This baktun-shift context reinforces the idea that calibrating the great cycles of time (e.g., the precession of the equinoxes) was very much on the minds of those unknown skywatchers who designed the Pyramid of Kukulcan at Chichén Itzá.

3. Sahagún's history of New Spain is translated in Anderson and Dibble (1953).

4. The November 14 New Fire date of A.D. 1507 was calculated by astronomer E.C. Krupp (1982). Mesoamerican scholar Johanna Broda recognized the dualistic dynamic between the events in May and November (1982b, 1992), but does not draw the potentially controversial conclusion that the Aztecs were really interested in calculating the future convergence of the ever-changing *exact date* of the sun-Pleiades conjunction with the static date of the solar-zenith passage. Furthermore, no scholars have recognized that the midnight zenith transit of the Pleiades defines the date of the sun-Pleiades conjunction six months later. Milbrath (1980a) also recognizes the May-November opposition, but, like Broda, only in a general way.

5. This suggests that the universal principles of Sacred Geometry underlie Mesoamerican science and calendrics. The pioneering astronomer Johannes Kepler used the Platonic Solids in his geometrical model of the solar system, wherein the orbits of the visible planets were accurately spaced according to the five Platonic Solids. These geometrical shapes are constructed from the sacred ratio known as the Golden Mean. In my book *Jaloj Kexoj and PHI-64* (1994) I explored the Tzutujil philosophy involving the concepts of regeneration and multiplication (Jaloj Kexoj) and compared this indigenous time philosophy with the mathematical principles I had determined were at the core of the Maya tzolkin calendar (one of which is the Golden Mean).

6. Sanchéz (1937).

CHAPTER 8: ZENITH IMAGERY IN MESOAMERICA

1. Santillana (1955:122-125).

2. Milbrath (1980b:452).

3. Milbrath (1980b:453). That these concepts may go as far back as Izapa should not be regarded as unlikely. Milbrath's evidence for this is the role played by the Pleiades and the zenith sun in the orientation of Teotihuacan (Dow 1967). Importantly, early Teotihuacan influenced early Kaminaljuyu, and the travel route between these two major Pre-Classic cities passed right by Izapa.

4. Aveni (1980:148).

5. B. Tedlock and D. Tedlock (1993:44). Of course, one cross is the zenith cross and the other is the Milky Way/ecliptic cross.

6. Milbrath (1980a:291).

7. Milbrath (1980a:292).

8. Milbrath (1980a:290).

9. Schlak (1989:260).

10. The South American Aymara Indian word *vilcacota* (literally, sun-Pleiades) shows that at least one Native American group thought of the sun and the Pleiades as a united entity (Sullivan 1996:371).

11. Schlak (1989:269).

12. Schlak (1989:265).

13. Kubler (1982:100).

14. Kubler (1982:111-112).

15. Kubler (1982:112).

16. Kubler (1982:112).

17. In this symbology, the two meanings for the serpent's tail are the year-sign and the Pleiades. Rather than assume that these meanings are completely unrelated, we are probably safer in assuming some form of metaphoric parallelism in which the year-sign and the Pleiades are, in fact, reflections of an underlying conceptual unity.

18. Joyce (1915).

19. Maldonado and Tio (1991).

20. It should also be noted here that archaeologists found cleft-head figurines in the early art of Teotihuacan (Hasso von Winning 1976:153). This motif continuity into the Toltec era suggests a conceptual link from the Olmec up through the Toltec and probably through the Post-Classic Mesoamerican cultures as well.

21. Digby (1972). Digby also mentioned that J. Eric S. Thompson pointed out to him that the Xiuhcoatl serpent has a trapezoidal year-sign symbol for a tail (Digby 1972:436). This gives us more reason for allowing a connection between the zenith and the year-bearer symbols. Not all scholars agree with Digby's hypothesis that the year-signs represent an astronomical shadow-measuring instrument. Sharon Gibbs, in her article "The First Scientific Instruments" (1979), briefly discusses Digby's claim and reproduces the trapezoidal year-sign from the Pyramid of Quetzalcoatl at Xochicalco. She calls the upper trapezoid design a "crown" that "seems to refer to a calendar year" (59). She writes that Digby claims this is an astronomical instrument "despite the lack of convincing evidence that Mesoamericans would have been interested in the information supplied by such an instrument" (59). This is really a surprising statement, especially when we consider that Gibbs collaborated with Anthony Aveni on the archaeoastronomical studies at Chichén Itzá (Aveni and Gibbs 1975), and should thus be aware of the astronomical interests of the Mesoamerican skywatchers. As can be seen in Diagram 43, the design in question shows a trapezoid "instrument" casting a shadow downward that has the form of a symmetrical cross. This kind of symmetrical shadow will be cast by the "instrument" only on the date of a solar zenith passage. In addition, there is a zenith tube at Xochicalco that has been examined and measured by archaeoastronomers. Thus, zenith observations were made at Xochicalco. As such, the trapezoid instrument portrayed on the Pyramid of Quetzalcoatl at Xochicalco is perfectly designed to identify the dates of solar zenith passages, information that Mesoamericans, especially the ones at Xochicalco, were in fact very interested in.

22. This is also what I feel the New Fire ceremony was designed to track. Scholars have described only part of what this ceremony meant—that it was concerned with observing the Pleiades pass through the zenith on a New Year's Day (at midnight). In this chapter, I synthesized additional material to reconstruct the full import of the New Fire ceremony, showing that it was really concerned with tracking when, in the distant future, the sun and the Pleiades join and pass through the zenith together.

23. Hugh-Jones (1982:191).

24. Urton (1981:122-123).

25. If Amazonia-Yucatan connections seem far-fetched, scholars have already discussed in great length the probable contact between the Olmec civilization on the Gulf Coast of Mexico and the Chavin culture in Peru, which took place around 1200 B.C. (Coe 1962; Evans and Meggars 1966; Opperman 1983). Michael Coe (1960) excavated a site named La Victoria on the Pacific Coast of Guatemala (quite close to Izapa) and saw probable connections with a contemporary culture in coastal Peru.

26. Santillana and von Dechend (1969:295, 407).

27. Susan Milbrath explored the opposition between Pleiades and Scorpius in Maya thought

(1980a:293, 297), and her conclusions support my comments on the opposition between the Pleiades (the rattlesnake rattle) and the dark-rift near Sagittarius-Scorpio (the snake's mouth). The Milky Way thus might be seen as a huge snake, as it is in South American cosmologies and in Mesoamerica. Its tail is the Pleiades and its mouth is the dark-rift. The Pleiades and the dark-rift are roughly opposed in the sky and both lie near the two crossroads formed by the Milky Way and the ecliptic.

CHAPTER 9: THE LONG COUNT: GALACTIC ALIGNMENT IN 2012

1. Carlson (1982).
2. Ridpath (1989).
3. This is obvious upon looking at any decent star chart, e.g., Ridpath and Tirion (1987).
4. For a good map of the southern Milky Way, see Schaaf (1996:66-67).
5. Modern scholars' emphasis on extreme accuracy in these matters is a form of misplaced concretism, which assumes that ancient people placed an equal importance on pinpoint accuracy, even when they were capable of it. The compelling nature of Maya end-date cosmology has potent mythological value; the thought complex that arises, like many other aesthetically appealing paradigms, can be scientifically invalidated because it does not fit modern science's criterion of accuracy. Clearly, this is a double standard, but it does serve to protect science's assumption that it belongs to the most advanced paradigm yet created by human beings.
6. Roylance (1997).

CHAPTER 10: MAYA CREATION: THE STELLAR FRAME AND WORLD AGES

1. Freidel et al. (1993).
2. B. Tedlock (1992) points out that the Orion nebula was not reported in Medieval astronomical sources, and thus may not have even existed during the Maya Classic period. This challenges Schele's interpretation of the Orion nebula as the primal fire of ancient Maya Creation mythology.

3. D. Tedlock (1985:334, 358).
4. Ethnographer and translator Dennis Tedlock explicitly offers this reconstruction in his translation of the Quiché *Popol Vuh* (1985:39, 334).
5. Furst (1981).
6. For additional information, Joann Roman Brisko's 1993 M.A. thesis (*Aztec Goddesses*) thoroughly explores the identity and role of female deities in Mesoamerican cosmology. Citlalinicue and Coatlicue have associations with the Milky Way. Also see Brundage (1979:35-37), "Star Skirt and Her Children," an Aztec story in which the Goddess Star Skirt (the Milky Way) gives birth to many deities, including Quetzalcoatl and Tezcatlipoca. Brundage writes, "She [Citlalinicue] was the Great Mother of the stars and as such was peculiarly incarnate in the Milky Way" (35). Citlalinicue was the Mother of the Gods, and "enthroned in the Milky Way Star Skirt [Citlalinicue] was the source of all wisdom. . . ." (35).
7. In *The Orion Mystery*, Robert Bauval discusses Egyptian cosmology and the astronomy near the Milky Way/ecliptic crossing point in Gemini, in which Orion, Sirius, and the Milky Way play key roles. It is quite thought-provoking that both the Egyptians and the Maya recognized Orion in their Creation mythologies, and an intuitive insight about that part of the sky may be at the root of the shared interest. The Gemini crossing-point indicates the direction to travel out of the Galaxy; in a sense, it is the doorway out of the local neighborhood. The Sagittarian crossing-point, on the other hand, points our way *into* the Galaxy—into the Galaxy's center and the mysteries of the origin of time and space that reside there. In other words, the Sagittarian crossroads signifies an inner orientation whereas the Gemini/Orion crossroads represents an outward looking, or objective, orientation to life. In the context of the model of a unified Zenith Cosmology and Galactic Cosmology presented in Part II, the polarity between the zenith-center passage of the Pleiades (near Gemini) and the Galactic Center passage of the December solstice sun refers to a polarity between inner orientation and outer orientation—the subject-object polarity in human thought, or the inner-

outer polarity present in philosophical models of reality. The synthesis of the Zenith Cosmology and the Galactic Cosmology, as achieved at ninth-century Chichén Itzá, thus represents a transcendence of dualistic thinking in general, a worldview in which inner and outer realities are understood and perceived to be inextricably interwoven. This view, of course, is recognizable as the ancient "as above, so below" doctrine. These considerations are beyond the scope of the present book, as they access more metaphysical aspects of Mesoamerican time philosophy; for more on this perspective, see Jenkins (1991, 1994a:8-21, and 1994c).

8. In my book *The Center of Mayan Time* (Jenkins 1995a) I demonstrated how One Ahau corresponds to the December solstice quarter. It is the primary year-bearer, the senior day-sign, corresponding to the senior seasonal quarter.

9. According to Lowe (et al. 1982), there are prototypal tun and katun glyphs at Izapa. The first Long Count dates in the archaeological record date to the first century B.C. One is from Tres Zapotes, one is from Chiapa de Corzo north of Izapa, and several other Cycle 7 dates are within the Izapan sphere of influence.

10. Freidel et al. (1993:89).

11. Sullivan (1996:371). Sullivan relates that the dimmest stars can be seen at heliacal rise when the sun is at least 20° below the horizon. For the dimmer contrast between the Milky Way and its dark-cloud formations, a further 4° is required, given clear stargazing conditions. This means that the last time the dark-rift was visible rising heliacally on the December solstice was about 1,700 years ago.

CHAPTER 11. THE COSMIC SYMBOLISM OF THE MAYA BALLGAME

1. Krickeberg (1966), cited in Fash and Kowalski (1991:59).

2. Braun (1982:65). Elsewhere: "[A] typical vertical cross section of a ballcourt graphically portrays the stepped 'jaws of the earth,' and again the entrance to the Underworld" (Parsons 1991: 197). Regarding Cauac monster symbolism, see Tate (1982).

3. This third level should be looked at closely. It involves the movement of the December solstice sun (as the gameball), but what does this mean? The "movement" of the solstice sun only occurs against background features such as stars and the Milky Way, and thus precession is an unavoidable factor in the cosmic symbolism of the ballgame.

4. Parsons (1991:197).

5. See, for example, James Brady's "The Sexual Connotation of Caves in Mesoamerican Ideology" (1988); Doris Heyden (1975); Bassie-Sweet (1991).

6. Laughlin (1975:132).

7. In addition to these sources, Peter Furst wrote "the triangular cleft, along with the ubiquitous U element, is a gender-specific female symbol in Mesoamerica. . . . As a kind of cosmic vaginal passageway through which plants or ancestors emerge from the underworld, it can be found in many places" (1981:151). Also, Matos Moctezuma (1995:32) relates that caves were perceived as wombs capable of giving birth to individuals or entire groups of people. Chicomoztoc, the Aztec origin place, is portrayed as a womb in the *Historia Tolteca-Chichimeca*. In other pre-hispanic art, walls of caves are depicted in the same way used to indicate skin. Bassie-Sweet writes: "A womb/vagina is represented in many Mesoamerican birth metaphors by a cave" (1991:77). The conceptual association between caves and the birth passage is universal and well-established. We can take this a step further and equate the dark-rift in the Milky Way (the cave in the sky) with the vagina of a cosmic female deity, whom we may call the Cosmic Mother. The Aztec goddess Citlalinicue (Star Skirt) is the Milky Way (Brisko 1993), and in fact gave birth to Quetzalcoatl and Tezcatlipoca (Brundage 1979:35-37). Clearly, the dark-rift would be her birthing passage.

8. This very same figure is called the Witz "mountain" monster in Schele and Freidel (1990:68).

9. On murals from Chichén Itzá and elsewhere, the gameball is depicted as a skull or containing a skull. Likewise, in the *Popol Vuh*, One Hunahpu's head is used as the gameball. One

Hunahpu's head represents the dead sun, prior to its rebirth. Among the present-day Maya in Guatemala, corn seed is thought of as "little skulls." When they are planted, it is as if they make a heroic journey through the Underworld, to be reborn as new plants. This connection reveals a major aspect of the ballgame's meaning. The ballgame is also about the resurrection of the Maize God, who ultimately is a reflection of One Hunahpu, the First Father. As I have explained elsewhere, First Father or One Ahau refers to the sun, specifically, the December solstice sun. The Maize Deity, as the agricultural symbol of fertility and life, is understood by the Maya to be an aspect of First Father. Typically, as in the Aztec pantheon, Maya deities have an array of identifications and attributes that are frequently shared. The most important thing to stress here is the idea that the Maize Deity must be killed before he can be reborn. Likewise, One Hunahpu is killed by the Xibalban Lords before he is eventually resurrected by his sons, the Hero Twins. In the ballgame symbolism of solar rebirth, the idea must have been that the sun must die, travel through a period in the Underworld, and can then be reborn. This relates to the important role played by sacrifice in the ballgame. Part of the ritual game involved the sacrifice of either the winner or the loser, reflecting the Mesoamerican idea that deities (or deity-impersonators) must be sacrificed prior to world-renewal. Simply put, death feeds new life.

10. Wren (1995).
11. Many scholars agree. See Fash and Kowalski (1991:66); Brundage (1979:10); Krickeberg (1966:248-249); Reilly (1995:31). Also, Klein (1976a:30), citing Thompson, discusses the reversibility of up and down concepts "depending on whether celestial or terrestrial matters were under consideration" (Thompson 1970: 196).
12. Wren (1995).
13. Wren (1991:51).
14. Of course, it equally portrays solar rebirth on the daily and annual levels; however, the goalring iconography is particularly suggestive of the dark-rift overhead and thus the World Age level of rebirth. The actual date on the Ballcourt Stone was deciphered by Wren (1995:3) as 10.1.15.3.6, which is November 15, 864 (Gregorian) via the 584283 correlation (the True Count).

15. Earlier, I described the sky over the Chichén Itzá ballcourt on the June solstice. Here, at Toniná, we may have an indication of the dark-rift "far below"—at the nadir—rather than overhead. The symbolism contained on the marker stone, as well as the hole underneath, certainly suggests this, for there is no "black hole" overhead at midnight on the December solstice; instead, like other hearths and offering holes, the "black hole" lies at the deepest point of the Underworld below. Rather than seeming contradictory, we may glimpse here a complex cosmovision that sees the dark-rift portal in the night sky (on the June solstice) and deep below the ground (on the December solstice). Furthermore, we should remember that the Maya perceived "the Underworld" as the night sky.

16. Schele and Freidel (1991:291).
17. Schele and Freidel (1991:309).
18. In the same essay, the authors discuss various Creation texts, pointing out that certain important events happen in the portal to the Otherworld, a location referred to with the hieroglyph that translates as "black hole" (Schele and Freidel 1991:291). This black hole is associated with cenotes, Underworld portals, sinkholes, skeletal and serpent maws, ballcourts, king accessions, and "birth" events. See Appendix 4 for a more detailed look at the black hole in Maya Creation texts.
19. I am grateful to Dawn Jenkins for suggesting this.
20. See Quirarte (1974).
21. The Toltec and Aztec version of the ballgame also has associations with their concept of the World Age "end-date." The gameball was large and made of rubber and, as mentioned, represented the sun. "Ol" means rubber, as in "Olmec" (the Rubber People). In the Aztec calendar, the seventeenth day-sign Ollin means "movement." In the Aztec cosmology, Ollin is the day-sign on which the present World Age or "Sun" is to end. Thus, the rubber ball rep-

resents the movement of the present World Age's sun.

22. The Aztec end-date was calculated by Tony Shearer (1975:115) to occur in August, 1987. However, his math is inaccurate by over one hundred days (see Jenkins 1996f). Interestingly, however, Shearer equates the tzolkin date 1 Imix with August 16, 1987 (1975:116, 154), revealing he used a correlation that was only one day out of step with the 584283 correlation.

CHAPTER 12: CHICHÉN ITZÁ COSMOLOGY: MAYA-TOLTEC RECONCILIATION

1. Schele (1995b:105).

2. Milbrath (1980a); Brundage (1979); Dow (1967). According to Miller and Taube (1993:141-142), the earliest appearance of the quetzal serpent in Central Mexico occurred at Toltec Teotihuacan in the third century A.D. That the Teotihuacano astronomer-priests were interested in the Pleiades and the zenith sun is evident in the orientation of the city, as outlined in Part I. Given these facts, a conceptual association between the Pleiades, the zenith sun, the New Fire ceremony, and the Toltec Plumed Serpent, Quetzalcoatl, is likely.

3. Miller (1977); Schele and Freidel (1990:371-376).

4. In my close scrutiny of the zenith-passage phenomenon, I realized that a range of days fulfills the "no shadow at high noon" criterion. The range depends upon one's latitude of observation. See Appendix 3 for the data.

5. The date is currently thought to be 10.0.12.8.0, equivalent to June 18, 842 via the 584283 correlation. See Schele and Freidel (1990:356) and Slayman (1996).

6. Coggins (1989).

7. See Jones (1995). This comprehensive book shows that the citizens of Chichén Itzá pursued and achieved a peaceful Maya-Toltec unification rather than a violent one. For a review of Jones's book, see Jenkins (1997b).

8. In Coggins (1984).

9. Milbrath (1988a).

10. As Milbrath wrote, "Astronomy and history may be fused if the figures are in fact co-rulers who claimed celestial patronage of heavenly ancestors, perhaps even the legendary founders of Chichén Itzá" (1988a:66). Clearly, Milbrath was on the right track.

NOTES TO PART III: MAYA COSMOGENESIS

CHAPTER 13: THE BIRTH OF THE HERO TWINS

1. These are: 1) Tedlock's translation of the *Popol Vuh* (1985); 2) "Myth, Math, and the Problem of Correlation in Mayan Books" in *The Sky in Mayan Literature* (1992); 3) "The Sowing and Dawning of All the Sky-Earth: Sun, Moon, Stars, and Maize in the Popol Vuh" (1988); and 4) "Where You Want To Be" interview in *Parabola* (B. Tedlock and D. Tedlock 1993a). Two of these sources identify Blood Moon as the waxing new moon (1985:40, 274 and 1988:12-13), while in a more recent essay, Tedlock corrects himself and offers a scenario suggesting that she is really the waning post-full moon (1992:258).

2. D. Tedlock (1992:258, 271).

3. D. Tedlock (1985:115; 1992:257).

4. D. Tedlock (1992:256). In this particular Maya context, One Hunahpu (1 Ahau) specifically represents Venus as morning star. In other contexts, One Hunahpu is the December solstice sun. Here we are reminded that Mesoamerican deities typically rule sectors of time or abstract principles or forces rather than objects. Overall, One Hunahpu represents the philosophical concept of new birth, which applies to the December solstice sun as well as the heliacal rise of Venus as morning star.

5. D. Tedlock (1985:39); B. Tedlock and D. Tedlock (1993a:44).

6. D. Tedlock (1985:334, 358).

7. B. Tedlock and D. Tedlock (1993a:49-50).

8. However, it is possible that the mytho-astronomical meaning behind the conception of the Hero Twins, and perhaps the whole episode itself, is a late innovation. We may even think it to be a specifically Quiché manifestation, perhaps eight hundred years old, but Tedlock deciphers these references at the Classic site of

Palenque (1992:250), as well as in the *Dresden Codex* and the *Popol Vuh*. Our other range, therefore, may be during the Classic Period prior to the dedication of Palenque's Temple of the Cross, say, A.D. 300 to A.D. 690. I favor the antiquity of sophisticated knowledge, and place the origin of the mytho-astronomical conception of the Hero Twins way back to Izapa.

9. EZCosmos 3.1 and Skyglobe 3.6 (both of which adjust for precession).

10. In the interest of thoroughness, we may choose to look at a Palenque context for the "syzygy in the mouth" signature of the Hero Twins' conception. I did a brief search for this and, frankly, found nothing in the seventh century A.D. so interesting as the second and first century B.C. dates examined. One exception is a very close conjunction of Jupiter-Venus-moon right in the dark-rift mouth, on December 10, 714 (Julian). The problem here is that the Temple of the Cross had already been dedicated decades earlier, and that is where D. Tedlock finds his Palenque source for the Hero Twins' conception. Ultimately, by the time Palenque came on the scene, it may have been an ancient ritual event, commemorated whenever it occurred, and deeply a part of age-old folk mythology. Neither should it be lost upon us that, in any language, the "conception" of the Hero Twins contains an implicit pun. In other words, the "conception" of the myth about the Hero Twins' "conception." (Punning is a wonderful trait of the Maya, modern or ancient.)

11. Aveni (1984:255).

12. David Fideler, in his book *Jesus Christ, Sun of God* (1993), explores the esoteric symbolism behind early Christian cosmology. The esoteric number for Jesus, 888, represents the Ogdoad, the Spiritual Sun "behind" the physical sun. Jesus, as the "Sun behind the sun" was an expression of higher truth for the early Christian gnostics (Fideler 1993:270-1). In reading Fideler's material on this esoteric understanding of Jesus, I could not help thinking about the Maya end-date cosmology. The "spiritual sun behind the physical sun" would be the invisible Galactic Center in conjunction with the December solstice sun. One might therefore suspect that the end-date conjunction is the "second coming" prophesied by early Christian astrologers.

CHAPTER 14: A HAWK, A CROSS, AND A MOUTH

1. Ethnographer Judith Remington gathered enough detailed information to understand that the Thieves' Cross is made up of stars belonging to Sagittarius. Barbara Tedlock followed this lead with information from her own field study of the Maya in "Hawks, Meteorology and Astronomy in Quiché Maya Agriculture." Tedlock confirms and clarifies the earlier information offered by Remington. Her observations were primarily made in Momostenango, Guatemala, in the mid-1970s. When the Swainson's hawks pass overhead in October or November on their way south, they are said to "drop the Cross" into the ocean, thus signaling the dry season. This cross is a constellation, a "bent cross" that is "not straight but rather was inclined to its left" (B. Tedlock 1985:83), which proves to be the Thieves' Cross in Sagittarius identified by Remington (1977:85-87). There are no illustrations of this constellation in either Remington's or Tedlock's papers, but a list of the stars in this cross allows us to chart it. The stars in the Thieves' Cross constellation are:

    a) Sigma (mag. 2.1)
    b) Phi (mag. 3.2)
    c) Delta (mag. 2.7)
    d) Gamma (mag. 3.0)
    e) Lambda (mag. 2.8)
    f) Epsilon (mag. 1.8)
    g) Eta (mag. 3.1)

2. Taube (1995).

3. D. Tedlock (1985:111).

4. D. Tedlock (1985:327); B. Tedlock (1982, 1983, 1985, 1986, 1992). All of these studies report the role of the dark-rift (*xibalba be*) in Maya thought.

5. Fought (1972:144-145).

6. D. Tedlock (1985:334).

7. Wisdom (1940:409-410).

8. D. Tedlock (1985:159-160).

9. In the Central Mexican *Borgia Codex*, an interesting picture portrays the birth of Venus in the

form of a rabbit. Rabbit, the eighth day-sign, is called Lamat in the Yucatec Maya language, and its glyph resembles a cross (see diagram below). The *Borgia* scene is very similar to the astronomical scenario sketched above. A bird is pulling the rabbit out of the mouth of a serpent:

***Lamat-Venus glyph and Birth of Venus in the* Borgia Codex**

Notice the cloud-scrolls along the body of the serpent, indicating that this is Mixcoatl, the Milky Way serpent (Miller and Taube 1993). The mouth must be the dark-rift. The bird, also "attached" to the Milky Way, may be the Xic (Hawk) constellation of the Quiché, the Old World Aquila. Again, this star group easily lends itself to being viewed as a bird. The *Borgia* scene shows the bird pulling Venus (the rabbit) out of the mouth of the Milky Way (the dark-rift). At the same time, the mouth of the bird may symbolize part of the dark-rift. The crosslike form of the Lamat glyph recalls the Thieves' Cross of the Quiché story, and the quincunx frog of the Chortí tale. The mytho-astronomical location of this event needs to occur on the ecliptic in order for Venus to pass by; the southern terminus of the dark-rift meets the ecliptic in Sagittarius. In sum, perhaps Venus-Quetzalcoatl was thought of as being born from the cleft in the Milky Way? My observations are supported by comments in Milbrath (1988b). For a Lamat glyph on an Olmec head where the cleft-head motif normally is, see Reilly (1995:37).

10. Thompson (1972:84); Thompson citing Roys (1933:103).
11. B. Tedlock and D. Tedlock (1993:44).
12. Fought (1972:265).
13. Fought (1972:265).
14. Fought (1972:274). If the Silent Day equals the night sky, the silent hour might mean the middle of the night. Midnight observations of astronomical features (perhaps the Pleiades?) might be implied. In this regard, Coggins (1987) mentioned that the New Fire observation of the Pleiades—originally a Toltec institution—

took place at Copán (near the present-day Chortí).
15. Fought (1972:274).
16. Fought (1972:336).
17. Fought (1972:336).
18. D. Tedlock (1993:229).
19. This situation is similar to the dramas surrounding the Tzutujil Maximón deity in the 1950s. See Mendelson (1959).
20. LaFarge (1947:124).
21. LaFarge (1947:113).
22. Sosa (1989).
23. Taube (1994:659).
24. Evon Vogt (1976) and Gary Gossen (1974) report a similar cosmological construct among the Zinacantecos and Chamulas of highland Chiapas.
25. A third "dark hole" near another cosmic center is the "smoking mirror" of the circumpolar deity Tezcatlipoca. See Hunt (1977).
26. Milbrath (1980a:291).
27. Milbrath (1980a:291).
28. Milbrath (1980b:452).
29. Milbrath (1980b:452).
30. Girard (1949:571).
31. In the work of Milbrath (1980b:452), we find an indirect acknowledgment of the three cosmic centers of Izapan-Maya cosmovision: the crossing-point of Milky Way and ecliptic in Sagittarius (which targets the Galactic Center), the zenith-as-center, and the polar center. All of these centers are represented at Izapa, in its monumental message and in the site's orientation to topographical features and sunrise positions along the horizon (see Part IV: Izapa Cosmos).

CHAPTER 15: THE MAN WHO WAS SWALLOWED BY AN ALLIGATOR

1. Norman and Raxuleu (1976).
2. In Quiché, walking "beside" the ocean is written with the word *ci:ʔ*, which means edge or mouth. Thus, he walked by the "mouth" of the ocean. The word for alligator is *ayi:n*.
3. In the same way that multiple layers of meaning are present in Maya folklore, multiple times are alluded to by the storyteller's alternate use

of past and present tense. The story ostensibly occurred in the past but its internal dynamics, which are the true point of the story, continue to occur in the present.

4. The original translator feels this motif is "obviously" due to "the influence of the story of Jonah and the Whale." However, this seems overly simplistic and nothing more is said.

5. Thus, in my revision of the translation, I retain capital "F" in Father as in a title, like First Father.

6. Specifically, the Tzutujil. Martín Prechtel related this information at a talk given in Boulder, Colorado, in February 1993.

7. Jenkins (1992b); Jenkins (1994a). My study of the Maya Venus Calendar showed that the Quiché and Ixil Maya may have adopted a Venus Calendar that changed the Sacred Day of Venus from 1 Ahau to 1 Manik (Deer). Manik was and is the primary year-bearer for the Ixil and Quiché calendar-priests, and Manik rules the sacred eastern mountain of Quijala (B. Tedlock 1982:100), the direction of the heliacal rise of Venus. According to my reconstruction, a thirteen-day correction was implemented circa A.D. 1246, thus bringing Lounsbury's November 18, 934 A.D. 1 Ahau 18 Kayab Sacred Day of Venus into alignment with Calendar Round beginnings (Lounsbury 1983), something not possible in the Venus Calendar evident in the *Dresden Codex*. Thus, the Maya would have then accomplished the synchronization of the Calendar Round with the Venus Round, as well as the vague Venus-Mars Round of 312 years.

8. Fash (1991).

9. D. Tedlock (1993).

10. As Claude Lévi-Strauss wrote, to understand the inner meaning of ancient legends, all poetic variants must be considered. Our understanding is enhanced when all the metaphors used in various redactions are taken into account. Another *Popol Vuh* variant, mixed with Bible references, was recorded by Oliver LaFarge in the Kanhobal Maya town of Santa Eulalia in the 1930s (LaFarge 1947). In addition, an unpublished Tzutujil version of the Quiché *Popol Vuh* is called "Of The Sweatbath" (mentioned in Carlsen and Prechtel 1988).

CHAPTER 16: SHAMANIC TOOLS, THRONES, AND BIRTH PORTALS

1. Wasson et al. (1986); Riedlinger (1990).

2. J. L. Furst (1978).

3. Borhegyi (1961:500).

4. D. Tedlock (1985:249-251).

5. Gordon Wasson, despite discovering the psilocybe mushroom cult in Central Mexico, tirelessly sought evidence for the ritual use of *Amanita muscaria*, the Indo-European soma, in Mesoamerica. There is some evidence that soma was known in ancient Mesoamerica and was used as an inebrient. For example, two terracotta figurines from Nayarit (in western Mexico) were identified by Peter Furst and clearly resemble *Amanita muscaria* (Wasson et al. 1986:51). Linguistic evidence summarized by Wasson (et al. 1986:47-53), based on the work of Bernard Lowy (1971; 1974), suggests that *Amanita muscaria* was associated with Kakuljá Hunrakan, the Quiché Maya deity of thunder and lightning strikes. (Mushrooms are traditionally associated with thunder and lightning strikes, as they seem to magically spring up after storms. Also, mushrooms have just one "leg," recalling lightning.) Furthermore, Lowy discovered evidence that the people of Chichicastenango, Guatemala, recognized *Amanita muscaria* as a poisonous mushroom, to be avoided. In a Tzutujil myth related by Martín Prechtel, Lowy (in Wasson et al. 1986:48-49) also found associations between the sacred tree, *palo de pita* (coralbean tree), lightning strikes, the Tzutujil Maximón cult-figure, and mushrooms.

6. Furst (1974a:191). Based upon information supplied by Barbara Tedlock and Dennis Tedlock, Furst (1974a:191) relates that *Stropharia cubensis*, "or one that closely resembles it in form and ecology," occurs plentifully in the Guatemalan highlands, where it was observed in the Quiché region growing in the droppings of sheep and goats. This confirms the likelihood that psilocybin-containing species could thrive in symbiotic relationship with ruminant animals other than Old World cattle.

7. Furst (1974a:193).

8. *Erythrina*, the coralbean, is reported to be an

effective sedative, and contains the alkaloids erysopine, erysovine, and hypaphorine (Orellana 1987:201-202). In Nahuatl it is called *tzompamitl*.

9. Orellana (1987:106).

10. Stross and Kerr (1981:349).

11. I believe that a direct stimulation of the colon may have given rise to visions of serpents; the colon, wound up in a snake-like configuration, being electrified by chemical stimulation, would possibly give rise to serpentine visions. Of course, this is a rather reductionistic interpretation, but serpent imagery in relation to vision rites is quite prevalent in Classic Maya art.

12. Harvilahti (1986).

13. Dobkin de Rios (1974).

14. Peter Furst mentioned Knab's work in Dobkin de Rios (1974:154).

15. Furst (1968).

16. Furst in Dobkin de Rios (1974:154).

17. Reichel-Dolmatoff (1982:167).

18. Reichel-Dolmatoff (1982:171).

19. Reichel-Dolmatoff (1982:176).

20. Davis (1991:249).

21. For the latest scoop on the Black Hole in the Galactic Center, see Schulkin (1997).

22. Stuart and Houston (1994:71).

23. D. Tedlock (1985:358).

24. D. Tedlock (1985:46).

25. Stuart and Houston (1994:71).

26. Stuart and Houston (1994:71-72).

27. "Similar shifts between title and toponym mark the use of the 'black hole' compound" (Stuart and Houston 1994:75). In other words, matawil and the black hole both serve to denote a title and a place: ruler and throne. A throne is a throne only when occupied and a ruler is a ruler only when enthroned.

28. Taube (1994).

29. Taube (1994:660).

30. Taube (1994:656).

31. Taube (1994:657).

32. Taube (1994:659).

33. Taube (1994:662).

34. Taube (1994:663).

35. Kaplan (1995).

CHAPTER 17: CONJURING CREATION

1. Harner (1980).

2. McKenna and McKenna ([1975] 1993). Their theory called Timewave Zero is based upon the "novelty wave" encoded into the ancient Chinese I Ching. Terence McKenna decoded the timewave and determined that the "zero point" of the wave, which determines the manifestation of the chaos attractor at the end of history, will be the December solstice of A.D. 2012. My research with the 2012 event emphasizes, based upon its astronomical nature, that we can consider the Maya prophecy to be about an era of transformation; fifty years on either side of 2012 might apply. Ultimately, a one-hundred-year period for a major shift in Earth's activities is but a nanosecond in the larger seasons of our planet's becoming.

3. Although the Milky Way had many mythic identities, its role as the Cosmic Birther or Great Mother emerges as the highest insight into its essential nature. Perhaps the most compelling words of support for this contention come from Mesoamerican scholar Burr Cartwright Brundage, who wrote, "The Milky Way was itself the body of that Great Mother out of whose tenebrous womb had once poured the sun and the moon and the stars" (Brundage 1979:9). Many scholarly sources provide the raw data for understanding how the Milky Way and its dark-rift represent the Great Mother Goddess and her birth canal. See, for example, Brady (1988); Heyden (1975); Bassie-Sweet (1991:77); Laughlin (1975:132), P. Furst (1981:151), Matos Moctezuma (1995:32); and Brundage (1979:35-37). Susan Milbrath (1988b) wrote about the Milky Way's role as a fertile and female road or river of stars and decoded the astronomical imagery in the myth of Venus-Quetzalcoatl's birth. Based upon Aztec sources, she saw Venus-Quetzalcoatl being "born" during Venus's passage through the Milky Way (near the dark-rift in Sagittarius). The conception of the Hero Twins also occurred in this same place, which I explored in Chapter 13. Milbrath concludes her study with these words: ". . . one of the principal sky mothers may be Citlalicue, the goddess of the Milky

Way" (1988b:164). The related Aztec Goddess Citlalinicue (Star Skirt) is the Milky Way (Brisko 1993) and gave birth to the twins Quetzalcoatl and Tezcatlipoca (Brundage 1979:35-37). There are more examples, but the point is clear: Meso-american people understood that the Milky Way was the Cosmic Mother. The reason I am em-phasizing this point is because its acceptance is crucial to appreciating how the Maya thought about the end-date alignment, which is an an-cient and fundamental mytho-astronomical idea-complex in Mesoamerican cosmology. As such, we can understand how the World Age transformation in A.D. 2012 is to be a cosmic insemination, and, ultimately, may result in the birthing of a new form of life on Earth.

NOTES TO PART IV:
IZAPA COSMOS

CHAPTER 18: CEREMONIAL CITY OF THE ANCIENT SKYWATCHERS

1. Burkitt (1924).
2. Thompson (1948); Proskouriakoff (1950).
3. Jakeman (1958:45-46). Subsequent researchers feel that Jakeman's ideas are flawed because of liberties taken with the reproduction of Stela 5. For example, Indo-European beards appear in his line drawings which seem to be Rorschach-like apparitions.
4. Refer to Marion Stirling's comments in *The Olmec and Their Neighbors* (1981).
5. Norman (1980:51) wrote that Stela 9 expresses an ascent into heaven through its alignment on Tajumulco volcano. This may be a secondary chance alignment of Stela 8 over Stela 9 (Nor-man 1980:52), whereas the primary alignment of Stela 9 is to the Tacana cleft in the north. Norman observed that Stela 89, a later find from the southeast corner of Group B, "depicts a man gazing toward the [December] solstice sunrise who appears to rise from his captive bands of death with the rebirth of the sun" (1980:53). This interpretation reinforces the idea of the Decem-ber solstice sunrise as a place of solar rebirth, which is critical to understanding the relevance

of the end-date precession-caused alignment as a World Age rebirth. However, I disagree with Norman's idea that the captive is rising from, or being freed from, his captive bands. More likely, he is one of many sacrifices required for facilitating solar rebirth (world renewal).

6. Parsons (1986); Cortez (1986); Miles (1965b); Quirarte (1973, 1974).
7. V. Garth Norman is one researcher who did in-clude these considerations from the start, though I cannot agree with many of his identi-fications. A general assumption present in Nor-man's commentary (1976), affecting a lot of his interpretations, is that the carvings are instruc-tive, priestly counsels toward afterlife fulfill-ment following a morally well-lived earthly ex-istence. As Lowe et al. (1982:315) point out, this idea "runs counter to the prevailing interpreta-tions of Mesoamerican religion and pre-hispanic world-view." Of course, this countering of con-ventional wisdom is not in itself lamentable; it is the overshrouding influence of Old World Middle Eastern religious ideas detectable in Norman's analysis. While comparisons between Old World and Izapan ideas can be argued, do-ing so does not help to identify the astronomi-cal content of Izapan monuments.
8. Thompson (1974:97).
9. Lowe et al. (1982).
10. Fash and Kowalski (1991:66); Brundage (1979: 10); Krickeberg (1966:248-249); Reilly (1995: 31); Klein (1976a:30); Thompson (1970:196).
11. In the text of this book, I will use the term "dialogue" for "dialectics." Isbell (1982) clari-fies the anthropological definition of the con-cept of dialectics. She proposes that the tropi-cal zone "provides a perceptual environment that promotes and enhances a particular 'sci-ence of the concrete'" (353). By "science of the concrete" she means that empirically per-ceived order in a given site's environment pro-vides the foundation for "systems of classifi-cations, epistemological structures, and cos-mologies" (353). Presumably the ambient framework that informs local cosmo-concep-tion includes topography, seasonal cycles, and astronomy. Having noticed the unique orien-tational properties of a specific location, hu-

man beings may found a site for precisely these reasons, and I believe this is what happened at Izapa. According to Isbell, environmental determinants inform cosmo-conception within the Tropics and lend themselves to ideas rooted in "dialectical, reversible dualism" (353). Importantly, she notes that "native philosophers, who are usually shamans or astronomer-priests, use methods and metaphorical language that are unfamiliar to us" (353). In other words, the logic underlying native thought-systems is dialectical rather than rationalistic. Rational or linear thought processes are limited by an either-or assumption that, in the end, does not model nature very well. A complementary, oppositionally inclusive, or reciprocal relationship between opposed categories of experience more accurately reflects native thought as revealed over many decades of ethnographic study. For example, see B. Tedlock (1982:2-5) and Jenkins (1994a:316-319).

Another concept related to this dialectical approach is "conflation." In my usage here, this means the purposeful mythologizing of dialectically opposed events so that they are understood as reflecting the same underlying unity. Opposites are conceptually "conflated" into a higher unity. We see this most clearly in the identification of Mesoamerican deities. The full moon is associated with the sun, being called a "little sun." In another example, the Underworld becomes the night sky when, after sundown, it rotates above the horizon. Here, the Underworld is actually above the Earth, a concept strange to either-or thinkers but perfectly compatible with the dialectical mind-set. The categories of sky and Earth are conflated into a higher unity in which, under certain conditions, the sky is below the Earth and the Underworld is above. Dennis Tedlock (1985 and 1995) stresses that the Quiché word *cahuleu* (sky-Earth) reveals a conflated concept in which sky and Earth are unified into one dialectical whole. This is a good example of how conflation and dialectical thinking works. And it can apply to extremely complicated levels of meaning, involving several levels of observations, including both temporal and spa-

tial categories. The unsung dimensions of knowledge encoded in Izapan stelae provide a great challenge of interpretation even when we are armed with such a progressive dialectical model.

For elucidation of dialectical thought, Isbell refers to Wagner (1975), who states that the anthropological usage of the concept of dialectics refers to "a tension or dialogue-like alternation between two conceptions or viewpoints that are simultaneously contradictory and supportive of each other" (52). According to Wagner, dialectical thought works by "exploiting contradictions against a common ground of similarity" (52). In comparison, "rationalistic or 'linear' logic" (52) appeals to a consistent meaning against a foundation of differences.

CHAPTER 19: SOUTHERN MESOAMERICA, 200 B.C.: THE IZAPAN CIVILIZATION

1. For example, Gilbert and Cotterell (1995).
2. Coe (1976:113).
3. Lowe et al. (1982:40).
4. See Edmonson (1988); Hall (1989-1993); Malmström (1997).
5. Coe (1962a:100).
6. Dutton and Hobbs (1943). These archaeologists identified the possible source of Plumbate ware and, on a dangerous and difficult ascent, they visited petroglyphs at a site called Piedra Pitayuda near the summit of the 13,800-foot-high Tajumulco volcano (1943:14).
7. Parsons (1972).
8. Séjourné (1957:Fig 7).
9. Jenkins (1995a:Bk. 3, 24-25).
10. Carlsen and Prechtel (1988).
11. Barba de Piña Chan (1988).
12. Norman (1976) and Lowe et al. (1982).
13. D. Tedlock (1985:330, 360).

CHAPTER 20: IZAPAN CALENDRICS

1. See Malmström (1973). Malmström was not the first to suggest that solar zenith-passage intervals at latitude 15°N might be responsible for

the origin of the 260-day calendar. See Nuttall (1928) and Apenes (1936). However, Malmström (1978) further supported Izapa as the origin place of the 260-day calendar by charting the chronological evolution and geographical distribution of Mesoamerican calendar systems and tracing them back to Izapa.

2. For the range of zenith-passage days at the latitude of Izapa, see Appendix 3.

3. This was calculated with the 584283 correlation, what I call the True Count. See Jenkins (1994a, 1996f).

4. The Tzotzil Maya of Chiapas (Vogt 1969:602) have a solstice cosmogram concept, as do the modern Tzutujil (Carlsen and Prechtel 1988). In addition, the present-day Zoque of Santa Maria Chimalapa believe that "the world is a square, with its corners at the points where the sun rises and sets at the solstices" (Muñoz 1977:140). Directional glyph blocks from a tomb at Río Azul confirm this conception for the Classic period (B. Tedlock 1992), as do the Uaxactun Group E alignments. Brotherston and Ades (1975) originally argued that the quadrated directional symbol of Mesoamerican cosmology conformed to the two solstice axes and the zenith, a breakthrough supported by Watanabe (1983), Coggins (1980) and others (e.g., Broda 1982b).

5. Using a 130-day interval, the moon passes through four phase cycles with twelve days left over. Two considerations allow us to extend this another two days to reach the new-to-full measure: 1) As mentioned, zenith observations cannot be made precisely to a day. At Izapa the range is at least three days, allowing us to add one-and-one-half days to twelve. It is true that the midpoint of the three-day range could have been calculated, adjusting for the vagueness in zenith-passage observations, but we cannot be sure that the Izapans were interested in this kind of accounting; they may have preferred to acknowledge the extreme limit of the three-day range. 2) Indigenous people (e.g., the Quiché) still measure the moon from its first appearance in the west as the new moon sliver, rather than from "moon dark." As such, this shortens the measure by one to two days, bringing us again to an accurate one-half lunar phase cycle.

6. Edmonson (1988:246) cites A.D. 292 as the first appearance of the Tikal calendar in the archaeological record.

7. Edmonson (1986a and 1988).

8. Jenkins (1995a:Bk. 3, 15-16).

9. Martin Pickands wrote his Ph.D. thesis on the Mesoamerican First Father legend. Pickands (1978) provides some startling perspectives regarding this ancient deity. He suggests that the ancient First Father figure Huracan unites two sub-aspects of himself, and is thus a kind of triune deity. This resembles the polar and zenith concepts combined under the category "north," both set in dialectical relationship to the Galactic Center in the "south." Pickands relates that the "Ahau cap" on certain deity figures is a parentage glyph meaning "Our Father" (129); we find this "Ahau cap"—a kind of inverted boat—on Stela 11, further evidence that the solar deity on Stela 11 is First Father.

10. My original argument is in Jenkins (1995a:Bk. 3, 16-19).

11. Coe (1976:121).

12. Malmström (1997:258).

CHAPTER 21: IZAPAN ASTRONOMY AND COSMOLOGY

1. According to Lowe et al. (1982) and Norman (1980), Izapa's main baseline, measured through Group H (Mound 60 over Mound 25), is 21° east of north. This points right at the peak of Tacana.

2. Norman (1980:51) states that the axis of Group B, just to the east of Group H, points "one to two degrees" further east. Looking at the picture of Tacana, we see a shallow cleft on the eastern flank, about 2° east of the peak. Thus, I suggest that the reason for Group B's deviated orientation is to emphasize this mythic cleft and the rising of the Big Dipper that occurs there. Similarly, the axis of Group A, which lies a short distance west of Group H, is deviated some "one to two degrees" *west* of the main 21° azimuth baseline of Group H. This, I believe, refers to astronomical events west of the peak—the falling of the Big Dipper. The North Celestial Pole is, of course, 21° west of Tacana peak, but the Group A reference holds as a general indicator.

Significantly, stelae 4 and 2 on the main axis in Group A depict the descent of the Seven Macaw bird deity, who is the Big Dipper (D. Tedlock 1985:330, 360).

3. Norman (1976:255-256).

4. Coggins (1982).

5. Coggins goes on to explore the northward orientation of Izapa to volcano Tacana. The oldest Mesoamerican rituals involve volcanos and the Old Fire God who lives inside them. This deity is associated with incensarios and is symbolic of the sun in the Underworld, at the nadir. Conversely, the volcano's peak is symbolic of the sun at zenith, in the exact center of the sky. At Izapa, the zenith-passage dates are May 1 and August 12 (with a three-day range of observation for both). Tacana thus represents geographical north, which orients the observer at Izapa to the polar region around which the sky revolves. Tacana also symbolizes the zenith, which was the fifth, central, direction in the Mesoamerican cosmogram bounded by the solstice axes.

6. Since Izapa is designed to mirror Tacana as the axis mundi, it might be more primary to place this 3-D grid over Tacana. When we do this the north-south axis points north to the "birth of corn" place near Cuilco, while the December

solstice axis points southeast to Tajumulco (see note 8 below). Furthermore, the horizon east of Tacana contains prominent peaks that correspond to the solstice and equinox sunrises, much like the manmade arrangement of pyramids at Uaxactun (Aveni and Hartung 1989). This compelling geographical fact explains why the ancient Izapan cosmologists mythologized Tacana as the navel of the cosmos.

7. See Freidel et al. (1993) and Schele (1995b).

8. According to Tedlock (1993:2, 235), the location of the semi-mythic origin place of corn is in the western Guatemalan highlands north of Cuilco and south of the Pan American highway. Teosinte, the original undomesticated corn, still

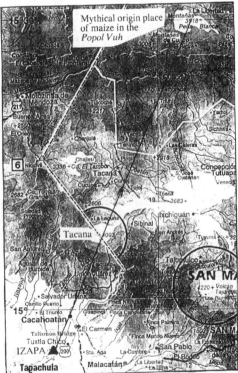

Cosmically oriented ley line: Izapa, Tacana cleft, origin place of corn, Big Dipper

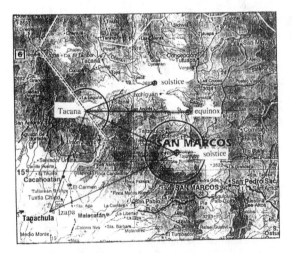

Peaks east of Tacana mark the solstices and the equinox

grows there. This is the area of the Montañas de Cuilco and the 3518-meter peak of the Montañas Peña Blanca which lies 45 kilometers beyond the Tacana cleft on the 23° east-of-north axis from Izapa. It is quite astounding that this mythic origin place of corn lies directly on the north-south axis that begins at Izapa and runs through the Tacana cleft (see diagram).

This axis continues northward (roughly) to Palenque (Coggins 1982). Since the cleft in Tacana, as a reflection of the witznal deity and the Olmec cleft head, is a symbolic emergence place of the maize/sun deity, it seems beyond coincidence that the Izapan axis points to the same origin place indicated in the later Quiché myths. Ultimately, this ley line is targeted on the Big Dipper (Seven Macaw in the *Popol Vuh*).

9. Horizon rise azimuths in this diagram are: a) Dubhe: 8.3°; b) Delta: 15.9°; c) Phecda: 20.3°; d) Alkaid 27.1°.

10. Sunrise in the northeast opposes the Milky Way dark-rift and crossroads setting in the southwest. The Big Dipper rises with the sun and thus is not visible at all during the night. On sunset the reverse is true: the sun sets with the Big Dipper in the northwest while the dark-rift and crossroads rises in the southeast. This suggests that around the December solstice, when the sun is weakest, struggling to be reborn into the new year, the Big Dipper is strongest, as Seven Macaw magnified himself falsely in the *Popol Vuh*, impersonating the sun. Conversely, around the June solstice the sun is "strongest," thus banishing the tricky Big Dipper from view. Echoed here is the cosmological belief, as evidenced in the *Popol Vuh*, that the polar area is a false center. Around the June solstice (bisecting the two zenith passages) the sun culminates overhead, north of the zenith; in effect, it has invaded the Big Dipper's realm of the north. In the same way that the Big Dipper is visible all night around the December solstice, the dark-rift and crossroads of the Milky Way/ecliptic are visible roughly all night long during the June solstice.

11. Jenkins (1994d, 1995a).

12. See Hatch (1971).

13. Only circa 2600 B.C. did the North Celestial Pole point to a star, but this is not relevant to the point being made.

14. Rise azimuth data for the stars given in this diagram are as follows. For A.D. 2000: a) 8.37°; b) 17.31°; c) 20.31°; d) 15.89°; e) 17.81°; f) 19.73°; g) 27.13°. For A.D. 11,400: a) 63.1°; b) 67.4°; g) 54.8°.

CHAPTER 22: THE MONUMENTAL MESSAGE

1. Norman (1976:264) explained these as planetary, moon, or star symbols. I think the best interpretation is that they are zenith gnomons, given the symbolism of their associated Throne 1 and Stela 9. Though crudely formed, they will indicate the zenith sun by casting no shadows at high noon, observable over a range of three days at the latitude of Izapa (see Appendix 3).

2. Because of its orientation northward to the Tacana cleft, this glyph also may have a secondary meaning of "north" (as in polar north). This seems to be a statement of equivalence between zenith and north that, as we explored earlier, is a widespread Mesoamerican idea. As mentioned, Group B's northward orientation is to the Tacana cleft, the emergence place of the north. However, the monuments of Group B seem to primarily address the zenith. Again, this seems to indicate the conceptual synthesis of "polar north" and "zenith."

3. Norman (1976:105) rejects the interpretation that the lower part of Stela 8 depicts the legs of a frog or toad, because of the "uniqueness" of these legs. However, the feet on the toad carving on Altar 1 and Stela 8 are very similar.

4. D. Tedlock (1985:330, 360).

5. Neither Lowe nor Norman concurs with Jakeman on the meaning of Stela 5, though Jakeman is often quoted and Lowe speaks in places of "our Canaanite model" (Lowe et al. 1982:272).

6. Schele (1992b:152, 212); Kelley (1989:92).

7. Stela 1 seems to depict a rain invocation. Lifting the fish out of the southern ocean might have invoked a sympathetic magic or ritual process through which the rains over Tacana to the north were assured. The fish on Stela 1 also are seen on Stela 5, and Stelae 67 and 22 in Group F. Their "ringed" tails resemble the breechcloth design on Stela 20 and elsewhere,

which in turn parallels the "bifurcated tongue" symbol (Norman 1976:122). The breechcloth design on the abstract Stela 20 is a symbol of male power and rulership, and the Freudian parallel between tongue and penis should not go unmentioned, as it provides a rationale for this symbolic parallel when we recall that, in Maya ritual, blood was let through both the penis and the tongue. The ring-tailed fish may represent the self-sacrifice of the Hero Twins, an event found in the *Popol Vuh* (they became fish for five days) that serves as the necessary precursor to their rebirth as celestial deities (the sun and moon).

8. Robertson (1967).

9. M. Miller (1995).

10. The three-spot motif also reminds one of the Ahau glyph as well as the "howl" phenomenon mentioned earlier in relation to vision enemas. In addition, it resembles the three-spot "solar face" on the tail of the *Crotalus d.* snake species, a key motif in the Zenith Cosmology reconstructed in Part II.

11. B. Tedlock (1982, 1992).

12. Lowe et al. (1982:285).

13. Laughlin (1975:132).

14. Lowe et al. (1982:285).

15. Kelley (1976:36); Lowe et al. (1982:295).

16. Schele (1992b); Freidel et al. (1993).

17. Cordy-Collins (1982) illustrates splay-legged females from Ecuador in the so-called "hocker" position of birthing and compares them to Tlaltecuhtli and other Central Mexican Earth Mother images. She postulates migration of this symbol southward from Central Mexico into South America circa A.D. 500. Several abstracted "ball and crescent" images from Ecuador resemble the Izapan sky-clefts, especially on Stela 88, which I propose is a male-female symbol of fertilization, a symbol with a primary astronomical reference at Izapa (the 13-baktun cycle end-date). In comparison, Cordy-Collins describes the Ecuadoran "ball and crescent" images as representing solely the Earth Mother (1982:218). Also see Klein (1976a) and Wilbert (1974).

18. Parsons (1986:142-143) provides a "sketch map" of Kaminaljuyu. The majority of the ball-courts, some seven of them, are oriented to the southeast horizon, about 4° south of the December solstice azimuth. The remaining three ballcourts at the site are perpendicular to this orientation. Despite the slightly skewed orientation (and there may be inaccuracies in the rough map used), one wonders if Kaminaljuyu imitated the earlier ritual-astronomical orientation of Izapa. Similarly, scholars have proposed direct Izapan influence in the founding of Copán (Aveni 1980). A detailed map of El Baúl shows a similar Izapan orientation of its ballcourt.

19. Wren (1995).

20. Freidel et al. (1993).

21. Izapa Stelae 22 and 67 both depict similar iconography involving a boat, a solar hero, and sky-ropes. The serrated edges on these depictions encircle the solar hero and are comparable to the "cosmic center" frame on the upper portion of Stela 8 in Group B, as well as to the serrated edge surrounding the crossband on Throne 1 in Group B. The serrated enclosure on Stela 22 thus may represent an Underworld portal or denote a cosmic center. The similarity between Stela 22 and Stela 67 suggests that the solar hero in "the middle" of the Milky Way canoe is in a cosmic center.

22. Norman (1976:272).

23. Schele (1992b, 1995b); Freidel et al. (1993).

24. This center-front position is comparable to the center-front glyph on Throne 1, which we identified as equivalent to the center or zenith direction in the cosmogram on Throne 1's top surface. This interpretation is reinforced by the overall symbolism of the zenith in the surrounding Group B monuments.

25. Klein (1976a).

26. In Tzutujil Maya time philosophy, *kexoj* is a concept of regeneration and renewal that operates on the collective spiritual level of humanity (see Jenkins 1994c).

27. Norman (1976:268).

28. As representative of the cosmic source and womb of creation, a male ruler's sexual identity is subsumed into his higher role as a birther and conjurer, which are normally female functions. Today, Quiché diviners speak of having

a "spirit wife," and the highest level of sha-man-priest daykeeper is a "mother-father."

NOTES TO PART V:
GAZING INTO THE GALAXY

CHAPTER 24: THE FORGOTTEN
GALACTIC PARADIGM

1. See Clow (1996:154-175); Eisler (1987); Thompson (1981).
2. Isbell (1982:353).
3. Isbell (1982:353).
4. Reichel-Dolmatoff (1982:176).
5. Reichel-Dolmatoff (1982:176).
6. Reichel-Dolmatoff (1982:176).
7. See DeKorne (1994); Ott (1994).
8. Halpern (1992).
9. Feuerstein et al. (1995) argue for the Indus River Valley civilization as being the cradle of civilization some 7,000 years ago. Interestingly, they see evidence for precessional knowledge and that the churning of the milky ocean (the Milky Way) was involved in Vedic cosmogenesis. See also Wilson (1996:284-286).
10. As explored in my books *Mirror in the Sky* (1991) and *Tzolkin: Visionary Perspectives and Calendar Studies* (1994), the 260-day tzolkin is a sub-unit of the 26,000-year precessional cycle. The former refers to individual physical unfolding and the latter refers to collective spiritual unfolding.

CHAPTER 25: BACK TO THE CENTER:
THE MEANING OF THE MAYA END-
DATE

1. See Roylance (1997). Roylance reports astronomical calculations that show, allowing for a margin of error, that the solstice meridian coincides most precisely with the Galactic equator between February 1998 and November 1999. However, precession is a very slow phenomenon, and it is clear that the Maya intended the 2012 end-date to mark this event. Nevertheless, the June solstices of 1998 and 1999 and the December solstices of 1998 and 1999 would appear to be critical turnabout points. We might consider ourselves to have "crossed the threshold" by the December solstice of 1999. However, as mentioned in the text, considering that the sun itself is one-half a degree wide, the December solstice sun will not completely clear the Galactic equator until roughly A.D. 2018.
2. See Eisler (1987:7-41, 80-103); Eisler and Loye (1993).
3. Gimbutas (1981).

BIBLIOGRAPHY

Adams, Richard E. W. (editor)

1977 *The Origins of Maya Civilization*. Albuquerque: University of New Mexico Press.

Aguilera, Carmen

1989 The Mexica leap year once again. In *World Archaeoastronomy: Selected Papers from the 2nd Oxford International Conference on Archaeoastronomy held at Merida, Yucatán, Mexico, 13-17 January 1986*, edited by Anthony F. Aveni, pp. 227-231. Cambridge, England: Cambridge University Press.

Anderson, Arthur J. O., and Charles E. Dibble (translators)

1953 *Florentine codex, General history of the things of New Spain. Book 7: The Sun, Moon, and stars, and the binding of the years*, by Bernardino de Sahagún. Monograph 14, part 8, book 7. Santa Fe, NM: School of American Research, Archaeological Institute of America.

Apenes, Ola

1936 Possible Derivation of the 260-day Period of the Maya Calendar. *Ethnos* 1:5-8. Mexico City.

Aveni, Anthony F.

1980 *Skywatchers of Ancient Mexico*. Austin: University of Texas Press.

1981a Tropical Archaeoastronomy. *Science* 213 (4504):161-171.

1981b Old and New World Naked-Eye Astronomy. In *Astronomy of the Ancients*, edited by Kenneth Brecker and Michael Feirtag, pp. 61-90. Cambridge, MA: The MIT Press.

1981c Archaeoastronomy in the Maya Region: A Review of the Past Decade. *Archaeoastronomy* 3:S1-S16. Journal for the History of Astronomy.

1984 The View From the Tropics. In *Archaeoastronomy and the Roots of Science*, edited by E. C. Krupp, pp. 253-288. AAAS Selected Symposium 71. Boulder, CO: Westview Press.

1989 Introduction: Whither Archaeoastronomy?

In *World Archaeoastronomy: Selected Papers from the 2nd Oxford International Conference on Archaeoastronomy held at Merida, Yucatán, Mexico, 13-17 January 1986*, edited by Anthony F. Aveni, pp. 3-12. Cambridge, England: Cambridge University Press.

1991 The Real Venus-Kukulcan in the Maya Inscriptions and Alignments. In *Sixth Palenque Round Table 1986*, edited by Merle Greene Robertson, pp. 309-321. Norman: University of Oklahoma Press.

Aveni, Anthony F. (editor)

1992 *The Sky in Mayan Literature*. New York: Oxford University Press.

Aveni, Anthony F., E. E. Calnek, and H. Hartung

1988 Myth, Environment, and the Orientation of the Templo Mayor of Tenochtitlan. *American Antiquity* 2:287-309.

Aveni, Anthony F., Sharon L. Gibbs, and Horst Hartung

1975 The Caracol Tower at Chichen Itza: An Ancient Astronomical Observatory? *Science* 188(4192):977-985.

Aveni, Anthony, and Horst Hartung

1981 The Observation of the Sun at the Time of Passage Through the Zenith in Mesoamerica. *Archaeoastronomy* 3:S51-S70. Journal for the History of Astronomy.

1989 Uaxactun, Guatemala, Group E and similar assemblages: an archaeoastronomical reconsideration. In *World Archaeoastronomy: Selected Papers from the 2nd Oxford International Conference on Archaeoastronomy held at Merida, Yucatán, Mexico, 13-17 January 1986*, edited by Anthony F. Aveni, pp. 441-461. New York: Cambridge University Press.

Aveni, Anthony, Horst Hartung, and Charles J. Kelley

1982 Alta Vista (Chalchihuites), Astronomical Implications of a Mesoamerican Ceremonial Outpost at the Tropic of Cancer. *American*

Antiquity 2:316-335.

Aveni, Anthony F., and Robert M. Linsley

1972 Mound J. Monte Albán: Possible Astronomical Orientation. *American Antiquity* 4:528-531.

Badaway, A.

1964 The Stellar Destiny of Pharaoh and the so-called Air-shafts in Cheop's Pyramid. *Mitteilungen des Instituts für Orientforschung Akademie der Wissenschaften zu Berlin*, 10:189-206.

Badner, Mino

1972 *A Possible Focus of Andean Artistic Influence in Mesoamerica*. Pre-Columbian Art & Architecture, No. 9. Washington, D.C.: Dumbarton Oaks.

Barba de Piña Chan, Beatriz

1988 *Buscando raices de mytos y leyendas Mayas*. Campeche, Mexico: Ediciones de la Universidad Autonoma del Sudeste.

Bardawil, Lawrence W.

1974 The Principal Bird Deity in Maya Art: An Iconographic Study of Form and Meaning. In *The Art, Iconography, and Dynastic History of Palenque, Part III: Proceedings of the Segunda Mesa Redonda de Palenque*, edited by Merle Greene Robertson, pp. 195-210. Pebble Beach, CA: Robert Louis Stevenson School.

Bassie-Sweet, Karen

1991 *From the Mouth of the Dark Cave: Commemorative Sculpture of the Late Classic Maya*. Norman: University of Oklahoma Press.

1996 *At the Edge of the World: Caves and Late Classic Maya World View*. Norman: University of Oklahoma Press.

Bauval, Robert, and Adrian Gilbert

1994 *The Orion Mystery: Unlocking the Secrets of the Pyramids*. New York: Crown Publishers.

Borhegyi, Stephan F. de

1961 Miniature Mushroom Stones from Guatemala. *American Antiquity* 4:498-504.

1965a Archaeological Synthesis of the Guatemala Highlands. In *Archaeology of Southern Mesoamerica*, edited by Gordon R. Willey, pp. 3-58. Handbook of Middle American Indians, vol. 2,

part 1. Austin: University of Texas Press.

1965b Settlement Patterns of the Guatemalan Highlands. In *Archaeology of Southern Mesoamerica*, edited by Gordon R. Willey, pp. 59-75. Handbook of Middle American Indians, vol. 2, part 1. Austin: University of Texas Press.

Boskovic, Aleksandar

1992 Great Goddesses of the Aztecs: Their Meaning and Functions. *Indiana* 12:9-13. Berlin.

Bove, Frederick J.

1991 The Teotihuacán-Kaminaljuyu-Tikal Connection: A View from the South Coast of Guatemala. In *The Sixth Palenque Round Table, 1986*, edited by Merle Greene Robertson, pp. 135-142. Norman: University of Oklahoma Press.

Brady, James

1988 The Sexual Connotation of Caves in Mesoamerican Ideology. *Mexicon* 10(3):51.

Braun, Barbara

1974 Southern Sources of Cotzumalhuapa, Guatemala. *The 41st International Congress of Americanists* 2:279-308.

1982 The Serpent at Cotzumalhuapa. In *Pre-Columbian Art History: Selected Readings*, edited by Alana Cordy-Collins, pp. 55-82. Palo Alto, CA: Peek Publications.

Bricker, Victoria

1988 The Relationship Between the Venus Table and an Almanac in the Dresden Codex. In *New Directions in American Archaeoastronomy*, edited by Anthony F. Aveni, pp. 81-103. Amsterdam: B.A.R. International Series 454.

Bricker, Victoria R., and Harvey M. Bricker

1992 Zodiacal References in the Maya Codices. In *The Sky in Mayan Literature*, edited by Anthony F. Aveni, pp. 148-183. New York: Oxford University Press.

Brisko, Jo Ann Roman

1993 *Aztec Goddesses: A Historical Perspective*. Master's thesis. San Jose, CA: San Jose State University.

Broda, Johanna

1970 Tlacaxipehualiztli: A Reconstruction of an

Aztec Calendar Fesitival from 16th-Century Sources. In *Revista Espanola de Anthropologia Americana*, vol. 5. Madrid, Spain.

1982a La fiesta Azteca del fuego nuevo y el culto de las Pleyades. In *Space and Time in the Cosmovision of Mesoamerica*, edited by F. Tichy, pp. 129-157. Latinamerika-Studien 10. Munich: Wilhelm Fink Verlag.

1982b Astronomy, *Cosmovisión*, and Ideology in Pre-Hispanic Mesoamerica. In *Ethnoastronomy and Archaeoastronomy in the American Tropics*, edited by Anthony Aveni and Gary Urton, pp. 81-110. Annals of the New York Academy of Sciences, Vol. 385. New York.

1991 The Sacred Landscape of Aztec Calendar Festivals: Myth, Nature and Society. In *To Change Place: Aztec Ceremonial Landscapes*, edited by Davíd Carrasco, pp. 74-120. Niwot, CO: University of Colorado Press.

1992 Astronomical Knowledge, Calendrics, and Sacred Geography in Ancient Mesoamerica. In *Astronomies and Cultures*, edited by Clive L. N. Ruggles and Nicholas Saunders, pp. 253-295. Niwot, CO: University of Colorado Press.

Brotherston, Gordon

1975 Time and Script in Ancient America. *Indiana* 3:9-40. Berlin

1976 Mesoamerican Description of Space II: Signs for Directions. *Ibero-Amerikanisches Archiv* 2:39-62. Berlin.

1979 *Image of the New World: The American Continent Portrayed in Native Texts*. London: Thames & Hudson.

1982 Astronomical Norms in Mesoamerican Ritual and Time Reckoning. In *Archaeoastronomy in the New World*, edited by Anthony Aveni, pp. 109-142. New York: Cambridge University Press.

1983 The Year 3113 B.C. and the Fifth Sun of Mesoamerica: An Orthodox Reading of the Tepexic Annals. In *Calendars of Mesoamerica and Peru*, edited by Anthony F. Aveni and Gordon Brotherston, pp. 167-221. B.A.R. International Series 174. Oxford.

1989 Zodiac signs, number sets, and astronomical cycles in Mesoamerica. In *World Archaeoastronomy: Selected Papers from the 2ⁿᵈ Oxford International Conference on Archaeoastronomy held at Merida, Yucatán, Mexico, 13-17 January 1986*, edited by Anthony F. Aveni, pp. 276-288. Cambridge, England: Cambridge University Press.

1992 *The Book of the Fourth World*. Bloomington: Indiana University Press.

Brotherston, Gordon, and Dawn Ades

1975 Mesoamerican Description of Space I: Myths; Stars and Maps; and Architecture. *Ibero-Amerikanisches Archiv* 1(4):279-305. Berlin.

Bruce, R. D., C. Robles U., and E. Ramos Chao

1971 Los Lacandones 2, Cosmovision Maya. *Instituto Nacional de Antropología e Historia, Departamento de Investigaciones Antropológicas, Publicaciones 26*. Mexico City.

Brundage, Burr Cartwright

1979 *The Fifth Sun: Aztec Gods, Aztec World*. Austin: University of Texas Press.

Burkitt, R.

1924 A Journey in Northern Guatemala. *University Museum Journal* 15(2):115-137. Philadelphia: University of Pennsylvania.

Campbell, Joseph

1986 *The Inner Reaches of Outer Space*. New York: Harper & Row.

Carlsen, Robert S., and Martín Prechtel

1988 Weaving and Cosmos amongst the Tzutujil Maya of Guatemala. *Res* 15:122-132.

1990 The Flowering of the Dead: An Interpretation of Highland Maya Culture. *Man* (N.S.) 26:23-42.

1994 Walking on Two Legs: Shamanism in Santiago Atitlán, Guatemala. In *Ancient Traditions: Shamanism in Central Asia and the Americas*, edited by Gary Seaman and Jane S. Day, pp. 77-112. Niwot, CO: University Press of Colorado.

Carlson, John B.

1981a Numerology and the Astronomy of the

Maya. In *Archaeoastronomy in the Americas*, edited by R. A. Williamson, pp. 202-213. Los Altos and Center for Archaeoastronomy, College Park, MD: Ballena Press.

1981b A Geomantic Model for the Interpretation of Mesoamerican Sites: An Essay in Cross-Cultural Comparison. In *Mesoamerican Sites and World Views*, edited by Elizabeth P. Benson, pp. 143-216. Washington, D.C.: Dumbarton Oaks.

1982 The Double-Headed Dragon and the Sky: A Pervasive Cosmological Symbol. In *Ethnoastronomy and Archaeoastronomy in the American Tropics*, edited by Anthony Aveni and Gary Urton, pp. 135-164. Annals of the New York Academy of Sciences, Vol. 385. New York.

1990 America's Ancient Skywatchers. *National Geographic* 177(3):76-107. Washington, D.C.: The National Geographic Society.

1991 *Venus-Regulated Warfare and Ritual Sacrifice in Mesoamerica: Teotihuacan and the Cacaxtla "Star Wars" Connection*. College Park, MD: Center for Archaeoastronomy.

Carlson, Ruth, and Francis Eachus

1977 The Kekchi Spirit World. In *Cognitive Studies of Southern Mesoamerica*, edited by Helen Neuenswander and Dean A. Arnold, pp. 36-65. SIL Museum of Anthropology, Publication 3. Dallas, TX: Summer Institute of Linguistics.

Carmack, Robert M.

1973 *Quichean Civilization: The Ethnohistoric, Ethnographic, and Archaeological Sources*. Berkeley: University of California Press.

1981 *The Quiché Mayas of Utatlán: The Evolution of a Highland Guatemala Kingdom*. Norman: University of Oklahoma Press.

1995 *Rebels of Highland Guatemala: The Quiché-Mayas of Momostenango*. Norman: University of Oklahoma Press.

Carrasco, Davíd

1990 *Religions of Mesoamerica: Cosmovision and Ceremonial Centers*. New York: Harper & Row.

Cholb'äl Q'ij: Agenda Maya. (Annual Calendar)

1994 Editorial Cholsamaj, 7a Avenida 9-25, Zona 1 Aprto. 4, Guatemala City; Editorial Maya Wuj, 4a Calle 1-74 Zona 7, Col Landívar, Guatemala City.

Closs, Michael

1983 Were the Ancient Maya Aware of the Precession of the Equinoxes? Review of *The Paris Codex: Decoding an Astronomical Ephemeris* by Gregory Severin. *Archaeoastronomy* VI (1-4):164-171. College Park, MD: The Journal of the Center for Archaeoastronomy.

Closs, Michael P., Anthony F. Aveni, and Bruce Crowley

1984 The Planet Venus and Temple 22 at Copán. *Indiana* 9:221-247. Berlin.

Clow, Barbara Hand

1995 *The Pleiadian Agenda*. Santa Fe: Bear & Company Publishing.

1996 *Liquid Light of Sex*. Santa Fe: Bear & Company Publishing.

Coe, Michael D.

1957 Cycle 7 Monuments in Middle America: A Reconsideration. *American Anthropologist* 59:597-611.

1960 Archaeological Linkages with North and South America at La Victoria, Guatemala. *American Anthropologist* 62:363-393.

1961 *La Victoria: An Early Site on the Pacific Coast of Guatemala*. Papers of the Peabody Museum of Archaeology and Ethnology, Harvard University, Vol. 53. Cambridge.

1962a *Mexico*. London: Thames & Hudson.

1962b An Olmec Design on an Early Peruvian Vessel. *American Antiquity* 27(4):579-580.

1966 *The Maya*. Great Britain: Thames & Hudson. Reprinted in 1971 by Pelican Books.

1972 Olmec Jaguars and Olmec Kings. In *The Cult of the Feline*, edited by Elizabeth P. Benson, pp. 1-18. Washington, D.C.: Dumbar-ton Oaks.

1976 Early Steps in the Evolution of Maya Writing. In *Origins of Religious Art and Iconography in Preclassic Mesoamerica*, edited by Henry B. Nicholson, pp. 107-122. UCLA Latin American Center Publications. Los Angeles:

Ethnic Arts Council.

1989 The Hero Twins: Myth and Image. In *The Vase Book: A Corpus of Rollout Photographs of Maya Vases*, vol.1, pp. 161-184. New York: Kerr and Associates.

1992 *Breaking the Maya Code*. London: Thames & Hudson.

Coggins, Clemency

1980 The Shape of Time: Some Political Implications of a Four-Part Figure. *American Antiquity* 45(4):727-739.

1982 The Zenith, the Mountain, the Center, and the Sea. In *Ethnoastronomy and Archaeoastronomy in the American Tropics*, edited by Anthony Aveni and Gary Urton, pp. 111-124. Annals of the New York Academy of Sciences, Vol. 385. New York.

1984 Murals in the Upper Temple of the Jaguars, Chichen Itza. In *The Cenote of Sacrifice, Catalogue*, edited by Clemency Coggins and Orrin C. Shane III, pp. 157-165. Austin: University of Texas Press.

1987 New Fire at Chichen Itza. In *Memorias del Primer Coloquio Internacional de Mayistas, 5-10 de Agosto de 1985*, pp. 427-484. Mexico City: Universidad Nacional Autonoma de Mexico.

1989 A New Sun at Chichen Itza. In *World Archaeoastronomy: Selected Papers from the 2nd Oxford International Conference on Archaeoastronomy held at Merida, Yucatán, Mexico, 13-17 January 1986*, edited by Anthony F. Aveni, pp. 260-275. Cambridge, England: Cambridge University Press.

1990 The Birth of the Baktun at Tikal and Seibal. In *Vision and Revision in Maya Studies*, edited by Flora S. Clancy and Peter D. Harrison, pp. 77-98. Albuquerque: University of New Mexico Press.

1996 Creation religion and the numbers at Teotihuacan and Izapa. *Res* 29/30:16-38. Cambridge, MA: The Peabody Museum of Archaeology and Ethnology.

Coggins, Clemency Chase, and R. David Drucker

1988 The Observatory at Dzibilchaltun. In *New Directions in American Archaeoastronomy*, edited by Anthony Aveni, pp. 17-56. BAR International Series 454. Oxford.

Cohodas, Marvin

1975 The Symbolism and Ritual Function of the Middle Classic Ball Game in Mesoamerica. *American Indian Quarterly* 2(2):99-130.

1978 *The Great Ball Court at Chichen Itza, Yucatan, Mexico*. Garland Series, Outstanding Dissertations in the Fine Arts. New York: Garland Publishing.

1991 Ballgame Imagery of the Maya Lowlands: History and Iconography. In *The Mesoamerican Ballgame*, edited by Vernon L. Scarborough and David R. Wilcox, pp. 251-288. Tucson: University of Arizona Press.

Cordy-Collins, Alana

1982 Earth Mother/Earth Monster Symbolism in Ecuadorian Manteño Art. In *Pre-Columbian Art History: Selected Readings*, edited by Alana Cordy-Collins, pp. 205-203. Palo Alto, CA: Peek Publications.

Cortéz, Constance

1986 *The Principle Bird Deity in Preclassic and Early Classic Maya Art*. Master's thesis. Austin: University of Texas.

Covarrubias, Miguel

1947 *Mexico South: The Isthmus of Tehuantepec*. New York: Alfred A. Knopf.

1957 *Indian Art of Mexico and Central America*. New York: Alfred A. Knopf.

Culebro, Carlos A.

1939 *Chiapas prehistórico: Su arqueología*. Folleto No. 1 (October). Huixtla, Chiapas.

Dahlin, Bruce H., Robin Quizar, and Andrea Dahlin

1987 Linguistic Divergence and the Collapse of Preclassic Civilization in Southern Mesoamerica. *American Antiquity* 52(2):367-382. The Society for American Archaeology.

Davis, Joel

1991 *Journey to the Center of Our Galaxy*. Chicago: Contemporary Books.

DeKorne, Jim

1994 *Psychedelic Shamanism*. Port Townsend, WA: Loompanics Unlimited.

Demarest, Arthur

1974 *The Origin of Izapan Civilization*. B.A. thesis. New Orleans: Tulane University.

Diaz-Bolio, José

1987 *The Geometry of the Maya and Their Rattlesnake Art*. Merida, Mexico: Area Maya.

1988 *Why the Rattlesnake in Mayan Civilization?* Merida, Mexico: Area Maya.

Digby, Adrián

1972 Evidence in Mexican glyphs and sculpture for a hitherto unrecognised astronomical instrument. *The 40th International Congress of Americanists* 1:433-442.

1980 Mesoamerican Astronomical Glyphs and Symbols Derived from the Sundial. In *La Antropología Americanista en la Actualidad: Homenaje a Raphael Girard*, vol. 1, pp. 183-190. Mexico: Editores Mexicanos Unidos.

Dobkin de Rios, Marlene

1974 The Influence of Psychotropic Flora and Fauna on Maya Religion. *Current Anthropology* 15(2):147-163.

Dow, James W.

1967 Astronomical Orientations at Teotihuacan, A Case Study in Astro-Archaeology. *American Antiquity* 32(3):326-334.

Dreyer, J. L. E.

1906 *A History of Astronomy From Thales to Kepler*. Cambridge University Press. Dover reprint 1953.

Drucker, D. R.

1986 The Teotihuacan pecked crosses: models and meanings. Paper presented at the 51st Meeting of the Society for American Archaeology, New Orleans.

Dütting, Dieter

1978 Birth, Inauguration and Death in the Inscriptions of Palenque, Chiapas, Mexico. In *Tercera Mesa Redonda de Palenque, vol. IV*, edited by Merle Greene Roberston, pp. 183-214. Palenque: Pre-Columbian Art Research, and Monterey, CA: Herald Printers.

Dutton, Bertha P.

1958 Studies in Ancient Soconusco. *Archaeology* 11:48-54.

Dutton, Bertha P., and Hulda R. Hobbs

1943 *Excavations at Tajumulco, Guatemala*. Monographs of the School of American Research, Number 9. Santa Fe: University of New Mexico Press.

Earle, Duncan M.

1986 The Metaphor of the Day in Quiché: Notes on the Nature of Everyday Life. In *Symbol and Meaning Beyond the Closed Community: Essays in Mesoamerican Ideas*, edited by Gary Gossen, pp. 155-172. Albany: State University of New York.

Eberhart, Stephen

1995 Babylonian vs. Maya Calendrics. Paper presented at the meeting of Natural Science Section at Michael Fields, Wisconsin, Nov. 17-19.

Edmonson, Munro S.

1982 *The Ancient Future of the Itza: The Book of Chilam Balam of Tizimin*. Austin: University of Texas Press.

1986 The Olmec Calendar Round. In *Research and Reflections in Archaeology and History: Essays in Honor of Doris Stone*. Middle American Research Institute Publication 57, pp. 81-86. New Orleans: Tulane University.

1988 *The Book of the Year: Middle American Calendrical Systems*. Salt Lake City: University of Utah Press.

Eisler, Riane

1987 *The Chalice and the Blade*. New York: Harper and Row.

Eisler, Riane, and David Loye

1993 Raising the Chalice. In *Mavericks of the Mind: Conversations for the New Millennium*, edited by David J. Brown and Rebecca McClen Novick, pp. 25-52. Freedom, CA: The Crossing Press.

Ekholm, Susanna M.

1969 *Mound 30a and the Early Preclassic Ce-*

ramic Sequence of Izapa, Chiapas, Mexico. Papers of the New World Archaeological Foundation, No. 25. Provo, UT: Brigham Young University.

Eliade, Mircea

1964 *Shamanism: Archaic Techniques of Ecstacy*, translated from the French by Willard R. Trask. Bollingen Series LXXVI. Princeton, NJ: Princeton University Press.

Ervast, Pekka

1992 [1916] *Kalevalan Avain*. Tampere, Finland: Kristosofinen Kirjallisuusseura ry.

1998 *The Key to the Kalevala*. Translated and edited by Tapio Joensuu and John Major Jenkins. Nevada City, CA: Blue Dolphin Publishing.

Evans, Clifford, and Betty J. Meggars

1966 Mesoamerica and Ecuador. In *The Handbook of Middle American Indians*, Vol. 2, edited by Gordon F. Ekholm and Gordon R. Willey, pp. 243-264. Austin: University of Texas Press.

EZCosmos, v. 3.1. Astrosoft, Inc. Desoto, TX. 1990.

Fabian, Stephen M.

1982 Ethnoastronomy of the Eastern Bororo Indians of Mato Grosso, Brazil. In *Ethnoastronomy and Archaeoastronomy in the American Tropics*, edited by Anthony Aveni and Gary Urton, pp. 283-302. Annals of the New York Academy of Sciences, Vol. 385. New York.

Fash, William L.

1991 *Scribes, Warriors, and Kings: The City of Copán and the Ancient Maya*. London: Thames & Hudson.

Fash, William L., and Jeff Karl Kowalski

1991 Symbolism of the Ball Game at Copán: Synthesis and New Aspects. In *The Sixth Palenque Round Table, 1986*, edited by Merle Greene Robertson, pp. 59-67. Norman: University of Oklahoma Press.

Feuerstein, Georg, Subhash Kak, and David Frawley

1995 *In Search of the Cradle of Civilization*. Wheaton, IL: Quest Books.

Fideler, David

1993 *Jesus Christ, Sun of God: Ancient Cosmol-ogy and Early Christian Symbolism*. Wheaton, IL: Quest Books.

Flem-Ath, Rand, and Rose Flem-Ath

1995 *When the Sky Fell: In Search of Atlantis*. New York: St. Martin's Press.

Fought, John G.

1972 *Chortí (Mayan) Texts 1*. Philadelphia: University of Pennsylvania Press.

Fox, John W.

1991 The Lords of Light Versus the Lords of Dark: The Postclassic Highland Maya Ballgame. In *The Mesoamerican Ballgame*, edited by Vernon L. Scarborough and David R. Wilcox, pp. 213-240. Tucson: University of Arizona Press.

Frawley, David

1991 *Gods, Sages, and Kings: Vedic Secrets of Ancient Civilization*. Salt Lake City, UT: Passage Press.

Freidel David, Linda Schele, and Joy Parker

1993 *Maya Cosmos: Three Thousand Years on the Shaman's Path*. New York: William Morrow and Company.

Furst, Jill Leslie

1977 The Tree Birth Tradition in the Mixteca, Mexico. *Journal of Latin American Lore* 3(2): 183-226.

1978 *Codex Vindobonensis Mexicanus I: A Commentary*. Institute for Mesoamerican Studies. Albany: State University of New York.

Furst, Peter T.

1968 The Olmec Were-Jaguar Motif in the Light of Ethnographic Reality. In *Dumbarton Oaks Conference on the Olmec*, edited by Elizabeth P. Benson, pp. 143-78. Washington, D.C.: Dumbarton Oaks.

1974a Fertility, Vision Quest and Auto-Sacrifice: Some Thoughts on Ritual Blood-Letting Among the Maya. In *The Art, Iconography and Dynastic History of Palenque Part III*, edited by Merle Greene Robertson, pp. 181-193. Pebble Beach, CA: The Robert Louis Stevenson School.

1974b Reply from Dobkin de Rios (1974). *Current Anthropology* 15(2):154.

1981 Jaguar Baby or Toad Mother: A New Look

at an Old Problem in Olmec Iconography. In *The Olmec and Their Neighbors*, edited by Elizabeth P. Bensen, pp. 149-162. Washington, D.C.: Dumbarton Oaks.

1986 Human Biology and the Origin of the 260-Day Sacred Almanac: The Contribution of Leonhard Schultze Jena (1872-1955). In *Symbol and Meaning Beyond the Closed Community: Essays in Mesoamerican Ideas*, edited by Gary Gossen, pp. 69-76. Albany: State University of New York.

1995 Shamanism, Transformation, and Olmec Art. In *The Olmec World: Ritual and Rulership*, pp. 69-82. The Trustees of Princeton University.

Garza, Mercedes de la

1989 Los Alucinógenos en la Religión Maya. In *Memorias del Segunda Coloquio Internacional de Mayistas*, pp. 1399-1409.

Gendrop, Paul

1978 Dragon-Mouth Entrances: Zoomorphic Portals in the Architecture of Central Yucatán. In *The Third Palenque Round Table, 1978, Part 2*, edited by Merle Greene Robertson, pp. 138-150. Austin: University of Texas Press.

Giamario, Daniel

1998 The May 1998 Galactic Alignment: A Shamanic Look at the Turning of the Ages. *The Mountain Astrologer* 11(2):57-61. Cedar Ridge, CA.

Gibbs, Sharon

1979 The First Scientific Instruments. In *Astronomy of the Ancients*, edited by Kenneth Brecher and Michael Feirtag, pp. 39-59. Cambridge, MA: MIT Press.

Gilbert, Adrian G., and Maurice M. Cotterell

1995 *The Mayan Prophecies*. Dorset, Brisbane, Rockport, MA: Element Books Limited.

Gillespie, Susan D.

1991 Ballgames and Boundaries. In *The Mesoamerican Ballgame*, edited by Vernon L. Scarborough and David R. Wilcox, pp. 317-346. Tucson: University of Arizona Press.

Gimbutas, Marija

1981 *Goddesses and Gods of Old Europe*. London: Thames & Hudson.

Girard, Raphael

1949 *Los Chortis ante el problema Maya*. 5 vols. Mexico: Antigua Librería Robredo.

1962 *Los Mayas Eternos*. Mexico City: Libro Mexico.

1966 *Los Mayas*. Mexico City: Libro Mexico.

1979 *Esotericism of the Popol Vuh*. Translated from the Spanish by Blair A. Moffet. Pasadena, CA: Theosophical University Press. Originally published in 1948 as *Esoterismo del Popol Vuh* by Editorial Stylo, Mexico City.

Goodman, Ronald

1992 *Lakota Star Knowledge: Studies in Lakota Stellar Theology*. Rosebud Sioux Reservation, SD: Sinte Gleska University.

Gossen, Gary

1974 *Chamulas in the World of the Sun: Time and Space in a Maya Oral Tradition*. Cambridge, MA: Harvard University Press.

1982 *The Transformation of the Hummingbird*. Book review by Eva Hunt. In *Archaeoastronomy* V(3):26-32. College Park, MD: The Journal of the Center for Archaeoastronomy.

Graham, John A.

1977 Discoveries at Abaj Takalik, Guatemala. *Archaeology* 30(3):196-197.

1978 Maya, Olmecs, and Izapans at Abaj Takalik. *The 42nd International Congress of Americanists* (8):179-188.

1982 Antecedents of Olmec Sculpture at Abaj Takalik. In *Pre-Columbian Art History: Selected Readings*, edited by Alana Cordy-Collins, pp. 7-22. Palo Alto, CA: Peek Publications.

Grove, David C.

1984 *Chalcatzingo: Excavations on the Olmec Frontier*. London: Thames & Hudson.

Guillén, Ann Cyphers

1993 Women, Rituals, and Social Dynamics at Ancient Chalcatzingo. *Latin American Antiquity* 4(3):209-224.

Hall, Robert L.

1989-1993a The Book of the Year: Middle American Calendar Systems. Review-essay by Munro Edmonson. *Archaeoastronomy* XI:118-121. College Park, MD: The Journal of the Center for Archaeoastronomy.

1989-1993b The Historical Identity of a Mass Conjunction Inferred from the Madrid Codex. *Archaeoastronomy* XI:101-103. College Park, MD: The Journal of the Center for Archaeoastronomy.

Halpern, Paul

1992 *Cosmic Wormholes: The Search For Interstellar Shortcuts.* New York: Penguin Books.

Hancock, Graham

1995 *Fingerprints of the Gods.* New York: Crown Publishers.

Hancock, Graham, and Robert Bauval

1996 *The Message of the Sphinx: A Quest for the Hidden Legacy of Mankind.* New York: Crown Publishers.

Harner, Michael

1980 *The Way of the Shaman.* New York: Bantam.

Hartner, Willy

1979 The Young Avestan and Babylonian Calendars and the Antecedants of Precession. *Journal for the History of Astronomy* X:1-22.

Harvilahti, Lauri

1986 Overtone Singing and Shamanism. In *Traces of the Central Asian Culture in the North,* edited by Ildikó Lehtinen, pp. 63-70. Mémoires de la Société Finno-Ougrienne, No. 194. Helsinki: Suomalais-Ugrilainen Seura.

Hatch, Marion Popenoe

1971 An Hypothesis on Olmec Astronomy, with Special Reference to the La Venta Site. *Papers on Olmec and Maya Archaeology: Contributions of the University of California Archaeological Research Facility,* No. 13, pp. 1-64. Berkeley: University of California.

Henwood, Lorne Somerville

1979 Notes on the Long Count. In *Katunob,* edited by George E. Fay, pp. 42-52. Greeley, CO: University of Northern Colorado.

Heyden, Doris

1975 An Interpretation of the Cave Underneath the Pyramid of the Sun in Teotihuacan, Mexico. *American Antiquity* 40:131-147.

1981 Caves, Gods and Myths: World-View and Planning in Teotihuacan. In *Mesoamerican Sites and World Views,* edited by Elizabeth P. Benson, pp. 1-40. Washington, D.C.: Dumbarton Oaks.

Hopkins, Nicholas A.

1991 Classic and Modern Relationship Terms and the 'Child of the Mother' Glyph (TI:606.23). In *The Sixth Palenque Round Table, 1986,* edited by Merle Greene Robertson, pp. 255-265. Norman: University of Oklahoma Press.

Hostetter, Clyde

1991 *Star Trek to Hawa-i'i.* San Luis Obispo, CA: The Diamond Press.

Hugh-Jones, Stephen

1982 The Pleiades and Scorpius in Barasana Cosmology" in *Ethnoastronomy and Archaeoastronomy in the American Tropics,* edited by Anthony Aveni and Gary Urton, pp. 183-201. Annals of the New York Academy of Sciences, Vol. 385. New York.

Hunt, Eva

1977 *The Transformation of the Hummingbird: Cultural Roots of a Zinacantecan Mythical Poem.* Ithaca: Cornell University Press.

Isbell, Billie Jean

1982 Culture Confronts Nature in the Dialectical World of the Tropics. In *Ethnoastronomy and Archaeoastronomy in the American Tropics,* edited by Anthony Aveni and Gary Urton, pp. 353-364. Annals of the New York Academy of Sciences, Vol. 385. New York.

Jakeman, M. Wells

1958 The Complex Tree-of-Life Carving on Izapa Stela 5: A Reanalysis and Partial Interpretation. *Publications in Archaeology and Early History, Mesoamerican Series,* No. 4. Provo, UT: Brigham Young University.

Jansen, Maarten E.R.G.N.

1982 The Four Quarters of the Mixtec World. In *Space and Time in the Cosmovision of Meso-*

america, edited by Franz Tichy, pp. 85-96. Latinamerika-Studien 10. Munich: Wilhelm Fink Verlag.

Jenkins, John Major

1989 *Journey to the Mayan Underworld*. Boulder, CO: Four Ahau Press.

1991 *Mirror in the Sky*. Boulder, CO: Four Ahau Press.

1992a *Tzolkin: Visionary Perspectives and Calendar Studies*. Boulder, CO: Four Ahau Press.

1992b Towards Reconstructing the Ixil-Quiché Venus Calendar. Four Ahau Press website: http://phidias.colorado.edu/jenkins.fourahau.html.

1993 *7 Wind: A Quiché Maya Calendar for 1993*. Boulder, CO: Four Ahau Press.

1994a *Tzolkin: Visionary Perspectives and Calendar Studies*. Revised with index added. Garberville, CA: Borderland Sciences Research Foundation.

1994b "Tzolkin: Visionary Perspectives and Calendar Studies" in *Borderlands, The Crossroads of Science & Spirit* L(3):1-5.

1994c *Jaloj Kexoj and PHI-64: The Dual Principle Core Paradigm of Mayan Time Philosophy and its Conceptual Parallel in Old World Thought*. Boulder, CO: Four Ahau Press.

1994d The How and Why of the Mayan End-Date in A.D. 2012. *The Mountain Astrologer* 8(1):52-57, 100-101. Cedar Ridge, CA.

1995a *The Center of Mayan Time*, (Book 2: Astrolo-Mythic Creation Day; Book 3: The Monuments of Izapa). Boulder, CO: Four Ahau Press.

1995b *Mayan Cosmogenesis 2012*. Audiotape presentation with illustrations. Borderland Sciences Research Foundation. Box 220. Bayside, CA 95524.

1995c Mysteries of Mayan Time Philosophy. *World Explorer* 1(6):33-34. Kempton, IL.

1995d Thesis. *Wacah Chan*, edited by Denise Lajetta, Issue #1. Rancho Santa Margarita, CA.

1995e The Finnish Sampo: The Stellar Frame and World Ages. In *Scenezine, Music, News, and Art*. August Issue. Chicago, IL.

1995f Review-Essay of *The Mayan Prophecies* by Adrian Gilbert and Maurice Cotterell. Four Ahau Press website.

1995g Taped interview with Adrian Gilbert, co-author of *The Mayan Prophecies*, November 1995. Louisville, CO: Four Ahau Press. Box 635, 80027.

1996a Interview with John Major Jenkins. *Esoterra: The Journal of Extreme Culture*, edited by R. F. Paul and Chad Hensley, 6:42-47. Berkeley, CA.

1996b Love Something? Look Into It. In *Zeitgeist*, edited by Nelson Axelrod, 1(4):25. Fort Collins, CO.

1996c The Pyramid at Chichen Itza: A Cosmic Myth in Stone. *The Mountain Astrologer* 9(5): 11-17. Cedar Ridge, CA.

1996d The Guile of a Plumed Serpent. In *Zeitgeist*, edited by Nelson Axelrod, 1(7):21. Fort Collins, CO.

1996e Visionary Perspectives. Interview in *Borderlands: A Quarterly Journal of Borderland Research*, LII(4):40-45. Bayside, CA.

1996f A Manifesto for Clarity. *Wacah Chan*, edited by Denise Lajetta, Issue #2. Rancho Santa Margarita, CA.

1996g Cosmic Alignments at Chichén Itzá: A Discussion with John Major Jenkins. In *Mayan Message*, edited by Jim Reed, 4:8-9 (Fall). 1-954-971-4691. Margate, FL.

1997a Chichén Itzá Cosmology: The Maya-Toltec Reconciliation. *World Explorer* 1(9):40-49. Kempton, IL.

1997b Book review of *Twin City Tales* by Lindsay Jones. In *Colorado Libraries*, edited by Carol Krismann 23(3):7. Boulder, CO.

1997c Creation Cycles in Maya Cosmogenesis. Radio interview on Liz Sterling's Innerviews, August 19, 1997. Margate, FL. 1-561-997-6343.

1997d The Astronomy of Baktun 13. Video presentation at the Institute of Maya Studies, Miami, FL, August 20, 1997. Louisville, CO: Four Ahau Press.

1998a Introduction. In *The Key to the Kalevala* by Pekka Ervast. Nevada City, CA: Blue Dolphin Publishing.

1998b Introduction to *Maya Cosmogenesis 2012* by John Major Jenkins. *Mayan Messenger*, edited by Mary Locke. Merida, Mexico.

1998c Mayan Kings as Shamans—and Shamanic Ballplaying. *Mayan Message*, edited by Jim Reed, pp.3, 6. Spring Issue.

Jenkins, Palden

1986 *Living in Time*. Bath, England: Gateway Books.

Johnson, Kenneth

1997 *Jaguar Wisdom*. St. Paul, Minnesota: Llewellyn Worldwide.

Jones, Lindsay

1995 *Twin City Tales: A Hermeneutical Reassessment of Tula and Chichén Itzá*. Niwot, CO: University Press of Colorado.

Joralemon, Peter David

1971 *A Study in Olmec Iconography*. Studies in Pre-Columbian Art and Archaeology, No. 7. Washington, D.C.: Dumbarton Oaks.

1976 The Olmec Dragon: A Study in Pre-Columbian Iconography. In *Origins of Religious Art and Iconography in Preclassic Mesoamerica*, edited by Henry B. Nicholson, pp. 27-72. UCLA Latin American Center Publications. Los Angeles: Ethnic Arts Council.

1981 The Old Woman and the Child: Themes in the Iconography of Preclassic Mesoamerica. In *The Olmec and Their Neighbors*, edited by Elizabeth P. Bensen, pp. 163-180. Washington, D.C.: Dumbarton Oaks.

Joyce, T. A.

1915 *Mexican Archaeology*. London: The Medici Society.

Kaplan, Jonathan

1995 The Incienso Throne and Other Thrones from Kaminaljuyu, Guatemala. *Ancient Mesoamerica* 6:185-196.

Keeler, Clyde E.

1957 The Cuna Indian Tree of Life. *The Bulletin of the Georgia Academy of Science* 15(1).

Kelley, David H.

1976 *Deciphering the Maya Script*. Austin: University of Texas Press.

1983a Review of *The Paris Codex: Decoding an Astronomical Ephemeris* by Gregory Severin. *Archaeoastronomy* 5:S70-S72. Journal for the History of Astronomy.

1983b The Maya Calendar Correlation Problem. In *Civilization in the Ancient Americas: Essays in Honor of Gordon R. Willey*, edited by Richard M. Leventhal and Alan L. Kolata, pp. 157-208. University of New Mexico Press and Peabody Museum of Archaeology and Ethnology.

1989 Mesoamerican Astronomy and the Maya Calendar Correlation Problem. In *Memorias del Segundo Coloquio Internacional de Mayistas* 1:65-95. Mexico: Universidad Nacional Autónoma de México.

Klein, Cecelia F.

1976a *The Face of the Earth: Frontality in Two-Dimensional Mesoamerican Art*. Garland Series, Outstanding Dissertations in the Fine Arts. New York: Garland Publishing.

1976b The Identity of the Central Deity on the Aztec Calendar Stone. *Art Bulletin* LVIII:1-12.

1982 Woven Heaven, Tangled Earth: A Weaver's Paradigm of the Mesoamerican Cosmos. In *Ethnoastronomy and Archaeoastronomy in the American Tropics*, edited by A. Aveni and G. Urton, pp. 1-36. Annals of the New York Academy of Sciences, Vol. 385. New York.

Köhler, Ulrich

1978 Reflections on Zinacantan's Role in Aztec Trade with Soconusco. In *Mesoamerican Communication Routes and Cultural Contacts*, edited by Thomas A. Lee, Jr. and Carlos Navarrete, pp. 67-74. Papers of the New World Archaeological Foundation, No. 40. Provo, UT: Brigham Young University.

1982 On the Significance of the Aztec Day Sign "Olin". In *Space and Time in the Cosmovision of Mesoamerica*, edited by Franz Tichy, pp. 111-128. Latinamerika-Studien 10. Munich:

Wilhelm Fink Verlag.

Krickeberg, Walter

1966 [1948] El Juego Mesoamericana y su Simbolismo Religioso. *Traducciones Mesoamericanistas* 1:191-313. Sociedad Mexicana de Antropología.

Krupp, E. C.

1982a The "Binding of the Years," The Pleiades, and the Nadir Sun. *Archaeoastronomy* V(I):9-13. College Park, MD: The Journal of the Center for Archaeoastronomy.

1982b The Serpent Descending. *Griffith Observer* 46(9):10-20. Los Angeles: The Griffith Observatory.

1983 *Echoes of the Ancient Skies: The Astronomy of Lost Civilizations*. New York: Oxford University Press.

1991 *Beyond the Blue Horizon*. New York: Harper-Collins.

Kubler, George

1962 *The Art and Architecture of Ancient America*. Revised 1984. New York: Penguin Books.

1982 Serpent and Atlantean Columns: Symbols of Maya-Toltec Polity. *Journal of the Society of Architectural Historians* 41(2):93-115.

Kushi, Michio

1980 *Visions of a New World: The Era of Humanity*. Brookline, MA: The East West Journal.

LaFarge, Oliver

1947 *Santa Eulalia: The Religion of a Cuchumatán Indian Town*. Chicago: University of Chicago Press.

LaFarge II, Oliver, and Douglas Byers

1931 *The Year Bearer's People*. Middle American Research Series, Publication 3. New Orleans: Tulane University.

Lamb, Weldon W.

1980 The Sun, the Moon and Venus at Uxmal. *American Antiquity* 45(1):79-86.

1981 Star Lore in the Yucatec Maya Dictionaries. In *Archaeoastronomy in the Americas*, edited by R. A. Williamson, pp. 233-247. Los Altos, CA: Ballena Press and College Park, MD: Center for Archaeoastronomy.

1995 Tzotzil Maya Cosmology. *Tribus 44*, pp. 268-278. Staatliches Museum für Völkerkunde, Linden Museum. Stuttgart, Germany.

Landa, Bishop Diego de

1566 *Relación de las cosas de Yucatan*. 1937 English translation by William Gates entitled *Yucatan Before and After the Conquest* published by The Maya Society of Baltimore and reprinted in 1978 by Dover Publications, New York.

Larsen, Helga

1936 The 260-day Period as Related to the Agricultural Life of the Ancient Indian. *Ethnos* 1:9-12. Mexico City.

Laughlin, Robert M.

1975 *The Great Tzotzil Dictionary of San Lorenzo Zinacantan*. Smithsonian Contributions to Anthropology 19. Washington, D.C.: Smithsonian Institution Press.

1977 *Of Cabbages and Kings: Tales From Zinacantan*. Smithsonian Contributions to Anthropology 23. Washington, D.C.: Smithsonian Institution Press.

León-Portilla, Miguel

1963 *Aztec Thought and Culture: A Study of the Ancient Nahuatl Mind*. Translated from the Spanish by Jack Emory Davis. Norman: University of Oklahoma Press.

Lincoln, J. Steward

1942 The Maya Calendar of the Ixil of Guatemala. *The Carnegie Institution of Washington, Publication 528*, Contribution 38. Washington, D.C.

Lounsbury, Floyd

1983 The Base of the Venus Table in the Dresden Codex, and its Significance for the Calendar-Correlation Problem. In *Calendars of Mesoamerica and Peru: Native American Computations of Time*, edited by Anthony Aveni and Gordon Brotherston, pp. 1-26. BAR International Series 174. Oxford.

1992 A Derivation of the Mayan-to-Julian Calendar Correlation from the Dresden Codex Venus Chronology. In *The Sky in Mayan Litera-*

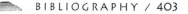

ture, edited by Anthony F. Aveni, pp. 184-206. New York: Oxford University Press.

Lowe, Gareth, Thomas A. Lee, Jr., and Eduardo Martinez Espinoza

1982 *Izapa: A Guide to the Ruins and Monuments*. Papers of the New World Archaeological Foundation, No. 31. Provo, UT: Brigham Young University.

Lowe, Gareth W., and J. Alden Mason

1965 Archaeological Survey of the Chiapas Coast, Highlands, and Upper Grijalva Basin. In *Archaeology of Southern Mesoamerica, Part 1*, edited by Gordon R. Willey, pp. 195-236. Handbook of Middle American Indians, Vol. 2. Austin: University of Texas Press.

Lowy, Bernard

1971 New Records of Mushroom Stones from Guatemala. *Mycologia* 63:983-993.

1972 Mushroom Symbolism in Maya Codices. *Mycologia* 64:816-824.

1974 Amanita Muscaria and the Thunderbolt Legend in Guatemala and Mexico. *Mycologia* 66: 188-191.

Maldonado, Ruben C., and Beatriz Repetto Tio

1991 Tlalocs at Uxmal. In *Sixth Palenque Round Table, 1986*, edited by Merle Greene Robertson and Virginia M. Fields, pp. 97-101. Norman: University of Oklahoma Press.

Malmström, Vincent

1973 Origin of the Mesoamerican 260-Day Calendar. *Science* 181:939-941.

1978 A Reconstruction of the Chronology of Meso-american Calendrical Systems. *Journal for the History of Astronomy* 9:105-116.

1997 *Cycles of the Sun, Mysteries of the Moon*. Austin: University of Texas Press.

Martínez, Gustavo Vargas

1990 *Fusang: Chinos en América antes de Colón*. Mexico, Argentina, Spain, Columbia, Puerto Rico, Venezuela: Editorial Trillas.

Matos Moctezuma, Eduardo

1995 *Life and Death in the Templo Mayor*. Niwot, CO: University Press of Colorado.

Matz, Martin, and John Major Jenkins

1995 *Pyramid of Fire: An Unknown Aztec Codex*. Translated by Martin Matz from Spanish explanation of a Borbonicus-style picture-book found in Ayautla, Oaxaca, Mexico in 1961. Interpretation by J. M. Jenkins and M. Matz. Four Ahau Press, Box 635, Louisville, CO, 80027.

McKenna, Dennis, and Terence McKenna

1993 [1975] *The Invisible Landscape: Mind, Hallucinogens and the I Ching*. New York: Harper Collins. Original 1975 edition by Seabury Press.

McKenna, Terence

1991 *The Archaic Revival*. New York: Harper San Francisco.

Meeus, J.

1983 *Astronomical Tables of the Sun, Moon, and Planets*, Richmond, VA: Willmann-Bell.

Men, Hunbatz

1990 *Secrets of Mayan Science and Religion*. Santa Fe: Bear & Company Publishers.

Mendelson, Michael E.

1959 Maximón: An Iconographical Introduction. *Man* LIX:57-60.

Meyer, Peter

1990 Mayan Calendrics. Date conversion software. Berkeley, CA: Dolphin Software.

Michelsen, Neil F.

1980, 1983, 1988, 1990 *The American Ephemeris for the 21st Century*. San Diego, CA: ACS Publications.

Milbrath, Susan

1980a Star Gods and Astronomy of the Aztecs. In *La Antropología Americanista en la Actualidad: Homenaje a Raphael Girard*, vol. 1, pp. 289-303. Mexico: Editores Mexicanos Unidos.

1980b A Star Calendar in the Codex Madrid. In *La Antropología Americanista en la Actualidad: Homenaje a Raphael Girard*, vol. 1, pp. 445-464. Mexico.

1981 Astronomical Imagery in the Serpent Sequence of the Codex Madrid. In *Archaeoastronomy in the Americas*, edited by R. A. Williamson, pp. 263-284. Los Altos, CA, Ballena

Press and College Park, MD: Center for Archaeoastronomy.

1988a Astronomical Images and Orientations in the Architecture of Chichen Itza. In *New Directions in American Archaeoastronomy*, edited by Anthony Aveni, pp. 57-80. BAR International Series 454. Oxford.

1988b Birth Images in Mixteca-Puebla Art. In *The Role of Gender in Precolumbian Art and Architecture*, edited by Virginia E. Miller, pp. 153-178. Lanham, MD: University Press of America.

1989 A Seasonal Calendar with Venus Periods in Codex Borgia 29-46. In *The Imagination of Matter: Religion and Ecology in Mesoamerican Traditions*, edited by David Carrasco, pp. 103-128. BAR International Series 515. Oxford.

Miles, S. W.

1965a Summary of Pre-Conquest Ethnology of the Guatemala-Chiapas Highlands and Pacific Slopes. In *Archaeology of Southern Mesoamerica, Part 1*, edited by Gordon R. Willey, pp. 276-287. Handbook of Middle American Indians, Vol. 2. Austin: University of Texas.

1965b Sculpture of Guatemala-Chiapas Highlands, and Associated Pacific Slopes. In *Archaeology of Southern Mesoamerica*, edited by Gordon R. Willey, pp. 237-275. Handbook of Middle American Indians, Vol. 2. (For corrections see Parsons 1986.) Austin: University of Texas.

Miller, Arthur G.

1977 Captains of the Itzá: Unpublished Mural Evidence from Chichén Itzá. In *Social Process in Maya Prehistory: Essays in Honour of Sir Eric Thompson*, edited by Norman Hammond, pp. 197-225. London: Academic Press.

Miller, Mary Ellen

1985 A Re-examination of the Mesoamerican Chacmool. *Art Bulletin* LXVII(1):1-12.

1995 Maya Masterpiece Revealed. *The National Geographic* 187(2):50-69.

Miller, Mary Ellen, and Karl A. Taube

1993 *The Gods and Symbols of Ancient Mexico and the Maya*. New York: Thames & Hudson.

Miller, Virginia E.

1989 Star Warriors at Chichen Itza. In *Word and Image in Maya Culture*, edited by William F. Hanks and Don S. Rice, pp. 287-305. Salt Lake City: University of Utah Press.

Mönnich, Anneliese

1982 The "tonalpohualli" of Codex Tudela and the Four Quarters of the World. In *Space and Time in the Cosmovision of Mesoamerica*, edited by Franz Tichy, pp. 97-110. Latinamerika-Studien 10. Munich: Wilhelm Fink Verlag.

Muñoz, Carlos

1977 *Cronica de Santa Maria Chimalapa; en las selvas del Istmo de Tehuantepec*. San Luis Potosi, Mexico: Ediciones Molinos, S. A.

Nelson, Diane M.

1996 Maya hackers and the cyberspatialized nation-state: modernity, ethnostalgia, and a Lizard Queen in Guatemala. *Cultural Anthropology* 11(3):287-309.

Nicholson, Henry B.

1971 Religion in Pre-Hispanic Central Mexico. In *The Handbook of Middle American Indians*, Vol. 10, edited by R. Wauchope, G. Ekholm, and I. Bernal, pp. 395-446. Austin: University of Texas Press.

Nicholson, Henry B. (editor)

1976 *Origins of Religious Art and Iconography in Preclassic Mesoamerica*. UCLA Latin American Center Publications. Los Angeles: Ethnic Arts Council.

1987 The "Feathered Serpents" of Copán. In *The Periphery of the Southeastern Classic Maya Realm*, edited by Gary W. Pahl, pp. 170-188. Los Angeles: UCLA Latin American Center Publications.

Norman, V. Garth

1973 *Izapa Sculpture, Part 1: Album*. Papers of the New World Archaeological Foundation, No. 30. Provo, UT: Brigham Young University.

1976 *Izapa Sculpture, Part 2: Text*. Papers of the New World Archaeological Foundation, No. 30. Provo, UT: Brigham Young University.

1980 *Astronomical Orientations of Izapa Sculptures.* Master's thesis, Anthropology Department. Provo, UT: Brigham Young University.

Norman, William, and F. Lucas Tepaz Raxuleu

1976 Quiché Text: The Man Who Was Swallowed by an Alligator. In *The International Journal of American Linguistics, Native American Texts Series, Mayan Texts I,* edited by Louanna Furbee-Losee, 1(1):40-60. Chicago: University of Chicago Press.

Nuttall, Zelia

1901 *The Fundamental Principles of Old and New World Civilizations: A Comparative Research Based on a Study of the Ancient Mexican Religious, Sociological and Calendrical Systems.* Archaeological and Ethnological Papers of the Peabody Museum, Vol. II. Harvard University. Salem, MA: Salem Press.

1928 *La Observación del paso del sol por el zenit por los antiguos habitantes de la America tropical.* Publicaciones de la Secretaría de Educación Pública, 17 (20), Mexico City.

Oakes, Maud

1951 *The Two Crosses of Todos Santos.* Bollingen Series XXVII. Princeton, NJ: Princeton University Press.

Oehler, Wolfram von

1996a Die Bedeutung des Kalendars: Ein Streifzug durch die Welt der Zeitbestimmung. Ortenberg, Germany.

1996b Die Hüter der Tage: Mesoamerikanische Kalendartradition und Maya Enddatum 13.0.0.0.0. Ortenberg, Germany.

Opperman, Renee

1983 The Olmec-Chavin Connection. *The University of Northern Colorado, Museum of Anthropology, Miscellaneous Series* 48: 73-82.

Orellana, Sandra L.

1987 *Indian Medicine in Highland Guatemala.* Albuquerque: University of New Mexico Press.

Ott, Jonathan

1994 *Ayahuasca Analogues: Pangæan Entheogens.* Kennewick, WA: Natural Products Co.

Pahl, Gary W.

1982 A Possible Cycle 7 Monument from Polol, El Petén, Guatemala. In *Pre-Columbian Art History: Selected Readings,* edited by Alana Cordy-Collins, pp. 23-32. Palo Alto, CA: Peek Publications.

Parsons, Lee A.

1967-69 *Bilbao, Guatemala: An Archaeological Study of the Pacific Coast Cotzumalhuapa Region,* Vols. I & II, Publications in Anthropology Nos. 11 & 12, Milwaukee Public Museum.

1972 Iconographic Notes on a New Izapan Stela from Abaj Takalik, Guatemala. *The 40th Congresso Internazionale Degli Americanisti* 1:203-212. Rome-Genova.

1983 Altars 9 and 10, Kaminaljuyu, and the Evolution of the Serpent-Winged Deity. In *Civilization in the Ancient Americas: Essays in Honor of Gordon R. Willey,* edited by Richard M. Leventhal and Alan L. Kolata, pp. 145-156. University of New Mexico Press and Peabody Museum of Archaeology and Ethnology.

1986 *The Origins of Maya Art: Monumental Stone Sculpture of Kaminaljuyu, Guatemala, and the Southern Pacific Coast.* Studies in Pre-Colum-bian Art and Archaeology, No. 28. Washington, D.C.: Dumbarton Oaks.

1991 The Ballgame in the Southern Pacific Coast Cotzumalhuapa Region and its Impact on Kaminaljuyu During the Middle Classic. In *The Mesoamerican Ballgame,* edited by Vernon L. Scarborough and David R. Wilcox, pp. 195-212. Tucson: University of Arizona Press.

Paxton, Meredith

1992 The Books of Chilam Balam: Astronomical Content and the Paris Codex. In *The Sky in Mayan Literature,* edited by Anthony F. Aveni, pp. 216-246. New York: Oxford University Press.

Pickands, Martin

1978 The First Father Legend in Maya Mythology and Iconography. In *The Third Palenque Round Table, 1978, Part 2,* edited by Merle Greene Roberston, pp. 124-137. Austin: University of Texas Press.

1986 The Hero Myth in Maya Folklore. In *Symbol and Meaning Beyond the Closed Community: Essays in Mesoamerican Ideas*, edited by Gary Gossen, pp. 101-124. Albany: State University of New York.

Pío Pérez, Juan

1864 "Cronologia Antigua de Yucatán y Examen del Método con que los Indios Contaba el Tiempo; Sacada de Varios Documentos Antiguos." In *Collection de documents dans les langues indigénes pour servir à l'étude de l'histoire de la philologie de l'Amérique ancienne*, by C. E. Brasseur de Bourbourg (Paris, 1864), 366-429. Also reproduced in J. L. Stephens, *Incidents of Travel in Yucatan*, i (N.Y., 1843, reprinted 1963), pp. 278-303.

Pollock, M.D. M.S., and Steven Hayden

1975 The Psilocybin Mushroom Pandemic. *Journal of Psychedelic Drugs* 7(1):73-83.

Prater, Ariadne

1989 Kaminaljuyú and Izapan Style Art. In *New Frontiers in the Archaeology of the Pacific Coast of Southern Mesoamerica*, edited by Frederick J. Bove and Linette Heller, pp. 125-130. Tempe: Arizona State University.

Prechtel, Martín

1993 *The Vision of the Female Principle in Contemporaneous Mayan Society and Cosmology*. Audiotape of lecture presented in Longmont, CO, March 28. Recorded by Four Ahau Press.

Proskouriakoff, Tatiana

1950 *A Study of Classic Maya Sculpture*. Carnegie Institution of Washington, Pub 593. Washington, D.C.

1963 *An Album of Maya Architecture*. Norman: University of Oklahoma Press. 1946 edition by Carnegie Institution of Washington.

Puleston, Dennis E.

1979 "An Epistemological Pathology and the Collapse, or Why the Maya Kept the Short Count." In *Maya Archaeology and Ethnohistory*, edited by Norman Hammon and Gordon R. Willey, pp. 63-71. Austin: University of Texas Press.

Quirarte, Jacinto

1973 *Izapan-Style Art: A Study of Its Form and Meaning*. Studies in Pre-Columbian Art and Archaeology No. 10. Washington, D.C.: Dumbarton Oaks.

1974 Terrestrial/Celestial Polymorphs as Narrative Frames in the Art of Izapa and Palenque. In *Primera Mesa Redonda de Palenque Part 1*, edited by Merle Greene Robertson, pp. 129-136. Pebble Beach, CA: The Robert Louis Stevenson School, Pre-Columbian Art Research.

1976 The Relationship of Izapan-Style Art to Olmec and Maya Art: A Review. In *Origins of Religious Art and Iconography in Preclassic Mesoamerica*, edited by Henry B. Nicholson, pp. 73-86. UCLA Latin American Center Publications. Los Angeles: Ethnic Arts Council.

1978 Sculptural Documents on the Origins of Maya Civilization. *The 42nd International Congress of Americanists* 8:189-196.

Raish, Martin

1984 *An Iconographic Study of Olmec and Izapan Monumental Stone Sculpture*. Ph.D. thesis, University of New Mexico.

Redfield, Robert

1950 *A Village That Chose Progress: Chan Kom Revisited*. Chicago: University of Chicago Press.

Redfield, Robert, and Alfonso Villa Rojas

1971 *Chan Kom: A Mayan Village*. University of Chicago Press. 1934 edition published by Carnegie Institution of Washington.

Reed, Jim (editor)

1996 The Reasons Behind the Mayan End Date. *Mayan Message* 1(3): 4-5. 6211 N.W. 20th St. Margate, FL 33063.

Reiche, Harald A.

1979 The Language of Archaic Astronomy: A Clue to the Atlantis Myth? In *Astronomy of the Ancients*, edited by Kenneth Brecher and Michael Feirtag, pp. 153-190. Cambridge, MA: MIT Press.

Reichel-Dolmatoff, Gerardo

1978 The Loom of Life: A Kogi Principle of Inte-

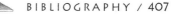

gration. *Journal of Latin American Lore* 4(1):5-27.

1979 Desana Shamans' Rock Crystals and the Hexagonal Universe. *Journal of Latin American Lore* 5(1):117-128.

1982 Astronomical Models of Social Behavior Among Some Indians of Columbia. In *Ethnoastronomy and Archaeoastronomy in the American Tropics*, edited by Anthony Aveni and Gary Urton, pp. 165-181. Annals of the New York Academy of Sciences, Vol. 385. New York.

1987 The Great Mother and the Kogi Universe: A Concise Overview. *Journal of Latin American Lore* 13(1):73-113.

Reilly, III, F. Kent

1995 Art, Ritual, and Rulership in the Olmec World. In *The Olmec World: Ritual and Rulership*, pp. 27-46. The Trustees of Princeton University.

Remington, Judith A.

1977 Current Astronomical Practices Among the Maya. In *Native American Astronomy*, edited by Anthony Aveni, pp. 75-88. Austin: University of Texas Press.

Ridpath, Ian (editor)

1989 *Norton's 2000.0: Star Atlas and Reference Handbook*. Longman Group, UK Limited.

Ridpath, Ian, and Wil Tirion

1987 *The Monthly Sky Guide*. Cambridge, England: Cambridge University Press.

Riedlinger, Thomas J. (editor)

1990 *The Sacred Mushroom Seeker: Essays for R. Gordon Wasson*. Historical, Ethno- & Economic Botany Series, Vol. 4. Portland, OR: Dioscorides Press.

Rivard, J. J.

1971 A Hierophany at Chichen Itza. *University of Northern Colorado, Miscellaneous Series, No. 26*. Fort Collins: Colorado State University.

Robertson, Merle Greene

1967 *Ancient Maya Relief Sculpture: Rubbings*. New York: New York Graphic Society.

Roe, Peter, G.

1982 *The Cosmic Zygote: Cosmology in the Amazon Basin*. New Brunswick, NJ: Rutgers University Press.

1992 The Pleiades in Comparative Perspective: The Waiwai *Shirkoimo* and the Shipibo *Huishmabo*. In *Astronomies and Cultures*, edited by Clive L. N. Ruggles and Nicholas J. Saunders, pp. 296-328. Niwot, CO: University of Colorado Press.

Roylance, James A.

1997 Galactic Alignments. *The Astrological Journal* 39(3):4-14. London: The Astrological Association.

Roys, R. L.

1933 *The Book of Chilam Balam of Chumayel*. Carnegie Institute of Washington, Pub. 438.

Sahagún, Bernardino de. See Anderson and Dibble (1953).

Sanchéz, P.C.

1937 Volcanic Activity along Latitude 19°30'N. *Proceedings of the 2nd General Assembly, Pan-American Inst. Geography and History*, pp. 215-217.

Santillana, Giorgio de

1955 *The Crime of Galileo*. Chicago: University of Chicago Press.

1968 *Reflections on Men and Ideas*. Cambridge, MA: MIT Press.

Santillana, Giorgio de, and Hertha von Dechend

1969 *Hamlet's Mill: An Essay on Myth and the Frame of Time*. Boston: Gambit. Reprint by R. Godine Publishers, Lincoln, MA.

Schaaf, Fred

1996 The Fabric of the Cygnus Milky Way. *Sky and Telescope* 92(4):64-67.

Schávelzon, Daniel

1978 Temples, Caves, or Monsters? Notes on Zoomorphic Façades in Pre-Hispanic Architecture. In *The Third Palenque Round Table, 1978, Part 2*, edited by Merle Greene Roberston, pp. 151-162. Austin: The University of Texas Press.

Schele, Linda

1992a *Workbook for the XVIth Maya Hieroglyphic*

Workshop at Texas. Austin: Department of Art and Art History and the Institute of Latin American Studies, University of Texas.

1992b *The Proceedings of the Maya Hieroglyphic Workshop, March 14-15, 1992*. Transcribed and edited by Phil Wanyerka. Austin, Texas.

1995a Trance States and Vision Quest in Ancient Maya Ritual. Videotape of slide-show lecture given at The 20th Annual Gordon Tomkins Lecture & Concert, November 10, 1995. University of California, San Francisco. Four Ahau Press: Box 635, 80027.

1995b The Olmec Mountain and Tree of Creation in Mesoamerican Cosmology. In *The Olmec World: Ritual and Rulership*, pp. 105-119. The Trustees of Princeton University.

1996 "Notes on the Correlation Question" and "A Note on the End Date." Email comments in response to questions. Cyberspace: http://copan.bioz.unibas.ch/meso/creationdate.txt.

Schele, Linda, and David Freidel

1990 *A Forest of Kings: The Untold Story of the Ancient Maya*. New York: William Morrow and Company.

1991 The Courts of Creation: Ballcourts, Ballgames, and Portals to the Maya Otherworld. In *The Mesoamerican Ballgame*, edited by Vernon L. Scarborough and David R. Wilcox, pp. 289-316. Tucson: University of Arizona Press.

Schlak, Arthur

1989 Jaguar and Serpent Foot: Iconography as Astronomy. In *Word and Image in Maya Culture*, edited by William F. Hanks and Don S. Rice, pp. 260-271. Salt Lake City: University of Utah Press.

Schmidt, W.

1931 Star Myths and Pan-Babylonianism. In *The Origin and Growth of Religion*, pp. 91-102. New York: The Dial Press.

Schulkin, Bonnie

1997 Does a Monster Lurk Nearby? Making a case for a massive Black Hole at the heart of the Milky Way. *Astronomy* 25(9):42-47.

Schwaller de Lubicz, R. A.

1982 *Sacred Science*. English translation, Rochester, VT: Inner Traditions. Originally published in 1961 by Flammarion.

Scofield, Bruce

1991 *Day-Signs*. Amherst, MA: One Reed Publications.

1994 *Signs of Time*. Amherst, MA: One Reed Publications.

Seaman, Gary, and Jane S. Day (editors)

1994 *Shamanism in Central Asia and the Americas*. Niwot, CO: The University Press of Colorado.

Séjourné, Laurette

1957 *Burning Water: Thought and Religion in Ancient Mexico*. Great Britain: Thames & Hudson.

Sellers, Jane B.

1992 *The Death of Gods in Ancient Egypt: An Essay on Egyptian Religion and the Frame of Time*. New York: Penguin Books.

Severin, Gregory M.

1981 The Paris Codex: Decoding an Astronomical Ephemeris. *Transactions of the American Philosophical Society* vol. 71, part 5. Philadelphia, PA.

Sexton, James D.

1981 *Son of Tecún Umán: A Maya Indian Tells His Life Story*. Tucson: University of Arizona Press.

1985 *Campesino: The Diary of a Guatemala Indian*. Tucson: University of Arizona Press.

Shao, Paul

1983 *The Origin of American Cultures*. Ames: Iowa State University Press.

Shaw, H. E.

1973 Astronomical Implications of the Meso-American Agricultural Calendar. Paper presented at the Seminar on Astro-Archaeology of the American Association for the Advancement of Science and Consejo Nacional de Ciencia y Tecnologia, Mexico, June 21, 1973.

Shearer, Tony

1975 *Beneath the Moon and Under the Sun*. Albuquerque: Sun Publishing Company.

Shook, Edwin

1965 Archaeological Survey of the Pacific Coast of Guatemala. In *Archaeology of Southern Mesoamerica, Part 1*, edited by Gordon R. Willey, pp. 180-194. Handbook of Middle American Indians, Vol. 2. Austin: University of Texas.

Skyglobe, v. 3.6. KlassM SoftWare. Copyright Mark A. Haney, 1989-1993.

Slayman, Andrew
1996 Seeing With Maya Eyes. *Archaeology* 49(4): 56-60.

Smith, Virginia G.
1984 *Izapa Relief Carving—Form, Content, Rules for Design and Role in Mesoamerican Art History and Archaeology*. Studies in Pre-Columbian Art and Archaeology, No. 27. Washington, D.C.: Dumbarton Oaks.

Sosa, John R.
1986 Maya Concepts of Astronomical Order. In *Symbol and Meaning Beyond the Closed Community: Essays in Mesoamerican Ideas*, edited by Gary Gossen, pp. 185-196. Albany: State University of New York.
1989 Cosmological, symbolic and cultural complexity among the contemporary Maya of Yucatan. In *World Archaeoastronomy*, edited by Anthony F. Aveni, pp. 130-142. New York: Cambridge University Press.

Spinden, H. J.
1916 The Question of the Zodiac in America. *American Anthropologist* 18:53-80.
1957 *Maya Art and Civilization*. Indian Hills, CO: The Falcon's Wing Press.

Sprajc, Ivan
1992 Venus-Rain-Maize complex in Mesoamerica: Associated with the evening star? *Indiana* 12: 225-257. Berlin.

Stephens, John L.
1841 [1988] *Incidents of Travel in Central America, Chiapas & Yucatan*. New York: Harper and Brothers. 1988 reprint edition by Century Hutchinson, London.
1843 *Incidents of Travel in Yucatan*. 1963 reprint edition by Dover Publications, 2 Volumes. New York.

Stirling, Matthew W.
1940 An Initial Series From Tres Zapotes, Veracruz, Mexico. *National Geographic Society, Contributed Technical Papers, Mexican Archaeology Series* 1(1).
1943 *Stone Monuments of Southern Mexico*. Smithsonian Institution Bureau of American Ethnology Bulletin 138. Washington, D.C.

Stirling, Marion
1981 Comments in *The Olmec and Their Neighbors*, edited by Elizabeth P. Benson. Washington, D.C.: Dumbarton Oaks.

Stratmeyer, Dennis, and Jean Stratmeyer
1977 The Jacaltec Nawal and the Soul Bearer in Concepcion Huista. In *Cognitive Studies of Southern Mesoamerica*, edited by Helen Neuenswander and Dean A. Arnold, pp. 126-159. SIL Museum of Anthropology, Publication 3. Dallas, Texas: Summer Institute of Linguistics.

Stross, Brian
1996 The Mesoamerican cosmic portal: an early Zapotec example. *Res* 29/30:82-101. Cambridge, MA: The Peabody Museum of Archaeology and Ethnology.

Stross, Brian, and Justin Kerr
1981 Notes on the Maya Vision Quest Through Enema. In *The Vase Book: A Corpus of Rollout Photographs of Maya Vases*, vol. 2, pp. 349-361. New York: Kerr and Associates.

Stuart, David, and Stephen Houston
1994 *Classic Maya Place Names*. Studies in Pre-Columbian Art and Archaeology, No. 33. Washington, D.C.: Dumbarton Oaks.

Sullivan, William
1996 *The Secret of the Incas: Myth, Astronomy, and the War Against Time*. New York: Crown Publishers.

Taladoire, Eric
1979 Orientation of Ball-Courts in Mesoamerica. *Archaeoastronomy Bulletin* II(4):12-13. College Park, MD: The Journal of the Center for Archaeoastronomy.

Tarn, Nathaniel, and Martín Prechtel
1986 Constant Inconstancy: The Feminine Prin-

ciple in Atiteco Mythology. In *Symbol and Meaning Beyond the Closed Community: Essays in Mesoamerican Ideas*, edited by Gary Gossen, pp. 173-184. Albany: State University of New York.

1990 Eating the Fruit: Sexual Metaphor and Initiation in Santiago Atitlán. *Mesoamérica: Journal of Plumsock Mesoamerican Studies and Centro Investigaciones Regionales de Mesoamérica* 19:73-82.

Tate, Carolyn E.

1982 The Maya Cauac Monster's Formal Development and Dynastic Contexts. In *Pre-Columbian Art History: Selected Readings*, edited by Alana Cordy-Collins, pp. 33-54. Palo Alto, CA: Peek Publications.

Taube, Karl A.

1994 The Birth Vase: Natal Imagery in Ancient Maya Myth and Ritual. In *The Vase Book: A Corpus of Rollout Photographs of Maya Vases*, vol. 4, pp. 652-685. New York: Kerr and Associates.

1995 The Rainmakers: The Olmec and Their Contribution to Mesoamerican Belief and Ritual. In *The Olmec World: Ritual and Rulership*, pp. 83-104. The Trustees of Princeton University.

Tedlock, Barbara

1982 *Time and the Highland Maya*. Albuquerque: University of New Mexico Press. Revised 1992.

1983 Quichéan Time Philosophy. In *Calendars of Mesoamerica and Peru: Native American Computations of Time*, edited by Anthony Aveni and Gordon Brotherston, pp. 59-72. BAR International Series 174. Oxford.

1985 Hawks, Meteorology and Astronomy in Quiché-Maya Agriculture. *Archaeoastronomy* VIII(1-4):80-88. College Park, MD: The Journal of the Center for Archaeoastronomy.

1986 On a Mountain Road in the Dark: Encounters with the Quiché Maya Culture Hero. In *Symbol and Meaning Beyond the Closed Community: Essays in Mesoamerican Ideas*, edited by Gary Gossen, pp. 125-138. Albany: State University of New York.

1992 The Road of Light: Theory and Practice of Mayan Skywatching. In *The Sky in Mayan Literature*, edited by Anthony F. Aveni, pp. 18-42. New York: Oxford University Press.

Tedlock, Dennis

1976 Winter Solstice. *alcheringa* 2(1):131. New York: J. Rothenberg and D. Tedlock.

1985 *The Popol Vuh: The Definitive Edition of the Mayan Book of the Dawn of Life and the Glories of Gods and Kings*. New York: Simon and Schuster. Revised 1996.

1988 The Sowing and Dawning of All the Sky-Earth: Sun, Moon, Stars, and Maize in the Popol Vuh. Paper presented at the University of Pennsylvania on April 5, 1987 in the University Museum Centennial Symposium, "New Theories on the Ancient Maya." Revised version completed on March 2, 1988.

1990 *Days From a Dream Almanac*. Urbana: University of Illinois Press.

1992 Myth, Math, and the Problem of Correlation in Mayan Books. In *The Sky in Mayan Literature*, edited by Anthony F. Aveni, pp. 247-73. New York: Oxford University Press.

1993 *Breath on the Mirror: Mythic Voices and Visions of the Living Maya*. New York and San Francisco: Harper San Francisco.

Tedlock, Barbara, and Dennis Tedlock

1993a Where You Want To Be. Interview in *Parabola: The Magazine of Myth and Tradition* XVIII(3):43-53. New York.

1993b A Mayan Reading of the Story of the Stars. *Archaeology* 46(4):33-35.

Thompson, Edward H.

1938 *The High Priest's Grave, Chichen Itza, Yucatan, Mexico*. Anthropological Series, Field Museum of Natural History, vol. 27, no. 1, pub. 412. Chicago: Field Museum of Natural History.

Thompson, J. Eric S.

1948 *An Archaeological Reconnaissance in the Cotzumalhuapa Region, Escuintla, Guatemala*. Contributions to American Anthropology and History, vol. IX, no. 44. Carnegie Institute of Washington.

1970 *Maya History and Religion*. Norman: University of Oklahoma Press.

1972 *A Commentary on the Dresden Codex.* Memoirs of the American Philosophical Society, Vol. 93. Philadelphia.

1974 Maya Astronomy. *Philosophical Transactions of the Royal Society of London*. A276:83-98.

Thompson, William Irwin

1981 *The Time Falling Bodies Take to Light*. New York: St. Martin's Press.

Thorne-Thomsen, Gudrun

1912 *East O' the Sun and West O' the Moon*. Chicago: Row, Peterson & Company.

Tichy, Franz

1981 Order and Relationship of Space and Time in Mesoamerica: Myth or Reality? In *Mesoamerican Sites and World-Views*, edited by Elizabeth P. Benson, pp. 217-245. Washington, D.C.: Dumbarton Oaks.

1982 The Axial Direction of Mesoamerican Ceremonial Centres on 17° N of W and Their Associations to Calendar and Cosmovision. In *Space and Time in the Cosmovision of Mesoamerica*, edited by Franz Tichy, pp. 63-83. Latinamerika-Studien 10. Munich: Wilhelm Fink Verlag.

1988 Measurement of Angles in Mesoamerica: Necessity and Possibility. In *New Directions in American Archaeoastronomy*, edited by Anthony Aveni, pp. 105-120. BAR International Series 454. Oxford.

Timms, Moira.

1994. Beyond Prophecies and Predictions. New York: Ballantine Books.

Tompkins, Peter

1976 *Mysteries of the Mexican Pyramids*. New York: Harper and Row.

Townsend, Richard Fraser

1982 Pyramid and Sacred Mountain. In *Ethnoastronomy and Archaeoastronomy in the American Tropics*, edited by Anthony Aveni and Gary Urton, pp. 37-62. Annals of the New York Academy of Sciences, Vol. 385. New York.

Tozzer, A. M. (translator)

1941 *Relacion de las cosas de Yucatan* by Bishop Diego de Landa. Papers of the Peabody Museum of Archaeology and Ethnology, Vol. 18. Cambridge: Harvard University Press.

Trimble, V.

1964 Astronomical Investigations concerning the so-called Air-shafts of Cheop's Pyramid. *Mitteilungen des Instituts für Orientforschung Akademie der Wissenschaften zu Berlin*, band 10, pp. 183-187.

Turner, Wilson G.

1985 *Maya Designs*. Dover Design Library. Mineola, NY: Dover Publications.

Ulansey, David

1989 *The Origins of the Mithraic Mysteries*. New York: Oxford University Press.

Urton, Gary

1980 Celestial Crosses: The Cruciform in Quechua Astronomy. *Journal of Latin American Lore* 6(1):87-110.

1981 *At the Crossroads of Earth and Sky*. Austin: University of Texas Press.

Valladares, Mark

1995 The Descent of Itzam Yeh. In *Maya Means Mother*. Kansas City. In manuscript.

Van Zantwijk, Rudolf

1981 The Great Temple of Tenochtitlan: Model of Aztec Cosmovision. In *Mesoamerican Sites and World Views*, edited by Elizabeth P. Benson, pp. 71-86. Washington, D.C.: Dumbarton Oaks.

Vogt, Evon Z.

1969 *Zinacantan: A Maya Community in the Highlands of Chiapas*. Cambridge, MA: The Belknap Press of the Harvard University Press.

1976 *Tortillas for the Gods: A Symbolic Analysis of Zinacanteco Ritual*. Harvard College. 1993 edition published by University of Oklahoma Press.

1981 Some Aspects of Sacred Geography of Highland Chiapas. In *Mesoamerican Sites and World*

Views, edited by Elizabeth P. Benson, pp. 119-142. Washington, D.C.: Dumbarton Oaks.

Wagner, Roy
1975 *The Invention of Culture*. Chicago: University of Chicago Press.

Waibel, Leo
1946 *La Sierra Madre de Chiapas*. Sociedad de Geografía y Estadística de Mexico.

Wasson, R. Gordon, Stella Kramrisch, Jonathan Ott, and Carl A. P. Ruck
1986 *Persephone's Quest: Entheogens and the Origins of Religion*. New Haven, CT: Yale University Press.

Wasson, R. G., and V. P. Wasson
1957 *Mushrooms, Russia and History*. New York: Pantheon Books.

Watanabe, John M.
1983 In the World of the Sun: A Cognitive Model of Mayan Cosmology. *Man* (N.S.) 18:710-28.

Waters, Frank
1963 *Book of the Hopi*. New York: Penguin Books.
1975 *Mexico Mystique*. Chicago: Sage Books.

Wertime, Richard A., and Angela M. H. Schuster
1993 Written in the Stars: Celestial Origin of Maya Creation Myth. *Archaeology* 46(4):27-30, 32.

Whitrow, G. J.
1974 The Cosmological Significance of the Milky Way. Essay-Review of *The Milky Way: An Elusive Road for Science* by Stanley L. Jaki and *The Discovery of Our Galaxy* by Charles A. Whitney. *History of Science*, xii, pp. 299-306.

Wilbert, Johannes
1974 *The Thread of Life: Symbolism of Miniature Art from Ecuador*. Studies in Pre-Columbian Art and Archaeology, No. 20. Washington, D.C.: Dumbarton Oaks.

Wilson, Colin
1996 *From Atlantis to the Sphinx*. New York: Fromm International.

Winning, Hasso von
1976 Late and Terminal Preclassic: The Emergence of Teotihuacán. In *Origins of Religious Art and Iconography in Preclassic Mesoamerica*, edited by Henry B. Nicholson, pp. 141-156.

UCLA Latin American Center Publications. Los Angeles: Ethnic Arts Council.

Wisdom, Charles
1940 *The Chortí Indians of Guatemala*. Chicago: University of Chicago Press.

Wren, Linnea H.
1991 The Great Ball Court Stone from Chichén Itzá. In *The Sixth Palenque Round Table, 1986*, edited by Merle Greene Robertson, pp. 51-58. Norman: University of Oklahoma Press.
1995 Chichén Itzá: The Rhetoric of Conquest and Creation. Paper presented at the 1995 Hieroglyphic Conference in Austin, Texas.

INDEX

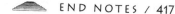

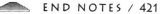

ABOUT THE AUTHOR

John Major Jenkins is a leading independent researcher elucidating the mysteries of ancient Mesoamerican cosmology and calendrics, who has authored five books and over a dozen articles on the Maya. Since 1986 he has journeyed to Mexico and Central America five times, thoroughly exploring the ancient sacred sites and the contemporary indigenous cultures.

Throughout this period, Jenkins researched the inner workings of Maya calendar science, writing his first book *Journey to the Mayan Underworld* in 1989. His book *Tzolkin: Visionary Perspectives and Calendar Studies*, published by Borderlands Science and Research Foundation in 1994, reconstructs the Mayan Venus Calendar and establishes that the "True Count" of the ancient tzolkin calendar is still followed by contemporary Maya daykeepers.

In August of 1997, Jenkins presented his pioneering research on the astronomy of the Maya calendar end-date in 2012 at the prestigious Institute of Maya Studies, associated with the Museum of Science in Miami. In March of 1998 he presented his reconstruction of the true meaning of the Pyramid of Kukulcan at *The Cosmic Serpent of the Ancient Maya Conference* in Merida, Mexico, having been invited to speak by the Indigenous Council of the Americas and the Mayoan Council.

John welcomes all correspondence, which can be addressed c/o Inner Traditions/Bear & Company, One Park Street, Rochester, VT 05767. For more information on John's books, tapes, current projects, and upcoming workshops, visit his website at http://edj.net/mc2012.

BOOKS OF RELATED INTEREST

Galactic Alignment
The Transformation of Consciousness According to Mayan,
Egyptian, and Vedic Traditions
by John Major Jenkins

Pyramid of Fire: The Lost Aztec Codex
Spiritual Ascent at the End of Time
by John Major Jenkins and Martin Matz

Beyond 2012: Catastrophe or Awakening?
A Complete Guide to End-of-Time Predictions
by Geoff Stray

2012 and the Galactic Center
The Return of the Great Mother
by Christine R. Page, M.D.

The Mayan Calendar and the Transformation of Consciousness
by Carl Johan Calleman, Ph.D.

The Mayan Code
Time Acceleration and Awakening the World Mind
by Barbara Hand Clow

The Mayan Factor
Path Beyond Technology
by José Argüelles

Time and the Technosphere
The Law of Time in Human Affairs
by José Argüelles

Inner Traditions • Bear & Company
P.O. Box 388
Rochester, VT 05767
1-800-246-8648
www.InnerTraditions.com

Or contact your local bookseller